Behind the Great Wall

Behind the Great Wall

A Post-Jungian Approach to Kafkaesque Literature

James Whitlark

Rutherford • Madison • Teaneck
Fairleigh Dickinson University Press
London and Toronto: Associated University Presses

Associated University Presses
440 Forsgate Drive
Cranbury, NJ 08512

Associated University Presses
25 Sicilian Avenue
London WC1A 2QH, England

Associated University Presses
P.O. Box 39, Clarkson Pstl. Stn.
Mississauga, Ontario,
L5J 3X9 Canada

The paper used in this publication meets the requirements of the American National Standard for Permanence of Paper for Printed Library Materials Z39.48-1984.

Library of Congress Cataloging-in-Publication Data

Whitlark, James, 1948–
Behind the great wall : a post-Jungian approach to Kafkaesque literature / James Whitlark.
p. cm.
Includes bibliographical references and index.
ISBN 0-8386-3427-3 (alk. paper)
1. Literature, Modern—20th century—History and criticism. 2. Kafka, Franz, 1883–1924—Influences. 3. Jung, C. G. (Carl Gustav), 1875–1961—Influences. 4. Psychoanalysis and literature. I. Title.
PN771.W46 1991
809′.04—dc20 90-55830
CIP

PRINTED IN THE UNITED STATES OF AMERICA

Contents

Behind the Great Wall

Acknowledgments

Part of chapter 3 has been adapted from my article, "Kafka's 'A Country Doctor' as Neo-Romantic Fairy Tale," originally published in *The Shape of the Fantastic: Selected Essays from the Seventh International Conference on the Fantastic in the Arts,* Olena H. Saciuk, ed. Westport, Conn.: Greenwood Publishing Group, 1990, pp. 43–49. Copyright © 1990 by Olena H. Saciuk. Reprinted with permission. Other material derives from my articles: "Kafka and the Taoist Sages," *Journal of the Kafka Society of America* 8 (June/December 1984); "A Post-Jungian Approach to Kafka," *Journal of the Kafka Society of America* 9 (June/December 1985); and "Kafka's Babel," *Journal of the Kafka Society of America* 13 (June/December 1989). Grateful acknowledgment to M. Luise Caputo-Mayr, editor, executive director, and founder of the Kafka Society of America, for permission to adapt these articles.

Introduction

In 1922, Franz Kafka (then thirty-nine) retired from business, accepted the imminence of his death, and directed that all his writings be destroyed; nonetheless, he continued to write. Imagine him seated at his desk, as, in a slightly shaky hand, he penned such disturbing parables as "A Commentary" *("Ein Kommentar")* composed late that year—a work worth considering as a prolegomenon to Kafkaesque literature in general.[1] In its first sentence, Kafka envisioned himself (or some persona) rising early, traversing dreamlike, empty streets. He next wrote that "suddenly" *(plötzlich)* there was an occurrence, a collapse. At this point, the manuscript shows, his pen paused in midsentence. Dostoevsky (translations of whose works much influenced the early Kafka) had already overused the expression "suddenly" *(vdrug)* to introduce emotions that swept away his characters' ordinary sense of time.[2] Kafka began again, crossed out this image,[3] and found a fresher one: the narrator thought that he had lost track of the time when he compared his watch to a public clock.[4] For whatever reason, he experienced not merely surprise but "terror" *(Schrecken)*. In shock, he next lost the "way" *(Weg)*—a term that Kafka repeated as if to give it more than its usual significance. "Luckily," there appeared a police- or "security"-man *(Schutzmann)*. But was it fortunate? When the narrator inquired the "way," instead of answering, the officer smiled, asked if the lost traveler were seeking the "way," and then ordered: "Give it up! Give it up!" As if "to be alone with his laughter," the policeman exited in a sweep or flourish *(Schwunge)*. Kafka paused again and changed the wording to a "great sweep" as if to stress the size and power of the law officer. Finally, Kafka penned a line at the end signaling that the paragraph-long narrative, however fragmentary, was finished.

In due course, his literary executor, Max Brod, unwilling to consign the manuscript to the flames, published it, but not without altering it. Apparently puzzled by the title, he deleted Kafka's and supplied his own. Similarly, Heinz Politzer, who devotes the whole first chapter of his tome, *Franz Kafka: Parable and Paradox* to interpreting "A Commentary," never explains the story's enigmatic title.[5] In one sense, since Kafka's writing tends to be self-reflexive, *"Ein Kommentar"* could be a commentary on Kafka's paradoxical persistence, his continuing to compose even though another part of himself (an internal censor or security officer) would have him give up, die, and obliterate his works that have become a burden to his tranquility. Considering the precision with which Kafka normally uses words, however, one would expect that when he says *"Ein Kommentar,"* he also intends to comment on some text. But which one? According to Kafka's young friend Gustav Janouch, Kafka owned and had been reading translations of Confucius's *Analects* and the works of Chuang Tzu.[6] Both contain the story of Chieh-yü, madman of Ch'û. According to the *Analects,* when Confucius was making one of his many journeys throughout China, the madman encountered him, said: "Give up! Give up!" *(I erh! I erh!),* and left mysteriously.[7] In the edition allegedly consulted by Kafka, Richard Wilhelm renders this phrase as, "Gib auf, gib auf," almost identical to Kafka's "Gibs auf, gibs auf."[8] In Chuang Tzu's version, the madman added that the Way *(Tao)* cannot be followed in any obvious manner but only "now going backwards, now crookedly."[9] Elsewhere in this scripture, a Taoist named Khang remarks, "When we walk we should not know where we are going"[10]—for only by surrendering conscious control can we be guided by the Tao, the indescribable way of the universe. In its various versions, Chieh-yü's story is prominent enough in Chinese folklore so that, given Kafka's well-documented sinophilia, a reasonable case could be made for Kafka's having known the tale, even if Janouch had not listed Kafka's readings. With Chieh-yü in mind, "A Commentary" gains a new perspective. From a Taoist vantage, encountering the policeman really is "lucky," since he discourages conscious pursuit of the man's "way." The triple repetition of the word "way" *(Weg)* becomes particularly meaningful since "way" is the most common translation of *Tao.* Even the narrator's destination, the railroad station *(Bahnhof),* means etymologically (in German) the court of the path or way. What, though, is the purpose of bringing a Taoist subtext into a European setting?

For the answer to this, we must turn to Kafka's attitude toward language and literature, which is very close to the Taoists'. Like Kafka, who published only when virtually coerced by his friends, so the legendary founder of Taoism, Lao Tzu, about to go beyond the preliminary stages of the Great Wall, the boundary of China, composed the *Tao te ching,* only to satisfy the pleas of his admirers. Like Kafka's writings, which lie under his own malediction that they should be destroyed, Lao Tzu offers his reluctantly, with the initial warning that they are not ultimately true. "The Tao that can be expressed is not the eternal Tao."[11] Kafka believed that "because language corresponds to the material world, it only suits what is related to possession [*Besitz*]" (*D* 40). However, he wanted to extend his writings to ineffable Reality (what the Taoists term *Tao*). Consequently, like the Taoists, he had to turn a language based on possession into a language of dispossession. What he sought was more than that general play with words attributed to literature by Paul de Man in his famous dictum, "The paradigm for all texts consists of a figure (or system of figures) and its deconstruction."[12] To see how Kafka's insight matched and then surpassed de Man's, begin, for example, with the narrator's "watch" *(Uhr).* That German word means primarily a timepiece, but in various expressions it assumes the more generalized sense of time itself, as if temporality could be an object, a clock to be owned. Kafka shows that it cannot be—that one chronometer will disagree with another; thus he presents a "figure" (time related metonymically to the clock) and its "deconstruction" (showing the problematic nature of that metonymy). Where Kafka transcends de Man's notion of literature is that Kafka then has the narrator, confused by this deconstruction, seeking help from a policeman, who is acting like a Taoist sage/madman. Kafka does not synthesize Austrian law enforcement and Taoism into "a figure" (or [one] system of figures)" for deconstruction; they never are united. That is why Kafka's parable sounds so strange, so *alien.* The French perceptively (albeit chauvinistically) use the term *aliénation* to mean both foreignness and derangement. The word has found its way into English and German. Indeed, such a grouping together of the foreign and insane is very old, probably anticipated by the ancient Greek term "barbarian" *(barbaros),* if that word derives from the idea that non-Greeks are forced to "babble" (make the sound "barbar"), because they lack human speech and reason. Reader and protagonist may feel a certain alienation and bewilderment, because Kafka introduces not merely Taoism but a number of systems. That he follows the title "A Commentary" not with an essay but with a narrative, probably derives from the Talmudic practice of sometimes using parables as commentary on the Hebrew Scriptures. The prose, however, is reminiscent of literary realism, except in its dreamlike minimalism. Through building a system (of science, law, etc.) people try to control and possess their environment. If Kafka had merely presented a "figure . . . or system" and its deconstruction, he would still be working within a fairly traditional logic. Instead, he jostles one system and its deconstruction against another, creating an *ungovernable world where any struggle for control becomes nightmarish*—the Kafkaesque. The very word *Kafkaesque,* which found its way into English as a synonym for the bizarre and mystifying, is itself a mixture of languages. "Kafka" comes from Jakob *(Y'QB)* with a prefix that may be either German or Czech;[13] "-esque" is French from the Italian suffix "-esco."

To understand what comment Kafka is making in *"Ein Kommentar"* requires an understanding of this polycultural, Kafkaesque condition. Since it is both a literary mode and an alienated state of mind, it requires a psychological as well as a literary analysis. The problem, at present, is that, like most literary criticism, the psychological has been undergoing frantic revision. Every branch of psychology itself has metamorphosed, ranging from the clinical to the psycholinguistic. The latter is evolving into neuro-linguistics, yielding odd new data as, for example, that polyglots (e.g., Kafka) may suffer from "mild to severe visio-spatial disabilities, particularly with respect to . . . orientation in space"[14]—evidence that could have bearing on the Kafkaesque motif of being lost or disoriented. In the late 1950s, Lacan's "Seminar on *The Purloined Letter*" set a new direction for literary psychology by *simultaneously* reinterpreting Freud and analyzing Poe's text.[15] Now, however, so much has changed in both literary criticism and psychology, that the revision must be more far-reaching, and, in the case of the Kafkaesque, the proper subject for such reinterpretation (or even correction) is not Freud but Jung. Kafka rejected Freudian analysis because it reduces psychic need mainly to sexual symptoms, while Kafka (like Jung) felt the basic problem was spiritual (*M;* 292).

In studying the Kafkaesque, my first step (chap. 1) sketches the more obvious connections between Jung's life and thought where they parallel those of Kafka. Since these writers' own experience of the Kafkaesque condition both sharpened their insights into it and removed their objectivity, this study commences here in order to allow for their personal limitations and to strip away their legends, particularly Jung's: he has been misrepresented as everything from an incredibly profound prophet to a Nazi quack. Despite a number of attempts to organize his findings, most notably the "Modern Psychology" lectures (1933–34),[16] he admitted in 1939, "My endeavors in psychology have been essentially pioneer work, leaving me neither time nor opportunity to present them systematically."[17] Next (chap. 2) begin the first stages of a post-Jungian (or updated Jungian) approach to the biographical elements in Kafka's works. Then three chapters treat the chief sources (Occidental lore, Jewish tradition, and Oriental tale) that Kafka, skillfully but disconcertingly, superimposes to create radical alienation.

If the Kafkaesque is to be seen as a basic human condition, it must be examined in relation to many authors. Consequently, part 2 is devoted to very brief summaries of (1) the more obvious biographical roots of alienation in each author's works; (2) the degree of difference between their Kafkaesque literature and Kafka's; and (3) the degree to which each one's version of the Kafkaesque supports or resists traditional Jungian analysis.

Finally, part 3 of the book reexamines the material introduced in parts 1 and 2 and applies it to the analysis of Kafka's story "At the Building of the Great Wall."

Part I

Kafka, Jung, and Collapsing Tradition

1
At the Frontier

> Against whom should the Great Wall defend? . . . Innocent northerners, who believed they gave rise to it! Venerable, innocent Emperor, who believed he ordained it! We wall builders understand that it was otherwise and remain silent.
>
> —Kafka, "At the Building of the Great Wall"

In his autobiography—or, as his disciple Aniela Jaffé calls it, his "religious testament"—C. G. Jung reveals the effect on his career of a period when his home seemed to be assaulted by forces from beyond the boundary of the explicable. He reports that, one day, a solid walnut table thunderously split; two weeks later, a steel knife, while lying in a drawer, exploded into fragments. Previously trying to decide between surgery and internal medicine as a specialization, he chose psychiatry, kept the knife remnants with him as souvenirs of what he termed "God's World" *(Gotteswelt),* and devoted his doctoral work to parapsychology (*Er* 4, 77, 111–13; *M x,* 72, 104–6). His dissertation concerned his cousin Hélène Preiswerk, a trance-medium whose voice, language, and accent changed to suit the character of whatever "spirits" allegedly possessed her. Her mediumism (which ended when she was finally caught at sleight of hand) fitted into a widespread, *fin-de-siècle* spiritualist fad, but Jung's interest in the esoteric continued long after that vogue and eventually included ghosts, magic, astrology, and flying saucers. Although he has inspired numerous literary theorists,[1] they have understandably sought a consistent system within his writings, while his most intriguing research was quite the opposite—speculations about numena transcending all systems.

In 1911, Franz Kafka, the other focus of this book, told Rudolf Steiner, "A major part of my being is aspiring toward Theosophy" (*T* 57). Kafka's friend Max Brod, in telling of this meeting, calls Steiner the "Anthroposophist" even though the Anthroposophical Society was not founded for two more years.[2] Unlike Anthroposophy, which seldom ranged far from relatively respectable Occidental sources, Steiner's 1911 affiliation, Theosophy, united East and West, as did Kafka and Jung. The Russian émigré Helena Petrovna Blavatsky, one of its founders, composed vast tomes with material drawn (some say "plagiarized") from Occidental folklore and from many Asian religions. She also allegedly received letters teleported to her by Tibetan masters, though the documents' mysterious materialization may owe something to legerdemain she learned during her own flirtation with mediumism.[3] Kafka's talk of aspiring to Theosophy belonged to a "set speech" he planned before meeting Steiner personally, an encounter that discouraged him from pursuing thoughts of joining, and Kafka also apparently found the few mediums he visited disappointing, but it is worth noting that his own pursuit of the transcendent involved an early brush with Oriental mysticism and the occult.

Occult interests tinge Kafka's writings, most obviously the description of a séance found among his literary fragments, but more importantly, his "Hunter Gracchus" narratives, tales of one of the undead. According to Wilhelm Emrich's monumental study, *Franz Kafka,* the "Hunter Gracchus" fictions represent "the pattern of all of Franz Kafka's stories and novels: the two worlds that cannot make themselves understood by one another."[4] Emrich thus astutely identifies a frontier between two realms as the typical Kafkan setting. In Kafka's story "The Warden of the Tomb" *("Der Gruftwächter"),* for example, a prince stations a sepulcher guard between "the Human and the Other" *(dem Menschlichen und dem Anderen, B* 290). In "The Burrow" *("Der Bau"),* a protagonist stealthily constructs his labyrinthine fortress against an unnamed, chthonic "Beast" (*Tier, B* 214). In the story, "At the Building of the Great Wall," the masons do not even reveal "against whom" they ineffectively erect their barrier. More problematically, Emrich trusts Kafka's characters (particularly the Hunter Gracchus) in their verdict that understanding cannot exist between the two worlds. How reliable is that mysterious hunter? He loudly despairs of communication, complaining that "no one will read what I record here" (yet we read it). In one fragment he asserts that all know of him but suppress or repress the Knowledge, while in another version he claims that nobody knows of him (*B* 107, 334–35). He insists that none can condemn his past: that his occupational killing and skinning of animals was perfectly innocent (a claim that Kafka, the ardent vegetarian, might have found less self-evident). This desire not to be judged provides a motive for mystifications, for Gracchus is resisting questions about his past. Similarly, in the description of a séance, the spirit first states that it wishes to go away, next argues that its coming was a mistake, then responds to questions with more questions, while the indefatigable medium tries to force an answer from it (*H* 235–36). In other words, Kafka's stories concern not precisely beings or worlds that "cannot" communicate, but ones that *will* not (as all of Jung's later studies have as their foundation his early researches into psychological repression).

The so-called "Language-crisis" *(Sprachkrise)* besetting Germanic intellectuals in the early twentieth century—a crisis that has since become far more general—did not arrive because anyone had proven the unreliability of language. As has so often been noted, since such a proof would have to be given in language, it would contradict itself. The ineffability of Reality forms one doctrine of a widespread, twentieth-century *Weltanschauung* accepted on faith for emotional, not logical reasons. And one of the clues to its origin is its frequent association with translation and cross-cultural or cross-generational contact. Significantly, the Hunter Gracchus, having learned many languages, acts (reluctantly) as an interpreter between the generations (*B* 332). Perhaps coincidentally, he is in the process of being corporeally transported to the heavens, i. e., to use the technical term, "translated."[5] At any rate, "translation," in one sense or another, serves as a paradigm for many of the occult arts, e.g., the transformation of letters into numbers in numerology and Kabbalistic *gematria,* or the decoding of metaphorical prophecies or secret writing. Mediums (such as Jung's cousin) often speak in accents or languages supposedly unknown to them or even "in tongues." From a Jungian point of view, such play with language becomes a means of breaking the hold of habit and opening the mysterious "Unconscious." Most importantly, creative literature has repeatedly viewed its origins as equally mysterious from the days when poets thought themselves to be recording or "translating" the voice of a muse, to the present when intellectual authors find themselves in a liminal, intertextual space collecting echoes from many times and languages. Kafka once noted that his writings were becoming a Kabbala. In a study of the manuscript of *Das Schloss,* Malcolm Pasley has detected markings suggesting that Kafka was indeed examining his own words for esoteric patterns.[6] In the "set speech" about Theosophy, Kafka associated his own writings with "clairvoyant" *(hellseherischen)* visions bringing him "to the boundary of the human" (*T* 57). The influence on him of his writing included such a trivial but intriguing effect as making him temporarily ambidextrous, or as he metaphorically added, "a double person" (*T* 109; *D 1* 105). Going further still, Jung even experimented with automatic writing. Fearing Jung's arcane proclivities, Sigmund Freud once told Jung to make Freudian sexual theory into a "dogma" as a dam against the "black tide of occultism," but Jung felt that the age of dogmatism was irrecoverably past (*Er* 156).[7]

Two Sides of Chaos

> At night along the wall, the dead called: We want to know about God. Where is God? Is God dead?
>
> —Jung, *Septem Sermones ad Mortuos*

With complementary personalities (in Jungian terms, "introverted" and "extraverted," respectively),[8] Kafka and Jung faced intellectual and political upheavals that the latter euphemistically called *Civilization in Transi-*

tion (*GW,* vol. 10). Kafka's life shows the strain of being quietly Jewish among loudly Christian and nationalistic Czechs. Learning Czech from his nurse, and French from a governess,[9] he acquired German and Yiddish from parents who mixed the two. He diligently studied Latin, Greek, English, and Hebrew, but felt at home with none of them, even complaining that he could not love his mother properly because he called her by the alien (German) word *Mutter* (*Ta* 116). He once wrote to his Gentile friend Milena Jesenská that the perennial "Jew baiting" made him feel like a cockroach being exterminated in a bathroom (*M* 24); however, he seldom complained about an anti-Semitism so obvious as to be not worth mentioning. The controversial poststructuralists Gilles Deleuze and Félix Guattari describe the historical moment thus:

> It is the situation of the Jews who have dropped the Czech language at the same time as the rural environment. . . . But there are only two ways [a German-speaking minority author at that time could have improved the situation]. One way is to artificially enrich this German, to swell it up through all the resources of symbolism, of oneirism, of esoteric sense, of a hidden signifier. . . . But this attempt implies a desperate attempt at symbolic reterritorialization, based in archetypes, Kabbala, and alchemy that accentuates its break from the people and will find its political result only in Zionism. . . . Kafka will quickly choose the other way, or, rather, he will invent another.[10]

If Kafka really was able to invent a completely other way (a complex question to be pursued for the remainder of this study), his success is, as Deleuze and Guattari imply, relevant to psychology, since, according to Jung, people do not escape the "archetypal." Indeed, in a 1935 diatribe against Jung, the Communist novelist Edward Upward singled out Kafka for particular scorn as a writer obsessed with the "archetypal."[11]

Jung himself (like most educated Swiss), came, like Kafka, from a multilingual background. Furthermore, he alienated himself by being a Christian parson's son drawn toward Jewish intellectuals. While confronting controversy in supporting Freud's almost exclusively Jewish circle in psychology, Jung brought strife to his marriage through an intimate friendship with a brilliant, young Jewish patient named Sabina Spielrein.[12] Based on equivocal evidence, the Freudian analyst Bruno Bettelheim contends, "[Jung] was still acting as her therapist [when], they became lovers."[13] Whatever the truth of the charge, Jung was at least indiscreet. As often occurs during the transgression of norms, he opened the situation to serendipity (the patient's unusually fast recovery) as well as to the anger of those with a vested interest in propriety (his wife and Sabina's mother). When the relationship cooled, Sabina began writing to Freud telling how the erotic teachings of Otto Gross (a Jewish patient of both Jung and Freud) had inclined Jung toward polygamy.[14] She also informed Freud of her plans to have (a real or symbolic) "Aryan/Semitic child" by Jung.[15] In the midst of this strain, a final break transpired between the latter and the young woman, and later, following doctrinal disputes, between Freud and Jung. Suffering a mental collapse that forced him to resign his academic post at Zürich University, Jung began conversing with the Old Testament prophet Elijah, who later appeared in Jung's writings as the Wise Old Man, a teacher, father, or God archetype—a trusted adviser such as Freud had been to him. Jung also envisioned a female archetypal figure, Salome, the Wise Woman or anima (which, according to the Jungian analyst Aldo Carotenuto, was at least partly derived from Jung's encounter with Spielrein).[16]

Among the many sources of contradiction within Kafka's and Jung's experience, Judaic/Gentile dichotomy certainly must be included. Kafka frequently passed as a Gentile; in a sense, Jung did the reverse, for, as if he were a rabbi, he tried to teach his Jewish parents how to be better Jews, even vehemently upbraiding one for having renounced the God of her Fathers (*Er* 144). In *The Slayers of Moses,* Susan Handelman examines one of the most abstract differences between Hebraic and Hellenic-Christian attitudes: the (neoPlatonic) tendency of the latter to distinguish between words and Reality.[17] Kafka and Jung combined this attitude with its opposite (building multilayered, quasirabbinic commentary as if truth lay exclusively in words interpreting other words, *ad infinitum*). According to Handelman, even vestiges of the rabbinic love of commentary suffice to bewilder Gentile critics and account for some of the hatred spewed on those who, like Freud and Jacques Derrida, preserve habits of Judaic exegesis (but in a secular context). Such writers as Kafka and Jung, whose inclinations led them into both camps, found themselves in limbo.

Germanic Jewry had generally been moving toward assimilation. According to German statistics, 12 percent of all Jewish marriages were interracial.[19] (With Kafka's encouragement, his beloved sister Ottla, for example, eventually married a Gentile.) Since the eighteenth-century beginnings of the Judaic Enlightenment or *Haskalah,* Jewish scholars had furthered the science and rationalism of the general culture as a possible cure for anti-Semitism. Solomon Grayzel comments;

> Civilized themselves, the Jews assumed that their opponents could be reached by civilized methods: calm protests, appeals to logic, the publication of books correcting the misconception of Jews and Judaism.[19]

Then world war came. Pogroms increased against Eastern Jewry, but this was less devastating than the heightened realization that European civilization suffered from worse than what Freud called "discontents"; assimilation into such a culture grew less attractive. Impetus accrued to

Zionism, a movement that (despite Deleuze's and Guattari's comment) slowly began to fascinate Kafka. (Strangely, in the nineteenth century, Jung's Judeophile grandfather, in between conversing with his dead wife and staving off the phantasms plaguing him during sermon writing, became "a precursor of Zionism.")[20] Acutely aware of the uneasy pluralism of Western civilization, especially after the break of depth psychology into Jewish and Gentile circles, Jung, just before the war, experienced visions of a great stirring in the Collective Unconscious, synchronous with his own psychic collapse.

> On August 1 the World War arrived. My duty was now clear: I must attempt to comprehend what had happened and to what degree my own experience corresponded to that of mankind collectively [*der Kollektivität*]. (*Er* 180)

At first sight, as usual, Kafka seemed almost oblivious to the outside world. He marked the beginning of what some were calling "Armageddon" with the nonchalant diary entry (one day late): "Deutschland has declared war on Russia. Afternoon, swimming school" (*T* 418). However, a week before, he had finally gathered the courage to announce his planned emigration to Germany to write full time.[21] War brought an end to that and continuation of a life he found intolerable. Both Kafka and Jung, then, encountered the mixed blessing of seeing others going to fatal battles while they agonized alone at their desks.

By 1917, Kafka was composing his most important collection of aphorisms and undergoing his most intense personal crisis, though one nearly opposite to Jung's. Where the latter apparently found monogamy restrictive, Kafka finally decided that marriage was beyond him and concluded his several-year, intermittent engagement to Felice Bauer. Her last recorded words about him were, "My Franz was a saint" ("Mein Franz war ein Heiliger"),[22] an opinion differing markedly from Spielrein's of Jung.[23] Where Jung vehemently broke with his professional father, Freud, Kafka suffered, primarily in silence, from an inability to escape from the "paternal sphere." While Jung experienced grandiose visions, Kafka, in 1917, contracted (eventually fatal) tuberculosis, which he believed to be the culmination of his lifelong death wish. Even Otto Gross plays a contrasting role in each case. In 1917, most unlike his allegedly leading Jung toward polygamy, Gross was working with Kafka on a magazine to be called the *Journal for the Suppression of the Will to Power (Blätter zur Bekämpfung des Machtwillens),* a Schopenhauerean title expressing a typically Kafkan renunciation of life (*Br* 179, 196; *L* 455, n. 65).

The aphoristic work that came from Jung's crisis arrived the previous year (1916) after a very Jungian prelude. According to his account, his children began seeing ghosts, and the doorbell, untouched, rang continuously. He sensed so many spirits in the air that he felt "barely able to breathe." They formed a chorus crying, "We are returning from Jerusalem where we did not find what we sought" (*Er* 194). Since the source of Judaism and Christianity failed to save the departed, they had visited him for a professional consultation. He obliged by writing for them *Septem Sermones ad Mortuos (Seven Sermons to the Dead),* which he attributed to the Gnostic "Basilides in Alexandria, the City where East touches West." He comments on the ghostly visitation.

> The intellect, of course, would like to arrogate to itself some scientific, physical knowledge of the affair, or, preferably, to write the whole thing off as a violation of the rules. But what a dreary world it would be if the rules were not violated sometimes! (*Er* 195; *M* 191).

With typical indiscretion, he had these mystic homilies printed and distributed to his friends. In 1925, he republished the *Sermons* in a larger edition. A copy eventually reached (Kafka's acquaintance) the great Jewish theologian Martin Buber, who, in 1952, publicly denounced Jung as a Gnostic. Jung hotly replied that he was neither a Gnostic nor (as another critic had accused) an agnostic, but an empiricist: he presented neither systems nor theories but facts. When in the *Sermons* he made statements about the "Hereafter" *(Jenseits),* he, unlike opinionated metaphysicians, meant them poetically, not literally (*GW,* vol. 18, pars. 1501–3). Despite Buber's attack, Jung later reprinted the *Sermons* in his autobiography—an excellent place for them, since, despite his attempts to hide behind poetic license or the mask of "Basilides" they, by his own admission, stem from a personal experience.

At first, both Kafka's 1917 aphorisms (later expanded and polished contemporaneously with the composition of the Great Wall stories) and Jung's 1916 *Sermons* were virtually unknown and unstudied; now, these works seem to be the best introduction to the metaphysical thought of each. But more important, because of the marked difference between the personalities and lives of Kafka and Jung, and because no evidence suggests that they ever influenced one another,[24] there is reason to believe that the similarities between these works reflect the limbo that human minds enter when they begin to step beyond their cultures.

As noted, the *Sermons* arose from an intense psychic experience that temporarily affected even Jung's breathing. In the seventeenth aphorism, Kafka also describes an evocative, paranormal moment.

> This is a place where I never was before: here breathing is different, and more dazzling than the sun is the radiance of a star beside it. (*D* 36)

Considering the attention paid to breathing by Taoists, Buddhists, and Hindu Yogis as a way of controlling thoughts, there is nothing surprising in

Kafka's and Jung's connection between a change in breathing and entering an altered state of consciousness.

In his autobiography, while discussing the ghostly visitation, Jung notes with some surprise that the departed have not progressed above their condition during life (a notion to which he often alluded); Kafka's fourth aphorism imagines ghosts who cling tightly to the vestiges of life until they return (though whether to haunt or reincarnate, Kafka does not say). This indeterminate Afterlife follows naturally from the idea that all boundaries are artificial: a Final Judgment would end the limbo. Thus the motif of an indecisive Hereafter has become a commonplace in late modern and postmodern fiction as in the delusory heavens described at the end of Heinlein's *Stranger in a Strange Land* or the spiritual "turkey farm" at the close of Kurt Vonnegut's *Slapstick*.

Jung's first *Sermon* begins with the usual caveat that Reality is ineffable: underlying everything stands an infinite, eternal, inexpressible "PLEROMA" that can as well be called "nothingness" *(Nichts)* as "fullness" *(Fülle)*. Where does Jung's notion of the PLEROMA (full/void) come from? Considering his interest in Hermetic philosophy, one may well turn to the second book of the "Poimandres [of Hermes's Trismegistus]," where Hermes explains that the "void" may equally or better be called "full" *(plērēstata)* because it is filled with air.[25] Similarly, the Buddhist term *sunyatâ* (denoting emptiness but connoting fullness) originally meant atmosphere. Thus the identity of fullness and void began as a riddle with air (a substance fascinating to the ancients because they did not entirely understand it) as the answer. Also in Jung's usage, the self-contradictory nature of the PLEROMA arises from something he cannot quite define, yet words can describe the qualities derived from the PLEROMA. Likewise, Kafka divorces words and Reality, then opens a back door by which the two may reunite: language can be used as an *Andeutung* (a hint, allusion, or pointing, *H* 45). At the end of the story, "At the Building of the Great Wall," he even suggests (perhaps ironically) that a time may come when people can contemplate the mysterious Beyond. Kafka, though, finds little utility in traditional religious language because he denies the validity of its mainstay—analogy.

Judaism and Christianity use analogies between terrestrial and Divine as the basis of dogma, presuming meaning in such images as Gen. 1.27: man's being made (as the *KJV* translates it) "in the image of God." In that verse, the Hebrew word rendered "image" *(SLM),* signifies also likeness, idol, or even, etymologically, an illusion.[26] This last fits Kafka's aphorisms, for, in discussing Gen., he sees the visible world not as an analogue of the Divine, but as an unreality covering an indescribable Source (*H* 49; *D* 43); Jung considers the Divine to be the rich, archetypal diversity ("multiple gods," *Vielzahl der Götter)* arising from the PLEROMA, i.e., as he was later to call it, the Collective Unconscious (*Er* 395). Orthodox theologians are uncomfortable with such views, as Kafka and Jung were painfully aware. Has orthodoxy managed anything absolutely convincing in the interpretation of religious analogies? Again and again, St. Thomas Aquinas (whose writings were officially declared "miracles" by the Catholic Church) addressed this issue of religious language but, as another Catholic theologian complains, Aquinas gave to religious discourse "no theory of analogy. He does not provide a method whereby one can be sure to speak responsibly of God."[27] According to Christian orthodoxy, speaking or even thinking irresponsibly about God risks damnation—terror of which beset Jung during his school years until he decided that blasphemy was a form of grace sent into his head by God himself (*Er* 45–46). Much blessed with such grace during his lifetime, Jung (like Kafka) further strengthened his heterodoxy by studying certain philosophers, including Kant, who believed that numena and phenomena share no classifiable qualities; thus Jung and Kafka concluded that logical analogy provides no way of describing Reality. Even since their time, such approaches to analogy as Mary Hesse's application of algebraic lattice theory still require a "common property" between the terms compared.[28] Thus, even though Kafka and Jung have arrived at their heterodox positions intuitively or emotionally, no one has entirely disproved their conclusions.

Because of human limitations, they considered the pursuit of Reality dangerous. Jung describes contemplation of the PLEROMA as a worthless process in which one "dissolves oneself" (*sich selber Auflösen, Er* 389; *M* 379), while, in aphorism 86, Kafka writes that in following Divine Knowledge, one "destroys oneself" (*sich Zerstören, H* 49). Similarly, in his later psychology, Jung termed the absorption of the ego by the "Unconscious" a "psychic disaster" (*GW* vol. 9, par. 45). As to literal self-destruction, however, Kafka discloses that if you desire to die, that is a good sign; you are beginning to understand what the world is really like—but you may mistakenly think that after death a Master will summon you to him. Also for Jung, as is evident in the ghosts' consulting him for therapy, beatific visions after death seem hard to achieve. Consequently, whether living or dead, you have no *conscious* access to Reality. Jung continues that we are part of the PLEROMA, yet infinitely distant from it. Kafka offers a notable image of this: one chain ties you to Heaven, another to earth; these leashes are only long enough to strangle you (*H* 46–47). Traditionally, mystics have sought to lose themselves in the Absolute, but in the modern Occident, individuality has become so important that annihilation of the self does not sound particularly attractive even to those preoccupied by the infinite and boundless (e.g., Kafka and Jung).

Since Jung's PLEROMA is infinite and eternal, every part of it contains it all. This paradox is reminiscent of William Blake, who perceived infinity in a grain of sand, eternity in an hour. Today, Jung's image sounds like holography, where every fragment of the photographic plate contains the whole picture. He is saying that since the all-embracing, timeless PLEROMA is in each person, you have past, present, and future within you. This old notion of a microcosm within man is the *terminus a quo et ad quem* of Jung's thinking, but his scientific writings attempt to prove it point by point. First, through his discussion of racial inheritance, he tries to amass evidence that the fruits of past wisdom are contained in the Collective Unconscious. He sees telepathy and precognition as involving knowledge of present and future, an awareness he eventually explained as "synchronicity," an acausal correspondence between the realms within and without.[29] Thus, Jung was not surprised when his dreams accurately foretold events. Kafka claims for mankind the Divine Knowledge of Good and Evil, which, in his version, is very comprehensive, including the future results of each act, so that one can choose correctly. Ethics usually circumvents this problem by focusing on motivations: if you try to do well, that is enough—but, in discussing this Knowledge, Kafka considers motivations *(Motivationen)* to be rationalizations repressing the unconscious omniscience. Kafka holds that what he calls the "Indestructible" *(Unzerstörbare),* an ineffable, indwelling presence, is common to all humanity, binding people together like Jung's Collective Unconscious and containing all knowledge, so, at best, words may act as vague hints or reminders of what you already unconsciously know. Since this indestructible Reality is timeless, all the events of your life are, from the viewpoint of the Eternal, "simultaneous" (*gleichzeitig, H* 50); thus fate is established as Jung also seems to imply. Despite all the seemingly fragmenting opposites on which Jung dwells, despite the intense fragmentation Kafka repeatedly expresses, they feel that all is ultimately one.

Finally, Jung and Kafka reveal the point of all these dizzying metaphysics—precisely to disorient the individual. Jung does this with a statement that nothing is fixed, and Kafka accomplishes it with the aphorism, "This feeling: 'Here I shall not anchor'—and instantly to feel the billowing, supporting swell around one!" (*D* 42). Mysticism traditionally seeks such a process of unknowing or going beyond all boundaries, often with another of Jung's and Kafka's points of agreement, belief that creation is continuous (*Creatur is immer und überall, Er* 390). In his aphorisms, Kafka plays with paradoxes of continuous creation, such as, since the significant moment occurs at each instant, nothing has really happened yet (*H* 39–40); thus, expulsion from Paradise is also perpetual: humanity is both saved and lost every moment (*H* 46). For Jung, continuous creation becomes a key corollary of synchronicity. In a work cowritten with the very reputable physicist W. Pauli, Jung leaps from the discontinuities of physics to "continuous creation," to which he appends a long theological note citing a string of Christian patristic fathers. He could also have justified his position by citing modern Jewish mysticism for, according to Buber, "The 'complete,' the legitimately religious existence of man, does not stand in a continuity but in the genuine acceptance and mastery of discontinuity."[30] If Jung, Pauli, and Kafka can convince the reader that the world is continuously being created anew, then they have abolished that mainstay of modern science, causality—one event's following another logically. In fanatical skepticism, Hume had long before deemed causality a superstition because it was philosophically unprovable. Jung agreed with Hume that causality and superstition could not be absolutely separated, but Jung proceeded one step further, establishing a kind of continuum (or, should one say, "discontinuum") of synchronously related events including both those that seem integrally joined (e.g., a struck match and flame) and those that may be less clearly associated (e.g., having a black cat cross one's path and suffering bad luck). Since such a continuum or discontinuum would have a psychological rather than physical reality, it would change from moment to moment and from observer to observer. Only the Collective Unconscious (a highly problematic entity) could give it unity.

Cognitive Dissonance

> The human essence, basically thoughtless, flighty as dust, can tolerate no confinement; if it restrains itself, it soon starts shaking insanely at the boundary; then wall, bonds, and one's very self are thrown apart in all heavenly directions.
>
> —Kafka, "At the Building of the Great Wall"

Kafka's adult life alternated between nocturnal, creative writing, and diurnal labor for an insurance company. He hated insurance, likening it to "the religions of primitive people who believe they can ward off evil by all kinds of manipulations."[31] In his first employment, these manipulations included arriving with "unconditional promptness," keeping no personal objects in his desk, and working for a shift of ten hours, six or seven days a week, plus "overtime without compensation."[32] After lengthy searching, Kafka found a six-hour-a-day position, a considerable improvement for some years until his father, long appalled by the son's light schedule, finally commanded the young man to run a family factory during the latter's spare time.

After a fairly ordinary childhood, Jung managed, without ill effects, equally occupied days (and sometimes nights) throughout his almost eighty-six-year life; but there was a significant difference: at least after he became famous, his business largely consisted of following his own whims. If patients bored him, he threw them out. Once, a bizarre chase scene occurred on the local lake, with a patient pursuing in one boat and Jung escaping in another.[33] Jung even found the opportunity to build sand castles and draw mandalas (all part of his psychological researches). Having married a rich and tolerant wife—two of the secrets of their relatively happy marriage—he could afford to keep the chains of routine sufficiently loose so that he did not completely tear them and himself to fragments.

To the extent that they could manage it, he and Kafka escaped alienation and the strictures of routine with religious fantasies. Jung's visionary notebooks (often a Blakean mixture of drawing and writing) occasioned a radical change in his psychology and Kafka's studies were sufficiently numerous so that they provided multiple sources for each of his works—one of the reasons for their universality and also for their strangeness, since they combine disparate cultures. In an enigmatic jotting about the Freemasons, he wrote the sentence fragment, "the possible truth that there is in every discourse and doctrine" (*T* 581; *D2* 230).

About seventeen years before the aphorisms when Kafka, himself, was seventeen (1900), he already distrusted language. "Words make awkward mountain climbers and awkward miners. They cannot lower treasure from the crag's summit, nor raise them from its entrails" (*Br* 9). The imagery of writing as being like scaling or burrowing within personified mountains comes from the (by-then-quite-out-of-date) German Romantic movement (e.g., E. T. A. Hoffmann's "Mines of Falun"). Throughout his life Kafka found more and more effective and contemporary ways of expressing that Romantic obsession with the ineffable. Authors from many disciplines cite him in connection with his fascination: how to bring within the system of language those unspeakable heights and depths, which, for want of any real name, he calls the "fabulous yonder" (*sagenhaftes Drüben, P* 10–11). The mathematician Rudy Rucker, for example, says of her great predecessor Kurt Gödel:

> The Kafkaesque aspect of Gödel's work and character is expressed in his famous Incompleteness Theorem of 1930. Although this theorem can be stated and proved in a rigorously mathematical way, what it seems to say is that *rational thought can never penetrate to the final ultimate truth.*[34]

Gödel's theorem implies the conclusion that no human system can simultaneously include everything in the universe and be consistent. In essence, Gödel draws a line through the world with the consistent (limited, practical, bureaucratic, and scientific) on one side and the inconsistent (universal, fantastic, and mystical) on the other. Typical of Romantics, Kafka and Jung, in their different ways, suggest that the two sides do not remain neatly separate but interpenetrate, so that any attempt at absolute consistency stands foredoomed to disastrous failure. For Emerson, "a foolish consistency" was merely "the hobgoblin of little minds."[35] This specter has since grown despicable with death camps that Kafka narrowly missed, bulwarks of that most pointless consistency, racial "purity." Jung indicted them as part of the "Nazi psychosis."[36] One scientific discipline after another has recognized the danger of another disastrous consistency, the hermeneutic circle. "The very language in which observations are reported is influenced by prior theories"; thus, one never assimilates value-free data with which to create, verify, or falsify a theory.[37] Attempting to break the circle, Jung and other psychologists have charted the repression of cognitive dissonance (untidy facts screened from consciousness because they cause anxiety by undermining current preconceptions). What Jung intuited but could not systematically describe, he generally relegated to the Collective Unconscious. Any attempt to apply Jungian analysis neatly to writers (as one might apply Freudian or Marxist theory to them) inevitably falsifies the basic looseness of his speculations. Admittedly, Lacan finds an almost Deconstructionist openness even in Freud, and Jung once prodded the latter until he acknowledged the intermittent operation of the censorship mechanism,[38] but Freud's general emphasis was on creating a clear, coherent system, with distinct boundaries. Jung writes, "Freud is seeing the mental process as static, while I speak in terms of dynamics and relationship."[39] Although Jung spent a lifetime gathering arcane data to try to prove the existence of the Collective Unconscious, ultimately it remained a mysterious storehouse of ineffable patterns; thus, he brought a *terra incognita* into the very heart of his psychology, thereby generating the suggestive incoherence that results from a mixture of known and unknown. His multiple-dimensional vision does not make for easy comprehension, but some obscurity is necessary in dealing with cognitive dissonance (that which defies systematization).

How can cognitive dissonance enter the system of language? For such a Zen poet as Basho, years of *zazen*—sitting attentively, carefully observing internal and external phenomena but without trying to systematize them—may have widened awareness, providing material for the startling juxtapositions and omissions of a successful *haiku*. Furthermore, because the Japanese written language contains both Chinese ideograms and characters representing the sounds of Japanese words, it often involves playing the one language (and culture) against the other. At least until recently, however, the situation in the West has been relatively different. Jung's therapeutic technique that he named "active imagination" (observing one's own fantasies) was a step toward Eastern meditation, but only a step. Jung insisted that his patients stop and try to understand their findings, a process that risked imposing a restrictive order on the perceptions. Intercultural contact, however, despite some conservative political efforts to prevent it, has fractured the traditional boundaries of every society, thereby allowing much of what was previously cognitive dissonance to enter consciousness.

Millions of bi- or multilinguals already stand at the frontiers of internationalism, though many may manage to compartmentalize the contrasting worldviews to which they have been exposed. For example, in a paper delivered at the 1987 Western Psychological Association Meeting, Philip V. Hull reported on the following research. To forty-one Spanish-English bilinguals, he administered the Spanish then, a few days later, the English version of the California Psychological Inventory, a personality test that has been repeatedly refined over the years to avoid cultural biases. Nonetheless, when taking the English version, the group scored higher in desire for personal achievement and other traits related to what, following Max Weber, might be called the "Protestant Ethic," while in Spanish they scored higher on self-control and other qualities that Weber associated with Catholicism.[40] Whether the bilinguals actually had two linguistically associated personalities or whether the test retained residual cultural biases, Hull's results at least serve to remind one that there are significant differences between cultures. Sanity tends to mean fitting into one's own group. If intercultural mingling continues to accelerate, will there come a time without any distinct culture?

Already, when the multicultural become professional authors, they may find themselves in the position of the bilingual Julien Green, who remarks:

> In reading the proofs of my book [*Memories of Happy Days*] I was struck by all that I had left unsaid and that I should most certainly have said in that book, had I written it in French. For instance, all that had to do with the development of religious feeling.[41]

An even more striking example concerns the critic Tzvetan Todorov. In Paris, his place of exile, he wrote a French speech against Bulgarian tradition, then returned to his native Bulgaria to deliver it. Once, however, he began translating it into Bulgarian, he found himself defending Bulgaria. He later realized:

> To my own eyes [my divided allegiance], rendered inauthentic both of my discourses, because each is only able to correspond to half of my being [*mon être*]; yet I am actually double."[42]

2
Autobiographical Investigations

> I am at the final boundary, before which I should perhaps sit for years, in order again perhaps to begin a new, again-unfinished story.
>
> —Kafka, *Diaries*, 30 November 1914

> Ever more filled with *ängst* in writing. Understandably. Each word, turned in the hands of spirits—this flourish of the hand is their typical movement—becomes a spike, bent against the speaker.
>
> —Kafka, *Diaries*, 12 June 1923

> Material . . . from the Unconscious had, almost literally, rendered me mute.
>
> —Jung

Kafka wrote much about his failure to write.[1] In a 1914 diary (early in his career), he seems lost, his extreme hesitancy marked by the awkward repetitions of "perhaps" *(vielleicht)* and "again" *(wieder)*. A few days later, he composed his most effective short fiction, "Before the Law" *(Vor dem Gesetz)*, also about someone sitting for years in front of an impassable boundary. Its plot, in turn, resembles other of his compositions including *The Castle*. In the next excerpt (from a 1923 diary—the last entry he ever made), he still seems lost, his style as convoluted as his thought. His image of being hampered by spirits or internal fragmentation, however, occurs throughout many of his striking works, most explicitly in the earlier parable, "The Invention of the Devil" *(Der Erfindung des Teufels)*. Its speaker wishes that he were possessed by only one demon. Instead, hellish legions war with one another. Kafka sometimes felt that he was trying to construct something from nothing. In one of the very earliest diary entries, he likens writing to Japanese acrobats who were climbing an almost unsupported ladder; however, Kafka adds that his ladder is completely without support, floating in midair (*T* 12). At other times (as already mentioned), he sees his problem as his own psychological fragmentation.

> Writing refuses to come to me. Thus design for autobiographical investigations. Not biography but investigation [*Untersuchung*] and discovery of the tiniest

> conceivable elements. From these I shall then build myself [*mich . . . Aufbauen*] . . . [but] if in the middle of the construction . . . energy fails . . . [m]adness follows. (*H* 388)[2]

In an article on St. Augustine's *Confessions* (a book with which Kafka was familiar), Lawrence Byrne sets forth the Augustinian model that has left its mark on the whole history of Occidental autobiography. Augustine considers his nature mysterious, "manifold, and quite immeasurable" *(varia, multimoda vita et immensa)*[3]—a spiritual fragmentation to be healed. Achieving coherence consists of finding how God "began to work out in time what [He] had predestined, so that [He] might reveal what was hidden and bring order into our disorder."[4] Byrne likens Augustine's hope to Roy Schafer's understanding of the psychoanalytic goal.

> The psychoanalytic "cure" . . . [is] a joint effort in storytelling, the analyst and analysand working to retell the analysand's past in a better, more acceptable story. And Schafer defines a "better" story here as one that possesses the virtues of coherence, consistency, comprehensiveness, and common sense."[5]

Augustine wishes to unify himself by discovering within himself the Divine image or pattern; Kafka seeks to find the elements so that he can build himself with the unity he elsewhere attributes to his impersonal God, the Indestructible. Instead of ever succeeding in constructing himself (the process of psychic unification called by Jung "Individuation"), Kafka, seeking help from neither analyst nor personal God, spent his life portraying his internal incoherence. The elements of his individual existence were trivial and boring. Wisely, he translated them into the larger, more universal ones of cross-cultural contact (which played a part in his fragmentation).

In *The Trial,* for example, "Before the Law" is prefaced by a multicultural disorientation of the novel's protagonist, Joseph K. First, he frantically spends the night reviewing an Italian grammar book to prepare him for an encounter with an Italian businessman. That meeting begins in a mixture of bad French and an obscure dialect from the south of Italy, almost incomprehensible to K. He must rely on his superior, the Bank Manager, to translate the Italian's words, presumably into German, even while K. fears the Manager is plotting against him. The latter asks K. to guide the visitor through the local Cathedral, famed for its art, so K. returns to his office and tries to memorize the Italian phrases he will need, but he is constantly interrupted. He reaches the Cathedral in time, but, perhaps because of a language problem, the Italian never arrives. Suddenly, K. becomes the object of a chaplain's preaching, as the context sharply turns from aesthetic to religious and then to legal: K.'s trial. By a further reversal, a "Scripture" quoted by the priest is no biblical passage but Kafka's parable, "Before the Law." It concerns a "man from the country" *(Mann vom Lande).* Ritchie Robertson observes:

> The phrase "Mann von [sic] Lande" itself represents a calque on [translation of] the Hebrew *'am ha-'arets.* This phrase was originally applied to the rural population of Palestine who did not understand the intricacies of the Law as it had been systematized by the rabbis; Kafka had already encountered the phrase in his reading. . . . He also knew the Yiddish derivative *amorets,* which had come to mean "ignoramus," and which he uses in his diary. ("Amhorez," *T* 177)[6]

Robertson's observation (an echo of similar ones by Politzer, Urzidil, and Robert),[7] may be an oversimplification because *Mann vom Lande* is a German idiom, used by Kafka previous to his diary entry, which looks as if it marked his first encounter with "Amhorez." The likelihood is that Kafka was initially intrigued by the confrontation of rural and urban cultures implied by *Mann vom Lande,* and this interest led him to note "Amhorez" in his Diary and perhaps also to pay attention to the cognate Hebrew phrase when he found it in his reading. At any rate, *Mann vom Lande* was for him a loaded phrase, suggesting a rusticated fellow away from his farm. This character encounters a doorkeeper with a Tartar *(tatarischen)* beard. In his reading, Kafka had run across Chinese tales of Barbarian (i.e., Tartar) doorkeepers. The *Mann vom Lande* cannot persuade the fearsome, possibly foreign guard to permit entry and the impasse lasts for years until the countryman's death. After the priest finishes recounting this parable, he and K. engage in a metaphysical exegesis of it, a kind of midrash (rabbinic commentary), though so parodoxical as to sound like a *Mondo* (Zen dialogue); thus the Catholic priest is made not only to say that "Before the Law" is part of the Scriptures, but to comment on it in the manner of a (Zenist) rabbi, a staggering juxtaposition of cultures. The priest argues that "the correct interpretation of a thing and the misunderstanding of it do not entirely exclude one another" (*P* 68–69 [W]), as if he were looking at matters from more than one perspective, i.e., from more than one cultural matrix. Finally, K. summarizes the priest's line of reasoning. "It makes lying [*die Lüge*] into the world order [*Weltordnung*]" (*P* 78–79 [W]). The key word is "lying." As in Kafka's aphorisms, the ultimate problem of language is deliberate deception or concealment, for, as previously noted, he believed that humanity possesses, indeed *is,* the Divine Knowledge but represses it (to avoid being torn between the heavenly and earthly frames of reference).

Certainly no single Ariadne's thread leads throughout the vast maze of universal lying, but Jung's earliest, most basic researches offer a beginning.

A Stylistic Polygraph

> How can we approach the dark sphere of man? As I have told you, this is done by . . . methods of analysis [including] the word association test. . . . I use this test . . . with criminal cases.
>
> —Jung, The Tavistock Lectures [originally delivered in English]

Near the turn of this century, Jung was still engaged in precise, clinical research: employing a one-fifth-second stopwatch to time the period elapsing between a researcher's pronouncing a word and the subject's response. This work delighted Freud because unconscious delays in response to emotionally charged items formed the first hard evidence that the mind actually did perpetrate those repressions Freud had theorized. Jung's procedure may have inspired the invention of the lie detector as well as the Rorschach test and may be related to the rise of semantic differential testing such as Charles E. Osgood's work with the comparative study of cultures or Osgood's and Zella Luria's tests of how each personality in a case of multiple personalities responds differently to the same words.[8] In Jung's hands, however, psycholinguistic research was far from dry. In a typical instance, a wealthy patron asked for Jung's help to investigate a theft possibly committed by the man's eighteen-year-old, live-in "protégé," who had recently been spending money with unaccustomed abandon. While (perhaps unethically) pretending to treat the youth for a neurosis (which might even have been inspired by the relationship between protector and protégé), Jung read a list of words, some of them associated with theft such as *steal, thief,* and *police*. The youth's reaction to these was slow and aberrant—a fact with which Jung confronted the lad; then the latter confessed (*GW,* vol. 18, par. 106; vol. 2, pars. 770–92).

As was stated earlier, Kafka based much of his writing on his inability to write, those emotional moments when a repressive force from beyond consciousness silenced him for far longer than the average subject undergoing word-association tests. Unfortunately, word association (like its child, the lie detector) gives ambiguous results. Furthermore, unlike speaking, writing usually conceals the delays of the composition process. The key problem is finding corroboration for any inference. Kafka provides one clue in *Hochzeitsvorbereitungen auf dem Lande*. Kafka's persona, Raban, recognizes that it is out of fear that he uses not the first but the third person to discuss his life. "And so long as you use 'one' in place of 'I', the situation is nothing and one can tell the tale, but if you accept that it concerns you yourself, you are run through and horrified" (*H* 162). Raban's feeling "run through" *(durchbohrt)* and "horrified" *(entsetzt)* is no calm, academic discussion of rhetoric. It sounds precisely like the kind of language-associated, emotional disturbance that Jung measured, except here the troubled moment is embedded in writing like an insect in amber.

Does Kafka's infamous letter to his father *(Brief an den vater),* which arose from Franz's inability to speak to the latter, manifest such psychologically charged substitutions? When Kafka's father, Hermann, asked why Franz even as an adult was afraid of him, the son, as he confesses, was too frightened to answer at the moment, so he wrote a forty-five page reply—a monumentally long "reaction time." Even while typing this missive, he says he felt hindered by fear (*H* 162), which becomes one of the main themes of the letter along with a theme to which emotional pronoun shifts relate it—his wavering sense of self.

The Shifting Self

> . . . when, during my last illness, you came tiptoeing to Ottla's room to see me, stepping in the doorway, craning your neck to see me in bed, and out of consideration only waved to me with your hand. At such times *one* would lie back and weep for happiness, and *one* weeps again now, writing it down [italics mine].
>
> —Kafka, *Letter to the Father*

Kafka shifts from first to third person, as if, in composing the letter, his bursting into tears accompanied a sudden desire to pretend that the situation was happening to anyone else, rather than to himself—exactly the same pretense that Raban makes. In his fiction, Kafka typically employs either relatively transparent personae (e.g., "K.") in the third person or more heavily disguised personae (e.g., the mouse narrator of *Josephine, die Sängerin,* the ape-narrator of *Ein Bericht für eine Akademie,* or the anonymous Chinese narrator of *Beim Bau der Chinesischen Mauer*) in the first person. Brod named one series of Kafka's autobiographical meditations "He" because Kafka so obsessively wrote of himself in the third person therein. That in such works he (like many other authors) required distancing is well-known, but less obvious is his desire for *sudden* distancing so acute that it vitiated his usually impeccable sense of style. Far from the artistic mastery of his fiction, the pronoun shift in this passage is a solecism. From a literary perspective, sentimentality and self-pity also mar the section, further corroborating what the crying suggests—that his objectivity was overcome by emotion.

The clue of the pronoun switch leads to a second point in the manuscript where Kafka states that his father's scoldings have furrowed his brain (*H* 183). After quoting a few of these cutting words (his father's view of how sinfully easy the son's life had been), Kafka suddenly shifts to the third person. Without noting this grammatical clue, Klaus Wagenbach comments, "The phrase Kafka uses about his father's words having 'traced furrows' in his brain is not only strange but incomparably more vivid than any other comment he makes on his childhood."[9] Wagenbach's sensitivity to the emotionally charged imagery corroborates the evidence of the pronoun switch that this is another passage to be singled out. Kafka himself says that the furrowing words generated an intense consciousness of guilt (*ein grosses Schuldbewusstsein,*" *H* 183). Sudden, guilt-induced anxiety may cause a polygraph needle to jump or produce the disturbed responses Jung sought and interpreted when he administered the word-association test in criminal cases. Admittedly, other emotions than guilt cause agitation, rendering the forensic application of polygraphs and word-association tests problematic, but here, where Kafka recalls a source of guilt, there should be no surprise in seeing a slight but real disturbance in the flow of his writing.

A third pronoun shift occurs in the following sentences:

> If I was to escape from you [Hermann Kafka], I had to escape from the family as well, even from Mother. True, *one* could always get protection from her, but only in relation to you. She loved you too much and was too devoted and loyal to you to have been for long an independent spiritual force in the child's struggle. [italics mine] (*BK* 208)

Thoughts of leaving his mother, memories of how dependent he was on her, and the realization that he can never compete with his father combine to make the section disturbing.

In "Letter to the Father," these three passages are not the only ones where Kafka moves from first to third person, but they are among the most abrupt ones, the points a composition teacher would probably mark as errors. In a continuum of passages, ranging from the most to least emotional, the next rank just below this triad would go to Kafka's discovery of the facts of life. This section (*H* 210–11) begins almost pleasantly as Franz walks on the Josefsplatz with his parents. He mocks his own pretended or "untrue" *(unwahr)* calmness. Gradually, he attacks his father for suggesting that the boy visit prostitutes. By the next paragraph, Franz is in white heat, five times calling sex "filth" *(Schmutz).* Then, as usual, he distances himself, retreating to the third person, this time in a whole paragraph, which describes his relationship to his father in terms of the letters *A* and *B.* By proceeding in a relatively controlled, gradual manner, Kafka avoids shifts as awkward as in those passages previously discussed. Furthermore, the algebraic paragraph concludes with the following words: "Since you are A and I am B," thereby fully accepting that the situation has happened to him, not to the anyone or everyone of the passages just cited. As throughout the letter, he speaks to his father with the familiar pronoun *Du,* unlike his father's habit, when angry, of referring to Franz in the third person very formally as "Mr. Son" (*Herrn Sohn, H* 178). Considering that Kafka thought that "coitus is the punishment of being close" (*T* 315), no one should be surprised by Kafka feeling somewhat nervous about sex. More interesting is that he appears to have been a shade more troubled at this triad of situations—situations that only a doctrinarily Freudian reading would consider erotic.

It is time to see what light that triad of passages sheds on the document's central puzzle: the relationship between Kafka and the one for whom he wrote the "Letter to the Father"—whomever that may have been (since the document is equivocal). The many candidates include his mother. According to *Franz Kafka: Eine Biographie,* he gave it to her, ostensibly to deliver to Hermann. After examining this overwhelming manuscript, she averted a collision between Franz and Hermann.[10] Did her son anticipate precisely this? How better could he try to win her to his side than through a work that mingles lavish praise of her with mild criticism, primarily for her not taking his part more openly?[11] Others to whom he showed the letter include Milena Jesenská and Max Brod, who eventually published it, as if it were for the general public. Kafka may have written the manuscript partly as therapy, i.e., for himself. And the conventional view assumes that he composed it for his father ("Letter to the Father" being Brod's title).

As usual, considered alone, the biographical facts do not illuminate the abyss of human intention, nor can even an ordinary close reading solve the enigma. Franz's sentences take on different shadings when one sees them as designed for himself, Father, Mother, Milena, or Brod, all of whom would have discovered much personal interest in the manuscript. What, then, do the triad of emotionally charged passages reveal about the intended audience of the document? First, that on one level it was meant for neither Father nor Mother. In the third passage cited, he admits that his mother is totally loyal to his father; thus there is little hope of winning her over or that she will endanger family tranquility by delivering the letter. It is, thus, most unlikely ever to reach the father. Styled differently, his admission might be a skillful ploy, a way of pressuring her into acting. In the partially uncontrolled passage, however, it is less likely to be a conscious strategy than a confession of despair. Comparably, Kafka stopped his typescript in midsentence with the despondent words, "You are unfit for life; but in order—" (*H* 450; *D* 405). Nonetheless, he took up pen and finished the missive, then submitted it as if one level of his mind continued to hope.

Further information comes from the second nodal moment in the letter, the father's furrowing words. Faced with Hermann's boast about his once-suffering economic hardship, Franz idiosyncratically complains of never being equally poor. According to Self-Psychologists (one of the groups whose findings contribute to the reinterpretation of Jung), a boy who cannot imitate and idealize his father invests psychological energy in vague, numinous parental images (a modern way of explaining some of the clinical evidence associated by Jung with "archetypes").[12] Seen in this light, Kafka's inability to imitate his father's life seems as important as the emotionally charged passage makes it. The form of his father's words—what the son calls "irony" (*H* 176; *D* 151)—also (in a vastly more polished style) characterizes Kafka's letter, indeed, much of his writing. When he asserts that all his works are about his father, he adds that in a sense his life and fictions have been "dictated" *(diktierte)* by the father, yet Franz likewise sees composition as a source of escape and freedom (*H* 203). His writing is a way of emulating his father by creating powerful words of his own, i.e., a way of finally growing up. At the end of the letter, Franz imagines what caustic reproaches Hermann will make in rejoinder to the manuscript; then Franz concludes that this imagined rejoinder comes not from the father but from Franz himself: Kafka has so perfectly portrayed and imitated the perspective of the father as, in a sense, to become the latter.

With this father/son fusion in mind, one cannot entirely agree with those critics who oversimplify Kafka's filial impiety, such as Ernst Pawel. The latter bluntly states, "Kafka quite obviously hated his father, and for some very good reasons, all of them developed at great length in this letter purportedly meant as a love offering."[13] Pawel directs attention to the best-written sections of the epistle, the "reasons . . . developed at length," but when Kafka acts like a lawyer constructing a brief for the prosecution he masterfully controls the writing rather than necessarily betraying his own deepest feelings. Thus, the carefully listed petty grievances against Hermann may represent a more conscious level than the solecisms do. Recall Kafka's slight awkwardness in telling how he weeps at the mere remembrance of his father's suffering in silence. Those tears sound more like love than like the hate presumed by Pawel. Without the pronoun shift, the reference to tears would be more likely a rhetorical trick than in their present context where they seem addressed to the father—not necessarily the actual father, but what John Hibberd calls "an archetypal parent."[14] The problem with Hibberd's otherwise perceptive remark is that he never defines "archetypal," a word used many ways in criticism, and several others by Jung, who eventually saw archetypes as the root of "feeling-toned complexes," the ultimate cause of disturbances in word-association tests. The ineffability that Jung frequently attributes to archetypes may remind one of the first paragraph in *Brief an den Vater,* where Kafka deems the subject of the letter to be beyond the power of his reason. A danger of the term "archetype," however, is that one might expect a single discrete entity (e.g., father archetype or mother archetype). Actually, mother and father appear so closely related in Kafka's letter, that they seem part of a single dynamic pattern—reminiscent of the point in *Das*

Urteil where the mother is said to have given the father her energy, so that he has become luminous with power.[15] Consequently, until psychology has explained Jung's "archetypes" more definitely, a safer Jungian term is *complex* (which the psychiatrist Theodore Ziehen had applied to disturbances in word-association tests even before Jung).[16] Since the nature of complexes is comprehensive, all of the candidates (Hermann, Julie, etc.) mentioned at the beginning of this section may have been addressed by different strata of the letter, which reflect Franz's many levels of consciousness. He likens the letter to a *Geduldspiel,* a children's toy where a ball goes through a labyrinthine series of levels. Then he concludes open-endedly that reality is not even this simple, but contains more than his art (*H* 223).

"Letter to the Father" embodies with unusual clarity the suggestive similarities between Kafka's chief personal problem (ambivalence toward following any model) and his metaphysical position (that language does not easily reflect Reality). Stronger even than sexual trauma is that loss of models—not only his strained relations with his father, but also the loss of all the other models his father denied him. Franz complains that Hermann derided Czechs, Germans, and Jews, leaving no one aside from Hermann's own person, whom the son found to be a "mystery" (*Rätselhafte, H* 169; *D* 145). Franz particularly complains that the father's nominal Judaism is unsatisfying and so the boy must seek elsewhere. He must produce his own personality without the usual guides—parents, family, orthodox religion, and country.

In "The New *Trahison Des Clercs:* Reflections on the Present Crisis in Humanistic Studies," Nathan A. Scott, Jr., astutely observes that to overcome the postmodern uncertainties of hermeneutics, an interpreter must "specify those patterns of emphasis which his sense of the whole leads him to regard as forming the essential ground . . . that distinguishes the vision of the world that the author has sought to convey."[17] If points of emphasis can be determined (as the foregoing attempts to do), a reader may find a way through the labyrinth of complex intentions and worldviews.

Personae

> All visible objects . . . are but as pasteboard masks . . . if man will strike, strike through the mask! How can the prisoner reach outside except by thrusting through the wall?
>
> —Melville, *Moby-Dick*

> The world will offer itself to you to be unmasked. It can't do otherwise; in raptures it will writhe before you.
>
> —Kafka (untitled aphorism)

In 1908, C. G. Jung introduced to psychology the decipherment of psychotic speech. He analyzed an aged schizophrenic who could only express herself by such weird circumlocutions as, "I am Socrates's deputy" to mean that she was persecuted as was Socrates. When Jung tried to explain his discovery to Freud, the latter listened "with an odd puzzled look." Finally, Freud remarked, "You know, Jung, what you have found out about this patient is certainly interesting, but how could you bear spending hours and days with this phenomenally ugly female?"[18] Jung, however, took no special note of her physical appearance, so fascinated was he by her observable mental condition, the mask, or in Jungian terminology, "persona," whose manifestations included her idiosyncratically metaphoric language.[19] For most people, the persona reflects one's place in the cultural matrix: doctor, lawyer, son, husband, daughter, wife . . . whatever the society requires, but the schizophrenic (for some yet-unknown reason) loses a sense of that matrix so that the persona becomes a hodgepodge of material gathered from practically anywhere (e.g., the allusion to Socrates).

Three or four years before Jung's discovery, the following passage from Kafka's "Description of a Struggle" *(Beschreibung eines Kampfes)* anticipated Jung's realization that deranged speech consists of circumlocutions. In it, Kafka's "persona" (in the literary sense, i.e., his projection of himself into the work) is addressed in the following derogatory way:

> The field poplar, called by you "Tower of Babel" since you did not wish to know it as a poplar, sways once more nameless, and you must term it, "Noah, when drunk." (*B* 43)[20]

Kafka's purpose for deriding his own persona's style, however, was not psychoanalytic but forms part of a section that he entitles "Entertainments, or Evidence that it Is Impossible to Live" *(Belustigungen oder Beweis dessen, dass es unmöglich ist zu leben).* In his 1917 aphorisms, he explains that phenomenal existence is a comforting lie projected by mankind as a protection against Reality, which would destroy us if we saw it directly. Paradoxically, he continues, people cannot endure without belief in this Reality, the "Indestructible." That is where fantasy proves its worth. It creates a sense of falseness, thus pointing beyond the phenomenal (the serpentine evil waiting to be unmasked) to the Indestructible, but without showing us how to reach it. As we have seen, for Kafka and Jung, not seeking Reality is important (though both want awareness to transcend what is normally conscious). Far less aggressive than Melville's Ahab, who wishes to strike through the mask, or Jung, who advocates *active* imagination, Kafka prefers a quietistic waiting. Kafka writes, "Theoretically, there is a perfect possibility of happiness: believing in the indestructible element in oneself and not striving towards it" (*D* 41). In the notebook from which this aphorism comes, he explains that believing means in a sense to become the Indestructible or more precisely, simply to *be* (*H* 89), a state beyond all striving. In one of his more difficult aphorisms he summarizes thus: "Our art is a means to be blinded by Truth: the light on the grotesque, withdrawing face is true, nothing otherwise" (*H* 47). Similarly, in a letter to Brod, Kafka wrote of how a story "destroys . . . or obscures itself, no, diminishes, moves away" (*L* 54), luring the reader on. Kafka makes his personae into caricatures constantly being unmasked so that, in the imagery of the aphorisms, the light of the Indestructible will shine through, blinding the readers to the visible world and awakening them effortlessly to the Reality beyond.

The passage about the poplar is part of a surrealistic section that powerfully generates such a sense of grotesque fantasy. The narrator arrives, riding on a friend, occasionally kicking the latter in the belly to urge him onward. When the human steed collapses, the narrator summons vultures from the sky to sit on the companion and "guard" *(bewachen)* him. Then, the narrator walks forward into the "unfinished" *(unfertigen)* landscape. With the 1917 aphorisms in mind, one may presume that the landscape is "unfinished" because it is continuously being generated by minds, and this presumption is substantiated by what happens next. Although the narrator has enjoyed the rugged scenery when he could ride, as a pedestrian he prefers that the hill become flatter and the (opposing) wind disappear. They obey. To improve the view, he adds pine trees to the slope and stars to the sky. When he closes his eyes, however, the road begins to become intangible beneath his feet, so he must look at it in order to bring it back into existence. Later, he sees an Oriental litter bearing a fat man who is talking to the landscape, bits of which float through his intangible flesh. There follows a subsection about the fat man's friend, Kafka's aforementioned persona, whose failings seem excusable, because he must live amid the preceding chaotic fantasies.

Kafka's depiction of this lunacy does not come from fieldwork at an asylum; he has been analyzing his own problems with language. Also early in his career (1910), Kafka complains in his first diary that when he tries to write, "my uncertainties surround every word; I perceive them sooner than the word, but what then! I am totally oblivious to the word, I invent it" (*T* 27). Like the persona who allegedly substituted images of a falling tower or of a tipsy man for the swaying tree, so Kafka says that he unintentionally projects fantasies between himself and language. He is lost in a dream. In the 1910 diary he presents this inability to communicate as a personal problem, but in his 1917 aphorisms he generalizes that language can never describe Reality. The latter is an ineffable Eden from which mankind is constantly falling (*H* 45–46). Similarly, in the poplar passage, the allusions to the Tower of Babel and Noah's drunkenness criticize the persona for the fallen condition[21] of the latter's language, his substituting an idiosyncratic association of ideas for objectivity. While, in his study of word association, Jung discovered that such a concatenation nonetheless possessed a kind of logic of its own, Kafka stresses the capriciousness of his own usage—a stress he maintains throughout all his works, for the peculiar sufferings of his many personae are all "evidence that It is Impossible to Live," that life in the visible world is unbearable and unreal.

Kafka's "persona" in the Jungian sense, his total adaptation to life, was sane and relatively successful, well-satisfying his employers, but his literary personae are enmeshed in personal myth such as the following fragment found among his papers:

> The Dream Lord [*Herr*], great Isachar, sat in front of the mirror, his back close to the surface, his head bent far back and sunk deep in the mirror. Hermana, the Lord [*Herr*] of Dusk entered and dived into Isachar's chest until he disappeared. (*H* 285)

Since virtually all of Kafka's fantasies show an obsession with his father Hermann, the name Hermana with its strangely feminizing final *a* certainly suggests some odd variant of his family problem (e.g., the fused father/mother already discussed). If Hermana is derived from Hermann, then presumably Franz, who himself saw his style as dreamlike, is the master of dreams, Isachar, named after one of Jacob's sons (Gen. 30:18).

By playing with the actual name of his father in the midst of a fantasy, Kafka (as often) slides from objective (the actual father) to subjective (Hermana). In his metaphysics, there is no obvious difference between sanity and madness (although, in his life, he sometimes fell into the conventional worry that he was going insane). In his fantasies, however, his erosion of boundaries between sanity and insanity was one of his principal ways of demonstrating that phenomena are unreal, but he did not arrive at this device quickly. In "The Judgment" *(Das Urteil),* he relies on a private code to relate his name to that of his literary persona, Georg Bendemann. In a 1913 diary (*T* 297), he deciphers it as follows: "Georg," he says, has the same number of letters as "Franz" while "Bende" is the same length as "Kafka." More mysteriously, he continues that the suffix "-mann" foreshadows the story's "not-yet known possibilities." What possibilities? In the same diary entry, Kafka explains that Georg "believes that he has his father within him" (*D1* 278). If some critic made so bold an interpretation, one would have a right to protest, but here Kafka himself reveals it, using the strange imagery of absorbing the father that he also employed in the fragment about Isachar and Hermana. How, then, is the suffix "-mann" a prefigurement? Even more strongly than in English, the

German word *Mann* suggests the adult, the husband—and for Kafka this is perhaps particularly true because it occurs in the first name of his father, the one who always seemed to Kafka lord *(Herr)*-man *(Mann) par excellence*. Georg thinks himself the man of the house, his father's role safely absorbed by the former with the latter in retirement. By the devilish irony of the story, he only has his father within him in the sense that he finds himself unable to resist his father's command to die when the father exposes the falseness of the young man's life. Kafka's reasoning is so cryptological that he has to explain it to *himself* in a Diary. He had no earthly reason to think that his readers would discover it since he did not know that his "friend" Brod would open these Diaries and other dirty linen to public scrutiny. In Kafka's last novels, *The Trial (Der Prozess)* and *The Castle (Das Schloss)*, however, the personae are both named K., so transparent a reference to their author that readers knew immediately. By this time, Kafka had so completely accepted the unreality of life that he had moved quite openly into his fantasies.

Even in his cryptological phase, however, Kafka has an *un*earthly reason to hope his readers might intuit the truth. If, as he contended, humanity is united in the Divine Knowledge, they could, perhaps, summon the omniscience to understand his "Evidence" by penetrating his strange disguises—and some of these are very strange indeed. The Kafka name sounded like the Czech word for jackdaw, a fact his father commemorated by painting an image of the bird on the sign of the family business to deceive his Czech customers into thinking he was of their ethnic group (a deception that worked well enough to spare the firm during one anti-Semitic riot). It is a commonplace of Kafka criticism that Franz used various dark birds of ill omen to represent himself, such as the title character of "The Hunter Gracchus" (from the Latin *Graculus*, jackdaw) or Raban (from the German *Rabe*, raven), the protagonist of "Marriage Preparations in the Country" *(Hochzeitsvorbereitungen auf dem Lande)*.[22] In the 1917 aphorisms, Kafka writes:

> The crows maintain that a single crow could destroy the heavens. There is no doubt of that, but it proves nothing against the heavens, for heaven simply means: the impossibility of crows. (*BK* 238)

This is eloquent admission of his own nonexistence if and only if one knows that crows like ravens and jackdaws represent Kafka.

The Yiddish etymology of his patronymic from "Jacob" provided Kafka with another series of associations. In nineteenth-century literature, Jacob's wrestling with God or the Angel[23] formed a type for encounters with anything actually or ironically considered Divine.[24] In an 1891 poem, for example, Herman Melville urges his readers to "fuse with Jacob's mystic heart, / To wrestle with the angel—Art."[25] Since by Kafka's period, the Angel could be virtually any person, thing, or idea, one should not be surprised in Kafka's novel, *The Lost One (Der Verschollene)* to find the character, Uncle Jacob, wrestling with the Angel, American commerce, for the blessing of vast wealth and for a seat in the senate, though, like his biblical eponym, Uncle Jacob arises from the struggle with an injured leg and altered name. (Like Hermann's change of the meaning of Kafka from Jacob to jackdaw, Uncle Jacob makes a subtle change of name, in his case switching his first name to his last one to Americanize himself.) The book calls particular attention to such vicissitudes of nomenclature. Because of Jacob's name change, Kafka's literary persona, Karl Rossmann,[26] at first refuses to believe Jacob to be his Uncle. However, the only reason why the Uncle wants to make the teenager Karl into a kind of foster son is that Karl has begotten a boy named Jacob after the Uncle. Kafka develops the image of Karl as Joseph (i.e., son of Jacob) through repeated references to Karl's condition as being like a bondage in Egypt.[27] The immature youth's name (on which much emphasis is also placed) means etymologically (and ironically) Man (Karl) Horse (Ross) man (Mann), something one must know to understand why Uncle Jacob irrationally and insistently forces Karl to live up to his name by rising at four-thirty every morning for horsemanship lessons. When the teenager once begs out of this activity to visit a family friend, the Uncle disowns Karl. In the last extant portion of the novel (which was never finished), Karl finds a position with the Theater of Oklahoma—Kafka's parody of Heaven—and is greeted with the blare of trumpets played by actors dressed as angels. Perhaps influenced by Authur Rimbaud calling himself "Negro" in *A Season in Hell,*[28] Rossmann then changes his name to "Negro," which, among other things, is a reference to invisible bondage in the Egyptian America like the blacks who were legally free without really being free.

In a relatively rational age, all of this obscure play with names—all of this slipping and sliding of idiosyncratic associations—must seem at least neurotic. Once, in a Diary, Kafka even writes that he felt upset playing cards partly because the German word for cards begins with a *K*, the first letter of his last name. He comments, "I find the 'K' hateful, almost nauseating, but I still use it in my writing, very typical of me" (*T* 375). Although his feeling ill at the sound of a single letter of his own name is a purely personal reaction, his combination of puns and religion has precedents. Also in a Diary, Kafka notes that, in an important question of religious duty, punning was used by Rabbi Eliezar, founder of Hassidism, a mystical Jewish movement that much interested Kafka (*T* 128). To take an English-language example, the Reverend John Donne's "Hymn to God the Father" is structured around a series of puns on Donne's own name, ending with the famous lines, "And having done that, Thou has done, / I have no more."[29]

Like Donne's yearning to be "done" with sinful mortal life, Kafka's personae generally fade into the void. "The Judgment," the story with which he was most pleased, ends with its protagonist's suicide. The title character of "A Hunger Artist" *(Ein Hungerkünstler)* starves himself to death as does Gregor Samsa in "The Metamorphosis" *(Die Verwandlung).* Isachar appears to be slipping through the mirror. The very title of *The Lost One* suggests Kafka's main theme, the disappearance of its protagonist. Although Kafka never finished the work, he writes in a Diary his intention that Rossmann should be "shoved aside" (*T* 481). The title characters of "The Bucketrider" *(Der Kübelreiter)* and "The Country Doctor" (*Ein Landarzt)* find themselves drawn to extinction in the vast, cold hinterlands. *The Trial* ends with the execution of Joseph K. As to his last novel, *The Castle,* not only did he reportedly intend to conclude the hopeless quest of his protagonist with the man's death, but the character is simply called "K" without even a first name. Jung's aforementioned patient liked to talk of herself as "Socrates' deputy" to show her importance, and many authors' personae are equally self-aggrandizing, but, for Kafka, projecting himself into his works was an act of radical humility, almost of suicide. He blots out one image of himself after another until only the Indestructible remains.

Mephistopheles

> Dare to break open the portals
> Past which everyone willingly creeps.
>
> —Goethe, *Faust,*
> *(quoted by Jung as a personal motto)*

In a 1918 notebook, Kafka writes that he represents only the "negative element of [his] age" (*D* 99). That negativity forms the common denominator of his major literary personae. In a sense, Kafka's favorite author, Goethe, created the predecessor or lord of most of them, Mephistopheles, who declares, "I am the spirit who negates" (*Faust,* part I, 1. 1338).[30] In a 1917 letter, Kafka likens himself to Mephistopheles at that point in *Faust* when the latter transforms himself into a dog (*BR* 182). When, in that drama, this animal again metamorphoses, Faust exclaims, "Then this was our poodle's core! / Simply a traveling scholar?" (*Faust,* part I, 11. 1323–24). Comparably, in "Investigations of a Dog," Kafka's persona is both traveling scholar and canine. Mephistopheles asserts lordship over mice and vermin (*Faust,* part I, 11. 1516–17), the species to which the protagonists of "Josephine, the Singer" and of "The Metamorphosis" belong respectively. Kafka frequently expresses his kinship with Mephistopheles' "relation, the snake" (*Faust,* part I, l. 2049), a phrase that Emrich cites as source of one of Kafka's serpent characters.[31] Mephistopheles keeps ravens for pets (*Faust,* part I, l. 2491), birds that Kafka sometimes uses as personae probably because of their similarity to the Kafka jackdaw. Large talking apes, like the protagonist of Kafka's story, "A Report to an Academy," serve Mephistopheles in the Witch's Kitchen (*Faust,* part I, ll. 2337–2604). In flying to the crags, Kafka's Bucketrider seems possessed by the same Mephistophelian magic that raises the Walpurgisnacht witches in their mountain ascent on levitating tubs, broomsticks, pitchforks, goats, etcetera. (*Faust,* part I, 4000–4010). In a Diary entry, Kafka speaks of himself as inspiring the terror associated with a cloven foot (*Pfederfusses, T* 484), one of the former appurtenances of Mephistopheles. In a 1922 letter to Brod, he wrote of suddenly realizing that writing was "service to the devil" (*Br* 384). If, as Brod asserts, Kafka read Goethe habitually, Kafka certainly knew that his personae connoted the demonic, but that connotation suited his vision of the visible world as evil and even art as a grotesque mask—far from the exalted place Goethe generally bestows on art. In references to Goethe, though, Kafka seems to suggest that the world might have been less fallen in the former's time. Brod summarizes, "To hear Kafka talk about Goethe with awe was something quite out of the ordinary, it was like hearing a little child talk about an ancestor who lived in happier, purer days and in direct contact with the Divine."[32] In a Diary, Kafka devotes a paragraph to Goethe's predicting the Messina earthquake by observing omens in the heaven (*T* [omitted]; *D1* 250–51), notes how his own admiration for Goethe sometimes keeps him from writing (*T* 244–45), and likens the atmosphere of Goethe's house to "dead grand-fathers" (*T* 654), the closest he actually comes to writing of Goethe as "an ancestor."

The meaning of Kafka's personae becomes clearer through contrast of his Goethe-mania with Jung's even more extreme case of it. In his autobiography, Jung twice mentions a rumor (completely unsupported, according to Aniela Jaffé) that Goethe literally was Jung's ancestor. The reason that this rumor fascinated Jung was because

> Goethe had composed almost a score and pattern of my inner dissonances and resolutions: the Faust/Mephistopheles dichotomy united within me into a single person, and I was he. (*Er* 237–38)

As Jung explains, he identified so strongly with Faust that the latter's murder of Philemon made Jung feel guilty, occasioning Jung to inscribe over the gate of his towered, medieval-style home: *Philemonis Sacrum—Fausti Poenitentia* (Shrine of Philemon—Penitence of Faust). Related by Jung to Faust's famous declaration, "Two souls, alas, are dwelling in my breast" (*Faust,* part I, l. 1113), Jung felt himself to be two people, one a finite being living in the twentieth century, the other infinite and eternal, but particularly attuned to the Faustian Middle Ages (*Er* 91). Jung considered Goethe to be part of the *Aurea Catena,* the "golden chain" of occult sages commencing with the god Hermes Trismegistus and continuing down (he implies) to himself (*Er* 192–93).

That Jung associated himself with a fictional ancestor may evidence an unease with his actual heritage, but Kafka is an even-more-marked outsider for whom all heritages are foreign. Little wonder that Kafka's alienation left him only castoffs for his personae: dog, roach, serpent, or the then-equally disreputable heathen Chinese of the Great Wall stories. The difference between a Jungian and literary persona is that the former can be a heterogeneous collection of imitated behaviors, not the latter, which requires a carefully honed focus.

In 1954, Roman Jakobson's famous article, "Two Aspects of Language and Two Types of Aphasic Disturbances" developed hints from Jung's association tests and others' later study of speech pathology into a two-category division of figurative language: metonymy and metaphor.[33] It is typical of our era that language would be classified in terms of aphasia (the inability to communicate). Kafka's personae are either metonymies (e.g., "K.") or metaphors (e.g., the dog-scholar), but they are used as apophasis, mentioning something while suggesting that one's own statements about it should not be taken literally. It particularly suits works such as *Faust,* where the multicultural wealth of allusion and erudition structures the work like a series of Chinese boxes or masks on top of one another, with the Ineffable beneath them all. In its first act, for example, Mephistopheles dons a mask of the title character and praises the pursuit of life and knowledge. Because the face of Mephistopheles lies beneath that mask, the audience recognizes his words as irony. Mephistopheles' face, however, is, in a sense, itself a mask of God, who works through the former, turning the devil's evil actions—the course of the play—into good (*Faust,* part I, l. 1337). At the end of part II, Goethe reveals that the visible world is not Reality.

> What is destructible
> Is but a parable.

Then, however, he affirms that in some manner he has been able to present the Real.

Here it was seen,
Here it was action.

Kafka's works follow this ambiguously apophatic tradition, perhaps coming even a shade closer to the final silence than *Faust*.

3
Myths and *Märchen*

I realized, "I now have a key to mythology and can unlock all the gateways of the Unconscious."

—Jung, *Memories, Dreams, Reflections*

What is jollier than belief in a household god!

—Kafka (a 1917 aphorism)

According to G. S. Kirk, Regius Professor of Greek at Cambridge University, "Myths are of their nature allusive."[1] One of the most noticeable difficulties of classical and Homeric Greek literature comes from the tendency of ancient authors to present myths in fragments, most often in tantalizingly brief references. Obviously, this means that the culture was saturated with myth so that the tales were too well-known to require complete narration. Even the surviving, elliptical allusions suffice to show that myths already existed in many variants; for the incompleteness with which myths were told partly concealed religious diversity, which otherwise might have strained social coherence. More intriguingly, the brief references by which authors presented myths acted in the manner that Kafka considers the only valid religious language, allusion or pointing (*Andeutung, H* 45). Typical of allusion is a certain brevity or rapidity. According to Marshall McLuhan, "Myth is anything seen at very high speeds."[2] While (despite Heraclitus) the world usually seems to change in a slow, predictable way, myth typically presents sudden cosmic changes, e.g., the moment that Phaethon created desert by scorching the earth with the runaway sun. Even as early as the time of the pre-Socratics, spreading commerce made the myths of neighboring peoples accessible to each other and literacy froze them in written forms susceptible to slow study. Traditions were shaken, as evidenced by rising philosophies taking the place of myths, which were beginning to be interpreted as allegory or simply dismissed—a process ever-more prevalent until the time of Jung. Surprisingly often, instead of allegorizing, Jungian analyses of myths consist simply of singling out those elements that point to the Unconscious, i.e., the Unknown (as will later be shown with Kerenyi's interpretation of Kronos). What lies at the heart of myth is this mystifying pointing, which makes it a precursor of the Kafkaesque, despite obvious differences between Kafka's revised myths and the originals.

The Pointing Finger

> If all things are in motion, every answer to any question whatsoever is equally correct.
>
> —Plato, *Theaetetus*

During the fifth century B.C. (according to a brief allusion in Aristotle's *Metaphysics*), a senior companion of Plato named Cratylus felt swept away in universal flux. Aristotle's Cratylus, in a modification of the philosophy of the still-older Heraclitus, said that every object *constantly* diverges from its previous configurations: you cannot step into the same river even once. From the instant your sandal enters until it reaches the streambed, water continuously flows. Because words do not change as quickly as the objects to which they refer, language misleads one into ignoring the real situation (causing what we now call "cognitive dissonance"). Consequently, Cratylus never spoke again. In lieu of verbalizing, he would "merely move his finger" *(dáktulon ekínei mónon),*[3] an act reminiscent of the "one-finger Zen" *(i chih t'ou ch'an)* of the Chinese abbot Chuh-Chih (ninth century A.D.).[4] In imitation of his teacher, T'ien-Lung, Chuh-Chih acquired the habit of raising a finger whenever anyone queried him about Zen (because the ultimate nature of Reality—the subject of Zen—cannot be described). At one time, when one of his teenaged pupils was asked about Zen, the latter also held up a finger. During his next interview with the youth, Chuh-Chih cut it off. After trying to raise the no-longer present finger in answer to a question about the Buddha, the boy attained enlightenment. Subsequent Zenists have frequently alluded to Chuh-Chih's nonverbal act,[5] and this act itself responded to a long tradition. A near-contemporary of Cratylus, Gautama Buddha, also considered the universe to be in constant flux *(anicca)*. As with Cratylus, this implied a distrust of language, particularly metaphysical language.[6] Centuries of Buddhist metaphysics later, a legend arose telling that Buddha preached the ineffable essence of his teaching by silently holding up a flower.[7] Since only one disciple understood, transmission was evidently almost impossible, perhaps requiring very special dedication. By the eighth century A.D., Zen tradition also included the story of Hui-k'o. He severed not a mere finger but a whole arm to evidence such commitment; then, when asked a Zen question, he became enlightened.[8] Cratylus's rejection of language would not have appeared as strange in certain Asian milieus. Indeed, even negative theology (a tradition that much impressed Kafka and Jung) is traceable to the East, largely to a treatise, *Concerning Mystic Theology*

(Perí Mustikēs Theologikhás) by Pseudo-Dionysius, who mixed Oriental, Christian, Jewish, and Greek lore (c. fifth century A.D.) in his discussion of how the nature of God transcends the power of words to describe. From a historical point of view, there is, however, little reason to trust Aristotle, Plato, or the Zen tradition. These stories about pointing appear to be philosophical myths—even to the elliptical, allusive way they are recounted. They rush away from tedious time toward attaining the Eternal. The years of meditating toward Enlightenment is reduced to the moment of looking at a flower or pointing with a missing finger. Cratylus's silent gesture substitutes for the vast prolixity of academic argumentation.

Jung's web of references to ancient and Asian obscurities is sufficiently vast to render his research almost unreadable. What did Kafka know of ancient learning? After studying philosophy in school, he continued to read Plato's and Artistotle's works, some in the original. In 1916, he tried to introduce his sister Ottla to Plato's dialogues.[9] It is difficult to determine the full extent of Kafka's considerable readings in Eastern, particularly Chinese literature, but its impact on his writings is often evident, as in a "Description of a Struggle" *(Beschreibung eines Kampfes).* The narrator encounters a yellow-skinned, fat man, seated in "Oriental fashion" *(orientalischer Haltung)* on a litter. His bearers try to carry him across a river, which, like Cratylus's stream, changes perceptibly. Indeed, so does the landscape; even the mountains move, for, as previously noted, the scenery reflects the mind (like the Mahayana Buddhist belief that nothing is real but thought). After the fat man drowns, "the riverbanks extended measurelessly, but with the palm of [his] hand [the narrator] touched . . . a distant signpost [*Wegzeiger,* which etymologically means way-pointer]" (*B* 59). Like Cratylus's paradox about not stepping into the same river even once and similar Buddhist imagery, Kafka exaggerates the speed in order to intrigue and confound the reader. Certainly, the rapidly metamorphosing body of the narrator leaves him so confused that his words break off suddenly, having reached the only possible conclusion for such anomalous flux: a flurry of answerless questions and mere pointing. In Buddhism "[t]he perception of the world in double-bind [i.e., self-contradictory] terms is due fundamentally to its temporal nature"—an idea of the world that, according to Janouch, Kafka attributed to Walt Whitman.[10] As to Kafka's knowledge of Buddhism, he owned Karl Neumann's version of *Die letzten Tage Gotamo Buddhos* and there is reason to suspect that Kafka also knew another Buddhist book translated by Neumann, *The Light of Asia,* which contains the following passage:

> Being's ceaseless tide,
> . . . ever-changing runs, linked like a river
> By ripples following ripples, fast or slow—

The same yet not the same—from far-off fountain
To where its waters flow.[11]

Finally, Kafka had a deep, long-noted affinity with Arthur Schopenhauer. The philosophy of this so-called "New Buddha" unites Oriental and Western sources, most certainly including the next stage in our inquiry, the Platonic theory of Ideas.[12]

Philosophic Myth

> And do you see, I said, men passing along the wall carrying all sorts of vessels, and statues and figures of animals made of wood and stone and various materials, which appear over the wall?
>
> —Plato, *Republic*

In *Metaphysics* (987a), Aristotle ridicules Idealists, a group traditionally assumed to include his teacher, Plato. According to Aristotle, they tried to save language from Cratylus's universal flux by presuming that words point beyond the visible world to a numinous dimension of the Eternal (*aidíois, Metaphysics* 1079a4) inhabited by unchanging Ideas (often considered predecessors of Jung's archetypes, partly because Plato was one of Jung's favorite authors). What, though, did Plato actually teach? In Plato's *Parmenides,* Socrates advocates a theory of Ideas and is defeated by Zeno and the title character, although in the process those two characters demolish their own position, leaving the nature of the universe unknown.[13] In Plato's Seventh Letter (341c4), he states that he had not nor ever would put a theory of Ideas into a *suggramma* (written work or treatise).[14] Plato's Socrates repeatedly criticizes the unreliability of writing, even though he does so in the midst of written works. A comparable paradox appears in the Chinese classic, *Tao te ching,* where Lao Tzu writes that people should abandon writing and return to knotted cord *(chieh sheng),* a mnemonic device, an allusion rather than a detailed record.[15] According to Taoism, babies are born as part of the Tao, the inexpressible unity of the universe, but as they grow they forget their source. Comparably, according to Plato's Socrates, it is through memory (*anámnēsis,* literally un-forgetting) that one can return to knowledge of the primal Ideas, encountered before birth and forgotten since then. For both Lao Tzu and Plato's Socrates, the cause of forgetting is apparently materialism, overly relying on objects (e.g., writings) instead of on one's natural abilities (e.g., memory), thereby weakening those abilities. Jacques Derrida considers Plato's distinction between natural memory *(mnēmē)* and writing or artificial memory *(hupómnēsis)* to be "something like the major decision of philosophy, the one through which it institutes itself, maintains itself, and contains its adverse deeps."[16] Actually, as Derrida himself has helped to demonstrate throughout most of his writings, there was no "decision." In both East and West, people continued to yearn for natural and artificial, Romantic and systematic, for even in the Occident, where consistency has become an obsession, few if any have ever managed to achieve it. Plato's most famous description of what is usually called his "theory" of Ideas is the ludicrous puppet show behind a mysterious wall, where unnamed beings carry objects that represent the Ideas. Plato's Socrates says that he is himself like those in the cave who do not see the truth (515a5) and that the Divine *(theós)* alone knows if the Ideas exist (517b6). Since only *theós* is left undoubted, one may well wonder if the puppeteers of the parable are meant to represent the gods (who serve as universal puppetmasters in Plato's *Laws* 644d–e). These gods are the true precursors of personified archetypes and figure prominently throughout all of Plato's works, which never completely exclude the mythical. Consider, for example, those early Platonic dialogues that Kafka, like most educated members of his generation, studied in school: *Euthyphro* and *The Apology.* Since, according to Brod,[17] it was Plato's irony that attracted Kafka, one should look afresh at these works to see the implications of their irony. The title character of the first of these preposterously maintains that he should model his relationship with his father on Zeus' attack on his. Plato's Socrates finally suggests that since the deities disagree with one another, no consistent ethics can be founded on them. The dialogue ends with Euthyphro exiting hurriedly to avoid admitting his foolishness, while Plato's Socrates comments, "You go away and leave me cast down from the high hope I had that I should learn from you what is holy" (16a)—a very open-ended conclusion. Multiple ironies and evasions similarly characterize *The Apology,* which does, though, affirm the deities' existence. Plato's Socrates asserts that there would be no spiritual matters—subjects to which he has devoted his life—without divinities or their children. If one links this affirmation of the gods' existence to Socrates statement in the *Euthyphro* about their warring with one another, the result is a universe with supramundane quarreling and inconsistency at its base. One can merely point to Reality, not explain it. This Kafkaesque aspect of Platonism has received less attention than it deserves. Even the militant agnostic Bertrand Russell carries the conventional view of Platonic harmony and unity to the following extreme:

> Ultimately there is one God, or the Good, to whom the ideas are adjectival. This, at any rate, is a possible interpretation of Plato.[18]

Much in Plato makes such an interpretation *almost* plausible. Plato's Socrates does not discard consistency capriciously but pretends to make it central to the reasoning process, until, always ironically, at the end of such typical dialogues as the *Euthyphro,* an unsolved or insoluble impasse is reached, and the speakers simply part. Throughout *The Republic,* Plato pursues the definition of some elusive virtue by which a person can harmonize the many facets of self and become "one out of many" (433c). Plato goes so far as to banish poets from his imaginary Republic lest his guardians identify with the many characters in the poems and become internally divided. In other words, he has an extreme fear of what is now called "Narcissism." In modern formulations (as previously noted), this condition consists not so much of self-love as of psychological fragmentation. It leaves its victims introvertedly trying to find themselves, since nothing seems quite real to them—the condition of Plato's Socrates, whose speculations about the Beyond consist of little more than allusions to what *theós* alone knows. In a classic study, Paul Shorey finds the Ideas to be ineffable.[19] According to the highly reputable classicist E. R. Dodds, what Plato says of the Ideas may derive from Shamanism, psychological experiences in which the mystic feels torn apart (cf., Narcissistic fragmentation). From this malady, he is healed and given power to heal by a dream of plunging to the primordial depths and learning from godlike ancestors.[20]

Even if, as Jungians assert, such experiences are universal, the languages in which they are originally formulated shape them. Consider, for example, Kafka's Platonic metaphor, "This life is lived between stage scenery. . . . [through the "tatters" and "junk" of which one must break free to reach] Truth" [*der Wahrheit, H* 351]. After "stage scenery" *(Kulissen),* he next focuses on light and dark in the theater. In *The Republic,* Socrates' friend Glaucon also likens the world to "stage scenery," literally, "shadow drawing" *(skiagraphía),* a word integrally connected to Socrates' preceding discussion of shadow and light. Transposing this imagery into German, Kafka ends with less metaphoric coherence, but then, lack of coherence was the (transcultural) condition he habitually remarked. Intercultural borrowings complicate unity, but their absence can have a worse effect on the credibility of an author trying to describe Reality, since universal patterns are by definition intercultural. It is hard, though, to know what such patterns may be when entities, which some philosophers take to be universal, actually vary according to convention. The division of the spectrum into colors, for example, differs from culture to culture, and, although the linguistic theorist Benjamin Whorf may have exaggerated the difference between Hopi and European languages, the former undoubtedly offers very different conceptions of time and space from the latter.[21]

How inevitable is ethnocentrism? Taking some hints from the Upanishads but much more from Kant, Arthur Schopenhauer produced a rhapsodically phrased, new philosophy including a theory of Ideas. After the first (1819) edition of his *Die Welt als Wille und Vorstellung,* he more and more associated his philosophy with Oriental thought, particularly Buddhism. His views do not sound parochial. His theory of Ideas, nonetheless, is largely an ad hoc explanation of animal species, believed to be immutable by a preevolutionary biology, which was still trying to demonstrate the generation of each creature according to its own kind (Gen. 1:25).[22] He could not quite escape his culture, nor could Jung (whose archetype-filled Collective Unconscious has Schopenhauer's unconscious, universal Will as one of its ancestors).

Imaginary Kinship

> All is fantasy—family, bureau, friends, the street, all fantasy, far or near, the woman; the corollary, however, is only this, that you are pressing your head against the wall of a windowless and doorless cell.
>
> —Kafka (diary entry)

> Those were better times, oh Zeus,
> When you delighted
> In boys and nymphs and hecatombs;
> Even the gods' reign does not last:
> The young replace the aged
> As you did to your senile father [Kronos].
>
> —Heinrich Heine, "The Gods of Greece"

Because of the tendency of myths to allude to one another,

> there is no way to begin with any "basic" myth or any "basic" theme, for the entire corpus interlocks and feeds back so that the total fabric resembles a piece of chain mail rather than the . . . structure sought by the text-historical analysts and some structuralists.[23]

Mythology refers to a vast family involving potentially every animate and inanimate being in the universe: sun, moon, earth, sky, and so on—considered the creation or progeny of gods and/or mortals, who interbred avidly. If one tries to construct a divine geneological chart, however, one must puzzle over the variant versions of who sired whom and when. Zeus' parentage, for example, is memorialized in the poetic formula, *Zeus Kronídēs,* Zeus, son of Kronos, which runs throughout the works attributed to Homer and Hesiod, the closest that Greece came to canonical literature. Since brief allusions can always be reconciled by anyone with sufficient imagination, and since the Greeks were not (with a few exceptions) inclined to heresy hunting, one should not be surprised to find in Crete the variant belief that Zeus was born every year.[24] Who, though, was Kronos? According to Kafka,

> [One] model parent [*Elternvorbild*] of Greek myth [was] . . . Kronos, who ate his sons—the most honest of fathers . . . maybe Kronos chose his method over the customary one out of compassion for his children. (*Br* 345)

The epigrammatic brevity of Kafka's little joke mirrors the conciseness of ancient allusions. The concept of a model or ideal (*-vorbild*) certainly recalls Platonism, perhaps by way of Goethe.

> During his last stay in Rome [Goethe] was occupied with [a search for] the *Urmensch,* the essence common to all humanity. The Greeks, he believed, had obtained an insight into that essence, and the types that represented the major gods gave expression to different qualities that belonged to it.[25]

The similarity of Jungianism to Kafka's statement is sufficiently obvious so that Richard and Clara Winston translated the word *Elternvorbild* in it as "archetype" (*L* 295). Kurt Weinberg's *Kafkas Dichtungen: Die Travestien des Mythos* even devotes a fifty-five page chapter to "Kafkas Archetypen,"[26] but Kafka's characteristically ironic treatment of stock images does not sound precisely the same as Jung's conversations with his "archetypal" figures or like Jung's evocation of their numinosity once he had read Rudolf Otto's works on the *Mysterium Tremendum*. What similarity, then, links *Elternvorbild,* Kronos, and Jungian "archetypes"? Answering this is a three-stage process, requiring, first, a quick survey of ancient references to Kronos; second, an understanding of Kafka's remark in context; and third, another glance at Jung's "archetypes."

Kronos was a usurper and castrator of his father, Uranus, yet also a god of fertility, a universal ruler during a primordial golden age and later over an island of heroes, when, in turn, the only one of his sons that he did not manage to devour (Zeus) usurped the more general sovereignty. His myth condenses into a domestic drama of mankind's decline from what for humanity was mythic perfection but what for his family was a hard time, indeed. As to the trustworthiness of two works that contain some of the first significant allusions to him, in *The Theogony,* the muses (the supernatural source of the work) recite, "We know how to speak many false things as though they were true; but we know, when we will, to utter true things."[27] In other words, they may be either attesting to the veridicality of *The Theogony* or denying it. The equivocal invocation of the other book, *Works and Days,* is only slightly more reassuring.[28] Plato urged that the myth of Kronos "be communicated only to a very few in some exceptional *mustērion* [mystery ceremony] and . . . be kept from the young."[29]

As to the context of Kafka's allusion, it forms part of a letter in which he tries to convince his sister Elli that her son should be sent away to a progressive school. Kafka wants the boy no longer "in Prague where wealthy Jews succumb to a spirit from which children cannot be guarded"

(*Br* 339). By implication, children are by nature uncorrupted, inheritors of the Kronian golden age, when the model parent was kinder by being more honest. According to Kafka, this activity, whereby modern fathers devour their children, "does not occur on the material level," which makes it all the more devastating (since, for Kafka, it is the spiritual that is the Real). To avoid the results of bad parenting, he relies on the professional educator, whose love is an "inscrutable mystery" *(unerforschliches Geheimnis)*. Once educated, the child may return and accomplish Elli's "deliverance" *(Rettung)*. Kafka tells a story to illustrate this and adds that the mother in it, being a "pious Catholic from Styria," was less in need of saving than a "Jewish woman of Prague." As part of his argument, he quotes from chapter 6 of Swift's *Gulliver's Travels*, where that churchman considers parents "the last of all others to be trusted with the education of their own children" (*Br* 342; *L* 293). As if Swift's multiple levels of irony were not enough, Kafka introduces the passage as evidence for his own position, yet with the disclaimer that he would not presume to agree *(nicht weil ich die gleiche Meinung zu haben wagte)* with so great a witness *(grossen Zeugen)* as Swift (*Br* 342). Thus the cynicism of the remark about Kronos is introduced as if it were merely a paraphrase of the misanthropic Swift, who fought in the Battle of the Books on the side of the Ancients against the Moderns. Consequently the allusion to Kronos is offered merely to be withdrawn, leaving only a vague pointing toward the past and the "inscrutable mystery" of education.

As to the Jungian approach to archetypes in myth, one of Jung's more prominent collaborators, Karl Kerenyi, gives the following account of an important episode in the myth of Kronos (one to which Kafka alludes in a parable to be discussed later):

> In his *Theogony*, Hesiod relates the birth of Aphrodite as follows. . . . [Kronos] cut off his father's procreative organ as his father was approaching his mother and threw it into the sea. From it there arose Aphrodite out of the foaming waters. In this version, as in a melody that utters the unutterable, the beginning and end of an ontogeny coincide: begetting and birth are identical, as also the begetter and the begotten.[30]

As is common in Jungian analysis, Kerenyi achieves a marvelous vagueness untroubled by tiny details of scholarship, e.g., there actually is serious doubt that Hesiod wrote the *Theogony*, and Uranus is not merely approaching Gaia: he is lying down fully stretched upon her *(etanústhē pántē, Theogony*, 177–78), so Kronos's blade interrupts him at a most embarrassing moment. Kerenyi continues, "The phallus is the child, and the child—Aphrodite, an eternal stimulus to further procreation." Instead, the *Theogony* provides an obscene pun. "Aphrodite . . . [is called] Philommedes [genital loving] because she sprang from the genitals." As Evelyn

White has observed, *philommēdéa* probably amounts to no more than a play on Aphrodite's more orthodox title, *philomeidés* (laughter-loving)[31]—thus Hesiod's pun may arise, not from the Muses' role as revealers, but as falsifiers. What Kerenyi is apparently trying to do is to reduce the myth to a series of paradoxical opposites, which cancel each other out, showing the story to be a pointing toward the "unutterable." Kerenyi may be true to the spirit of Hesiod—the same spirit that Kafka also evokes. In a style again fraught with qualification and divagation, Kafka elsewhere affirms that human unity is evidenced in the way each life recapitulates the evolution of mankind as a whole, "even in the most secret emotions of the individual" (*DI* 316–17). This is the essence of Jung's speculations about archetypes as in some unclear way constituting a racial heritage. It explains the sense of kinship felt by Kafka and Jung toward the Greeks and their gods, whom Germans had honored as if they were ancestors ever since the *History of Ancient Art (Geschichte der Kunst des Altertums,* 1763). Germany established an imaginary kinship with Greece's equally imaginary deities, from whom the Hellenic tribes once fancied themselves descended. Long after Goethe's classicism and Hegel's preference for Greek religion over Judaism, even after Heine's debunking of the Immortals, and Nietzsche's Dionysian reinterpretation of them, Kafka presented his own version.

Sirens

> Non-being can put on an alluring face, and the goddess of the dead can appear in the form of a hetaera. Such were the sirens.
>
> —Karl Kerenyi

About two months before his final break with his long-term fiancée Felice Bauer (December 1917), Kafka wrote a narrative that Brod later entitled, "The Silence of the Sirens" (*P* 88–91). Instead of Kafka's many-year relationship with Felice, it treats a mythic moment, Ulysses' escape from the allurements of clawed seductresses. The core of the work is a jocular argument. He presents the myth as "proof" *(Beweis)* that "insufficient, indeed, childish means" *(inzulängliche, ja kindische Mittel)* may achieve "deliverance" *(Rettung).*

One of the common objections to Jung's methodology is that he relies for proof on myths, which can mean virtually anything. Paradoxically, Kafka makes insufficiency the core of his evidence. Underscoring the tenuousness of his data, he presents not an ancient version of the tale, but his own parody of it (and of biblical Hermeneutics). Despite probably having heard that the sirens' song can "pierce anything" *(durchdrang*

Alles), Ulysses, with "innocent joy" *(unscheuldiger Freude)* trusts wax and chains for protection. The *Odyssey* (Xii, 44) calls the singing "clear-toned" or "shrill" *(ligurē)* and "magic" *(thélousin).*[32] This description probably suggested the all-piercing song of Kafka's Sirens, but, in the *Odyssey,* the spell does not reach wax-deafened crewmen, while Odysseus, who applies no wax to his own ears, clearly hears it. Kafka's Ulysses, nonetheless, temporarily deafens himself with wax while, ironically, the Sirens remain silent. Thus, in another paradox, "Ulysses, however, if it may be so expressed, did not hear their silence."

This sentence suggests at least two radically different kinds of metaphysical language. The clause, "if it may be so expressed" recalls the tradition of the Athenian Academy: that there is a Reality, which language with varying degrees of imprecision tries to describe. Words are either imperfect imitations (Plato's Socrates, *Cratylus* 423b) or conventional names (Aristotle, *De interpretatione,* 16a19). The clause, "Ulysses . . . did not hear their silence," recalls another kind of language—a rabbinic commentary on the Bible, which must resolve seeming contradictions, since Judaism traditionally held its Scriptures to be perfect. Thus here, the irresistible power of the silence and Ulysses having resisted it are (facetiously) reconciled by his not having heard the silence. Kafka's surreal juxtaposition of these incompatible conceptions of language undermines both, making the Athenian assumptions of verbal fallibility render communication doubtful, while his travesty of rabbinic devotion to verbal infallibility reduces it to rationalization and casuistry. In the process, Kafka defamiliarizes the story of Odysseus, leaving one wondering how, after all, mere wax did suffice against magic.

In the *Odyssey,* the allurement of the Sirens' enticements lies in their promise to disclose all that occurs on earth. For Kafka, no more-than-human voice offers such a revelation, nor does Circe appear to instruct Ulysses on how to deal with the ineffable, yet deliverance remains possible—even from the Sirens' greatest weapon, their silence. The danger here is less the silence itself than *Überhebung,* a masterfully chosen word meaning both exemption and presumption. To be exempt from the Sirens' song is to feel more than human, what the Greeks called *hubris,* overweaning pride, bringing madness and destruction. Unlike the Nietzschean *Übermensch,* who gloats in his ability to endure the meaninglessness of the world, Ulysses innocently assumes that the Sirens are still singing. Not pride but faith—trust in his own childish machinations—radiates from his "great eyes" *(grossen Augenpaar),* striking the Sirens dumb. In letters to Felice, Kafka agonized that her seeming to be quiet and unintelligent in his presence was somehow his fault. Ulysses, however, remains unaware of his effect on his inhuman admirers—or does he? Based on a codicil added to the parable, Kafka's exegetical voice speculates, "Maybe he actually realized, although human understanding cannot comprehend it, that the Sirens were silent, and raised the above-noted pretense against them and the gods merely as a sort of shield." Like ancient Greeks (Hassids, traditional Chinese, etc) who avoid praising their children and possessions lest all be punished for pride, Ulysses may pretend not to notice the degree of his success. The most inadequate defense, a mere pretense or fiction (no more real than Kafka's story itself), has brought deliverance. The same year as the parable (1917), Brod's *Paganism—Christianity—Judaism* calls such an event a "this-worldly miracle." For Brod, divine grace permits an inadequate human effort to succeed, but the result is not, as in Christianity, a turning away from the world but toward it, as here where Ulysses proceeds on his worldly way. Brod confines such miracles to Judaism, but, in a 1920 letter, Kafka complains that Brod has overstressed the differences between it and paganism (*Br* 279).

As to the Sirens, themselves, in a 1921 epistle to Robert Klopstock, Kafka thus describes an (unidentified) girl's letter, "These are the seductive voices of night, this is how the sirens sang" (*L* 310). He continues that they do not intend to seduce, but their lamentation at their own sterility sounds so beautiful that men fall in love. In a note to Milena Jesenska, Kafka denounces his own impurity, adding that she has overrated him because of his literature. "None sing with purer voices than those dwelling in the profoundest Hell; what we mistake for angels' song is theirs." There is enough in common between this remark and "The Silence of the Sirens" to suggest that Kafka empathizes with the Sirens (as well as with Ulysses). Left to their own devices the Sirens will sing and Ulysses will voyage into the unknown, but in each other's company, the first are silenced, the second in peril.

Heroes

> Each one of us must choose some hero
> To emulate in striving for Olympus.
>
> —Goethe, *Iphigenia in Tauris* (a drama seen by Kafka in 1910)

> Released from jail, the heroes awkwardly formed a line, having lost their agility through incarceration.
>
> —Kafka (untitled fragment)

During an Olympic boxing match, the judges refused the prize to Cleomedes of Astypalaea, condemning his manslaughter of his opponent as an error *(adikía)*. In an insane rage, Cleomedes rushed from the stadium and attacked a nearby school where he murdered sixty children. Fleeing the incensed populace, he took refuge in a temple, then mysteriously disappeared. The Delphic oracle informed the citizens: "Last of the heroes is Cleomedes of Astypalaea. Honor him with sacrifices as one no longer mortal."[33] Since he fairly well represented the moral level of Hellenic heroism, the populace should have been overjoyed to hear that he was the last of his kind. Greek heroes were chthonic beings, worshiped in nocturnal services. Raised on Christian paragons who save children instead of massacring them, Goethe idealizes his ancient heroes, none of them very close to the Greece with which he associates them. Kafka achieved slightly greater authenticity because of his sensitivity to paganism. In the aforementioned letter about *Paganism—Christianity—Judaism,* Kafka objects to Brod's case against Greece. The former writes that all Brod had demonstrated was that people like the two of them would have been "desperate" if they lived in ancient Hellas, "but even then not quite" (*L* 242). Kafka continues that what he respects in the Greeks is their humility, their obsequiously prostrating themselves before degenerate gods and heroes. Thus, one suspects, he was inspired to write about even more wretched heroes, thereby achieving a deeper humility than the Greeks. This is a sufficiently strange variant of idealization so that one may well turn to Jung—or rather to an analysis of Jung—for clarification.

Several years prior to his death, while conversing with Richard Evans, Jung disclosed that he had first discovered "archetypes" while considering how people find ideals and behavioral models in myths and legends.[34] Perhaps the seeds of his discovery go back as far as his childhood, but a datable part of it was his writing "On Psychological Understanding" (1914). It argues that each introvert constructs "a new world . . . a *Weltanschauung*" and everyone should do so, in order to relate psychological to eternal life (*GW,* vol. 9). Thus it posits the notion that role models (emphasized by Freud) are not enough; people should discover ideals and *raisons d'être* within them. In *Jung in Context,* Peter Homans examines this stage according to recent developments in self-psychology made by the American analyst Heinz Kohut. Having just undergone his famous, emotionally charged breach with Freud (marked by Freud's fainting, their exchanging stormy letters, and Jung's retreating into fantasy), Jung, according to Homans, was experiencing what Kohut calls "Narcissism":

> [the need] to differentiate a sense of self from the sense one has of another, whom the self has previously idealized or with whom the self has previously merged. Jung's experiences were struggles to establish a sense of "otherness" and, conversely, a sense of a coherent self.[35]

Homans implies that at least some of the numina called by Jung "archetypes" are not the universal patterns that he eventually considered them, but effects of the idealization/deflation process. Plato, similarly, focuses on Socratic education: youths following "the gadfly of Athens" as his questions deflate pompous elders and lead his followers to imagine that they are discovering eternal ideas within themselves. The dialogues have enduring appeal because they speak to times (not confined to adolescence) when idealized parents, leaders, and peers no longer seem fit models, so the emotion formerly invested in them transfers to ideas (or better Ideas and Archetypes). Kafka's *Weltanschauung* (his speculations about the "Indestructible") however, are so far removed from phenomenal existence that they offer no clear way to live; therefore, he must return to deflation and write of unheroic heroes, figures who despite (or because of) their imperfections manage to point away from this world.

Composed in the year of the aphorisms (1917) and of such mythic pastiches as "The Silence of the Sirens," Kafka's story, "The New Lawyer" *(Der Neue Advokat),* begins with a brief allusion to the self-proclaimed god and hero Alexander the Great. First reducing Alexander into an unfilial son and murderer of friends, Kafka then reveals Alexander's only claim to admiration: he could point toward India's gates *(Indiens tore)*—even though he could never enter them. As an individual, Alexander is demeaned even below what history would allow (since he actually did reach India), while the mystical Goal, the mysterious Indian gates, is idealized. Then Kafka characteristically denigrates modern leaders even below the level of Alexander, for, according to Kafka, they pridefully and impatiently brandish their swords, so that their entourage sickens in trying to follow the moving point. As he writes elsewhere: "Which of us would not have been happy under Alexander's radiant gaze?" (*D* 301). According to the 7 August 1920 letter, the reason for such contentment is that a pagan god (and one may assume a deified hero like Alexander) helps one have faith that a Divine Reality lies beyond, but he stands in between his followers and the Goal, protecting them from destroying themselves in individual struggles to reach it.

What would happen, though, if a modern were to attempt such concentration as Alexander manages in pointing steadily? Only two days before writing "The Silence of the Sirens," Kafka composed an answer to this question in the form of a now-celebrated narrative beginning with the phrase, "an everyday heroism" *(ein alltäglicher Heroismus).* In the posthumous publication of the parable, unfortunately, Brod added the title, "An Everyday Confusion." The most extensive and scholarly treatment of the parable, Ruth V. Gross's *PMLA* article entitled "Rich Text/Poor Text: A Kafkan Confusion," briefly notes Brod's tampering, then continues to refer throughout to Brod's title, ignores the theme of heroism, and focuses on confusion.[36] The story itself concerns a remarkable character who is simply called A. Representing a *reductio ad absurdum* of heroism in everyday life, he achieves the absolute concentration of Kafka's Greek heroes, but with disastrous results. On leaving for a trip to H, A is encountered by B in the doorway, but A, concentrating fanatically on the need to reach H to see B, brushes B aside without recognizing the latter. Similarly, in "The Silence of the Sirens," when Ulysses came closest to the Sirens, his heroic concentration drove them from his mind. A perceives no difference between the travel conditions when the trip took ten minutes and when it required ten hours, but since he has largely managed to obliterate the external world from his consciousness, neither the readers nor the protagonist will know what really happened to him during this forgotten time. Finally, like Achilles, Oedipus, and Jacob, his adventures bring him a leg injury, but A does not accomplish any great purpose (as he has been little more than an algebraic letter from the beginning). He lies on a staircase, down which B, insensitized by rage, loudly descends. The pain renders A mute and powerless, while the darkness makes unclear (*undeutlich,* uninterpretable, unpointable) how close B really is. A's Alexander-like concentration breaks when most needed. Gross perceptively remarks that A's "pulled tendon" *(Sehnenzerung)* is a German pun, also meaning "pull of longing." Certainly, longing, greed, above all, pride, are stronger among Kafka's moderns than his ancients. The character A is guilty of boasting and impatience.[39] Ulysses' success depends on his seeming completely unaware of his remarkable effectiveness. Alexander manages to point his sword decisively, while moderns grandiosely brandish theirs. As was commonplace in German (and not only German) tradition, Kafka shows a decline from ancient to modern, but, as was also common from Heine on, Kafka stresses the imperfection of the classic heroes as well. Indeed, not content with the evident foibles of mythic heroes, even in his own versions of their tales, he "[s]ometimes . . . imagine[s] an anonymous Greek who comes to Troy without ever having intended to" (*L* 270). By anachronistic references and by an allusion to "rooms in the parents' home," (Kafka's abode for many of his adult years), he suggests that this Greek is a persona of Kafka, killed at the beginning of the war, when "even the gods do not yet comprehend the issue." In other words, the heroes' actions precede their understanding of what they are doing, and if they had waited for clarification "global history would have remained limited to two rooms in his parents' home and the threshhold linking them." Kafka sometimes saw his own process of writing as moving from nebulous feeling to words and then to an understanding of what in meditative concentration he had managed to write.

According to "The New Lawyer," Alexander's famous horse, Bucephalus, has declined into a mere human being—a lawyer like Kafka. However, with the heroic age past, "it may really be best, perhaps, to do as Bucephalus has done and bury oneself in the law books." To have mere books instead of events at first appears unfortunate, but he is now, for the first time, "free," unencumbered by a rider, lacking someone to lead him to death. Indeed, one of Kafka's aphorisms equates thinking about the inevitability of death with seeing a mural of Alexander in battle (*H* 50).

Being a hero can be painful, as with Prometheus. Kafka provides four versions of that myth: (1) Prometheus was tortured for having revealed *(verraten)* the gods; (2) the pain caused him to unite himself with the rock (eventually identified as the "Inexplicable," *Unerklärliche);* (3) all was forgotten; and (4) everyone grew weary of the meaninglessness. This parody of the "higher criticism" of the Bible and of other religions is itself a religious statement, though a complex one. The first version is such a brief allusion to the myth that instead of a theft of fire, Prometheus's crime appears to be showing the divine world to mankind. Kafka's second version offers a mystical religion of pain, bringing union with the Inexplicable. The third leads away from the phenomenal through forgetfulness and meaninglessness. Unlike Deconstruction, Kafka discovers beneath the words a "substratum of truth [*Wahrheitsgrund*]." The four versions each show a different (inadequate) way of coming to terms with the rock until the readers are trained by frustration to renounce an impatient reaching for categories. Only then does he allude to the rock as something in and of itself. In Zen, the deliberate frustration of trying to solve a *Koan* (a question impossible to solve logically) is intended to lead to the Great Doubt opening the devotee to Enlightenment, which cannot be expressed but only shown as through pointing. Jung also believed that psychic progress required a suffering that mystics often call "the dark night of the soul."

Brod was less content with frustration. His *Paganism—Christianity—Judaism* exemplifies ignoble suffering as a "bookkeeper permanently attached to his armchair."[38] For Brod, such agony stems from capitalism and thus is not heroic but due for elimination. During the period when Kafka was commenting on and criticizing that book, he composed another revised myth, "Poseidon." It transforms that deity into a master clerk, endlessly checking figures in the administration of the oceans. Capitalism never enters the matter: someone has to administer, and since Poseidon becomes physically ill at the thought of leaving the water, his attempts to change posts are fruitless. His position is the one that fits him, the one he was granted in the beginning. Indeed, the chief source of his vexation is people's assumption that he may ride about freely. Being told that one's frustration is avoidable (as Brod was doing to Kafka) is not necessarily comforting. Largely because of annoyance, Poseidon becomes deeply weary and depressed, ceasing all activity. In collapse, he manifests the Divine "presence" *(Gegenwart)* around which a seagull flies, as, according to another of Kafka's fragments, art itself circles the Light. Alexander, Prometheus, and the character A also manifest their "heroism" (their introverted concentration) in a kind of collapse (a moral one for Alexander, a mental one for A, and a physical one for Prometheus).

Märchen

> If one tells a fairy tale [*Märchen*], then everyone knows that one has confided oneself to alien powers and excluded the jurisdiction of our own day.
>
> —Kafka (untitled fragment)

Kafka's first German teacher, Ferdinand Deml, enthusiastically taught fairy tales as part of the course, and, at least from that time forward, Kafka loved that genre, even undergoing, in adolescence, what Ernst Pawel calls a "Teutonic folklore phase."[39] At Kafka's death, books in his possession included the *Kinder—und Hausmärchen* of the Brothers Grimm as well as collections of Chinese, Turkish, Jewish, and other once-oral narratives.[40] Critics often call Kafka's works "anti-fairy-tales,"[41] yet as Max Luthi observes, "[Despite being] out-and-out anti-fairy tales . . . they have much in common with fairy tales."[42] The classification problem arises partly from the diversity of folk stories of which oral fairy tales are themselves a heterogeneous subvariety. The latter have drifted from continent to continent and been committed to writing in myriad forms, which, in turn, have influenced later oral versions until spoken and literary styles mingle inextricably. One way of picturing this subvariety is as a continuum. On one side are arrayed oral narratives, e.g., the kind Vladimir Propp tried to describe in his controversial *Morphology of the Folktale* (which might be thought of as a methodical arrangement of some structures that Jung treats as archetypal images). Near the middle appear nineteenth-century literary imitations of oral tales, such as Hans Christian Andersen's works. On the other side lie Kafka's dreamlike fictions. Instead of a simple dichotomy of fairy tale and antifairy tale, the continuum suggests that Kafka transforms folk images from both myth and *Märchen* in a manner comparable to but more extreme than Romantic writers of *Kunstmärchen* (literary fairy tales). To show the general dynamics of this process, it is sufficient to compare Kafka's story, "A Country Doctor" *(Ein Landarzt)* with a few tales collected by the Brothers Grimm and some written by Andersen in books that Kafka used to read to his roommate Dora Dymant.[43]

According to Propp's study of Russian folktales, works of that genre commonly begin with a family (the microcosm of society) torn by conflict, though he only specifically mentions the quarrel of brothers.[44] Almost as typically, in the Grimms' original (1810) transcription of "Hansel and

Gretel," the two siblings are allied together against an evil mother.[45] By the Grimms's fifth edition, the mother has become a stepmother.[46] In the *Kunstmärchen* "The Snow Queen" (a story sharing much with "Hansel and Gretel"), Andersen writes of the children Gerda and Kay, who "were not brother and sister, but who loved each other quite as much as if they had been."[47] The story develops from their quarreling and separation. Finally, in "A Country Doctor," a villainous groom, confronting the narrator and his maid, cries, "Holla, Brother, Holla, Sister," and two horses crawl from a pigsty (*E* 147). Readers may, for an instant, presume that he is addressing the two humans since there is apparently no one else around. Then he acknowledges kinship with the animals—or, more precisely, the five figures constitute a strange pseudofamily. The "unearthly" *(unirdischen)* steeds answer the doctor's desire to open windows by doing so in some uncanny way. Next he senses that "the horses [are] summoning [him]" through an unspoken rapport between them. He feels not merely protective of his servant-girl, but bereft or robbed *(beraubt)* of her—a more possessive emotion—when he cannot save her from the groom. She flees toward the doctor's house, where she happens to live. The groom pursuing her is apparently also an inhabitant of the property, though he is, nonetheless, a "stranger" to the doctor. This pseudofamily, scattered in the cold, contrasts with the real family of the sick child, all huddled together in the stiflingly hot room.

By beginning with the pseudofamily and moving to the real one, Kafka reverses the *Märchen* pattern, which commences with the protagonist(s) (with whom one is to identify) in a real family and then shifts to the false one. In the 1810 "Hansel and Gretel" transcription, the witch, a projection of the wicked mother, first seems to adopt the children, then seeks to devour them; and when she dies, so does the real mother. More elaborately, "The Snow Queen" contains four different witch figures including the title character. Changing from benevolent to malevolent matriarch from moment to moment, she sometimes seems far from motherly as when she is first attracted to the boy by seeing him "half undressed." Kafka's groom is a libidinous projection of the doctor, who has a sexual fantasy of the maid lying beneath the former.

The uncanny beings from Andersen's literary imagination are more multifaceted than those from oral tales recorded by the Grimms, and Kafka's bogeys transcend both as can be seen by further examining the pigsty incident. Propp identifies violation of a prohibition as a common second episode in fairy tales, and, in his system, the prohibition may either have been stated or not (Propp 121, et passim). Thus the category includes such oral tales as "Bluebeard," where the wife opens an explicitly forbidden door, and "Hansel and Gretel," where the children nibble at a gingerbread house without being warned against such behavior.

The pattern becomes even more nebulous when Andersen imitates and adapts it in his "Snow Queen." Kay boasts that he would melt the title character if she entered his home. Not until that evening does he see her for the first time—a greater time delay than oral fairy tales usually exhibit—and even then she merely frightens him. The full punishment comes much later still, and is barely traceable to the boast. In "A Country Doctor," the protagonist meets the uncanny groom by opening a supposedly long-unused pigsty. Is one to focus on the fact that he has opened a door that should have been left shut? Or, considering Kafka's own Jewish heritage, should one see the existence of a pigsty on the doctor's property as taboo? Or is the problem that the latter's despair has betrayed him to demonic forces? Actions connect even less clearly than in "The Snow Queen."

Next, the groom's "brother" and "sister," the horses, crawl from the sty. The interrelationship of people and animals forms a common theme in fairy tales, sometimes obviously, as in stories of metamorphosis, but also more subtly, as in the 1810 "Hansel and Gretel," where the boy is placed in a stall to be fattened like a "little pig" *(Schweinchen)* (Rolleke 74). In Andersen's fable "The Pigs," the title characters use a horse's carriage as their sty. All three stories have a theme of degeneration, but are treated in a progressively abstract manner. In the 1810 "Hansel and Gretel," hunger reduces a family to such a level that the parents willingly abandon their children; then a witch treats the latter like domestic animals. More philosophically, in "The Pigs," a Rose King laments that "the beautiful has departed," while an old godfather prophesies the Second Coming of Christ when the world will again bloom with beauty (Andersen 174). Still more elaborately, "A Country Doctor" not only has such evidences of decay as horses forced into a pigsty, but also the meditations of the title character, who notes that magic ceremonies have taken the place of organized religion. Rather than the simple Christian reassurance of Andersen, Kafka writes of faith having assumed complex patterns.

In giving these horses to the doctor, Kafka's groom resembles what Propp calls a "Donor," the one granting a magic gift. Usually, Donors are simultaneously Good and Evil figures, such as the cannibalistic witch Baba Yaga, the most common Donor in Russian folklore. Similarly, in the Grimms' "Iron John," the title character is probably a mass murderer of huntsmen and certainly a kidnapper of the prince, yet he becomes a foster father to the latter and gives him a remarkable steed. In "The Snow Queen," the chief Donor is the little robber-girl, who keeps a reindeer so that she can torture it with a knife. She repeatedly threatens Gerda with the blade and draws the latter to bed with her. In the morning, though, the robber-girl helps Gerda onto the reindeer and sets both free. While the story "Iron John" did not try to reconcile the title character's two sides,

Andersen says that the little robber-girl's mother "filliped [her daughter's] nose till it was red and blue; and it was all done for love" (334). The explanatory phrase "all done for love" suggests that likewise the girl's treatment of Gerda and the reindeer is a kind of rough affection. More obviously, in "A Country Doctor," the groom, who lasciviously bites the maid, falls into that perverse category. Furthermore, his gift of the horses is both harmful and helpful—which adds an additional ambiguity to the situation.

After receiving the steeds, the country doctor is swept away, and no longer seems to have much control over his life. Such passivity is characteristic of fairy-tale heroes. The great deeds attributed to them are typically performed by supernatural helpers according to advice given by parent-surrogates. After the hero or heroine has shared a crust of bread with a wise old dwarf, wept at a mother's grave, or performed some equally unspectacular act, magic will kill the dragon, save the princess, or whatever else needs to be accomplished. Andersen's "Snow Queen" also evidences a transition from trivial activity to significant inactivity. Like his playmates, Kay ties his sled to a sledge, in his case that of the Snow Queen, who drags him faster and faster through the swirling snow. Andersen hints that Kay might have broken free if he could remember his prayers, but his eyes and heart had previously been pierced and frozen by broken pieces from a demonic mirror; thus he can only recall his multiplication tables, which prove useless against the supernatural. This incident serves as a more developed transition than oral tales usually provide. Furthermore, in those tales, the heroes' passivity almost always forms a state of grace. Having himself struggled from penury to affluence, Andersen generally seems uneasy with passivity as here, where Kay's imprisonment in the Snow Queen's frozen world means virtual damnation. Being a product of the same bourgeois culture that requires individual initiative, Kafka cannot quite see surrender to magical forces as grace, yet, as his autobiographies generally agree, he had a strong predisposition toward passivity. Characteristic of Kafka's protagonists, the country doctor enters a world even more hellish than Andersen's. Instead of having the voluptuous but chilling Snow Queen for company, the doctor is stripped and placed in bed with a hostile boy, then sent naked into the storm. Kay is inured to the frost and deprived of memory by the kisses of the Queen as they fly together in her coach. The fact that we glimpse his mind at all differentiates him from most heroes of oral tales. Kafka's doctor is plagued by thoughts and memories as the unearthly horses speed him into the cold.

Indeed, the cold itself functions differently in each kind of fairy story. In folktales, as Propp observes, there is usually a need to be remedied. Consequently, the imagery of hunger and cold appears again and again, but seldom rises above the literal level. In "The Snow Queen," however, cold symbolizes science—a part of life that Andersen fears may freeze out affection and imagination. In a typically Romantic passage, Kay sits bewitched in what Andersen calls "the icy game of reason," trying to piece splintered ice into the word "Eternity." He can do so only after Gerda kisses him, thawing his heart. Kafka's country doctor, lamentably, has no one to save him from what he deems "the frost of this most ill-fated epoch" (*E* 153). The key term is fate *(Glück)*. Previously the doctor blamed the gods for his fortune. Kafka echoes sources even before the Grimms' fairy tales. He recreates the mood of Nordic myth, the *Gotterdammerung* of growing cold and predestined doom—a world of malevolent powers untamed by Christianity. And in the midst of this darkness, Kafka places the very human, even comic doctor.

The fusion of comedy and drama is a characteristic of fairy tales (which generally escapes Propp and Jung). In the 1811 manuscript of "Rumpelstilzchen," for example, that little man is described both as "ridiculous" and "dangerous" (Rolleke 241). On the one hand, we hear of his silly dance in the forest and, on the other hand, of his ability to kick through thick stone—a power many martial artists might envy. As Romantic writers expanded the length of the fairy tale, they naturally stretched the comic sections—not always with results that seem very skillful today. Andersen making gentle fun of his little heroes and heroines appears sentimental or even patronizing. At times, one does not know how to interpret a bizarre detail, such as the robber-girl biting her mother's ear. Among the Romantic fairy-tale writers, E. T. A. Hoffmann most uses humor, often at the risk of leaving readers unsure of his attitude toward his characters' hyperemotional ramblings. In "A Country Doctor," however, Kafka demonstrates a perfect control of tone. The protagonist is a typical Kafkan character—one so hypersensitive that he would even be miserable at a garden party, yet he is thrust into a supernaturally hostile environment.

The scene in the patient's bedroom combines farce and dark comedy. Previous critics have also noted folkloric elements in it. Hartmut Binder points out that Kafka read a Polish legend about a doctor who first despaired of healing his patient, then tried again successfully.[48] Kafka changed it to a doctor who first despaired of finding anything wrong, then tried again so successfully that he found the patient to be incurable. The Polish doctor could not leave because of the press of visitors in the sickroom. Kafka's crowd of characters not only holds the doctor prisoner but strips him naked and puts him to bed with the invalid. John Hibberd cites Flaubert's version of the legend of St. Julian the Hospitalizer, where the saint lies in bed with a leper and is transfigured as a heavenly reward (94). What is important, though, is the burlesque that Kafka makes of it all, with the little patient threatening to tear out the country doctor's eyes as the little robber-girl in "The Snow Queen" threatened to stab her bed companion.

His comedy, however, never undercuts his tragedy. Like the Grimms' story, "The Poor Boy in the Grave" about a youth who commits suicide, the country doctor's patient longs for death. He suffers from a worm-infested, pink *(rosa)* wound, which commentators have rightly connected with the name of the maid, Rosa, whose relationship to the doctor is now only a festering memory. This link, however, does not explain why the doctor first could not see the large sore and then found it glaringly present. The fairy-tale tradition offers a possible answer. In "The Snow Queen," Gerda and Kay see the same rose differently. To her it is beautiful; to him it is hideously worm-riddled because his sight has been affected by the demonic mirror. Consequently, he only appreciates the deathly beauty of ice. The influence of imagination in shaping perception is a common theme in romanticism, but it is perhaps nascently implied in the sympathetic magic so often depicted in fairy tales. Viewed thus, the wound appears because the doctor searches for it—a common notion in some faith-healing traditions. At the end of the story, the doctor describes the call as a "false alarm"—hardly an appropriate phrase if the patient were really dying when the physician was summoned. One may recall that Kafka's aphorisms deem mankind to be simultaneously expelled from paradise and still there depending on the point of view. In seeking after disease even with the laudatory purpose of curing it, the country doctor has permanently expelled himself from his home. The tragedy is that like virtually all of Kafka's protagonists, he is fixed in his wrong perception, and the other characters' attempts at magic are equally fruitless, for the age itself seems to blame.

In the Grimms' story "Godfather Death," faith is already staggering. An impoverished man rejects God as a godparent for his child and chooses Death because this latter treats rich and poor alike. The tragic tale ends with the child's becoming a famous physician, who tries to cheat Death and is killed for the attempt. The father's blasphemous rejection of God may be only his personal idiosyncrasy. In Andersen's "The Snow Queen," however, the demonic mirror of reason has infected many as science erodes faith. Kay is saved, but in some of Andersen's other stories (e.g., "Under the Willow Tree") the protagonists freeze to death. In "A Country Doctor," the minister stays at home unraveling his robe, for faith itself is unraveling and no one knows how to control the imagination, whether it turns toward lust as with the groom or toward disease and decay as with the boy.

The beginnings of this decay can be traced at least as far back as myth—the doom awaiting the Nordic gods or the series of Divine rulers in classical mythology: Uranus, Kronos, and Zeus in that unstable succession to which Kafka alludes in his letter to Elli, deeming Kronos to be "the most honest of fathers." Such "honest" depiction of familial relations in terms of primary processes (hunger, lust, etc.), characterizes myth, and—usually in almost but not quite as forthright a way—oral fairy tales. Instead of Kronos, the devouring parent, one finds in "Hansel and Gretel" the child-eating witch, a pseudoparent. In contrast, Kafka portrays the mysterious groom biting the maid before chasing her in prelude to an undisclosed act. As society itself has evolved toward greater complexity, impersonality, ambiguity, and indirectness, so also, in a general way, have its fantasies. In the reputable fiction of Kafka's time, the formulaic epithets and hyperboles of orality had largely given place to the elegant variations, qualifying phrases, and greater detail typical of literary narrative, yet a thread of continuity runs from myths to *Volksmärchen* to Romantic *Kunstmärchen* to Kafka's neo-Romantic fairy tales.[49]

4
A New Kabbala

Thou shalt not make any graven image.
—Exod. 20:4 (copied by Kafka into a notebook)

I am to pose nude for the artist Ascher as model for a St. Sebastian.
—Kafka

In *The Trial,* young girls deride Josef K. with the phrase, "He permits himself to be painted!" Detecting that there must be something derogatory about the charge, Evelyn Beck equates Kafka's persona with Kafka himself and tries to turn the puzzling phrase into evidence about his sex life. She concludes:

> I have not been able to discover whether the expression "sich malen lassen" [permit oneself to be painted] was indeed slang among homosexuals for a sexual episode, but I have a hunch it may have been, or was intended to suggest some phrase like it.[1]

In 1912 (about two years before beginning *The Trial*), Kafka, who thought enough about the second commandment to copy it in a notebook, posed in the nude for a Christian icon despite Judaism's nervousness about icons, Christianity, and nudity. Even should Beck uncover concrete evidence of homoeroticism, that would simply be one more religious taboo broken. Kafka not only posed for a graven image but occasionally dabbled in visual imagery himself, filling his notebooks with doodles and drawing the cover for one of Brod's books (a design that the publisher was unable to reproduce to Kafka's satisfaction so that it is no longer extant). More importantly, Kafka created religious literary imagery, even though he doubted the ability of words to portray the Divine Reality. This doubt, this fear that exoteric words are mere idols emptily pretending to portray the Indestructible, also underlies Kabbala, a form of Jewish, mystical hermeneutics. The modern Kabbalist Carlo Suarés writes:

> It is impossible to speak of the unknown in our common tongues (including Hebrew), without changing it arbitrarily into recognizable images. . . . It is

> inevitable that our tongues desecrate all that they discuss, because they have being only in the measurable, in images, appraisements, comparisons.[2]

Kabbala even denies that God is conceivable, as, for example, the great sixteenth-century Kabbalist Isaac Luria reputedly stated, "There is no intellect created which could conceive of him, since he has no place, and no boundary, and no name."[3] Kafka once described his works thus:

> This whole literature is an onslaught against the frontiers, and would have, if Zionism had not interrupted, developed into a new Secret Doctrine [*Geheimlehre*], a Kabbala. The first stages [*Ansätze*] of that exist. (*T* 553)

The one unifying thread through the maze of Kabbala is the belief that a secret wisdom or secret language, adequate to describe the inconceivable Infinite, lies within Scripture. Most commonly, this secret is sought through the substitution of symbolic numbers for letters in a process called "Gematria," where the correct combination of letters is called a "gate."[4] As previously mentioned, Kafka explained that Georg equals Franz because they have the same number of letters. Actual Gematria is vastly more complex. Fortunately, Kafka never went beyond the first stages of Kabbalistic thinking or we would have to transliterate his words into Hebrew letters, change those to numbers, and proceed onward, pocket calculators in hand. During his final illness, Kafka called for Kabbalistic texts, stating that he did not know in what language they were written—strong evidence that any previous acquaintance with Kabbala must have been slight and based on hearsay. He did, though, encounter much of the latter—vicious attacks on Kabbala in Heinrich Graetz's *History of the Jews,* indirect treatment of Kabbala in books on Hasidism, and perhaps, as Robertson speculates, a bit of secondhand information from Kafka's friend Georg Langer, who eventually wrote *Dir Erotik der Kabbala* (1923).[5] A mystical hermeneutics may also have been implied by the phrase "a new Secret Doctrine" *(einer neuen Geheimlehre).* The word *Geheimlehre* was the common way of translating the title, *The Secret Doctrine* (1888), a vast work by Helena Petrovna Blavatsky, cofounder of the Theosophical Society (1875). Her writings mix esoteric interpretation of various Scriptures, Judaic, Christian, Hindu, and Buddhist, with Kabbalistic, Gnostic, and other elements. In *The Secret Doctrine,* for example, she envisions the "Monad or Jiva" ("the immortal part of man")[6] scaling the evolutionary ladder through a series of prehuman incarnations until the reincarnating "spark of the Divine" attains self-consciousness, "the principle, or the intelligence, of the Elohim [a word in biblical Hebrew usually translated as God]." To gain this, an individual "has to eat of the Tree of Good and Evil." Thereafter, one flourishes only so long as one dwells under the "protecting shadow" of that Tree (i.e., remembers the primeval, arcane knowledge).[7] After attending a few lectures, Kafka disassociated himself from the society, so there is no reason to interpret his works in a dogmatically theosophical manner. He had, though, begun an esoteric approach to scriptural language, as his reference to Kabbalism also suggests.

Kabbala means tradition. Kafka's "new . . . Kabbala" involves a radical reinterpretation of a tradition he spent a brief lifetime studying. His readings included both Hebrew ("Old") and Greek ("New") Testaments, as well as works by St. Augustine, Meister Eckhart, Pascal, Kierkegaard, Nietzsche, Dostoyevsky, Tolstoy, and twenty-three volumes from a series entitled "People's Books of Religious History for the German Christian Present," covering such subjects as *The Fairytale* [*Märchen*] *in the Old Testament, The Ancient Mystery Religions and Christianity, The Gnosis,* and *The Philosophy of the Old Testament.* He even sent Felice extracts from a biography of Erdmuthe, the wife of the founder of the Moravian Brethren. Kafka made a number of abortive attempts to align himself with his Jewish heritage through his transcient enthusiasm for the Yiddish theater, his distant interest in Eastern Judaism, his struggles with Hebrew, and his growing acceptance of Zionism; but even with Zionism there is a question of how seriously he took it, as, in 1922, when he grouped it among his hobbies along with "anti-Zionism" and the piano (*D2* 209). One may also wonder what he meant by it. He wrote Milena that since he would never leave his hospital room in Czechoslovakia, "why shouldn't I travel as far as Palestine?" (*M* 236). Thus Palestine was for him something like the Taoist land of Hua-hsü, which, according to the *Lieh Tzu* (allegedly read by Kafka) could only be reached by a mental journey.[8] He informed Felice that Zionism was "but an entrance to something more important" (*F* 482). Nonetheless, his relation to Hebraic tradition was stronger than is implied by his famous pronouncement:

> What have I in common with Jews? I have hardly anything in common with myself and should stand very quietly in a corner, content that I can breathe. (*T* 350; *D2* 11)

One way of assessing the impact of Judaism on his writings is to contrast his conception of religious language with the following biblical attitude toward language and with Jung's own reinvention of Kabbalistic hermeneutics, his analytic psychology. Jung wrote:

> The Jew has the advantage of having long since anticipated the development of [the study of] consciousness in his own spiritual history. By this I mean the . . . Kabbalah.[9]

Silence

> Then Ahimaaz ran by the way of the plain, and overran Cushi . . . and the watchman went up to the roof over the gate unto the wall, and lifted up his eyes, and looked, and behold a man running alone.
>
> —II Sam. 18.23–24

> "I ran past the first watchman. Then I was horrified, ran back again and said to the watchman: I ran through here while you were looking the other way." The watchman gazed ahead of him and said nothing.
>
> —Kafka (untitled fragment)

As in this passage from II Sam. (when the news of Absolom's death is brought to David), a moment in the Bible when no one speaks usually sets the stage for a revelation. The vast weight of subsequent commentary (Mishnah, Talmud, Kabbala, etc.), however, reflects a growing hunger for meaning so extreme that every pause in the text itself is "read" as having its own significance. In his *Answer to Job,* for example, Jung imagines that Job's morality raised the latter so far above God that Job could "see Yahweh's back, the abysmal realm of 'shards.' " Then Jung discusses why Job remained silent about this alleged vision (*GW,* vol. 11, pars. 595–96). In a note, Jung explains that these shards are remnants of the vessels into which God poured forth his energy, according to later Kabbalism, particularly that of the *Zohar* (thirteenth century A.D.) and of Isaac Luria (sixteenth century A.D.). Considering that Job presumably lived almost two thousand years before this doctrine of shards was first promulgated, minds less Kabbalistic than Jung would not see Job's silence about them as evidence that Job was, as Jung concludes, just too "canny" to mention them. Jung treats Job the same way Kafka does Ulysses, whose alleged canniness lay in not revealing that he had heard the silence of the Sirens. Particularly in the hands of Kafka and Jung, hermeneutics becomes a richly creative activity, though they are not alone in this.

"In the days of King David, innocent children could interpret the Torah in forty-nine ways positively and forty-nine ways negatively" (*Midrash Leviticus Rabbah* 26).[10] According to the rabbinical tradition (from which this statement comes), not just the Bible but also such exegesis was considered part of revelation. The Jerusalem Talmud makes the startling pronouncement, "All that a faithful disciple will expound in the future in front of his master was already disclosed to Moses at Sinai" (*Yerushalmi Peah* 6:2).[11] It is difficult to imagine that God discussed Kafka's interpretations with Moses, but for the great anthropologist Levi-Strauss (the son of a rabbi) all versions of a myth, including interpretations, are considered equally authentic. With five of these, I shall contrast André Neher's *L'Exil de la parole* (winner of the 1978 Remembrance Award in Jerusalem),[12] because it studies in a relatively orthodox manner a side of the Bible that is particularly relevant to Kafka: silence as language. With Neher as foil, one can better assess the heterodoxy and originality of Kafka and Jung.

Neher's approach is best seen in his treatment of a passage from 1 Kings (19:11–12). The Scripture begins with a storm followed by an avalanche, earthquake, and fire, but God speaks through none of these. Only after they have passed does he manifest himself in a *QOL DMMH*, which Neher boldly translates as "voice of silence." ("voix du silence," Maisel 42; Neher 42—although the Hebrew might be rendered as a "whisper," contrasted with God's often thunderous revelations). Neher sees the Divine as characterized by stillness, both in the Bible and in history, particularly during the Holocaust, when gas soundlessly seeped into crowded, extermination chambers. With academic precision, he discovers a "morphology," "syntax," and "semantics" of the ineffable void.

> In terms of "morphology," he discusses silence as a background, barren as lunar terrain—yet he connects it to Psalm 19.2–4: The heavens declare the Glory of God, and the firmament showeth His handiwork; . . . there is no speech, there are no words, neither is their voice heard. (Neher 10)

By providing a blank surface on which the Holy Words are written, the inaudible *Te Deum* described in the Ps. provides a space for revelation (though it is not itself revelation). As previously noted, according to Kafka's 1917 aphorisms (about Eden, The Tree of Life, etc.), one may await in silence the intuition of the Indestructible, but that Entity is not precisely "God" and the visible world is illusion, not revelation. The original transgression, according to Kafka, transformed the human essence into the Knowledge of Good and Evil,[13] so the Divine is immanent, while for Neher's Judaic orthodoxy, God is transcendent. Kafka's interpretations have even more in common with Jung than with the Gnostics (to whom they are both commonly compared). A Gnostic text entitled "On the Origin of the World" (103.9–20), for example, affirms that an evil demiurge created the earth and that mankind needs secret knowledge *(gnosis)* in order to reach the true God, Immortal Humanity *(anthropos)*.[14] Kafka considers mankind rather than the demiurge to be the creator of the (illusory) visible world, and Kafka argues that Knowledge is suicidal, not salvational. More emphatically than the Gnostics, Kafka stresses that Knowledge cannot be conveyed with words, which belong to the realm of visible illusion (*H* 45). While Neher and Gnostic believers in a divine *anthropos* talk in terms of a personal God or gods, Kafka and Jung make their cosmic forces more impersonal, resembling those Kabbalistic works that speak of emanation rather than creation and that prefer to envision God as *'YN* (emptiness)[15] rather than in anthropomorphic images.

As to Neher's Syntax of Silence, he distinguishes three basic forms: absence, trial, and providence. The first manifests itself in the Book of Esther, where God is not even mentioned. Neher remarks, "Rabinnical tradition is justified in seeing a close connection between the etymology of the name Esther and the concept of the hidden God, since Esther, in fact, signifies "hidden one" (Neher 22). Neher exemplifies trial with the sacrifice of Isaac and praises Kierkegaard's (Christian) interpretation of it as well as Martin Buber's (Jewish) hermeneutics (Neher 15, 23). For providential silence (God withholding his intervention during a seeming misfortune that turns out to be a blessing), Neher chooses Joseph's exile, which raised that patriarch to such wealth, status, and power that he could save the people of Israel.

As with morphology, so with syntax, Kafka's silences assume most unorthodox forms. In one parable, it is at Mount Sinai, the place where God formerly revealed his Word, that Kafka depicts the apparent absence of the Divine Voice. "Many beings" *(Viele)*—whether people, animals, or others, Kafka does not tell us—slink, creep, crawl *(umschleichen)*—any of these translations are possible—"around Mount Sinai" (*H* 348). They speak "indistinctly" (*undeutlich,* not pointing), resorting to verbosity and screams or remaining restrained—literally, "closed" *(verschlossen).* The sacred connotations of Sinai contrast with these slithering creatures. This contrast generates an uncanny resonance rather than the mere obliqueness that Neher finds when Scripture omits God. In a 1953 letter to Pére Bruno, Jung sees Moses on Sinai as part of the same "archetype" as Elijah on the mountain and continues listing other manifestations of the "archetype" including Christ, "Baal, El-Elyon, Mithras, Mercurius, and Allah personified as al-Khadir" (*GW,* vol. 18, par. 1529). By the time Jung has listed all the variations, they seem to have nothing in common but some vague association of human and divine. Having rendered the "archetype" indistinct by these smothering details, he makes it creep and crawl in his "Transformation Symbolism in the Mass." There he focuses on medieval portraits of the crucified Christ as a serpent (based on "the comparison of Christ with the serpent of Moses in John 3:14"). Thus, through wide-ranging scholarship, Jung's excess evokes a result comparable to Kafka's absence of the Divine Voice—a daemonic chaos equivalent to silence.

Exemplary of the second structure of syntax (the trial), both Neher and Kafka discuss God's strange command to Abraham that the latter sacrificially kill his heir, the child of his old age. Essentially, Neher's point is that from the moment God ordered his own Law violated by this immolation, the reader remains in suspense waiting for explanation. Only at the last moment is the silence broken by divine intervention, stopping the murder and giving the whole incident meaning as a proof of Abraham's faith. Kafka's theology follows a different approach. As his skepticism about language turns the Law delivered at Sinai into a babble of voices, his doubting human adequacy to divine purposes causes him repeatedly to rewrite the story of Abraham, each time making the patriarch less heroic. Kafka had been reading Kierkegaard's *Fear and Trembling,* where the latter posits God's freedom from ethics and Abraham's heroic "leap of faith" in recognizing this divine transcendence. Not the divine freedom (which fitted Kafka's own metaphysics) but the heroic Abraham bothered Kafka, so, in a June 1921 letter to Robert Klopstock, Kafka imagined several versions of Abraham, ranging from an automaton to one who could not have even become "an old clothes dealer" (*Br* 333). For Neher, the trial of Abraham's faith beautifully structures the Divine silence into mounting suspense, ending in the jubilation of victory; for Kafka, despair intensifies until the moment of utter frustration—the inability of Kafka's Abraham even to begin the appointed task. In regard to one of his versions of Abraham, Kafka likens this agony to an awards ceremony where, by mistake or professional malignity, the worst student is called and rises to the derision of his peers. Comparably, an image of error or sadism is central to Jung's version of Abraham. According to Jung, a Midrashic commentary explains that the shofar used at the Day of Atonement sounds in order to remind God that he should never have cruelly asked Abraham to sacrifice Isaac. Jung adds that the "idea of God" must be clarified to recognize that if God is All, then he must be both Good and Evil (*GW,* vol. 18, par. 1551).

Kafka and Jung see providential silence very differently than Neher. Where the latter ends the structure with seeming misfortune turned into Good, Kafka does the reverse in "The Building of the Temple" *(Der Tempelbau).* That edifice rises with miraculous ease, but with disturbing decorations. It is desecrated with the scribblings of children or barbarians—graffiti on the quarried blocks predating the temple and destined to outlast it by an eternity *(Ewigkeit).* In *Psychology and Alchemy,* Jung discusses an even stranger temple building. When Tibetan lamas feel disturbed or come upon a problem on which tradition is silent, they construct a mental mandala, a magical, circular design. According to Jung, the mandala is really a "*building* . . . a house or temple," comparable to the patterns he sees in Occidental figures that he also calls "mandalas"—circular, symbolic art, particularly works by medieval alchemists and by his own patients (*GW,* vol. 12, pars. 123 and 166). After the mandalas seem entirely real to the lamas, the latter deconstruct the mental constructs, created entirely so that they could better understand the formlessness, which (like Kafka's graffiti) precedes, undermines, and follows all structure.

Finally we come to Neher's most elaborate classification: semantics. Here, I particularly beg your patience (Kafka's cardinal virtue), for Neher achieves a truly rabbinical complexity. Again he relies on a threefold division, this time: inertia, energy, and masking, but he further divides each category into two parts, each associated with a Hebrew term for silence.

The first kind of inertia is designated by the Hebrew word *DMH,* which he likens to "the dark night of the soul" of St. John. It is what we viewed structurally as "absence," but now, semantically, it reveals its emotional meaning—one's feeling abandoned to the mute creation—Kafka's Sinai. Neher, though, presumes this absence to be temporary. The second kind of inertia is *STQ,* the condition of the sea when God miraculously abates a storm, allowing the surface to grow calm. Neher adds that the Bible never applies this term to people. However, it best suits Kafka's Abraham, who does God's will only because of "inertia" *(Schwerbeweglichkeit).* Thus dehumanized, he loses any "advantage" *(Vorteil)* he might otherwise have gained.

The next large division is silent energy. Its first form is *HRSh,* the concentration of the artist as he sits quietly bringing chaos into unity. One of Kafka's versions of Abraham, despite faithfulness, cannot journey to Mount Moriah because he must first "put his house in order"—a potentially endless process. Therefore, because of human weakness, the seeming virtue of organization, which for Neher helps man to serve God, here has the opposite effect. The second kind of mute energy is *ChShH,* which Neher interprets as quiet expectation, particularly Israel awaiting the Messiah. Indeed, Neher takes pride in Judaism's deep understanding of this aspect of Sacred Silence. On this subject, Kafka states that the Messiah will arrive when "the most unbridled individualism of faith" *(zügellosete Individualismus des Glaubens)* comes (*P* 80–81). Such individualism sounds like what used to be called "heresy." Kafka quietly awaits the time when individualism in religion runs so wild that even the dead will not stay safely buried but come back to join the debate. Then he inventively speculates that this is the Christian doctrine (while Neher carefully defends Judaism's difference from Christianity). Recall that considering each man as partly divine, allows Kafka to see some truth in the Incarnation. Jung interprets the Messiah as the archetypal goal of the process of Individuation, a remarkably similar paradox. To be entirely individual, a nonconformist, independent of any specific culture, is to identify with what is common to all humanity, the link (or Mediator) between it and the Divine.

Finally, Neher considers ironic silences as masks. If the disguise is human—as with a hero concealing his purpose until the decisive moment—Neher applies the Hebrew term *'LM,* the dumbness of the tongue-tied (whom he humanely sees as potentially heroic). One might first think of the inarticulate creatures roaming Kafka's Sinai, but, sadly, they may possess no minds to conceal. More relevantly, Kafka says of one group of his imaginary Abrahams that they "are hiding their faces . . . so as not to have to lift their eyes and see the mountain" (*L* 285). Characteristically, Neher exemplifies the mask as a way of preparing for divine service; Kafka, as a way of avoiding it. Neher's last meaning of silence is the "hidden God," or "concealed face," a phrase for this veiling used over twenty times in the Bible (Maisel 45; Neher 45). Since this aspect of the silence of God interests him most, he subdivides it into yet three more levels: psychologically, man's horror at the silence that leaves him feeling abandoned by God; historically, the lack of a satisfying explanation for the repeated destruction of Israel; and, metaphysically, the doctrine of negative theology that the Divine transcends words. "Thou art a God that hidest Thyself," as Is. complains (45:15). In these terms, examine Kafka's theologizing. "The Messiah will come only when he is no longer necessary" (*P* 81). Where Neher longs to have God send his final messenger, the Messiah, Kafka (like Jung) envisions the Messiah (the redeemed individual) as the result of salvation (Individuation), not its cause; thus the Messiah comes only after he is unnecessary (after all have saved themselves).

During the psychedelic 1960s, I once reencountered a rock musician sitting in a library. Since I had previously mentioned Jung to him, he eagerly showed me a passage from a Jungian tome, which he said had helped him to understand his father. After some discreet questions, I found that he had no literal comprehension of the words. They had worked like an inkblot, a series of nebulous images, triggering his own memories, with excellent therapeutic effect. Comparably, for Kabbalists, *gematriya* (playing with the letters of Scripture) is not merely a hermeneutical device but also a meditational exercise. Perhaps, the ultimate value of silence in any text is to form a kind of empty margin, leaving room for the reader's own fantasies (as, according to one Kabbalistic doctrine, God opened space for the creation by withdrawing himself from it). However close silence comes to revelation, silence is only an overture.

Imagery

> Before setting foot in the Holy of Holies you must take off your shoes, yet not only your shoes, but everything; you must take off your traveling garment and lay down your luggage; and under that you must shed your nakedness . . . and then even the glimmer of the undying fire. Only the fire itself is absorbed by the Holy of Holies.
>
> —Kafka (untitled fragment)

> He will depict in his mind only the divine energy which derives from the supernal root so that its light will be of infinite greatness.
>
> —Rabbi Dov Baer of Mezritch (1710–1772)

The renowned Hasidic and Kabbalist "Maggid" (master) Rabbi Dov Baer suggests in this passage that the Kabbalist engage in vivid visualization of imaged energy as a way of experiencing the Divine, a state beyond imagery. Despite some significant differences,[16] Kafka's hypnotically repetitive stripping down to the primal fire seems to be a comparable visualization technique, also involving a self-negating, a mystical procedure sufficiently widespread so that Jung considered growth beyond the ego to be a universal part of spiritual development.

What is the relationship of visualization imagery to biblical language? The prototype of Kafka's novel *The Trial,* the Book of Job, a canonical work that obsessed Jung, will serve as well as any for a few examples. Indeed, the modern reader who approaches it as an exposition of Divine Justice will probably lose patience because it does not consist primarily of logical argument. Rather it presents vivid, repetitive imagery of human weakness and Divine Power, as if tempting one to disassociate from the former and identify with the latter. For Job, however, such an identification was only possible when God was physically present, not merely mentioned by the comforters (a point worthy of later consideration). For the moment, though, compare the Joban and Kafkan attitudes toward language in the following instances:

> He hath made me also a byword [*MShL*] of the people.
>
> —Job 17.6[17]

> You yourselves would become images [*Gleichnissen*].
>
> —Kafka

Kafka probably first gained public attention with his tale of a man metamorphosed into an insect, but this line about being transformed into a *Gleichnissen* (originally meaning a likeness) is even more intriguing. Job's concern about being changed to a *MShL* (also at one point meaning a likeness) at first seems a drab cliché unworthy of close attention, but with scrutiny it leads into a very similar mystery—the figurative transformation of flesh into language, almost the inverse of the Incarnation, where the Word becomes flesh. A terminological investigation is necessary. The relationship of Job and the Incarnate Word underlies Jung's highly controversial work, *Antwort auf Hiob* ("Answer to Job," 1952, *GW,* vol. 11), but before plunging into a study thereof, one should confront this problem of likenesses or analogies. Since Kafka believes that language cannot treat Reality analogously *(vergleichweise, H* 45), critical opinion has recently turned against the word *parable* (i.e., allegory) to describe Kafka's short stories and to translate his term *Gleichnissen*. Not "parables" nor "likenesses," but "imagery," a less common meaning of *Gleichnissen,* best suits Kafka's statement, "all this imagery *(Gleichnissen)* means is that the unknowable is unknowable." Like Tantric visualizations, Kafka's *Gleichnissen* lead into emptiness. In a fragment, he wrote, "Void, merely an image, no more than that, absolute oblivion" (*H* 349). Azriel of Gerona says of mystical prayer that it "drives away all obstacles and impediments and reduces every word to its 'nothingness.'"[18]

According to Jung's *Answer to Job*, effective religious language not only seems to point to the Divine but also convinces the believers that it embodies Reality through its magical energy ("mana," *GW*, vol. 11, par. 558). How, though, does one measure "magic"? In Japan, where calligraphy is believed to embody varying levels of *ki* (virtually the same as *mana*), there have been microscopic studies of Zen works to show that ink forms clearer, more integrated lines after the calligraphers obtain Enlightenment.[19] Unlike Jung's measurement of how nervousness impedes word association, these integrated lines ostensibly flow from a superior psychological orientation. Such research into calligraphy, however, is completely alien to the alphabetical writing of the Bible, where not only cannot the modern reader judge the *mana* with which *MShL* was written, but where even the difference between it as meaning either laughingstock or profound utterance depends entirely on vowels that were not originally recorded. Nonetheless, The Book of Job is primarily about energy—the omnipotence of God versus the laughably weak condition of suffering humanity. In Job's enervating agony, he cries:

> What is my strength that I should be quiet,
> and what my end, that I should be patient. (6:11)[20]

Even silence requires a modicum of energy and hope. At first, Job's friends wordlessly sat with him in a place of refuse and burned dung. Derided or rebuked by most people, he had these faithful ones to comfort him—for a week, then, human strength gave out: he cursed the day on which he was born, and with understandably frazzled nerves, they started gently rebuking him, sparking his indignation and their ire. Like Joseph K.'s writing vast autobiography as self-defense, Job longs for his story to be written (19:23) as eternal testimony; for he trusts in the power of writing to convince people of the truth, so he will no longer be a byword. This trust does not mean, though, that he is literally truthful. In chapter 19, he testifies:

> For I know that my Redeemer lives,
> though he be the last to arise upon earth
> Deep in my skin this has been marked,
> and in my very flesh do I see God
> I myself behold Him,
> with my own eyes I see Him, not with another's.

Twenty-three chapters later, after God has actually appeared, Job confesses: "I have heard of You by hearsay, / But now my own eyes have seen You." Evidently, his earlier testimony was not literally true, perhaps merely a visualized hope, but God accepts variations from the literal, for he acquits Job. In finding Job innocent, the Divine Whirlwind empowers Job to perform a ritual for the community, fills him with healing energy, and provides him with those ancient tokens of power: wealth and a large family. Not truthfulness but successfully evoking the Divine saves him.

In regard to Truth, the rabbinical *Genesis Rabba* (8.5) contains this striking incident:

> Truth said, "Let [man] not be created, because he is compounded of falsehood." . . . What did the Lord do? He took Truth and cast it to the ground.

Kafka wrote, "Truth is indivisible, hence it cannot recognize itself; anyone who wants to recognize it has to be a lie" (*D* 43). Similarly, the central point of Jung's *Answer to Job* is that in ancient times God (or the God concept) being largely unconscious (or being the "Unconscious") could not recognize himself (itself). In confronting Job and seeing himself through human eyes, God realized the value of (human consciousness)—even as untrustworthy as it is—and decided to become human himself (the Incarnation). Jung acknowledges that he is not describing Reality but merely presenting a largely subjective view, a personal myth (*GW,* vol. 11, par. 559), one based on his arcane readings (including two allusions to Kabbala) and his psychological discoveries. In other words, from the literal point of view, his psychoanalysis of God is a lie, one that he realizes will upset many people (though he never expected the public to become as angry as it did). Like Kafka's previously mentioned understanding of art as grotesque, the very offensiveness of a religious untruth may stimulate the energy necessary to turn one's attention from the physical to the transcendent. In *The Trial,* a priest remarks that the Scripture he has been reading and interpreting need not be considered "true" but merely "necessary." K. complains that this transforms lying into a "world order" (*Weltordnung, Pr* 264), and in a deleted passage recognizes that people have only been alluding to the truth, but his understanding goes no further. The Whirlwind never comes. At the book's close, in a light from a distant window, K. sees a "dim and insubstantial" figure stretching hands toward him. While K. ponders the meaning of this enigma, he is placed on a rock (in a parody of human sacrifice) and killed with a knife.

According to Harold Bloom's *Kabbalah and Criticism,* "In Hebraic tradition, all literary representation partook of transgression, unless it were canonical," so that each new work occasioned anxiety.[21] In describing the numinous energy of archetypal imagery, Jung meant not merely the ecstatic joy evoked by it but also its association with awesome terror. Kafka feared his writing as a daemonic power. He typically sentenced his personae to death as with the sacrifice of Joseph K. slain by his contact with the Law. According to Kabbala, when God created the universe, his energy filled a series of vessels, which shattered from the strain.

Repetition

> Within one week, I had cured that anxiety neurosis, and that is not a lie (I am too old to lie!)—that is a fact.
>
> —Jung, *The Symbolic Life*

Speaking in English to the Guild of Pastoral Psychologists, London, Jung thus concludes a notable case history. One night he dreamed of an attractive woman with a "father complex." On meeting a new patient the next day, he thought, "perhaps she is the one!" Even though he could not find any evidence of such a complex, he kept probing until he learned that she had broken from Judaism despite her grandfather having been a great Hasidic Kabbalist, a miracle-working rabbi. This information inspired Jung to accuse her of being "untrue to your God" (i.e., betraying her Divine Father), the decisive moment in the "cure."

If I encountered this in a novel, I would be impressed by the artistry with which the author had created a distinctly unreliable narrator. The very word *cure* sounds suspicious, since prudent physicians do not make such claims, particulary about so nebulous an ailment as neurosis. Jung often falls under this suspicion. In the case of his treatment of the physicist Wolfgang Pauli, for example, Jung proclaimed that therapy "cured" the patient's excessive drinking, yet Pauli's assistant H. B. G. Casimir recalls the terror of subsequently driving with Pauli, who chortled, "Ich fahre ziemlich gut" ("I drive pretty good") as he drunkenly zigzagged from one side of the mountain road to the other.[22] Even this behavior, though, marked an improvement over his previous collapse.

Considering the hyperbolic nature of the word *cure,* one may wonder if Jung's repetitive phrasing is not merely rhetorical but also symptomatic of nervousness (the way he interpreted repetition in his word-association test). Consider his fourfold assertion of the cure: (1) by stating it, (2) by adding "that is no lie," (3) by parenthetically interpolating "I am too old to lie!" (4) and by concluding "that is a fact." In a novel, I would also note the subtle implication of the narrator's self-image as himself a wonder worker. Like a Kabbalist, Jung derives revelations from his own dreams. Directly before the anecdote begins, he quotes another patient's remark. "Dr. Jung is a god." Like this patient, Kafka himself easily fell under the spell of a charismatic person while in the latter's presence. Then he would typically submit the experience to his irony while alone writing his Diary, as in the following entry: "The influence of a tranquil face, a quiet speech, particularly from a strange man, not yet seen through. God's voice out of a human mouth" (*T* 346; *DI* 324).

The issues of repetition, orality, and charisma are integrally connected, as with idolized popular singers who raise their audiences to ecstasies on waves of repetitive clichés. Before literacy became common, it was easier to believe in "cures," total returns to lost health, repetitions of primal perfection. Now, when all the written records can be consulted, belief becomes more difficult. Similarly, in Kafka's novel *The Trial,* total acquittals are said to be legendary, actual acquittals being at most presumptive. Only in a moment of faith, as under the sway of a charismatic figure, do the past "archetypes" seem totally manifest in the present. Kierkegaard's theological novel *Repetition* (1843)—which Kafka read—struggles with this problem. Its protagonist makes a journey in hope of recovering the past, but without success. Then he realizes that "only spiritual repetition is possible, although in the temporal life it is never so perfect as in eternity, which is the true repetition." In life, two kinds of almost timeless moments happen—the aesthetic's escape into seemingly eternal beauty leading to selfish disinterest in the world and the saint's mystic encounter with the truly Eternal, leading away from self to altruistic commitment. Kierkegaard calls the first of these "recollection" (his interpretation of Plato's *anamnesis*); the second he terms "spiritual repetition."[23]

Given a particular example of repetition, however, the question of whether it is spiritual or not depends on context. In an article entitled, "New Directions in the Psychology of Religion," Michael Argyle contends "religion is not just a set of metaphors, but perhaps its additional meaning is conveyed by the powerful non-verbal and contextual signals that accompany those metaphors and messages,"[24] i.e., what one repeatedly sees or senses as its frame. Kafka cannot literally employ "non-verbal" cues in a text, but he is skillful in using context, including the association of his works with their sources. If Kafka wrote poetry in a repetitive biblical style, this intertextuality of his repetition would be easy to chart, but the relationship of his prose to the Bible is mediated by other prose writers, certainly including Dickens, to whom he gives credit for inspiring *The Lost One*. Thus, before analyzing an example of Kafkan repetition and its tie to Scripture, there is a need to take a fairly protracted look at a work by Dickens to see what is relatively new and what is traditional in Kafka's approach. In *Dickens and the Broken Scripture,* Janet Larson thus characterizes his ironic use of biblical echoes:

> Dickens is satirizing empty forms or—quite a different reason— . . . is unconcerned . . . with the full traditional meaning of the ritual. Such silences and inattentions, paradoxically occurring within contexts that attend carefully

> otherwise to biblical tradition, must also be accounted for, as must lapses like the botched allusion in Great Expectations that Julian Moynahan has made famous: Pip's inadvertent "pharisaic rewording of the publican's speech" while he is attending the dying Magwich ("I thought I knew there were no better words I could say beside his bed, than 'O Lord, be merciful to him, a sinner!' ")[25]

Dickens's change of "me" to "him" in Luke 18:13 was prepared for through the following pattern of repetition that so thoroughly relates Pip to Magwich that the former is not pharisaically patronizing Magwich. The story begins the day that the protagonist "found out for certain, that this bleak place overgrown with nettles was the churchyard . . . and that the small bundle of shivers growing afraid of it all and beginning to cry, was Pip." This discovery of himself occurs through the sudden, disorienting advent of a terrifying, almost supernatural figure named Magwich (perhaps derived from Magus and witch), who literally turns the boy upside down. Pip sees "the church . . . go head over heels before me, and . . . the steeple under my feet. . . ."[26] Not just the whirling makes him aware of his feet and heels but the fact that the man has "a great iron on his leg." Pip's mind fixates on leg images—perhaps all the more so because, being so small, legs are the part of adults closest to him, though this alone does not explain the motif. In addition to the frequently mentioned leg iron, Magwich has "broken shoes," and being "lamed by stones" he is also characterized by an often-mentioned limp (2). As he "limped toward the low church wall," he "looked in my young eyes as if he were eluding the hands of the dead people, stretching up cautiously out of their graves, to get a twist upon his ankle and pull him in." Since Pip has been examining the graves of his dead family, Magwich seems like a ghostly father or some more sinister apparition. Pip runs home only to be plagued by thoughts of the "fugitive . . . with the ironed leg." Out of fear of reprisal, Pip steals food for the criminal, thereby becoming a criminal himself. He stuffs a "hunk of bread and butter down the leg of [his] trouser." Then, "the secret burden [of guilt] co-operates with another secret burden down the legs of his trousers"(p. 10). Every time he moves to do his chores, the bread starts to slip out by his ankle: "the load upon [Pip's] leg . . . made [him] think afresh of the man with the load on *his* leg." (11). Fearing that he will soon be caught and sentenced to the prison ship from which the man has escaped, Pip asks about the inmates. He is told, "People are put in the Hulks because they murder, and because they rob, and forge, and do all sorts of bad; and they always begin by asking questions" (12). Significantly, Pip recalls, "I was in mortal terror of my interlocutor with the iron leg; I was in mortal terror of myself." In returning to the graveyard, Pip "couldn't warm [his] feet to which the damp cold seemed riveted as the iron was riveted to the leg of the man." Although crural imagery runs throughout the novel—e.g., the irony of Magwitch's daughter's scorning Pip because of the latter's coarse boots—there is no point in citing it all. The point is that, by the ending, identification between Pip and the father-figure Magwich is sufficient so that Pip's words about "him, a sinner" are not necessarily pharasaic condescension, but a prayer for Magwich and himself as criminals, inextricably implicated in the same crimes. Pip is an accessory after the fact, engaged in helping Magwitch escape, so that, for all Pip knows at the moment, he and Magwich may die on the same gallows.

With Pip, the reader enters a world of childish superstition, the strange fancies that the boy "religiously entertained" (1), so that at first the frightening repetitions are part of a child's religion of fear, not Kierkegaardian "recollection" or "spiritual repetition" (since both are pleasant). This chain of repetition, however, transforms Pip's prayer from pharisaical to genuinely Christian, thereby retroactively linking the whole chain to spiritual repetition. The pattern follows Dickens's essentially unitarian theology, a belief that mankind should grow beyond superstition to a moral humanism, though one emphasizing the sinfulness of humanity. By choosing a Dickensian pattern for *The Lost One,* Kafka creates the expectation that the repeated imagery will be extremely commonplace—not openly religious—but that it will eventually become associated with a recognizable biblical echo, the religious grounding of traditional novels.

The first chapter prepares for Karl to meet his limping protector, Uncle Jacob, whose need for a cane and whose alteration of appellation, although never fully explained, nonetheless, appear to be due to less profound causes than the biblical Jacob's divinely wounded thigh and changed name. *Great Expectations* begins with a church seemingly inverted, then righted; Kafka opens with a stranger symbol, the Statue of Liberty called "Freedom-goddess" *(Freiheitsgötin)* holding not the actual torch but a sword—the threat of freedom itself. Instead of docking, Karl wanders back into the shelter of the ship, ostensibly to look for an umbrella *(Regenschirm),* the word for which signifies etymologically a rain *(Regen)* protector *(Schirm).* The latter word is also used with human protectors (e.g., *Schirmherr,* patron). Fairly soon, though, he himself is lost in the labyrinthine passages. He realizes the danger of having left his luggage in the care of a stranger, and (like Pip's neurotic fascination with the "iron leg") this event occasions further worry—twenty-three repetitions of the word "luggage" *(Koffer)* in eight pages, as Karl recalls how he had previously lost sleep trying to guard it. (Recall Kafka's aphorism about the holy of holies, where luggage must be stripped away along with everything else before the mystical moment of unity.) Without any resolution to the matter of the luggage, Karl joins forces with a chauvinistic stoker who wants preferential treatment because he is German. Years later, Jean-Paul Sartre famously denounced racism as a cowardly flight from freedom back into the protective tribe.[27] Kafka anticipates this idea, for each of Karl's concerns is a symbol of protection, *Regenschirm*, luggage (property), racist Stoker bent on a right-wing revolution aboard ship, and, finally, the rich uncle, Senator Jacob, who criticizes Karl's parents for having sent the boy away unprovided, with no hope but America's "signs and wonders." As previously noted, in the Torah this phrase refers to the plagues of Exod. It is the biblical echo that explains the repeated search for protection. Dickens's biblical moral was extraverted (the need for identification with others) while Kafka's is introverted and mystical (stripping away the protection of physical existence). Dickens's presentation of the leg imagery was largely metaphoric, but Kafka, who rarely uses metaphors and distrusts them, simply repeats either quite exactly as with the twenty-three occurrences of *Koffer* or by substituting one of Karl's concerns for another, yet showing each to arise from the same immature craving for security.

Kafka's "new . . . Kabbala" should not be confused with the old one. The latter, in interpreting the Bible, focuses on moral action as a way of identifying with God's moral attributes, for Kabbala presumes that a repetition between the heavenly and earthly is possible. If traditional Judaic interpretation of the Bible ever shies away from the idea of repetition, this reluctance is because the Torah is seen as an eternal plenum of meaning. As the Talmud Pesahim proclaims, "There is no 'before' or 'after' in Torah" (6b). What seem like repetitions to secular critics (e.g., the creation of man recounted twice, the Ten Commandments listed twice) is part of a divine fullness of meaning where every letter has something different to teach. Since Kafka for more modern reasons considers repetition extremely problematic, his repetitions generally highlight the need for the spiritual rather than its manifestation.

The Incarnate Word

> Is the fact that there are religions proof an individual cannot remain good? The Founder [*Grunder*] breaks Himself away from the Good to incarnate Himself. Does He do it for others or because He is convinced that only with others can He remain what He has been, for He must negate the "World" to avoid loving it.
>
> —Kafka (untitled fragment)

One might misread the first sentence to mean merely that a person cannot remain good without religions, but such an interpretation does not even make sense of that sentence, let alone what follows it. For Kafka, evil is a necessity *(Notwendigkeit)* during part of human development (*H* 44). If people could remain perfect on their own, religions would not have arisen to preach them into that condition. The ordinary word for Creator is *Schöpfer,* but Kafka believes that man, not God, creates the (illusory) world. Thus God is Founder or, even more literally, Grounder, the One providing the "Ground [*Grund*] of Being" (Eckhart's phrase), while "the Good" is a Platonic term meaning the Eternal. As previously mentioned, Kafka sees each person as the Divine Knowledge incarnate, but he must mean something more special than this Incarnation of everyone or else he would not talk of "others." Consequently, the special Incarnation must be of those like Jesus who do not repress Divine Knowledge but express it as nearly as words may, i.e., by pointing to the truth, thereby leading people away from worldliness. Their entering physical existence prevents even them from being Good. Kafka writes in another fragment, "Christ suffered for mankind, but mankind must suffer for Christ" (*H* 117; *D* 97). This statement was originally part of an aphorism proclaiming that since all people are One, they must each suffer all the world's sufferings. This is not as dreadful as it first sounds, for another aphorism explains that what appears to be suffering is Really "bliss," i.e., it seems painful because it draws one away from worldliness but the same movement is bringing one closer to Being (*H* 51). What does this mean for the individual? As soon as he identifies with the One, thereby uniting wtih the Good, the highest Individuality, the Indestructible element (*H* 89; *D* 78), he must move back into the muck of illusion to try to save others, even though this involves suffering and absence from the Good. The Kabbalist Luria taught that people may cooperate in the salvation of the world through a life of concentrated prayer, Kavvanah, for which labor some people supposedly reincarnate into this world of pain. Robertson sees Kafka's humility and mysticism as constituting Kavvanah,[28] but Kafka here associates his metaphysics with Christianity, or rather a parody of Christianity, particularly of the belief that "the Word was made flesh" (John 1:14) because "God so loved the world that he gave his only begotten Son" (John 3:16)—where, for Kafka, the Founder incarnated to avoid loving the world.

According to Gustav Janouch's possibly apocryphal account, Kafka once remarked: "[Christ] is an abyss filled with light. One must close one's eyes if one is not to fall into it."[29] On another occasion, according to Janouch, Kafka employed a similar imagery: "The truth," Kafka said, "is always an abyss. One must . . . dare to dive from the quivering springboard of everyday experience and sink into the depths." (154). Considering Kafka's occasional interest in the writings of Meister Eckhart, St. Augustine, and Kierkegaard—considering also the fact that many of Kafka's personae are Christian—one might wonder why he never made the Kierkegaardian leap into Christianity itself. Although there have been too many attempts to read the Kafkan corpus as Bunyan-like allegory, the very real question of Kafka's attitude toward the Incarnate Word that he parodied needs further exploration.

In beginning such an examination, one may well focus on one of his most suggestive aphorisms from 1917, a year when he was studying Hebrew, composing a mystical mythology comparable to Blake's, and recovering from the shock of discovering his (eventually fatal) tuberculosis. On 25 February 1917, writing in the fourth Octavo Notebook, he laments that the Commandments, the ground beneath his feet, the very air around him—all no longer exist; he must recreate them through his art. In his own version of the God-as-Maker motif *(deus artifex topos),* which has dominated literary criticism from at least the time of Petrarch,[30] Kafka interprets artistic creation as a reflection *(Abglanz)* or even part of the primal work *(ursprünglichste Aufgabe)* of Creation (*H* 120). The word *Aufgabe* not only means work but also giving up, a secondary sense that may be relevant here in two ways: (1) Kafka sees his own literary creating as a kind of surrender, marked by his growing weakness, disease, and alienation; (2) Kabbalism (of which Kafka has often been suspected) envisions Creation as an act of Divine Withdrawal. On 24 February, in the same notebook, he had written that the world is constantly created, moment by moment springing into existence and then, presumably, being annihilated moment by moment. In the 25 February entry, he suggests that everything created from nothing is worthless, i.e., all phenomena are worthless. He continues that the constant recreation of the world leaves it devoid of continuity and tradition. He is, he says, a representative of the negativity of his age, because he has neither been guided to Life *(Leben)* by Christianity's "weak sinking hand" *(schwer sinkenden Hand)* nor by the Jewish prayer shawl, which is flying away along with the Zionists. Here, again, Christianity appears as something pulling one downward, like the hand of a drowning swimmer, though the depths are in some sense—ironic or otherwise—bestowers of Life. Kafka concludes with the portentous words, "I am the End or the Beginning" *(Ich bin Ende oder Anfang).* The sentence strangely echoes Christ's "I am Alpha and Omega, the beginning and the ending." (*Egō eimi to Alpha Kai to Omega,* Rev. 1:8).[31] The idiom in Rev. is a Hellenized version of the proverbial Jewish way of describing the whole of a matter as being from *aleph* to *tau,* the first and last letters of the Hebrew alphabet. Kafka's changing "and" to "or" conforms to his mystical system, according to which life is a series of creations from nothing, their connection being that they reflect the Divine Reality. In his stories, by showing life as a sequence of disconnected, dreamlike encounters, Kafka strips away rationality in order to depict visionary epiphanies of this Divine Reality.

One part of his mythology—his seeing himself as half a Christ (first or last) is quite relevant to his attitude toward Christianity. One might, of course, counter that he is not speaking about Christianity at all. After all, the imagery of God as First and Last occurs in Isa. 41:4 and, thus, belongs to Judaism as much as to Christianity. Kafka, though, has just been talking about *both* Christianity and Judaism. His 1917 aphorisms are in a strange hinterland combining elements of the two. In one of these gnomic sayings, as we have seen, he asserts that because Adam ate of the tree of the knowledge of Good and Evil, humanity "became . . . Divine Knowledge" *(wurden . . . das göttliche Erkennen)* but without Divine Power; thus, again, Kafka images man as a demi-god, this time with the potential to become like God, himself (*P* 30). Raising humanity so high runs counter to the central thrust of Judaic thought—the uniqueness of God—but it is not precisely the Christian Incarnation. Most certainly it is no simple antithesis to Christianity, as can be seen from one of his most famous parables. In it, children are given a chance to choose between being kings or royal messengers. Craving activity, they all opt for the latter. In describing their paradoxical state (messengers without a message), Alan Udoff simplistically explains, "If the figure of the Messiah is the embodiment of the archetype of the Messenger, then Kafka's courier is nothing less than its antipodal disfiguration, the archetype of the anti-Messenger—or anti-Messiah."[33] Actually, as will be later discussed (chap. 10), Kafka disliked antitheses. He is not trying to create anything as superficial as anti-Messiahs or anti-Christs. Art, for him, has no such simple message, but (according to his 25 February aphorism) generates a thin mountain air where one may "step suddenly into the light." Seen from that altitude, what, then, is his attitude toward his Christian characters?

One of the first of these is the Supplicant, in *Description of a Struggle* (c. 1904–5). He spends his time in church splashing his emaciated body with holy water or beating his skull against the stone floor. Since Kafka thought of himself as repellently thin, and gave that appearance to a number of his personae, such as the hunger artist in the story of that name, the Supplicant is probably a comic self-portrait. Upon being questioned, the Supplicant protests:

> "I do not know under what suspicion you hold me, but I am guiltless." Then he reiterated: "Naturally, I do not know under what suspicion you hold me." (*B* 40; *C* 31)

Thus, he prefigures one of Kafka's most famous personae, K., who protests his innocence throughout *The Trial* despite his not knowing the charge. Eventually, the Supplicant admits why he prays so zealously. To him everything seems to "sink down like a snowfall." Here, again, Kafka associates Christianity with the imagery of sinking into the abyss underlying the world of appearances. The Supplicant continues that he has been struck by this sense of unreality while overhearing a conversation (indeed, a conversation that Kafka himself actually heard and recorded in his Diaries as having impressed him in the same way). Next, the Supplicant ecstatically proclaims: "The Virgin Mary's cloak is coiling around her pillar and the wind is tugging at it. Does no one notice this?" (*B* 46; *C* 36).

Not much can be made of the mere fact that Kafka employed a visionary, possibly mad Christian as a persona. "Description of a Struggle" remains in a fragmentary state. During the period of its composition, Kafka (like the Supplicant) was in his early twenties and (also like the ecstatic Supplicant) not in full control of his words. Kafka's first major works were completed in 1912 (*Das Urteil* in September; *Die Verwandlung* in November) after a July vacation in the Harz Mountains. There he apparently attended Christian church, for he mentions the Ambrosian chants during a 14 July service. Despite the urging of a member of a Christian community, Kafka, however, refused to convert, saying that he was not yet ready. The Christian expressed faith that Kafka was "close to grace" but Kafka cryptically "referred him to the inner voice," thereby winning the argument; nonetheless, it was at this period that Kafka consented to serve as a model for a statue of St. Sebastian. Kafka mentions reading the Bible (presumably a Christian translation) in his room each day after meals. The year 1912 was a year of religious ferment for Kafka—admittedly not as extreme as 1917—but marked by Kafka's tentative exploration of Christianity and by his first readings of Jewish history. It is, thus, not entirely a coincidence that two of his works that have most fascinated the religious imagination were written during that year.

The first of these, *"Das Urteil,"* ends with a father condemning his son to drowning. As the boy obediently rushes out to plunge into the river, a charwoman screams "Jesus!" (*C* 87). The son hangs for a while with "weakening hands" and then dies faithful to his father's will. Certainly, this suicide would not strike any Christian as comparable to Christ's atoning death, but the juxtaposition of the charwoman's "Jesus!" with the boy's weakening hands and fall into the abyss does recall the imagery complex by which Kafka described Christianity on 25 February 1917.

In *"Die Verwandlung,"* Gregor Samsa longs for Christmas Day, when he plans to insist that his sister be allowed to attend the music conservatory. As a bug, however, he loses all track of the Christian calendar, which previously had been marked by his father's promenading on Sundays and Holy Days. Now, confronting the bleak timelessness of existence beyond the human condition, Gregor comes to the decision to disappear, largely out of love for his family, who are troubled by his presence. Just as the first dawn rays spread over him, he dies.

In the cathedral scene in *The Trial,* K. has come to act as a guide for an

Italian businessman, who never arrives. The day grows dark and stormy. Just as he is about to leave, a light is lit over a mysterious pulpit, designed so that the priest must bend agonizingly forward all the time that he preaches—Kafka's motif of the suffering messenger. "K. crossed himself and bowed, as he ought to have done earlier." This is the way the passage reads, but who is saying that K. should have crossed himself? In a typical Victorian novel, particularly in the works of Trollope, one would have little doubt that a narrator's reference to obligation was an authorial interjection, upholding propriety. In some twentieth-century novels, a similar reference might be no more than a reflection of the character's own sense of guilt. With Kafka, though, guilt never seems to stay confined to an individual, but spreads in the manner of original sin. Man cannot fulfill the demands of the Absolute as the preacher reaffirms with the celebrated parable, "Before the Law." A man from the country comes in search of the Law but is permitted to go no farther than the portal. Human strength was insufficient to gain admission, but just as Gregor Samsa perceived the morning light as he died, just as the son in *"Das Urteil"* dies in a realization of hopeless love, and just as Kafka envisions creative artists stripping away all earthly concerns in order to reach a mystic light in the thin air, so the man from the country finally sees a radiance from the guarded portal. This light is like the Divine Knowledge, which, according to Kafka, man *became* upon eating of the Tree of the Knowledge of Good and Evil. This Knowledge is his True Self, realizable only when the false, worldly self disappears, i.e., in death—either literal death, as with his characters, or figurative death, as with the discipline of self-abnegation he expects from writers.

The process of stripping away false selfhood is his characteristic theme as in "A Country Doctor," which is worth summarizing again here. Its protagonist has a respectable position in the community, but to fulfill his duty he must make a house call and his horse has died. This is but the beginning of his misfortunes. Stripped of everything—position, respect, home, companionship, even clothing—he succumbs to "the frost of the most unhappy of ages." The doctor feels that he is being "misused for sacred ends," because the people "have lost their ancient beliefs; the parson sits at home and unravels his vestments, one after another" (*C* 224). The minister's unraveling vestments, of course, parallels the stripping of the doctor. Even in its decline, indeed, particularly because of its decline, the parson's Christianity, like the doctor's practice, produces a sense of emptiness, a prelude to spiritual truth.

Unfortunately, that truth brings with it no power to improve earthly conditions as can be seen from "The Bucket Rider" *("Der Kübelreiter"),* a tale much like the preceding one. The protagonist of "The Bucket Rider" is hopelessly poor, lacking even the coal to warm himself in midwinter. His coal bucket is so empty, so light, that he can ride on it, which he does to the coal dealer, who significantly lives next to a church. According to the Law "Thou shalt not kill," the dealer must provide fuel to those on the point of death, but bundled away in his overheated house, the dealer can barely hear the cries of the protagonist. The dealer's wife insists that there is no one there, even when she can see the poor man, and so, in the very shadow of the church, his claims go unrecognized. In his suffering, he realizes the Law, but it cannot help him because those in power and therefore comfort are blinded by that comfort from seeing the cold emptiness around them. As the doctor rides into the killing "frost of this most unhappy of ages," so the bucket rider flies through the air to "the ice mountains and [is] forever lost."

Does Kafka's metaphysic of emptiness have anything in common with actual Christianity? In trying to find common ground between Zen and Christianity, the modern mystic Thomas Merton discovered a Christian theology linked to the "emptiness without manner" of the fourteenth-century visionary John Ruysbroeck and also the Christian doctrine of kenosis, the "self-emptying" of God in Jesus' Incarnation (*heauton ekenosen,* Phil. 2:7).[34] Kafka encountered this Christianity of emptiness in the writings of Meister Eckhart, whom he praised in 1903 for revealing a new room in Kafka's own castle (*Br* 20). For Eckhart, knowledge is the same as being, a probable source of Kafka's odd belief that man *became* the Divine Knowledge.[35] What apparently attracted Kafka most in Christianity was what was common to many religions. He could not go beyond this to accept Christ as God Incarnate, Beginning *and* End. For Kafka, beginnings and endings are like a gestalt picture. Looked at one way, the picture is a young woman, a Beginning; seen from another perspective, it is an old woman, an Ending. Thus, for instance, Gregor Samsa's end begins a new day for his parents but he will not live to see it. He is gone with no Christ to resurrect him and restore him to human form. Because of Kafka's austere—one might even say bleak—mysticism, his Christian characters must lose virtually everything, including at least most of their Christianity, before they can glimpse the truth, and realize that truth brings the destruction of their temporal selves.

What is of interest is that, through almost Kabbalistic reinterpretation, he sees truth even in a religion he finds as uncongenial as Christianity. In *Psychology and Alchemy,* Jung suggests that there is truth in all religions and that Christians should stop chiding him with inconsistency for such a position since a religion affirming that Three are One and that a virgin gave birth ought to enjoy paradoxes (*GW,* vol. 12, par. 18). In *Aion,* Jung adds a bit of occult trivia that may be particularly applicable to Kafka: since opposites tend to resemble each other, the raven (one of Kafka's birds) not only traditionally represented the Devil but also Christ (*GW,* vol. 9, par. 127).

5
Oriental Tales

> Gustav Wyneken and his friends spell out—as you can see [in their publications]—transcriptions of reality from translations of ancient Greece. . . . [O]nly [in the immediate moment] can [reality] be won or lost. [O]ne must break through [the facade].
>
> —Kafka (according to Janouch)

> Rather than memorizing Eastern spiritual techniques and imitating them in a totally Christian way—*imitatio Christi!*—with a correspondingly forced manner, far more valuable would it be to discover if the Unconscious embodies an introversion comparable to what has arisen as the leading spiritual principle of the Orient.
>
> —Jung, "On 'The Tibetan Book of the Great Liberation' "

The pluralism of modern Europe, a classical education (including familiarity with Graeco-Roman myth), and a fascination with Jewish tradition, all contributed to Kafka's and Jung's disorientation, so they sought a new *orientation* outside of that chaos—in the East, even though they realized that neither they nor others could actually reroot themselves. On the one hand, Jung used yoga to keep his mind from being swamped during his mental breakdown. He also spent hours under a pear tree in his garden casting auguries with the *I ching* (a Chinese classic of meditation and divination). Once he even stayed up all night "playing with the *I ching*" in company with its translator Richard Wilhelm, and Jung used the *I ching* in treating at least one patient.[1] Indeed, Jung's theory of synchronicity was partly inspired by that book. Under Oriental influence, he made statements such as, "Matter is [only] a hypothesis," coming close to Hindu (and Kafkan) belief that the visible world differs radically from Reality (*GW,* vol. 11, par. 762). Among Jung's articles on Eastern religions are his prefaces for the *I ching, Introduction to Zen Buddhism, The Tibetan Book of the Great Liberation,* and *The Tibetan Book of the Dead,* the last of which he described as his "constant companion . . . [to which he owed] numerous intriguing ideas . . . discoveries [and] insights" (*GW,* vol. 11, par. 833).

On the other hand, he frequently warns his readers against slavish imitations of Eastern practices, not merely because he did not want Occidentals to go for spiritual guidance to a yogi instead of to him, but also because he feared they would end with a mishmash of cultures, the limbo he had himself experienced. He particularly worried that, for a Westerner, joining an Oriental religion amounted to an *imitatio Christi,* because the Occidental would continue to use willpower (the method of the *imitatio Christi*), thereby rigidifying the ego rather than joining it to the "Unconscious" as (he believed) an Oriental would. (His advice against will power comes from *Tao te ching,* chap. 33.)

According to Janouch, Kafka owned and had studied a collection of books on Chinese religion, which he was holding in his hand even while ridiculing their editor, Wyneken, for turning toward the East. Considering that Kafka met Janouch after stopping work on the unfinished Great Wall series, there is the possibility that Kafka's interest in the Orient had partly waned or soured, but records of his subsequent readings and book purchases show that it had not vanished. Nonetheless, in the biography *Franz Kafka,* Ronald Gray contends:

> Unlike many of his contemporaries Kafka was seldom inclined to oriental religious speculations . . . so far as he reads or writes about religion, it is the Judaeo-Christian tradition that is in the forefront; he reads the Bible and the Talmud, Kierkegaard, Pascal, as well as Nietzsche (often a disappointed Christian) rather than the Upanishads or the Bhagavad-Gita.[2]

Kafka quotes from the Vedas in a 1922 Diary (*T* 581). According to Janouch, Kafka did read the Bhagavad-Gita, was conversant with the works of Rabindranath Tagore, and had some general knowledge of Hinduism, though he apparently found it less appealing than Taoism (Janouch 85 and 153). Phrases from Orientalist readings slip casually into the speech of Janouch's Kafka, as, when discussing mysticism, he coins the metaphor, "the . . . drop of water [entering] . . . the infinite sea" (Janouch 142). The image probably comes from Sir Edwin Arnold's life of the Buddha, *The Light of Asia,* which had a widely selling German edition in Karl Neumann's translation.[3] Kafka is known to have owned Neumann's rendering of another Buddhist work, *The Last Days of Gautama Buddha* (Wagenbach 251). As to Gray's characterization of Nietzsche as "a disappointed Christian," that may have some truth as far as it goes but, at the turn of the century, Nietzsche's reputation linked him to the Orient, as where Alexander Tille in his introduction to the first English version of *Also Sprach Zarathustra,* compares it to the Buddhist Scriptures.[4] In translated works of Chuang Tzu (owned by Kafka, according to Janouch), Wilhelm likens that ancient Taoist to Nietzsche.[5] More recently, in *The Buddhist Nirvana and Its Western Interpreters,* Guy Welbon argues that Nietzsche's belief in "eternal return" and in "transvaluation of values" should be seen in a Buddhist context, because they are reminiscent of reincarnation and the Buddhist doctrine of constant change *(anicca).*[6]

Nietzsche learned Sanskrit, and named his hideaway "Nirvana," but his closest link to the East was via Schopenhauer. The latter's myriad affinities with Asian religions have been noted since the beginning of his reputation, John Oxenford's 1852 article "Iconoclasm in German Philosophy," which speaks of Schopenhauer wavering "between Brahmanism and Buddhism."[7] Typically, Max Nordau's very popular book *Degeneration* (1895) claims,

> The degenerate and insane are the predestined disciples of Schopenhauer and of [Karl Robert Eduard von] Hartmann [a follower of the former] and need only to acquire a knowledge of Buddhism to become converts to it.[8]

Despite the disrepute of Schopenhauerism, not only did Kafka own the complete works of Schopenhauer and a biography of the latter, but the indebtedness of Kafka's pessimism to Schopenhauer's is a critical commonplace.[9]

Kafka's interest in China is undeniable. One of his favorite books was Hans Heilmann's translation, *Chinese Lyrics.* He quoted from it in a letter to his fiancée Felice, animatedly read aloud from it on occasion, and gave a copy of it to Max Brod.[10] Another of his favorite tomes was Martin Buber's translation, *Chinese Ghost and Lost Stories.* In 1920, along with an extract from the *Chinese Lyrics,* he copied into his notebooks two passages from Buber's work, a volume he recommended to Felice.[11] These two books mention such common Taoist concepts as *yin* and *yang* (Buber xiv), the spiritual power of nature (Buber ix), Taoist magic (Buber 32), and the Tao itself (Heilmann 82). A fragmentary collection of Kafka's books remaining after his death contains other translations from the Chinese such as Richard Wilhelm's *Chinese Folktales* and Hans Bethge's rendering of Far Eastern poetry, *The Chinese Flute.*[12] His collected letters include reference to his ordering Friedrich Perzynski's *Concerning Chinese Gods: Travels in China* and Otto Fischer's *Chinese Landscape Painting* (*Br* 467; *L* 400). Janouch remarks Kafka's perusing Wilhelm's translations of Lao Tzu's *Tao te ching (The Way and Its Power)* and of two other Taoist works: Chuang Tzu's *Nan hua dschen ging (True Book of the Southern Blossomland),* and of Lieh Tzu's *Tschung hu dschen ging (True Book of the Spring of the First Cause),* the latter of which includes material attributed to the fellow Taoists Lia Yu Kou and Yang Tzu (Janouch 152–55).

Kafka would have been even more idiosyncratic than he was if he refused to read the Orientalism current in his circle, and he usually could summon the courage to face the pages of strange books. In another of the myriad biographies entitled *Franz Kafka,* Meno Spann acknowledges Kafka's "Exoticism" but suggests that it was simply "the yearning to escape" like the "young poet Brand" who screamed the single word "Cairo!" on his Prague deathbed—a summation of all his frustrated desires in a vision of one fabled fleshpot of the East.[13] Perhaps Kafka's Asian readings may have begun in mere escapism or curiosity, but they brought him in contact with profound and puzzling mysticism (sometimes especially puzzling because of Western errors in the presentation).

The Lure of Asia

> I dreamed . . . before the altar sat a yogi . . . with my face. . . . [I] thought: 'He is meditating me. I am his dream.' "
>
> —Jung, *Memories, Dreams, Reflections*

Jung interpreted this yogi as the Unconscious producing the ego, a yogi being chosen for that role because, as we have noted, Jung believed that the East represents the Unconscious. He found Asia engrossing since early childhood when he used to stare at pictures of Brahma, Vishnu, and Shiva (*Er* 23). What for Jung (and Kafka) were the alluring psychic riches of the East have for centuries connoted a more literal affluence to the general public. Austria owes its German name, *Osterreich* (Eastern kingdom or Eastern wealth) to its origin as a small extension of the Carolingian empire toward fabled Asian treasures. Even by the twentieth century, though, the Austrian empire stretched little farther toward the dawn than Kafka's birthplace, Prague (from *Praha,* the Czech word for "threshhold"). According to the exotic novel *The Golem,* by Gustav Meyrink (his precursor and fellow native of Prague), that provincial capital was founded by an "Order of the Asiatic Brothers."[14] In the midst of its crowded streets, where Oriental and Occidental architecture meld, Meyrink places the Golem. A product of magic in the shadowy Jewish ghetto, it is, nonetheless, Mongolian in appearance (43). Meyrink mixes its story with Asian images even to introducing the tale with a parable of the Buddha. This syncretic fantasy tells little about the prosaic Prague of commerce, *Gemutlichkeit,* Czech nationalism, and Austrian bureaucracy, but it is a good introduction to the oneiric city that underlies Kafka's urban narratives, and it forms one of many links between Kafka (familiar with the work of Meyrink) and the eclectic Orientalism they both practiced.

Kafka himself once began a short story about a golem, but to place Kafka within the development of Orientalism, we need to begin further back than Meyrink, with the first major encounter of East and West, the invasion of India by Alexander the Great. Kafka evokes that event in "The New Attorney" *(Der Neue Advokat),* composed in January 1917 and included at the very beginning of his volume entitled *A Country Doctor*

(Ein Landarzt), which he compiled between July and August of that year and published in 1919. The story sets the tone for the rest of the book by contrasting a glorious (though unsatisfactory) past with a drab present. Binder mentions Kafka's acquaintance with several versions of the Alexander stories including *Taten des grossen Alexander* (a modern recension of the medieval legend) and another work containing a Talmudic tale of Alexander's reaching the gates of Paradise but finding them closed.[15] Binder looking for a few sources follows the scholarly assumption that *specific* readings influence a writer in a *specific* manner—but since, like Jung, Kafka tends to be interested in general patterns, one may wonder if some grand design underlies Alexander tales virtually regardless of specific source. The value of this approach (used previously in the section on *Märchen*) is that the exact extent of an author's readings is indeterminable, so that viewing an author in terms of a tradition is at least as valid as charting demonstrable borrowings. One common denominator of the Alexander sagas is a legendary border, whether in his trips down the Ganges to Paradise or in gates that he allegedly constructed in some mysterious Eastern pass to defend civilization from barbarians. His chief enemies, Gog and Magog, have been identified as the lost Tribes of Israel, the Mongols, and so many others that the exact identity hardly seems to matter.[16] In a 21 December 1910, Diary notation, Kafka mentions Alexander imprisoning them (*T* 32). According to one scholar, the tales of gates built by Alexander to defend civilization are confused accounts of the Great Wall of China, constructed for the same purpose.[17] Jung records two Armenian tales in which divine intervention or a vast sea preserves one-fourth of the world from Alexander (*GW,* vol. 14, n. 514)—legends that Jung (seized by one of his stranger, numerological obsessions) adduces as proof of the archetypal difficulty of going from the number 3 to the number 4. Looked at as a whole, however, the Alexander material offers no such specific pattern, merely the idea that some barbarian or paradisiacal culture invariably lies beyond civilization. A hero to Hebrews (because he temporarily eased the problems of Israel) and thence to Christians, Alexander was eventually seen as "a fore runner of Jesus, earlier representations of whom portrayed him in Alexander's likeness, and the conception of Alexander Cosmocrator in time grew into Christ Pantocrator."[18] Jung adds the place of Alexander in alchemical texts as an *illuminatus* (*GW,* vol. 14, n. 410). Gregory Triffit provocatively dubs Kafka's Alexander "the transcendent Absolute['s] . . . human representative."[19] As Jung spent much of his career preaching that Good and Evil are inseparable, Kafka's parable may present a murderous, half-mad guide to the Beyond. The most popular facet of the legend, the connection of East and West, so strongly implies a gateway to the Orient that the stories give us two entries: one to

danger, the other to Paradise—and the pointing sword of Kafka's Alexander does not distinguish between them (as Kafka never resolves whether the Beyond is, in human terms, Good or Evil).

After the medieval Alexander romances, the next major phase of Orientalism was that eighteenth-century mania called "Chinoiserie." One English enthusiast even "determined to have all the white cows [on his estate] stencilled with a blue Chinese pattern, but the animals were so obdurate and perverse as in the end to oblige him to abandon his scheme."[20] Ultimately, the West proved equally resistant, unwilling to transform itself into a pseudo-Chinese fairyland, among other reasons because Orientalism and xenophobia have always existed in close proximity. In James Thomson's conservative, indeed, deliberately archaic poem *The Castle of Indolence* (1748), for example, "soul-dissolving" (I, 39) temptations from "Turkey and Persia Land" (I, 33) are associated with a place of "perfect Silence" and "blank Area" (I, 29), where "a sleepy Horror" (I, 5) waits under the control of an "Arch-image."[21] Here already appear many of the themes of later Orientalism (the dissolving self, emptiness, the mysterious archimage or archetype), but all are treated as evil traps with "Arch-image" an echo of Spenser's "Archimago," a personification of hypocrisy in the form of a pilgrim returned from the East.

The Oriental vogue came early to Prague. Rudolph II stored there perhaps the largest collections of Asiatic objects in seventeenth-century Europe (Impey 57–58.). In 1709, as a setting for Far Eastern porcelains, Count von Sternberg of Prague constructed one of the first lacquered or "japanned" rooms on the Continent (Impey 166). Kafka could not have seen Rudolf's wonder room *(Wunderkammer)*, its contents long previously dispersed; but other remains of Eastern European Chinoiserie in curio shops, public architecture, and old books were virtually unavoidable, particularly Pu-tais (Chinese figurines resembling a monk of legendary proportions).

> Even today, hardly an antique store lacks the moronically grinning features of Pu-Tai [which were] . . . absorbed wholesale into the great grammar of European ornament and scattered, later, indiscriminately over the most unlikely surfaces and with the most extraordinary effect. (Impey 93)

Unknowledgeable Occidentals tend to confuse Pu-tais with images of Gautama Buddha and wonder why the founder of an ascetic faith is so well fed, but Pu-tais come from a later, Chinese syncretism. According to legend, the obese, shaven-headed monk they caricature spent most of his time sleeping. If, at first light, he still dozed in the open, the day turned out invariably fair; if he slumbered under a bridge, rain fell by evening.

Consequently, his countrymen considered him one with the Tao. To the eighteenth-century Occident, however, he was simply an example of Eastern degeneracy and Western superiority. A nightmarish version of Pu-Tai appears in a previously discussed section of Kafka's story, "Description of a Struggle" (*"Beschreibung eines Kampfes,"* version A). Borne on a litter in "Oriental fashion," the "monstrously fat," bald, yellow-skinned grotesque has "the artless expression of a man who meditates" (25). He is distraught because the scenery is so attractive that it almost draws his eyes open, troubling his concentration. Indeed, the initial subsection of the story is entitled "An Address to the Landscape," for he engages in a long apostrophe, imploring the world to recede. Obediently, mountains move away, covering themselves with fog. The dream parodies common features of Chinoiserie: the charm of the landscapes (paintings of scenery being an artistic genre once almost unknown in the West);[22] the oppressiveness of the palanquin (emblematic of Eastern tyranny); the indolence of Pu-Tai (evident at a glance even to those ignorant of his history); and the dreaminess associated with Asia (reputedly a continent of quaint myths and superstitions). Kafka portrays him as wishing to withdraw from nature like an Indian Buddhist, the variety of that faith best known at that time partly because of its association with Schopenhauer, or, as the Victorian poet Robert Buchanan called that philosopher, "The New Buddha."[23] Kafka's yellow-skinned "fat man" is so disturbed by the landscape that it makes his thoughts "sway like suspension bridges in a furious current." Eventually, the tale's progress reifies this simile when waters carry him away. While he floats to his destruction, he rhapsodizes, recounting anecdotes about the insubstantiality of life. In a probably unintentional irony, Kafka ridicules the Pu-Tai-like figure for trying to separate himself from nature; the original Pu-Tai, however, stood for union with it, because of a Taoist component in Chinese Buddhism. In other words, in 1904 or 1905 when he wrote the fragmentary story, Kafka already had a nascently Taoist perspective (though probably little knowledge of that faith). "Description of a Struggle" certainly evidences his deliberation about man's relationship to nature as with his aphorism, "If [the lungs] pant they smother from internal poisons; if they breathe slowly they smother from unbreathable air, from outraged things. But if they attempt to seek their own rhythm, they expire from the search" (*C* 46). Since conscious attention to breathing rhythms is a relatively modern concern in the West, inspired by growing knowledge of Hindu and Taoist yoga, Kafka's words must allude to some ultimately Eastern breathing technique (though, probably filtered through some popularization, e.g., Theosophy). The reference to "outraged things" sounds particularly modern, suggesting the fear that if a balance between man and nature be not preserved, the very air will not maintain us. While

Chinoiserie did not so completely reshape the East as did the Alexander romances, it was more complacent than Kafka's nightmare, though, even there, a Chinoiserie-like laughter at the East predominates.

Only partly Chinese, Chinoiserie also imitated other Asian styles, most certainly including the Near Eastern, much in vogue because of Antoine Galland's (incomplete) translation of *The Arabian Nights* (1706–17). Kafka employs its setting in "Jackals and Arabs" *(Schakale und Araber)* as well as "In the Caravansery" *(In der Karawanserei).* The first of these (composed January 1917), is, like several of the *Arabian Nights,* a tale of talking animals pitted against mankind, except in Kafka's story the jackals only despise the local humans and look to a foreigner as a savior, who might cut an Arab's throat. They have their own matrilineal, relatively peaceful society, but with "a very old quarrel . . . in the blood" against Arabs, who kill animals before eating them instead of following the "natural" course of eating carrion, like the jackals. Here as often, Kafka burlesques the tendency of people to see their own customs as universal laws. Critics have debated whether it is an allegory of Jewish/Arab relations, of moral dualities discussed by Nietzsche, or of Kafka's own obsession with purity. In summarizing this critical diversity, Triffit observes, "This very multiplicity of equally valid or invalid equivalents makes the whole process [of trying to find sources] futile."[24] From the Jungian standpoint, however, the ubiquity of a pattern is what is interesting, as is also its development. In *The Arabian Nights,* for example, a merman, even though "all things God hath made fear the son of Adam," first attempts friendship with a human being, but finally rejects him because of a difference in their customs. Kafka ridicules both the humans' slaughtering and the scavengers' consuming carrion. Overcoming any temptation to introduce his own vegetarianism as a neat alternative, he concludes with the swooning or powerlessness *(Ohnmacht)* into which the sight of blood drives the jackals, for their "quarrel [is] . . . in the blood."

Equally sordid, the parable entitled "In the Caravansery" describes a small, filthy oasis, where ill-mannered merchants water their camels and wreak havoc on one another. As one character in *The Arabian Nights* once observed, "Never knew I of elegance in the desert."[25] Nonetheless, the caravansery gate has beautiful statues of angels on it (as *The Arabian Nights,* itself, actually features marvelous doorways and other treasures, including Paradise itself, found in the wild). Before Kafka's angelic gates, merchants wait in "powerless fury" *(ohnmächtigen Zorn)* until they are permitted to enter in an incomprehensible ceremony, perhaps instituted by the caravansery owner, though none has even seen him (*P* 114–15 [*W*]). This is one of the few cases where Kafka's characters ever manage to transit portentous portals, and the ugly violence beyond may make one wonder if those left outside are really unfortunate.

Since Kafka's allusions suggest his attraction to some Orientalism, why did he not lard his prose with dancing girls and pagodas? In this case, the answer may lie partly in his precise sources but even more in his interests (which determined those readings). He was, after all, an admirer of Voltaire.[26] On perusing such *contes orientales* as Voltaire's *Zadig* and the Asian portions of *Candide,* a modern reader probably remarks, as does Martha Conant in her study *The Oriental Tale,* "The background is pale and shadowy . . . and references to Eastern places and customs are rare."[27] W. Burns and Hartmut Binder have demonstrated the considerable indebtedness of Kafka's story "In the Penal Colony" to Octave Mirbeau's novel *Le jardin des supplices,* set in the Orient, particularly China, yet, despite the great number of borrowings, Kafka strips away the specifically Asian setting, preserving only the *mood* of confronting a radically different culture—what apparently most fascinated Kafka in the East, though that was not his only interest in it.

China

In the cold night, bending over my book,
  I have forgotten to go to bed.
The perfumes of my gold-embroidered bed-covering
  have dissipated. The hearth no longer burns.
My beautiful friend, who has previously mastered her anger
  only with difficulty, snatches the lamp from me
And asks: Do you know how late it is?
—Jan-Tsen-Tsai (1716–1797), "In the Depths of Night"

In this poem, which Kafka included in a letter to Felice Bauer, he likened its author to himself and later wrote to her, "I am Chinese" (*F* 657). His Sinophilia places him not precisely in the avant-garde of the period, but at least among the *au courant*. In 1905, as a preface to the source of this poem *(Chinesische Lyrik),* Hans Heilmann felt obliged to explain that his title was not a contradiction in terms, for the "yellow devils" *(gelben Teufeln)* actually had produced verse.[28] There were, nonetheless, already other Sinophiles. In Vienna, August Pfizmaier (1808–87), for example, was so engrossed in Asian studies that he did not learn of the Franco-Prussian War until it was well under way, and only then by reading of it in a Chinese newspaper.[29] His fellow Austrian, Joseph Strygowski (1862–1941), argued that Northern European art was less integrally connected to Mediterranean than to Central Asian.[30] A little later, a third countryman, Albert Ehrenstein, "took spiritual flight from 'Barbaropa' [barbaric Europe] to immerse himself in Chinese culture."[31] Jung's Sinophilia grew gradually as he explains in his commentary on *The Secret of the Golden Flower.*

> When I began my life work in the practice of psychiatry and psychotherapy, I was completely ignorant of Chinese Philosophy, and it is only later that my professional experiences have shown me that in my technique I had been unconsciously led along that secret way which for centuries have been the preoccupation of the best minds of the East.[32]

Master of the kind of impressionistic writing popular in Kafka's day, Robert Walser states, supposedly in a job-application form, "I am Chinese . . . [I believe what] is big and exacting is fearsome and horrid . . . your respectful servant, positively drowning in obedience."[33] In a foreword to his *Selected Stories,* Susan Sontag likens Walser's style to "the free, first person forms that abound in classical Japanese literature: pillow book, poetic diary, 'essays in idleness' " (viii). Since Kafka's early style struck his contemporaries as very like that of the then far-better-known Walser, one may note a Far Eastern quality to the former's as well—and for good reason. As Wagenbach has observed, Kafka's interest in both Far Eastern art and poetry probably helped him toward a technique of subtle omissions and intimations.

Above all and from whatever sources, Kafka developed a playful ambiguity, as in "The Green Dragon" *(Der grune Drache).* Western readers are used to voracious dragons, frequently with Satanic associations (as in Rev. 12.9). Unlike its Western counterpart: "The Eastern dragon is . . . the genius of strength and goodness. He is the spirit of change, therefore of life itself."[34] Being Divine, no creature can kill it, so it chooses its own death.[35] Because of its marvelous qualities, it appears in many legends, including references to its being eaten, as in *Chuang Tzu* (since various reptiles are sometimes represented as dragons in Chinese menus). Kafka's dragon is "half embarrassed, half treacherous" *(halb verlegen, halb tuckisch)* but "tastely juicy" *(gut im Saft)* or, as one translator renders the phrase, "fat and succulent" (*P* 150–51). Has the dragon come to eat or be eaten? He says that he offers himself to the narrator because of the latter's longing, but, in the unpredictable stories of Kafka, one might conceivably find either a man or dragon who wishes to be consumed. Jung tends to associate dragons with matriarchs, a connection that fits nicely with Kafka's previously mentioned fragment about the gigantic Madame Snake, but is quite inapplicable to the Green Dragon, described with a masculine pronoun. In *Psychology and Alchemy,* however, Jung also links dragons to the primal chaos, specifically the abyss of Gen. 1:2 (*GW,* vol. 12, par. 26). Kafka calls attention to the Green dragon's awkward size (too large to fit in the room), its swelling sides, and lack of feet, so that it seems vast and ungainly, suggesting an alien, chaotic presence. Because of the traditional link between dragons and snakes (as in Greek where *drákōn* can mean either dragon or large serpent), this fragment is reminiscent of another of Kafka's about a chaotically vast reptile. It begins:

> Sweet snake, why do you remain so distant, come closer, still closer, enough, no further, remain there. Alas, for your limits do not exist. (*D* 116).

The critic Franz Baumer says that Kafka's lack of fear or loathing for serpents "transcends the Western mind, to which the snake simply appears evil and alien."[36] In these two reptile fragments, however, it is the alienness of the creatures that is stressed (the dragon is gigantic; the snake seemingly infinite). The question of Evil is left open, as, in the second one, where the narrator, perhaps ineffectively, tries to stop the serpent's advance. In yet another fragment (*H* 56–57), it is the old and corpulent narrator who is "gigantic" and too large for the low-ceilinged room. The visitor this time is not a German-speaking dragon, too large to pull all its bulk within the small room, but a tiny Chinese scholar, who knows no German. As so often, Kafka apparently presents variations on the same pattern—confrontation with an alien being, and with no simple moral that the unknown is Good, Evil, or even comprehensible.

His fascination with the indefinite and ineffable makes Taoism the Chinese faith most like his writings. Sometime during the third, fourth, or perhaps even as early as the sixth century B.C., sages of Southern China composed texts of what is called "Taoist Philosophy" *(Tao chia).* The oldest of these texts, the *Tao te ching,* is attributed to Lao Tzu, a name that could mean "old one" or "old boy," the latter connected with the legend that he spent eighty years in his mother's womb after having been sired by a falling star.[39] Perhaps, as Leo Wieger argues, Taoism originally came from India (since another legend has Lao Tzu discover it in documents from the Western frontier of China),[38] or perhaps, it was of Chinese origin. Its teachings are as controversial as its beginnings. N. G. Giradot uses an intriguing analysis of Taoist imagery to try to show that its fundamental attitude is a preference for "primal chaos" over the artificial order of society,[39] but he may be slightly oversimplifying. The *Tao te ching* affirms that the Tao is constantly in motion (chap. 25); thus, it seems chaotic and is frequently compared to the primal lack of obvious order. Lao Tzu, however, deems the movement of the Tao to be circular (chap. 25), so there is a pattern to it (a mandala). Furthermore, Chuang Tzu gives frequent examples of men in society who, nevertheless, manage to follow its extremely nebulous designs (e.g., a butcher who cuts meat with incredible speed and ease because he intuits the patterns of its grain). Tao and order are not opposites but maintain a *yin/yang* relationship: each side includes a trace of the other, like the *tai chi* symbol (a circle divided by an s-shaped line and with a spot of light in the dark portion as well as a spot of dark in the light). One term for Tao, "the great image" (*tai hsiang, Tao te ching,* chap. 35), suggests a primal pattern. Since classical Chinese does not distinguish between singular and plural, Tao sometimes is referred to as "images" (i.e., archetypes) by Wilhelm,[40] perhaps suggesting archetypes because his renderings have a Jungian flavor—to the amusement of later Sinologists. In "Introduction to the Causeway Edition" of *The Secret of the Golden Flower (T'ai i chin hua tsung chih),* Charles San upbraids Jung and Wilhelm for "consciously or unconsciously" ignoring the main point of the work, sexual yoga, and substituting Jungian doctrine. For instance, "when the translator refers to *anima,* a concept deriving from Jungian psychology, we should understand rather the sexual force *ching,* which is then transformed into *chin tan,* the golden elixir of life" (xii). According to San, "For Western man the intellect is paramount, and understanding life is equated with intellectualizing it. For the Eastern mystic, however, *experience* is paramount" (ix–x). The irony is that Jung spent most of his life making the same point, and Wilhelm brought a greater sense of Chinese experience to his translations than most previous translators, yet by the standards of Sinology in 1976, when San wrote, both Jung and Wilhelm were admittedly too prudish, abstract, and European. Over a decade after San, one can only wonder if his emphasis on the actual experience of Eastern meditations (so popular in the 1970s) will itself eventually seem quaint and dated.

Kafka allegedly owned the Wilhelm translations of Taoist texts. Both because of the Jungian shading that Wilhelm gives them, and because Jung's teachings have a marked affinity with Taoism, Kafka's contact with that faith presented something very like Jungian psychology. Consider, for instance, Wilhelm's rendering of the *Tao te ching.* His introduction identifies one of Lao Tzu's main themes as

> the Self [*Selbst*] (the "pure I" which belongs to man-as-man). In order to progress from the empirical ego to this supra-individual entity a great deal of abstraction from everything accidental and distinctively individual is required. (Wilhelm xvii; Ostwald 15)

The *Self* is also a key Jungian term for a supraindividual "archetype." Does Lao Tzu actually discuss the Self? The term that Wilhelm usually translated thus is *shên,* which means "the body, the trunk, one's self, personal."[41] In Wilhelm's rendering of *shên* as Self (*Selbst* or *'reine' Ich*) there may be some loss of the corporeal connotations of the original (which derived from the picture of a pregnant woman). Also in his preface, Wilhelm makes the wise man *(shêng jen),* or, as he renders the phrase, "the Man of Calling" into another archetypal image of the Self, specifically identified by Wilhelm with "the idea of the Jewish Messiah, an idea in which everyone can participate according to his inner adaptation" (Wilhelm xx; Ostwald 18). This notion that all people should inwardly adapt themselves to become a Messiah or express, as Wilhelm adds, a "cosmic power" does not sound so very different from Kafka's interpretation of the Messiah. In yet another version of the supraindividual Self (chap. 10), Wilhelm has Lao Tzu ask: "Can you educate your soul so that it encompasses the One without dispersing itself?" The original Chinese actually concerns two souls, one mortal, the other immortal. Although Wilhelm's *Tao te ching* certainly does not offer all of Jungian psychology, it contains a few hints, particularly in connection to the Self.

A number of Kafka's contemporaries had some knowledge of Taoism, including Bertolt Brecht, Thomas Mann, Hermann Hesse, several Dadaists, particularly Tristan Tzvara, and a few philosophers, among them Fritz Mauthner.[42] As previously mentioned, Kafka was, according to Janouch, critical of Westerners turning to the East. Nonetheless, after Janouch bought one translation of the *Tao te ching,* Kafka allegedly presented him with others as if to urge the latter to approach Taoism with scrupulous care (Janouch 151–56). This cautious attitude sounds similar to Taoism itself, which repeatedly warns that readers should not regard its Scriptures as some clear map to be literally followed but as an inspiration to individual discovery. Kafka reportedly puzzled over epigrams by the Taoist philosopher Lao Tzu.

> I am fascinated by them, but their kernel remains hidden from me. I've re-read them several times. I discovered that—like a little boy playing with glass marbles—I followed them from one cranny of thought to another without in any way getting any further. In these aphoristic marbles, I only discovered the hopeless shallowness of my own intellectual categories, which couldn't define or accommodate [Lao Tzu's] marbles. (Janouch 153–54)

In his parable, "A Patience Game" (*Ein Geduldspiel,* or as Ernst Kaiser and Eithne Wilkins translate it, "A Chinese Puzzle"), Kafka also uses this imagery of balls in tight crannies. He describes a small sphere that finds the "ways" *(Wege)* of its toy maze uncomfortably narrow for it, so that the ball stays away from the labyrinth whenever possible (*P* 176–79). The similarity of images may evidence that, as authors often do, Kafka was working through one of his compositions mentally while chatting with Janouch.

Janouch is but one of many who connect Kafka to Taoism. In *Franz Kafka: A Biography,* Brod identifies Kafka's "chief theme" as a fear of losing the "right way" *(Weg),* "Law" *(Gesetz)* or "Tao" *(Tao).* Borges likens Kafka's works to Han Yu's account of the ineffability of unicorns and also to Jung's reference to unicorns, whose appearance accomplishes "the Tao of the king."[43]

The now-popular Marxist critic Walter Benjamin wrote an essay guessing at a connection between Kafka and Taoism. He discussed the essay with Bertolt Brecht, who improvised the following conversation between Lao-Tzu and Kafka:

Lao-Tzu: Well now, disciple Kafka, the organizations, leaseholds and other economic forms in which you live make you uneasy?
Kafka: Yes.
Lao-Tzu: You can't cope with them any more?
Kafka: No.
Lao-Tzu: A stock certificate worries you?
Kafka: Yes.
Lao-Tzu: And now you are looking for a leader to hold on to, disciple Kafka.[44]

Brecht then deems this Kafka (of his own invention) "despicable." Brecht likens him to stunted trees that the Taoist Chuang Tzu praised because they escape the "pains of usefulness," i.e., being cut down for lumber. Denouncing such "obscurantism" as contrary to the Communist cause, Brecht proclaims, "I reject Kafka."

The case of Brod and Benjamin can be significantly strengthened by more detailed comparison. In addition to general similarities between Taoism and *The Castle,* there are also occasional verbal coincidences. An early version, for instance, contains the sentence:

> The art of [dealing with the Castle] consists fundamentally [or only] in doing nothing, allowing the apparatus to function by itself and compelling it to function by standing here irremoveable in one's earthly weight. (*S* vol. 1, 198–99; *Ca* 425)

This reference to weight *(Schwere)* provides a clue to Kafka's many references to that image (e.g., one of Kafka's Alexanders who cannot cross the Hellespont because of his weight). Conventional Western assumptions do not suit Kafka's weight imagery. Judeo-Christian tradition, for example, often associates weight with the burden of sin, particularly in the weighing of the soul, originally an Egyptian motif present in both Hebrew and Greek Testaments of the Bible.[45] The *Tao te ching* (chap. 26), however, associates lightness with foolish restlessness and esteems heaviness as "the root of the light."[46] Taoism advocates not doing *(wu wei),* simply allowing the Tao to take its course, and, as in Kafka's sentence about "doing nothing," Taoists see weight as an aid to *wu wei*. Alexander, for example, should not restlessly roam the earth destroying, but allow his weight to hold him and draw him into the contemplation of the Indestructible. As marks on the manuscript demonstrate, Kafka hesitated between considering "doing nothing" to be the only or the fundamentally right course; then he deleted the entire sentence. In the final version of *Das Schloss* (if any manuscript of an unfinished work may be called final), K. (the constantly frustrated protagonist) lacks an understanding of "doing nothing," which would presumably solve his problem, thereby draining the novel of its pathos. When, for example, his landlady asks him to "do nothing" on his own until the Castle has acted (thus providing an opening and direction for his actions), he refuses (*S* 138; *Ca* 110). In his commentary on *The Secret of the Golden Flower,* Jung writes that *wu wei* is an important part of his therapeutic technique where (in a characteristically Western manner) this passive meditation is called "active imagination" and given an intellectual component (analyzing one's own fantasies). Jung explains that he originally learned to let the psyche take its own course from Meister Eckhart, another place where Kafka encountered the spiritual technique of doing nothing (90).

In one series of aphorisms, Kafka describes the expulsion from Eden as eternally repeated; thus man is still in Paradise though he may have difficulty realizing it. According to Taoism, everyone already instinctively possesses the knowledge of the Tao and thus has the potential for a paradisiacal oneness with all nature. According to Kafka, man's mortality springs from the attempt to act according to the knowledge of Good and Evil, an effort that transcends his strength and ultimately destroys him. By transcending the individual differences of beings, including those between Good and Evil, the superior man obtains union with the whole. In legend, some Taoist sages even became immortal in their oneness with the imperishable Tao. In his aphorisms, Kafka maintains, "The Indestructible is One: each individual man is it and at the same level is it all together, thereby the imcomparably indivisible union of mankind" (*D* 42). One of the principal images of the aphorisms is an unmeasurable "Way" (*D* 38)—Way being, according to Wilhelm, the most literal translation of the equally unmeasurable Tao.[47] In Taoism, the problem is to avoid struggling or assertively striving. Kafka writes, "Theoretically a possibility of perfect happiness exists: to believe in the Indestructible without striving towards it" (*D* 41).

In "Metamorphosis" *("Die Verwandlung"),* waking from disturbing dreams, the protagonist, Gregor Samsa, finds himself transformed to an unspecified insect in an experience he first finds dreamlike until he decides it "was no dream" *(war kein Traum).* The situation has a few points in common with the most famous Taoist parable (one resembling Jung's own nightmare about the yogi!): Chuang Tzu dreamed that he was an insect (a butterfly); on awakening, he wondered whether he was Chuang Tzu, who had dreamed himself an insect, or a bug that now dreamed it was Chuang Tzu. He concluded, "This is a case of what is called the Transformation [*Wandlung*] of Things" (Wilhelm 21; Legge 245). In other words, all that distinguish the phenomena of the world are states of mind, which change into one another, for all existence is no more real than a dream. Kafka also found life unreal. For instance,

> Once while visiting his friend Max Brod, young Kafka awakened Brod's father, who was asleep on a couch. Instead of apologizing, Kafka gently motioned him

to relax, advanced through the room on tiptoe, and said softly: "Please—consider me a dream."[48]

Kafka's title, *"Verwandlung,"* means, among other things, "the scene change on a theater stage."[49] The story concerns the alternation from one of life's illusions to another.

Clemens Heselhaus has compared Kafka's "Metamorphosis" to the *Metamorphoses* of Ovid,[50] but there is at least one important difference. In Ovid's *Metamorphoses* (as in fairy tales), transformation typically has some supernatural agent who performs the change. In Kafka's tale, as often happens in Taoist parables, the transformation occurs without explanation, as if it were an ordinary part of nature. One Taoist sage, for example, states that if his arm were changed to a rooster, he would use it to salute the day[51]—as strange a transformation as Samsa becoming a giant insect. At first glance, though, there may seem to be a significant difference between what Chuang Tzu calls his "transformation" into a beautiful butterfly and Samsa's into "vermin" *(Ungeziefer)*. This German word, however, recalls one of Chuang Tzu's central themes. As Kurt Weinberg has noted, the word etymologically means a creature unfit to be sacrificed.[52] As Brecht remarked, Chuang Tzu paradoxically preaches the value of uselessness, saying, for instance, that one is fortunate to be afflicted with some seeming deformity that renders one unfit for human sacrifice. From the Taoist point of view, Samsa's suffering stems less from his transformation than from his unwise desire to be of service. He castigates himself for lying "useless" *(unnutz)* in bed, because he wants to go on sacrificing himself for his family, even though his transformation exempts him from such efforts. At last, though, he attains to "empty and tranquil contemplation" *(leeren und friedlichen Nachdenken)* as he fasts himself to death.

Throughout many of Kafka's writings, as also in those of Chuang Tzu, fasting forms a common motif. Chuang Tzu advocates not literal fasting, but fasting of the heart *(hsin-chai)*, emptying the mind of disturbing emotions (Kaltenmark 98). One continues to live in the world, eating and drinking like an ordinary human being, yet figuratively fasting, because one's heart remains empty. In one fragment, Kafka writes of "certain ascetics" who expect a voice to tell them "now you may eat like the others and it will not be accounted unto you as eating" (*D* 300). These "ascetics," however, are not really Taoists, but "insatiable" fellows who expect that literal fasting will bring them to eating without corruption, a state that only *hsin-tai* entails. Considering Kafka's own abstemious diet, one may feel surprised at the negativeness with which he typically depicts fasting, but his ridicule is for the ostentatious, self-assertive abuse of this activity. Chuang Tzu also condemns such hypocrisy, specifically deriding "people [who] even keep fasts to talk about them."[53] The title character of Kafka's story, "A Hunger Artist," has the unenviable position of fasting for notoriety. The protagonist of "Investigations of a Dog" actually fasts in order to talk about it, offering his account of his fasting to canine scientists. He incorrectly believes that through "the highest effort" he can achieve the highest results: thus this dog literally fasts, hurting health and life. According to Chuang Tzu, the Taoist Hsu Wu-Kuei gave the following appraisial of dogs:

> A dog of the lowest quality thinks only of catching its fill of prey. . . . One of middling quality seems always to be looking up at the sun [i.e., being proud]. But one of the highest quality [translated by Wilhelm-Tsingtau as a hunter] acts as though it had lost its own identity.[54]

Coincidentally, perhaps, Kafka's story follows a similar pattern. His canine narrator separates himself from those dogs dominated by appetite. As a pup already expecting to achieve greatness, he one day "glancing upward saw . . . bright day" and observed dogs that, from disdain or some other cause, would not speak to him. The protagonist's investigations began then and with them, his increased pride. Finally, he meets a "beautiful" dog, "a hunter," that will not answer questions but considers his judgments "natural self-evident things." He seemingly sings "without knowing it"; indeed, he completely lacks the investigative consciousness of the protagonist, yet possesses a "power" that compels the latter to obey him. Actually, fasting harms the health of the protagonist, particularly in his search for the origin of food. In contrast, Chuang Tzu states, "[When] they have a sufficiency of food and drink [the sages], know not from whom they get it" (Wilhelm 91; Legge 372). They neither alienate themselves from nature by analyzing it, nor do they engage in long, unnatural fasts. Kafka's protagonist recalls a conversation between a sage *(Weisen)* who considers forbidding fasting and another who deems fasting so unthinkably unnatural that no prohibition is necessary.

There really is a wealth of analogues between Kafka and Taoism. In Kafka's first surviving work, "Description of a Struggle" *(Beschreibung eines Kampfes),* one of its versions contains the fragment, "Excursion into the Mountains" *(Der Ausflug ins Gebirge").* Its narrator begins by realizing that he can expect help from no one—this sense of an unhelpful world matches Lao Tzu's attitude in the fifth poem of the Tao Te Ching. "Nature is unkind: it treats the creation like sacrificial straw dogs." At first, such a world sounds unequivocally hostile, but more profoundly considered it is not so, either in Taoism or in Kafka's fictions. Lao Tzu fills poem five with ecstatic praise of the emptiness of nature; Kafka continues his "Excursion" by personifiying the no-one who will help him and imagining a joyous trip with a group of no-ones *(diese Niemand)* into the mountains. Such a personification of negative abstractions also occurs in

Taoist texts, e.g., in the twenty-second chapter of Chuang Tzu's work, Not-doing dwells on the mountain of steep mystery. The same chapter contains the character Nonexistence. As to the mountains, they so often served as Taoist retreats that the Chinese ideograms for mountain and man when placed together signify a Taoist immortal. In the mountains, these sages reputedly found a tranquility so beyond the limits of language that it could only be expressed in such words as "nothing," "non-doing," or "nonexistence." All one can say is that the state brings the feeling of joy, unity, and freedom that Kafka's narrator experiences walking arm and arm with the "numberless" no-ones. Even Kafka's metaphysical humor is here reminiscent of Taoist whimsy, for Taoist sages (usually depicted laughing) sought to transcend the stereotypes most people take so seriously. Unfortunately, it is hard to believe that Kafka's "long study of Taoism" really extended as far back as the 1904–5 period when he was writing "Description of a Struggle," before Wilhelm's translations were published (though there were others he might have read). I shall limit myself to one more comparison.

Lieh Tzu states:

> To him who dwells in his nothingness . . . all beings manifest themselves. He is as sensible to them as still water; he reflects them like a mirror; he repeats them like an echo.[55]

In his famous letter to his father, Kafka mentions a "sense of nothingness that often dominates me (a feeling that is in another respect, admittedly, also a noble and fruitful one)." How could nothingness be "noble and fruitful"? Perhaps like Lieh Tzu, the nobility is this virtuous humility and the fruitfulness is the sensitivity to all existence—a particularly productive condition for a writer. For Kafka, Taoist mysticism apparently remained a tantalizing, unrealizable way to transform his negativity into union with the One. Unfortunately, clear manuals on Taoist yoga were not available in Kafka's day.

Part II
In the Ruins

Khrobu/K mogile/Zum Grabe/To the Grave of/á la tombe de/FRANZE KAFKY

—Sign in five languages pointing the way to Kafka's grave, Prague, Czechoslovakia

6
Leopards

> Leopards invade the temple and empty the sacrificial flagons; this recurs again and again; eventually, one can predict it and it becomes part of the ceremony.
>
> —Kafka

In "Généalogie de la culture Japonaise," Karatani Kōjin perceptively defines postmodernism as the "anti-Occidental tendencies within the Occident."[1] Similarly, in a *PMLA* article, Uta Schaub sees these tendencies as an "Oriental Subtext" in postmodernism, particularly within the works of Foucault.[2] Like these definitions of postmodernism, Kafka's imagery concerns foreign elements subverting the old traditions. He makes these invaders animals. The so-called "Modern" period of literature defined the human condition as an evolutionary progress raising mankind above its animal ancestors, an ascent built on the development of language and individuality. By losing faith in this progress (as well as in rational language and individuality), precursors of the postmodern seemed, from the modernist viewpoint (of Kafka's period), to be retreating toward animality. The leopards are the most aggressive of Kafka's creatures. The next two chapters will examine less assertive postmoderns who better resemble other of Kafka's animals, but, at present, consider the leopards. Whether drawn by some otherwise-unsatisfied hunger or by curiosity, they find themselves having become a part of an archaic ritual—and rituals, Jung insists, embody a quest for "Individuation." Furthermore, according to Jung, identification with an animal may signify integration of the psyche and revivification (aspects of Individuation)—the more elementary the animal, the deeper the psychic strata involved (*GW,* XII, 158). Obviously, this Jungian interpretation is almost diametrically opposite to the listless, psychically drained Gregor Samsa/insect but Jung's general attitude toward animals comes close to being suitable for Kafka's big cats, for example, the leopards or the caged panther, which, at the conclusion of "The Hunger Artist," "seemed" to exude vitality and freedom.

Before examining the more truly Kafkaesque (and therefore complex) "leopard"-like authors, begin with a relatively simpler one, reputed to embody vitality and freedom—Gary Snyder. His relationship to foreign traditions is clearest in one of his first publications, "Cold Mountain," (the T'ang Dynasty poems of Han Shan that Snyder very freely translated from Chinese to English). Snyder's friend Jack Kerouac has recorded the translation process in *The Dharma Bums,* a fairly transparent *roman à clef.*[3] To intensify the Beats' identification with Han Shan as an ancient model, a purveyer of perennial wisdom, "Japhy Ryder" (Snyder) Englishes one of Han-shan's phrases *(ch'en mi)* with the words, "high as a junkey." Ryder makes this state sound almost praiseworthy. He then explains to Kerouac's narrative persona (Smith) that the Chinese idiom really means "high as the sensualists in the city below." Snyder (in his published version), renders *ch'en mi* as "high on mountains," a less vivid image than "high as a junkey," but even further from the original. The Chinese phrase actually means being sunk in *maya* (illusion), to most Buddhist sects the depths of spiritual degradation. Yet, according to tantric Buddhists, ritual contact with such appealing distractions as sex, and sometimes even drugs, may permit the devotee to transcend illusion. Not scholarship but Ryder's own tantric practices (discussed at length in *The Dharma Bums*) may be the reason for the idiosyncratic rendering of the Chinese. In an introduction to "Cold Mountain Poems," Snyder remarks of Han Shan and his friends, "You sometimes run onto them today in the skidrows, orchards, hobo jungles, and logging camps of America." That Snyder turns Han-shan into a hero of the American counterculture may owe something to the quasi-Jungian Joseph Campbell, whom Snyder had been reading before beginning the translation. Like Campbell (and Jung), Snyder believed that mythic heroes undergo a predictable series of trials.[4] Snyder selected and rearranged the Han Shan poems so that they represented such a traditional pattern of movement toward Enlightenment, including an expected dark night of the soul. Snyder's Han Shan, for example, sees himself become a "naked bug"—a simultaneously literal and strange translation (and transformation). In China, describing oneself as a naked bug *(lo ch'ung)* is a commonplace; in the West, it sounds Kafkaesque, so translators usually suppress it. Snyder, however, includes it, because he wishes to stress non-Western elements (though elsewhere he does not always include the same non-Western imagery as the original). This bug of Snyder and the Chinese, by the way, is no Gregor Samsa, but exuberant in watching his human self pass away, bringing him closer to his goal of Buddhist selflessness. If Snyder's Han Shan is no longer quite in control of his life, he struggles little, accepting guidance from the Tao and adapting the old rituals to his iconoclastic disposition. Like Ursula Le Guin's Taoism (which led her to rediscover independently some of Jung's concepts)[5] and Doris Lessing's Sufism (linked to what she discovered about herself through successful analysis by a Jungian),[6] Snyder's syncretic Zen poses no serious challenge to Jung, indeed seems to run along Jungian lines.

The following authors evidence more of the Kafkaesque difficulties that may arise from invading foreign traditions.

Mircea Eliade

> It is . . . tendency toward the archetype, toward the restoration of the *perfect form*—of which any myth or rite or divinity is only a variant, and often rather a pale one—that makes the history of religions possible.
>
> —Eliade, *Images and Symbols*

> [Eliade] is the one scholar who has offered a comprehensive system for explaining all religious behavior and thought.
>
> —Guilford Dudley, III, *Religion on Trial*

His mother an Oltenian, his father a Moldavian [Gheorghe-]Mircea Eliade (originally Iremia), once said that he himself combined Oltenian and Moldavian strands of Rumanian culture, drawing energy from the former, and from the latter, during adolescence, a "melancholy, sometimes almost amounting to real clinical depression."[7] He had unusually much to alienate him during his life, even before his final expatriate decades of commuting each year between Paris and Chicago. He was nursed by a Tartar woman, "so," as he writes, "a contact between myself and the Orient was established when I was a mere suckling."[8] In grade school, World War I meant that instead of being able to rely on his father (who was away in the army) for assistance, he found himself in a household where the only men were enemy German soldiers billeted there. He turned to one of them for aid with German homework, but this soldier, like some educated Germans of the age, insisted on speaking nothing but French.[9] During this period, Eliade would run away from home and not return for days.[10] At the same time that Eliade had to be polite to these "guests," he was engaged in ferocious fantasies of leading Rumanian troops against the enemy—visions that became so vivid and uncontrollable he could barely separate them from reality. He began jotting them down—the beginnings of his creative writing.[11] Like Jung's few ventures into fictionalizing, Eliade's significant outpouring of novels and short stories generally did not arise from laborious drafting and repeated rewriting, but from "inspired" composition. Indeed, of one novel, *The Light that Failed (Lumina ce se stinge),* he eventually admitted that he could not remember how it ends, because he found himself unable to reread its stream of consciousness.[12] This memory lapse, however, may owe something to the disorientation of emigration, for after only three years studying yoga and Sanskrit in India he spoke his native tongue, Rumanian, "badly and with a foreign accent"[13]—this despite (or because of) being a talented linguist, who, during adolescence, taught himself Hebrew, Persian, and Italian, and finally came to know an uncounted number of Eastern and Western languages.

In "The Forbidden Forest: Eliade as Artist and Shaman," Edward P. Nolan observes:

> Eliade, a life-long quester in exile, is both poet and theoretician of the outsider, and can appropriately be seen as linked not only to such modern connoisseurs of chaos and experts in futility as . . . Kafka . . . but also to their precursors.[14]

Eliade not only inherited the Kafkaesque mode but also furthered its development as, for example, in one of his later novels, *The Old Man and the Bureaucrats (Pe strada mantuleasa).*[15] It begins with a man hesitating before a building where he must confront the law (a member of the Ministry of Justice). He enters, though, and through what seems at first a misunderstanding, is at dawn waked by an agent of the court (like Joseph K.). Where Kafka's novel *The Trial,* however, shows an ordinary man confronting an incomprehensible court, Eliade depicts seemingly ordinary bureaucrats interrogating an incomprehensible individual. The old man's prolix reminiscences—an inextricable mesh of verifiable, mundane fact, and occult occurrences—lead to bureaucrats' arrest, dismissal, or suicide. A growing proportion of the government tries to decipher his vast, digressive memoir. In the end, there is an ambiguous hint that the bureaucrats themselves may have ties to the supernatural, but this final twist is less impressive than the spiritual terrain Eliade explores throughout the bulk of the book. Previous writers have generally located the sacred in vivid images or in the ineffable. In contrast, *The Old Man and the Bureaucrats* finds "hierophany" (Eliade's term for the sacred made manifest) in the power of the digressive, frustrating, and boring to disrupt quotidian life. In the nightmarish result, neither the old man nor bureaucrats ever gain control. Perhaps the old man's ability to bluff and confuse them may owe something to the protagonist of Kafka's novel *The Castle,* but Kafka usually confines the power of equivocation and confusion to his religious authority figures, such as the priest (in *The Trial*).

Before his death in 1977, Eliade spent his mature years trying to create what he called "The History of Religions"—even though it has more to do with atemporal archetypes than with actual history. He was, however, entirely capable of the latter. At the University of Chicago, after he had delivered a factually unimpeachable history of East-West contacts, I overheard a graduate student complaining that for once Eliade had omitted controversial, poetic insights. These latter have placed him in the same quasi-scientific hinterland as Jung, and for almost the same reason—an attempt to comprehend all religious imagery in terms of a few patterns. Controversy is exciting, and Eliade has ventured boldly. Eliade's encyclopedic command of anthropological material, though occasionally erroneous in minor details, has garnered academic respect. As far as the meaning of individual images, however, Eliade offers no advance over Jung. Eliade's *Patterns in Comparative Religion* can only provide meaninglessly vague categorization, for example, water—"the whole of potentiality"—since it has actually meant so many different things in different cultures. In his ensuing discussion of aquatic symbolism, nonetheless, he offers an interesting statement about baptism.

> There can be no question here of "influences" or or "borrowings," for such symbols are archetypal and universal; they show man's position in the universe, while at the same time evaluating his position in regard to his god (to absolute *reality*), and to history.[16]

The interest does not lie in the first part of the sentence, affirming as it does the usual, unproven (and probably unprovable) theory that fixed patterns (e.g., baptism) arise from unconscious (or in Eliade's terminology "transconscious") archetypes. (Here, as often, Eliade uses the word "archetypes" in essentially its Jungian sense despite elsewhere proposing his own, more limited definition: the "paradigms" believed by a specific culture to have been "revealed" long ago.)[17] Far more suggestive is the remark about man using symbols to establish his place in the universe (to which Eliade applies the psychological term "orientation"). This concept lies behind Eliade's best-documented work, his study of symbols that orient man (e.g., the ubiquitous images of time's repeating itself, the so-called "eternal Return"). Jung's compendious examination of mandalas (symbolic circles) found them connected to an orientationlike process of self-formation. Kohut saw self-formation largely as orienting oneself in relation to human images, comparable to another class of common "archetypes" (e.g., the wise old man). A dynamic process of orientation seems most likely to underlie religious symbolism. Eliade deserves credit both for his scholarly works that delineate this issue, and even more for his fictional ones that thrust readers into the labyrinth of disorientation and problematic reorientation.

Eugène Ionesco

Born in Rumania of a French mother and Rumanian father, Eugène Ionesco spent his early childhood in La Chapelle-Anthenaise (a small town in France), next lived in Paris, later emigrated to Rumania for secondary and higher education, and finally returned to France. Interviewed by Claude Bonnefoy, Ionesco said that his Rumanian-French background "did result in tensions: but the anguish was sometimes a good thing," because his entering cultures that initially seemed alien to him involved his learning, partly forgetting, and relearning languages more than once.[18] In his teens, his attitudes simply switched from one culture to the other. At eleven, he had written "*French* patriotic plays," one of which, at fourteen, he transformed into a Rumanian patriotic play, both in language and subject matter (*Entretiens* 64; *Conversations* 56). As he grew older, however, he ceased to identify closely with the shibboleths of either culture. His literary breakthrough came when he began to study English. Being forced to memorize the clichéd expressions of the primer, awakened him to the large extent such banalities play in ordinary conversation (a realization probably fostered by his years of French/Rumanian language study). Suddenly, he saw people as automatons mouthing the idioms of their cultures, a vision he dramatized in *The Bald Soprano (La cantatrice chauve),* his first published play.

Rhinoceros (Le rhinocéros), another of his best-known dramas, may owe much to his reading of Kafka's *Metamorphosis.* Ionesco told Bonnefoy that, whatever Kafka's intention, Ionesco interpreted the latter as portraying a savage truth: our socially established roles and personalities are not as fixed as they seem; any moment we may become monsters. Bonnefoy remarked that this insight is central to Ionesco's *Rhinoceros* (where the people turn into rhinoceroses). Ionesco agreed, but without telling whether he had read Kafka before writing the play (*Entretiens* 44–46; *Conversations* 38–40). At any rate, according to Ionesco, the Kafkaesque condition is "man wandering without purpose—forgetful of his purpose, cut off from his essential, transcendental roots. (*Entretiens* 148; *Conversations* 127). This description manifests genuine understanding of Kafka (as well as describing one of the chief characteristics of Ionesco's own absurdist theater).

This sense of deracination also forms a leitmotif throughout his conversations with Bonnefoy, but it not only reminds Ionesco of Kafka; more often Ionesco associates it with the religious-historical studies of his personal friend Mircea Eliade and the psychology of Jung. In his autobiography *Fragments of a Journal (Journal en miettes),* Ionesco writes:

> I prefer Jung to Freud. Jung does not ban religion. We know that he asserts that it is a psychological need and that since it is a need, it corresponds to truth. What truth? Is this truth, itself, the symbol of something else, does it conceal something else? That's not what I mean. I dare not: I'm not bold enough to believe.[19]

Raised a Catholic, Ionesco, by the very incoherence of this passage, may manifest anxiety about his religious uncertainty, poised awkwardly between unbelief and faith. He told Bonnefoy that his obsessions inspire his incoherence and contradictions that he does not want to resolve, because

Reality transcends any system. Consequently, instead of composing logical arguments, he writes plays (he says) so that he can explore both sides of every question (*Entretiens* 71–72; *Conversations* 62–73). He feels severed from the "transcendent roots" of certainty except for occasional mystical experiences characterized by light—a luminousness that Ionesco (following Eliade and Jung) sees as a universal archetype. Those experiences, particularly one during his teens, inspired the radiant city at the beginning of his play *Killer (Tueur sans gage)* (*Entretiens* 33–37, et passim; *Conversations* 29–32, et passim). Indeed, he sees his plays as explorations of "archetypes," such as the "archetype" of the sphere (the mandala, signifying to him Paradise), which he contrasts with the "archetype" of the labyrinth (connoting to him time, space, hell, alienation, and Kafka) (*Entretiens* 45; *Conversations* 39). He considers "archetypes" (man's roots in a common humanity) to be the opposite of stereotypes (parochial conventions) (*Entretiens* 131; *Conversations* 113). More like Jung and Eliade than Kafka, Ionesco believes that an author may communicate with his audience by evoking the "archetypal" ties with the past, yet he is equally interested in satirizing and exposing the Kafkaesque absurdity of everyday life.

Hermann Broch

Born three years after Kafka, his fellow countryman Hermann Broch reflected much the same multicultural, decadent Austrian milieu and was acutely sensitive to Kafka's vision of humanity as overwhelmingly weak and alienated. Broch deemed Kafka the only "true" representative of our age:

> [Ours is] the situation of extreme helplessness, and Kafka, not Joyce, has done it justice; in Kafka we find the beginnings of an adequate countermyth [where] what really matters is the symbolization of helplessness per se, which means the symbolization of the child.[20]

Consequently, Broch rated his own writings below Kafka's, an appraisal that will sound inevitable, indeed, almost an understatement to English-language readers for whom Broch is hardly a household word. Ernestine Schlant, however, reflecting a Germanic perspective, counts Broch "among the foremost novelists of the twentieth century."[21]

American neglect of Broch is ironic since his greatest work, *The Death of Virgil (Der Tod des Vergil),* begun in Nazi-dominated Austria and written partly in prison there, was completed during his exile in the United States. Broch subtly transmutes Virgil into a Kafkaesque antihero. According to legend, Virgil, on his deathbed, wanted to destroy the *Aeneid,* because he would not have a chance to revise it thoroughly. Broch's Virgil goes much further, desiring to "burn everything that he had ever written or composed," not merely because he no longer has time to perfect his poems, but because of Kafka-like doubts about the value of any human activity, particularly art.[22] The real Virgil died of a sudden fever; Broch's version of Virgil suffers from symptoms (particularly coughing up blood) suggestive of Kafka's death from tuberculosis. Broch's Virgil also bears a certain resemblance to Kafka's Hunter Gracchus. Both begin their stories lying between life and death as they are carried from a ship through an intricately described crowd where children play a notable part. In addition to "Hunter Gracchus," Kafka wrote a fragment about that character who expatiates at length about the problem of coherence, the same theme of unity that runs throughout *The Death of Virgil.* This is perhaps merely to say that in both the Gracchus and Virgil narratives, the wandering mind of a half-dead protagonist leads to discussion of the universe and of death. Gracchus travels blown by winds from the "lowest Regions of Death" (*B* 107; *C* 230); Broch's Virgil descends in a fever vision to those depths.

At least since Aniela Jaffe's 1955 essay on the "Individuation" process in *The Death of Virgil,* the Jungian influence on it has been obvious.[23] After meeting Jung in 1932, Broch began a series of "Zodiac Stories" based on analytic psychology.[24] These stories represent an early, naive attempt to reconcile Jung and Kafka. "Archetypal" images appear as little more than Wagnerian leitmotifs announcing the characters' presence, while, in the story, "A Slight Disappointment," Broch imitates a labyrinthine Kafkaesque dreamworld (as Schlant has remarked).[25] Why did Broch try to reconcile the Kafkaesque and the Jungian? In his early twenties he had converted from Judaism to Catholicism and then in middle age he returned to Judaism. He saw them as differing in manner more than in substance, for he considered each a human attempt to approach the One (the mystic Unity sought by Kafka and Jung). In *The Death of Virgil,* this One is what the protagonist attains at the end of his Individuation process, when led by *puer* and *anima* archetypes he reaches "the word beyond speech."[26] Broch says of his process of composition:

> I concentrated most exclusively upon the experience of death, worked myself completely into dreamlike states of trance, and wrote everything down almost automatically.[29]

This auto-intoxication sounds very Jungian. However many nightmares Broch's Virgil endures, the novel has less to do with real weakness or suffering than with a series of revelations raising Virgil ever higher above ordinary mankind. Moreover, *The Death of Virgil* contains other incoherences, particularly the tension between the Roman past described and the Austrian present that infuses his description. As he mentioned in his afterword entitled "Sources" *("Quellen"),* he has woven over one hundred translated passages by the real Virgil into the novel, yet not these but free verse, jarringly different in style from them, purportedly encapsulates Virgil's philosophy. Broch employs classical gods as "archetypal" images in Virgil's mind, then, anachronistically adds an "angel" *(Engel).*[28] Admittedly, medieval piety misread the *Aeneid* as evidence that Virgil was secretly a Christian, but Broch has not adequately prepared for a Judeo-Christian angel appearing to an otherwise pagan Virgil. Indeed, this angelic manifestation sounds like the assumption that since the same "archetypes" produce images in all people, thus anyone, regardless of culture, may hallucinate any image. If that was Broch's intention, then even *The Death of Virgil* represents a fairly naive level of "archetypal" theory—but he later progressed further, perhaps even beyond Jung, as a result of his interest in languages.

In *The Death of Virgil* itself he confronted the problem of translating Virgil into German, and, upon reaching America, due to financial and other reasons, he was forced to English his own novel in collaboration with Jean Starr Untermeyer. George Steiner says of this translation:

> Taken "straight," this bit of prose suggests Gertrude Stein seeking to transcribe and parody Kant. But it is hardly meant to stand alone. It forces us back to the original which it in turn illuminates; its own opaqueness induces the original to declare its meaning more fully.[29]

In Broch's last decade, speculation about translation, its limitations and implications, inspired him to write "Some Remarks on the Philosophy and Technique of Translation." He distinguishes between "Logos" (the universal patterns of logical relations) and "Archetypes" (the patterns specific to a particular language). Although he died before he could incorporate this insight into his psychological speculations, it is extremely suggestive. For Jung, universals (i.e., "archetypes") are ineffable patterns that cannot be studied directly. If, instead, the universals are logical patterns (series of relations traceable to the concept of the One), then they can be directly observed, their existence verified, and their manifestations precisely analyzed. Furthermore, if the manifestations (Broch's "Archetypes," Jung's "archetypal images") are seen as taking their forms largely from local tradition, then each tradition needs to be examined very carefully, rather than merely compared to others throughout the world. Section 3 attempts to work out some of these implications.

Octavio Paz

The Mexican, twenty-two-year career diplomat and Nobel Prize winner, Octavio Paz writes works of multilingual intertextuality. They reflect his travels in the United States, Spain, India, Japan, France, Switzerland, Britain, and, of course, Mexico—or rather the two Mexicos, ancient and modern. When asked about himself in interviews, he typically begins by identifying himself as "mestizo," Indian and European, for he feels drawn both to the Aztec past (of which he is quite knowledgeable) and to Europe. From the 1950s on, he has added Asian researches to his former fascinations, translating the Japanese poet Basho and studying Buddhism, particularly Nagarjuna's metaphysics and Tantrism. In 1968, as an act of political protest, he resigned from the ambassadorship to India. Long before that, however, he had really abandoned commitment to any single country (even his beloved Mexico). He has found himself continually attempting to transcend boundaries like the modern artists he describes in *Alternating Current (Curriente alterna).*

> When the furthest limit has been reached, another painter arrives on the scene, makes the crucial leap, discovers yet another free space beyond, and once again is stopped short by a wall—a wall that he must leap over in order to reach the open spaces beyond.[30]

In the early poem "Prologue" *("Prologo"),* like the narrator of Kafka's juvenile narrative "Description of a Struggle," Paz fantastically invents a landscape, called into being detail by detail, but this sense of freedom from what is ordinarily called "reality" has its nightmarish side as in another of Paz's early poems, "The Endless Instant" *("¿No hay salida?").* The poem's speaker remains in Kafkaesque suspension.

> The walls are enormous,
> the glass of water is thousands of miles away, it
> will take me a thousand years to cross my room again.[31]

Paz's *oeuvre* is constantly trying to escape from this stagnation, that is, from Kafka. In *Alternating Current,* Paz contrasts Apuleius's *Metamorphoses* and Kafka's "Metamorphosis."

> [Apuleius's character] Lucius represents Mediterranean common sense and truculence, gastronomy and a sensuality that has a faint tinge of sadism, Greco-Latin eloquence and Oriental mysticism—the Phallus and the Idea. All of which culminates in the glorious vision of Isis, the universal mother, one night on the seashore.[32]

For Kafka's Gregor Samsa, however, "abjection is his permanent state." With Kafka as an example of a modern writer, Paz continues:

> In the past, continuity consisted in the prolongation or the persistence of certain archetypal forms of features in works of art; today, this continuity takes the form of negation or opposition.[33]

By implication, Paz's "continuity" with Kafka consists of a revolt against the latter, a quest to traverse the Kafkaesque labyrinth of solitude further than even Kafka had done in order to reach "the reunion of languages, spaces and times," where modernity itself will be destroyed in the annihilation of all time, but this reunion is always problematic, deferred by the modern ambience of rebellion.[34] In his major prose work, *The Labyrinth of Solitude* (*El laberinto de la soledad,* 1947), Paz articulates his desire for a postmodern return to a pagan ethos like that of Apuleius, or as Richard J. Callan has shown in a 1977 *Hispania* article, like that of Jung. In Jungian fashion, Paz conceives of consciousness as racked by loneliness and by tension between opposites, once, he believes, peacefully reconciled in the comfort and tranquillity of the womb. Authentic life can only come from a dangerous and heroic trip through some kind of symbolic maze to find the Center, the vivifying Unconscious—an idea Paz takes from the crypto-Jungian authors Toynbee and Eliade (as well as, presumably, from his own introspection). Finally, Paz describes the symbolic function of woman in a manner reminiscent of the Jungian anima.[35] Callan could have found even more parallels if, instead of confining himself to *The Labyrinth of Solitude,* he had looked at a larger sample of Paz's works, particularly the later ones. Between 1956 and 1967, Paz's readings in Saussure, Jakobson, and Chomsky led him to conclude that language had a life of its own,[36] so that it became for him a kind of Collective Unconscious shaping human values and preserving archetypal vestiges of the past. Also, *The Labyrinth of Solitude* is slightly untypical of Paz's writings in that the book's central thesis—man's quest for unity—made him less appreciative than usual of the advantages gained by there being many "gods," that is, many "archetypal" forces pulling mankind in various directions. Like the so-called archetypal school of Jungians, Paz often sounds nostalgic for polytheism. Finally, Paz, like Jung, benefited from greater knowledge of Eastern meditation than Kafka, so that Paz apparently took some of his notions from the same Oriental sources as Jung such as their common fascination with the mandala (the inspiration for Paz's justly famous poem "Blanco," written in two different colors of ink with geometrical blocks of verse).

Carlos Fuentes

Born in Panama, son of a Mexican diplomat, Carlos Fuentes spent his sixth to twelfth years in the United States, where he became bilingual, indeed, thought that Mexico was "a nonexistent country . . . invented by his father."[39] He later wrote his first (unpublished) novel in English, the rest in Spanish, beginning with his move to Chile. Echoing Bakhtin, he remarks, "I always tried to tell my critics . . . do not look for . . . one language [in my novels] but for many languages at odds with one another."[38] Politically, he generally sympathizes with the left, but he denounced Russian intervention in Czechoslovakia (thereby, at least implicitly, allying himself with the Czech revival of Kafka, which served as a symbol of resistance to Soviet communism). After all, his first amorous encounter was with a Czech woman.[39]

Like so many authors in Latin America, he writes in the Kafkaesque tradition called "magic realism," which has become the characteristic style of the region, though not without opposition. When he was in school, one of his teachers told him that it was "un-Mexican" even to read Kafka, but this warning did not deter Fuentes.[40] Eventually, he associated the Kafkaesque with the decline of the "degraded Ego [into] exhaustion, self-doubt, and finally, self-forgetfulness. . . . Kafka's man has been forgotten; no one can remember K. the land surveyor."[41] In the story "At the Building of the Great Wall of China," Kafka momentarily made "you" the protagonist, thus deviating from the novelistic convention of depicting characters in the third person as egos that can be objectively observed by the reader. Comparably, in Fuentes's monumental novel, *Terra nostra,* and in his most famous novella, *Aura,* the protagonist is frequently spoken of in the second person.[42] Typical of Fuentes, both works feature the juxtaposition of contrasting cultures: a mélange of mythical past and speculative future in the former; an alternation between Spanish narration and brief passages of (untranslated) French text in the latter.

Gloria B. Duran's Jungian book *The Archetypes of Carlos Fuentes* identifies a borrowing from Kafka's story "The Silence of the Sirens" in the following passage from Fuentes's *Holy Places (Zona sagrada):*

> The bound chieftain said that he had listened and resisted. He lied. It was a question of prestige, of awareness of the legend. Ulysses was his own P. R. man. This time, and only this time, the sirens did not sing . . . Ulysses, was able to pass by without danger.[43]

Like Kafka, Fuentes treats myth with sophistication and irony, rather than with the naive fascination Jung assumed to be typical of authors. Fuentes, nonetheless, was willing to see his works as reflections of a Jungian process of Individuation. He wrote to Duran (in English) saying that her Jungian interpretations of *Holy Places* "sound very, very valid."[44] Fuentes makes a point of denying any prior knowledge of Jungian theory (though, considering his friendship with Paz, he may have absorbed archetypal theory under another name). As an example of Duran's Jungianism, consider her treatment of Fuentes's character Claudia.

> She is in fact all women, or the archetype of woman as mother, mistress, wife. What remains to be seen is that Claudia . . . is herself a double, part female and

> part male. Again I must refer to June, who pointed out that "man in his myths always manifested the idea of the coexistence of male and female in one body."[45]

In Jungian theory, the "archetype of woman as mother, mistress, wife" is the *anima,* while that of male and female in one body constitutes the hermaphrodite. Are these the same archetype? Jung assumed that actual women combined masculine and feminine characteristics; however, an anima is not an actual woman but the feminine side of a man, so it should not in itself be hermaphorditic. Jung, though, sometimes talks of archetypes undergoing "contagion" (mixture together) and he described the anima as involving what is "equivocal, and unrelated in woman" (*GW* 15, par. 521). Thus, for Jung, feminine can mean masculine or practically anything else. The advantage of this looseness is that Duran can produce with it a "very, very valid" description of the surface features of Claudia without having to distort her analysis to fit some consistent psychological system. At any rate, the year after Duran's book appeared, Fuentes wrote of "archetypes" in *Don Quixote*.[46]

Thomas Mann

Although Thomas Mann may be discussed profitably within the confines of German literature, as his Nobel Prize suggests, his work looms beyond any national border. Indeed, foreign experiences stand behind the composition of his books. Only upon moving to Italy for three years did he begin his first major work, *Buddenbrooks.* Thereafter, the Italian or Latin given name and German patronymic of some of his best-known characters (e.g., Tonio Kroger, Felix Krull, and Serenus Zeitblom) evidence an attraction to both cultures, a conflict anatomized in many of his books, most obviously *Death in Venice (Der Tod in Venedig).* Another common motif is a contrast between turbulent Germany and pacifist Switzerland. His short stay in a Swiss sanitarium (1912) inspired *The Magic Mountain (Der Zauberberg).* From 1933 to 1938, he lived in Switzerland, beginning the most voluminous and time-consuming project of his career, the Joseph saga, a tranquil rumination about the ancient Middle East, troubled then as ever. He finished that multivolume masterpiece during his twelve-year stay in America, after which he lived as an American citizen in Switzerland.

During his later years, he championed German-language authors, using his influence to see that they were recognized and published abroad, but these efforts were in no way confined to "Aryan" writers. The "definitive" English edition of *The Castle,* for example, bears Mann's homage to Kafka in its preface (1940). Therein, Mann calls Kafka "a religious humorist" *(eines religiösen Humoristen).*[47] The phrase could also be applied to Mann, though in various manners, as his art developed. In *Buddenbrooks,* the humor—religious and otherwise—is principally irony, his viewing the northern, Protestant Germany of his childhood from the urbane vantage of Italy, but the mode is realistic. Only as time and travel further distanced him from his prosaic roots does his writing become more fantastic, mystical visions at first offered almost apologetically as the dream or delusion of his characters. In what he considered his last major work, *Joseph the Provider* (*Joseph, der Ernährer,* 1943), however, he begins with a celestial "Prelude in the Upper Circles" *(Vorspiel in Oberen Rängen).*[48] Where most of the Joseph saga avoids speaking of God except in terms of skeptically presented, often contradictory human speculations, this section gives the angel's superhuman testimony. One model is, of course, Goethe's "Prologue in Heaven" but instead of Goethe's contrast between the devil's doggerel and the angels' hymnlike verse, Mann presents heaven from the perspective of seraphic bureaucrats reminiscent of *The Trial* and *The Castle.* He praised both books in the "Homage" published shortly before he began the last volume of his Joseph saga. Like Kafka, Mann's angels consider the creation of the world a demonically inspired mistake, but they view God as an essentially unconscious Power using mankind for his Consciousness, the argument of Jung's answer to Job. Ignace Feuerlicht writes:

> In his last years, Mann often spoke of grace, and without any humorous overtones. . . . Yet it is difficult to see what grace means to somebody like Mann, who does not believe in a personal God.[49]

In Jungian psychology, the same combination occurs, an impersonal, Collective Unconscious producing synchronicity, having much in common with grace.

Perhaps Mann's courage to break into fantasy derives both from Kafka and Jung, for the latter's thought had an ever-increasing impact on the later fictions of Mann. In voluminous correspondence with Jung's collaborator Karl Kerenyi, Mann testifies to his own fascination with "myth plus psychology . . . [a combination of which he had] long been a passionate adherent."[50] He continues by remarking his pleasure to find that Kerenyi and Jung see the psychopomp "as essentially a child divinity," an image that recalls to him one of the motifs of his own *Death in Venice* (101). In other words, he prides himself on having discovered that allegedly "archetypal" pattern. Although, in a certain sense, Mann may be said to believe in archetypes, he sees their repetition as a source of religious humor, by contrasting with modern emphasis on individuality those primitive people's ritually enacting archetypal reoccurrence. Mann comes closest to Jung when the latter talks of the *changing* images inspired by the same archetypes. Like Jung, Mann considers the Old Testament God a Trickster figure, Mann's own *Joseph, the Provider* constituting "a divine rogue's tale," but Mann's emphasis on the humor and on the historical changes ultimately renders the "archetypal" patterns equivocal. At the beginning of *Joseph and His Brothers,* Mann deems the past "bottomless" *(unergrundlich).*[51] This Kafkaesque sense of life without a fathomable foundation fits Jung's speculations about the evolution of the Collective Unconscious but it contradicts Jung's tendency to see his "archetypes" as relics of the past, ancient grounds on which an objective psychology could be fashioned.

Hermann Hesse

> And when they came to [Djü-dschi] with their questions
> . . . he remained silent,
> Only pointing quietly with his finger.
>
> When I finished [Hesse's] poem, I glanced over at [him] and saw him raise his finger. . . .
>
> I gave [Hesse's] regards to Professor Jung. He smiled and asked about [Hesse]. We talked about many things, and learned that he also knows how to make the gesture of Master Djü-dschi.
>
> —Miguel Serrano, *Jung & Hesse*

Despite coming from a seemingly homogeneous Pietist enclave in Swabia, Hermann Hesse had an exotic family history. In 1835, his Stuttgart-born grandfather, Hermann Gundert, an accomplished theologian and linguist, had accompanied a British missionary to India. There, Gundert married a French-Swiss woman, who learned Indian dialects, but never her husband's language, German. Consequently, her daughter, Marie, Hermann Hesse's mother, corresponded with her in French or English—corresponded more than spoke because after a very brief childhood in India, the girl was sent from one European home or school to another. Finally, though, Marie returned to India, where she first married a Britain, and then Johannes Hesse, a German-speaking Russian, with a fondness for linguistics.[52] Their son Hermann made cultural interaction one of his primary themes and directed his later writings toward the fabulous East—the hemisphere about which people came to consult his maternal grandfather "in English, French, Indian, Italian, Malayalam [about] . . . the secret, age-old mystery . . . [of which his mother] could speak and sing in Malayalam and Kanarese."[53] Hesse's family background *per se* did not necessitate this Orientalism (for none of his siblings took that course). His ancestor's covert pluralism, nonetheless, offered an avenue of escape from their overt Pietism—a welcome avenue since Hermann Hesse was as troubled by Johannes Hesse as Kafka by his father.

The most Kafkaesque of Hesse's Orientalist fictions is *The Journey to the East* (*Die Morgenlandfahrt,* 1956). Influenced by Kafka's projection of himself into his later novels as K., Hermann Hesse calls the protagonist H. H. The book concerns a mysterious League, a fantastic, paternalistic organization functioning outside of the normal political and legal channels like the court in Kafka's novel *The Trial.* Indeed, in one of its functions, Hesse's League serves as "an omniscient Court of Law"—an even more-obvious echo of Kafka.[54] Like so many of Kafka's narrators, H. H. foregrounds the difficulties of knowing and expressing the truth in a world of unverified or unverifiable experiences. Like the High Command in Kafka's Great Wall stories, the court officials in *The Trial,* and the higher bureaucrats in *The Castle,* the leadership of the League is sometimes known only through rumor.[55]

As to Jung, Hesse had over sixty psychoanalytic sessions with the Jungian analyst Josef B. Lang, read a number of Jung's works, and had sessions with Jung himself. As Ralph Freedman tentatively suggests, it was this Jungian therapy that seems to have triggered Hesse's turn eastward.[56] During his psychoanalysis with Jung, Hesse wrote friends praising the treatment and defining its goal as "to create a space within ourselves in which God's voice can be heard."[57] Despite the many similarities between Hesse and Jung, they argued over the term *sublimation*. Hesse held that an artist sublimates his personal problems and neuroses into art—that the very difficulties of individuation had positive value, at least for the artist. In contrast, Jung insisted that true art was not a personal matter but a "primary instinct" from deep in the Collective Unconscious.[58] In other words, Hesse, whose fictions are more or less thinly disguised autobiography, could not believe that they were essentially the work of archetypes—that his sensitive interweaving of words, ideas, and personal experiences amounted to little more than a butterfly weaving a cocoon. He also suffered the embarrassment that his psychoanalysis had not been entirely successful. There were too many subsequent periods of personal chaos such as the drunken collapse that inspired his nightmarish *Steppenwolf.* Hesse's most ambitious work, *The Glass Bead Game,* began as a nostalgic fantasy, concerning a Utopian future organization devoted to playing games with fragments of a partly mythological past. Hesse finally realized the psychological dangers of such an escape from his own age. He made the book into a warning against narcissistically pursuing one's own individualistic isolation from society as a whole. The complex vision of his magnum opus finally brought him the Nobel Prize in 1946.

Tommaso Landolfi

> Just as French logic precipitated something essential in Samuel Beckett, and English latter-day romanticism released something quirky in Jorge Luis Borges, so Russian literature, both classic and modern, gave Landolfi that particular form and accent, that special approach to his material, which makes him unique among contemporary Italian writers. For even the best Italian writers, such as Moravia, Gadda and Pavese, regard the metaphysical question as settled; they end their books precisely at the point where Landolfi begins his.[59]
>
> —Raymond Rosenthal, "A Note on Landolfi"

Since Rosenthal published these words in 1971, the rising prestige of other Italian fantasists (e.g., Italo Calvino) makes Tommaso Landolfi no longer seem unique, but since Landolfi has become known as "Italy's Kafka,"[59] he can hardly be ignored in a study of the Kafkaesque. The most obvious similarity between Kafka and Landolfi is style—their detailed descriptions of anxious vascillation coming from their common roots in Dostoevsky. The resemblance between Kafka and Landolfi goes further, however, involving their fascination with fantasies of nonhuman persons or of people treated inhumanly. In Landolfi's "Fable" *(Favola),* a canine narrates as in Kafka's "Investigations of a Dog," and in an untitled story by Landolfi, people convicted of some mysterious fault or imperfection are subjected to a torture machine as in Kafka's story "In the Penal Colony."[60]

Landolfi's stories vary greatly including both simple, psychological sketches (easy to analyze in Jungian terms) and anomalous works, closer to Kafka. Consider, for instance, two of his fictions that seemingly focus on the anima. In his story "The Mute," a fifty-year-old lunatic imagines that a fifteen-year-old, aphasic girl represents ideal femininity. She has "a terrible, unconscious beauty." He imagines her possessing the "nocturnal archetypes." Nonetheless, he shies from profaning "[her] eternal limbs, eternal as the light, fecund as the dust of stars, inexhaustible as the hidden fount of life."[61] Then,

> a friendly celestial power [gives him] a sign that [a solution] existed, that there could be a way for [him] to possess the child wholly and eternally; but [the solution] would not make itself known. ("The Mute")

After considering this enigmatic revelation, he believes he understands: he must kill her (which he does). Eventually, he lies on death row tortured by guilt and fear of damnation.

Perhaps Landolfi intended this narrative as a parody of, or tribute to, Romantic literature of madness, but his tale never truly escapes those Romantic patterns that obsessed Jung. "The Mute" describes a man in the latter half of life—the period when, according to Jung, the anima (typically associated with the eternal, feminine, and nocturnal) may appear in its last role to summon a man toward self-discovery, a gradual preparation for death. Landolfi's narrator, however, misunderstands this summoning and projects the anima image on a real girl, her youth and muteness facilitating the projection. Since, however, no actual girl (subject to the vicissitudes of growth and maturation) can eternally represent the anima, he kills her. Only two sentences in the story complicate this textbook example of Jungianism. "Nothing of what I said is true. Not because it is not true but because I said it." If developed, this paradox could have been interesting. In context, however, it is precisely what a Jungian analyst would expect. Because of who and what the narrator is (a psychotic with particular complexes), he will inevitably distort the world, perhaps even suspect his own prevarication (as he apparently does); but he will also (unknowingly) manifest the truth about himself, by narrating psychologically revealing fantasies.

In contrast, Landolfi's story entitled "Gogol's Wife" is much more resistant to psychologizing. The narrator, allegedly a Boswell-like biographer named Foma Paskalovitch, discloses that the great Russian author Nikolai Vassilevitch Gogol married a human-size balloon. At first, the tale seems to be just another case of anima projection. In Pygmalion-fashion, Gogol can shape, paint, and dress the inflatable doll into his image of perfect womanhood. It offers even less resistance than the mute fifteen-year-old of the before-mentioned story. Then the biographer casually mentions that he once heard the doll asking to go to the bathroom. Who is insane? Gogol? Paskalovitch? Both? Or is the problem that, as always in fantasies, the laws of quotidian existence do not apply and dolls can talk as readily as the animals of Aesop? The doll, named "Caracas"—the narrator has no idea why—also eludes classification by constantly changing due to Gogol's ministrations and to the natural slippage of air from the balloon. Paskalovitch repeatedly focuses on this problem.

> At the beginning of this chapter I cast some doubt on the propriety of considering Caracas as a unitary personality; nonetheless I myself could not quite, whenever I saw her, free myself of the impression that, however unheard of it may seem, this was fundamentally the same woman.[62]

This contains two jokes: first, the idiocy of the narrator wondering if she was one woman or many, when, of course, she was not a woman at all. Second, and more interesting, is the comedy of Gogol constantly remaking his wife as if his idea of perfection were also in flux. In relation to Jungian psychology, the question becomes: How can one "archetype" (the *anima*) be represented in such a variety of ways and still be called a single "archetype"? Finally, Gogol overinflates Caracas and after her explosive demise, he destroys their child, a baby doll—or so Paskalovitch presumes, though that biographer had only a brief look at the object being destroyed. Despite having actually made Gogol appear totally depraved, Paskalovitch piously hopes to have dispelled the slanderous rumor that Gogol abused his wife. "And what else can be the goal of a humble biographer such as the present writer but to serve the memory of that lofty genius who is the object of his study?" (384). Where "The Mute" imported Russian Romanticism wholesale into modern Italian, "Gogol's Wife" anachronistically combines the nineteenth-century Russian sensibilities of Paskalovitch with a story reminiscent of Federico Fellini's modern obsessions. Intercultural combinations mark Landolfi's best work. Since he has a degree in Russian literature and has translated several books from that language, his grotesqueries are most often Russian-Italian. Being a typical European, however, his knowledge is not limited to those two lands. In his story "Hands" *("Mani"),* for example, it is apparently the study of French that expands the protagonist's sympathies until he no longer tolerates even the extermination of a mouse (a situation reminiscent of the rat-killing scene in Hoffmannsthal's *Der Brief des Lord Chandos*). The important points are that intercultural relations inspire Landolfi to fantasies of dehumanization or identification with the nonhuman and that, strangely, his postmodern vision is fed by a fascination with Victorian literature.

Bruno Schulz

> And while the sky clears gradually from the west and becomes translucent, servant girls walk out in their Sunday best, in threes, in fours, holding hands. They walk in the empty, Sunday-clean and drying street between the suburban houses bright in the tartness of the air which now turns crimson before dusk; rosy and round-faced from the cold, they walk with elastic steps in their new, too tight shoes.
>
> —Schulz, *Sanatorium under the Sign of the Hourglass*

> And people in their Sunday best
> Stroll about, swaying over the gravel
> Under the enormous sky
> Which, from hills in the distance,
> stretches to distant hills.
>
> —Kafka, "Description of a Struggle"

According to Isaac Bashevis Singer, the Jewish/Polish, author/visual artist Bruno Schulz "wrote sometimes like Kafka, sometimes like Proust, and at times succeeded in reaching depths that neither of them reached."[63] Schulz, who rendered Kafka's novel *The Trial* into Polish, greatly admired the latter's fantasies, perhaps partly because of the similarity of their lives. Despite their both being multilingual, Jewish intellectuals in a provincial, anti-Semitic Eastern Europe, they seldom managed to leave their places of birth and remained under the shadow of their fathers. As Kafka had an intense friendship, possibly an affair, with the Catholic Milena Jesenská, so Schulz was for a time engaged to a Catholic woman but religious differences and family problems brought the relationship to a depressing end. Their writings, nonetheless, contrast more than one might expect.

Despite the striking similarity of the scenes recorded in the previously cited passages, Schulz is more pleasant and effusive. In "Description of a Struggle," Kafka's poem introduces a hypersensitive victim of *fin-de-siècle* alienation. Schulz's narrator is a relatively cheerful pensioner in second childhood (who adapts to his new condition by enrolling in a grade school). At the end of the chapter, the pensioner's body, shrunken with age, grows so light that he floats away into the "unexplored yellow [autumnal] space" *(zólte, neizbadane, jesienne przestworza).*[64] His flying into the void may remind one of Kafka's story "The Barrel Rider," but unlike the morose protagonist of that tale, Schulz's pensioner praises the disastrous wind that sweeps him away. "It was woven of softness and gentleness, but it pretended to be brutal and fierce" (*Klepsydra* 338; *Hourglass* 170). Like Schulz's pictures that accompany his writings—lightly etched, doll-like figures with oversized heads—his stories introduce a children's world where parents—indeed, all adults—appear to be too childlike to threaten or punish. Inured to disorder in a childhood of family troubles, Schulz seems less frightened of chaos than Kafka.[65]

Schulz's own father slowly declined into madness, a fact obliquely mirrored throughout Schulz's second (and last) book, *Sanatorium under the Sign of the Hourglass.* In that work, the father becomes gradually more eccentric, entertaining such a notion as that "beauty is a disease," albeit, one that brings him "bliss" *(szczéscia).* In the chapter entitled "Dead Season" *("Martwy Sezon"),* the narrator, Joseph N. (his name an obvious tribute to Kafka's Joseph K.), describes the father, Jacob, as sleeping with another man and seemingly wrestling with him. To innocent, young Joseph, this recalls the biblical Jacob's struggle with the Angel, and the episode actually ushers in a period of creativity and prosperity for the father. (Schulz tends to link eccentricity and imagination—another reason, perhaps, why he finds chaos congenial.) In the next chapter, though, the father has entered the Sanatorium of the title. In a striking metaphor for madness, Schulz describes the father as dead, yet suspended outside of time so that he seems alive only because of the miraculous clinic. Finally, the father turns into a crab or scorpion. It lies on its back, legs clawing the air (like Gregor Samsa as an overturned insect at the beginning of "Metamorphosis"). Closing with a transformed *(metamorfozy),* helpless father and slightly disgusted son forms the antithesis of Kafka commencing his most famous work with the father disapproving and son metamorphosed (*Klepsydra* 345; *Hourglass* 175).

According to Schulz's friend Arthur Sandauer, the former's works consist of a series of antitheses "arranged along a chronological line, which reduces in the end to an opposition between a childhood free from complexes and a poisoned maturity, or, generally, between the nineteenth and twentieth centuries."[66] Perhaps as a result of his friendship with Schulz, Sandauer possessed private information about the former's intentions, but in what is published, Schulz seldom vituperates against anything. In particular, he seems delighted with antitheses. In the chapter entitled "Spring" *("Wiosna"),* for example, Schulz's pubescent persona says that contemplating that season (and an attractive, young girl) leads his thoughts "into tantalizing regions of contradiction, into blissful antinomies" (*Klepsydra* 181; *Hourglass* 39). Indeed, he wonders if self-division is not inevitable. "Who hasn't a brother under one form or another who follows him like a shadow, an antithesis, the partner in an eternal dialogue?" (*Klepsydra* 201; *Hourglass* 56). Kafka considered antitheses to be superficial rhetorical tricks. Schulz, however, like Jung, sees the strain of facing the antithesis of life as leading the sufferer rather far into the psychic depths. "[A]lmost demented from contradictory feelings," Joseph imports from the realm of "unborn tales" (i.e., the Unconscious) a dream in which he brings wax statues of past dignitaries (quasi-archetypal figures) to life. In this story within a story (blended vertiginously into the main narrative), he seeks to lead a waxwork army in defense of the girl until he ultimately admits that he has acted ignorantly, missing the total picture. He is then arrested for his dreams. What is wrong with them (aside from a peculiarity they share with most dreams)? Perhaps the best explanation lies in Schulz's first book, *Cinnamon Shops (Sklepy Cynamonowe).* The father says that although the very nature of this world and the next is the infinite profusion of life, man, like the Gnostic "Demiurge" who created him, has fallen in love with matter (in particular, with trash) and so reduces all to this condition. It makes no demands; it is like a mannequin, free from the complexity of a living being.[67] These wax images are obvious mannequins to whom the boy turns because he is incapable or unwilling to undertake a demanding, living relationship with the girl. Or, more precisely, the images are idols, and their link with human depths makes them no less idolatrous. Despite the borrowings from Gnosticism, the father's theology is essentially Judaic, an attack on the idolatrous substitution of matter for spirit as an object of reverence. Reluctantly, he even condemns beauty, the attractive quality in some objects that tempts one to turn them into standards, archetypes of perfection. Although Schulz's works manifest what John Updike has called "a religious saturation, entirely heterodox, unknown in literature since William Blake,"[68] a Judaic (anti-archetypal) current underlies the divesity.

It was partly for his Judaic heritage that Schulz died. One day in 1942, having temporarily left the Jewish ghetto in which Third Reich law confined him, he was slain by a Gestapo agent. The murder was committed to spite a rival of that agent within the German heirarchy, a Nazi *friend* of Schulz,[69]—thereby bringing to a close (but not necessarily a conclusion), Schulz's lifelong engagement with contradictions and "blissful antinomies."

John Steinbeck

Winner of the 1962 Nobel Prize for literature, John Steinbeck, in his writings, managed a sometimes impressive, sometimes uneasy juxtaposition of journalistic and scholarly tendencies. The latter inclination began when a childhood reading of *Morte d'Arthur* gave him what he called a "secret language."[70] This personal version of Middle English along with the Latin and Greek he studied in school earned him special access to a realm of myth and legend; in contrast, the bits of Spanish and Tagalog he picked up in youth from fellow manual workers[71] helped him principally in his reportage as he moved from one culture to another.

The combination of imaginary past and actual present naturally plays some part in all his writings, but no more so than in his *The Winter of Our Discontent* (1961), the novel that directly preceded his receiving the Nobel Laureate. He described his novel as "a strange book . . . part Kafka."[72] During the composition of that work, Steinbeck had been reading Kafka's short stories, and there is a particular affinity of it with Kafka's story "The Judgment." The opening sentences of each set them in the spring (a startling season for Steinbeck's novel considering the "Winter" in its title), but he chooses to develop the Kafkaesque irony of hibernal desolation in the midst of vernal weather. Kafka's story concludes with the protagonist, Georg, a young businessman, leaping to a watery death at the order of his father. *The Winter of Our Discontent* climaxes when the protagonist, Ethan, also a young businessman, enters the sea with the intention of killing himself (though he changes his mind). He is driven almost to death by a sense of having failed his forebears, particularly his father and grandfather. In portraying the latter, Steinbeck adopts the Kafkan technique of describing authority figures with exaggerated ambivalence: both Georg's father and Ethan's grandfather are outlandishly, even comically demanding, larger than life beings. Ethan loved the grandfather so much that he "ached from it"[73] and Georg's devotion to the father is so intense as to be ultimately suicidal. Another pattern linking the two stories is the motif of a nebulous former companion as the protagonist's alter ego. It is a commonplace of Kafka criticism that Georg's friend, languishing in Russia, life apparently ruined, serves as Georg's psychological double or complement. Ethan and his friend Danny Taylor were boys together, "same age, same size, same weight" (103–4), and they remain "close" in spirit, despite their moving in different circles since Danny has declined from rich kid to town drunk.

In a letter, Steinbeck wrote that his novel was Kafkaesque in its oddness.[74] Comparably, his character Ethan senses "strangeness" within himself, his acting partly from unconscious motivation. In a 1978 article, Donald Stone has analyzed this motivation in Jungian terms, seeing Ethan's daughter and the seductive Margie Young-Hunt as anima figures, embodiments of the internal forces. Stone justifies such an analysis largely on the grounds of Steinbeck's discussion of Jungian theory with Dr. Evelyn Ott in 1930 and with Joseph Campbell in 1932. The problem with Stone's approach is not that *The Winter of Our Discontent* is totally unrelated to Jungian theory, but his reductive use of it.[75] Indeed, Stone ignores much evidence within the novel of such a connection, including the following. At the beginning of chapter 6, Ethan speaks of an ineffable inner realm like a cavern in which "faceless" beings decide his fate. "This secret and sleepless area in me I have always thought of as black, deep, waveless water, a spawning place from which only a few forms ever rise to the surface" (98). This certainly sounds like Jung's "Collective Unconscious." Furthermore, the character "old Doc Peele" once told the protagonist that this darkness contains inherited instincts from the early history of humanity (99), an even clearer reference to Jungian speculation about archetypes. Ethan himself describes his dreams as "like men dancing, wearing the horns and masks of animals" (42), the kind of comparison between modern unconscious and prehistoric ritual that Jung often made. Ethan says that some people might confuse this interest in the unconscious with the Freudian "back to the womb and the death wish" but, like Jung, Ethan sees such ideas as not universally applicable. "I don't think they are true of me, except as easy ways of saying something that isn't easy" (52).

Ethan's expression of these archaic instincts, however, is heavily influenced by his scholarly proclivities, his having "luxuriated in languages, bathed in the humanities, lodged in the old, the beautiful, the obscure" (48). His whimsical utterances, many of them parodies of Scripture and religious ritual, include whimsically fractured Latin and Middle English. Not only polyglot but pluralistic, he advocates a reader-response approach to literature. "A story has as many versions as it has readers" (80). His hermeneutic pluralism extends to the problem of archetypes. He remarks that to him the Tarot arcana The Hanged Man looked right side up while to Margie Young-Hunt it appeared upside down (94). Thus a pat reduction of the novel to any system, including one derived from Jung (as Stone does), ignores too much. *The Winter of Our Discontent* treats a time of Kafkaesque strangeness, a midlife crisis when the protagonist feels possessed by inner powers, and Steinbeck fills it with the kind of images that Jungians among others find attractive (e.g., suspected poltergeists, clairvoyance, the Tarot, and astrology), but it is no more a doctrinaire Jungian work than a slavish copy of Kafka.

Joyce Carol Oates

Valedictorian of Syracuse University in 1960, Joyce Carol Oates received an M.A. from the University of Wisconsin in 1961, taught at the University of Detroit until 1968, then at the University of Windsor until 1978. The subtle difference between Canadian and American culture has become a motif in many of her stories, while the more general theme of borders figures prominently in others, including her book, *Last Days,* part 2 of which (entitled "Our Wall") describes cross-cultural contact in Eastern Europe. Even after moving back into the United States, she continued editing her Canadian journal, *The Ontario Review.*[76] In a book composed during her Canadian stay, she writes:

> The world has no meaning; I am sadly resigned to this fact. But the world has meanings, many individual and alarming and graspable meanings, and the adventure of human beings consists in seeking out these meanings.[77]

This complex contrast between "meaning" and "meanings" underlies the relationship between her works and those of Kafka and Jung. She begins her highly perceptive article entitled "Kafka's Paradise" with the statement:

> Kafka is not only one of the finest writers of this century, now legendary and saintly, and bearing, as Auden remarked in 1941, the same sort of relation to his age that Dante, Shakespeare, and Goethe bore to theirs, but he has become for many of his readers a kind of perpetual riddle, a Zen koan—the ultimate, interior, soul-transforming experience, to "solve" which would be to "solve" the problem of existence itself.[78]

Her tone gently condemns those who would seek ultimate "meaning" from one author's works. She continues her genial satire by pointing out the irony that the meaning most critics have attained is a despairing one while "Kafka asserts boldly that in 'reality' we always win" (268).

> Kafka's mysticism is primarily one that intuits unity (though it experiences—or seems to experience—only fragments); it makes a distinction between the

> unifying mind and the mind that reasons this very distinction between self and object.[79]

She interprets Kafka as someone like herself, acutely aware of the fragmentary meanings of life but able to intuit an ineffable coherence behind them. She describes "Kafka's mysticism" as merely "one" kind; thus, she maintains a skeptical attitude toward his conclusions. Her article "Kafka's Paradise," the climax of *New Heaven, New Earth,* overflows with a nostalgia for paradisiacal unity, a condition of undifferentiated "Being." Her word "Being" (used throughout the book) is tied to a twice-repeated quotation from the *Tao te ching.* "Being is born of not being."[80] Strangely, this quotation does not support Oates's use of "Being" as the primal origin, but instead gives "not being" as the Source. Furthermore, the translation she uses (that of Gia-Fu Feng and Jane English) may be misleading. The words translated as "being" *(yu)* and as "not being" *(wu)* may mean more precisely "having" and "not having," echoing the first poem in the *Tao te ching,* which contrasts the possessive state of mind (attuned to the phenomenal world) and the nonpossessive state (attuned to the Tao). In other words, although Oates has tried very hard to allow for human diversity, she posits only one characteristic—an affirmation of Being—as linking together her mystics, yet even this slender thread exaggerates the real case, where "not being" (or not having) may describe the mystical experience as well as "Being." In *New Heaven, New Earth,* the intellect—for example, Kafka's desire to explain himself in writing (282)—becomes the villain, spoiling relations between the sexes and leading to misery. Actually, however, there is more reason to think that writing was for Kafka the principal form of meditation, his chief means of evoking those blisses that he occasionally mentions. Oates, though, is quite correct that writing also brought problems for him, both through the time it required and through the alienation inherent in intellectual activity.

Although she has perhaps come closer to solving the Kafkan "riddle" than many specialists in his writings, her slight oversimplification sometimes compromises the use she makes of Kafka in her own narratives. Her short story "The Metamorphosis," for instance, concerns "Matthew [who] woke suddenly from a daydream that was not his."[81] This sentence well expresses an idea central also to *New Heaven, New Earth* that an impersonal consciousness beyond the ego shapes our lives and troubles our dreams. In this insight she echoes Kafka's own "Metamorphosis." Disappointingly, the transformation in her story is simply an illness rather than the mind-jolting *Verwandlung* in Kafka's. True to her assumption that writing should express Being (what actually exists), she reduces the story to realism, the literary mode she employs most often, while, on the other hand, following Meister Eckhart, Taoism, and certain other extreme forms of mysticism, Kafka describes experiences that cannot all be pigeonholed as expressions of Being (even though he sometimes uses that word). Her short story "The Transformation of Vincent Scoville" reduces Scoville's transformation to easily explained insanity, partly because "like Franz Kafka, Vincent had weighed the joys of marriage against the incontestable joys of privacy—and of course privacy had won."[82] Her poem "A Report to an Academy (after Kafka)," however, moves beyond realism by simply paraphrasing Kafka's story.[83] By placing it in her volume entitled *Invisible Woman,* she subtly suggests that the ape being forced to imitate a man's world is like the condition of women in a male-dominated society. As she says in her preface to Kafka's *Complete Stories and Paradoxes,* "In the end [the ape] is neither animal nor man."[84] Only at her best does she manage to convey experiences that cannot be categorized.

Also in regard to Jung, she shies only slightly from psychological categorization. Concerning the anima, for example, she writes that the "soul . . . is usually identified with the feminine, though that interpretation is probably not necessary."[85] What is the meaning of "probably not necessary"? Similarly, in commenting on Sylvia Plath's use of the word *archetypes,* Oates writes,

> Between the archetypes of jealous, ruthless power, represented by the Father/Son of religious and social tradition, and the archetypes of moronic fleshly beauty, represented by these smug mothers, there is a very small space for the creative intellect, for the employment and expansion of a consciousness that tries to transcend such limits.[86]

She continues that readers may find this subjection to archetypes overly passive but it is part of a very old "predicament" (124). She seems restive with the conservatism inherent in archetypal theory, yet she is sufficiently well-read to realize that the contemporary problems of woman have analogues throughout the world.

Jorge Luis Borges

Because of a British grandmother, the Argentine polymath Jorge Luis Borges grew up bilingual, following the family tradition of using English for scholarly, and Spanish for other purposes. Before reaching his teens, he published a Spanish translation of Oscar Wilde's story "The Happy Prince."[87] At fifteen, he accompanied his family to Geneva, where he officially studied French and Latin (and learned German without a teacher). His best friends there were Jewish (foreigners like himself), perhaps the source of his pronounced Judeophilia, although one might also mention his aunt's Jewish husband. He acquired enough Italian to study *The Divine Comedy* and began writing sonnets in English and

French, one of the latter entitled, "Poem to Be Recited with a Russian Accent" *(Poeme pour être recité avec un accent russe).* After a year in Spain imitating the ultraists, Borges returned to Argentina, where he was a librarian until political problems forced him to become a traveling lecturer around the world.

One of his last appearances was at the 1983 Modern Language Association convention in New York, where he gave an address entitled, "Conversations with a Writer." In an accent alternating between British and Argentinian, Borges spoke—his sightless eyes turned upward, seeming to converse with the subject of his lecture: Franz Kafka. After his ghostly dialogue, discussion ensued, focusing on Borges's essay, "Kafka and his Precursors" *(Kafka y sus precursores).* It identifies predecessors of Kafka ranging from the Chinese sage Han Yu to the anonymous composers of Chinese myths analyzed in C. G. Jung's *Psychologie und Alchemie*—a work published two decades after Kafka's death. Borges's essay, however, does not try to prove that Kafka ever heard of his "precursors"; such proof, Borges implies, would be irrelevant, since "every writer *creates* his own precursors"; a new genius so transforms his readers' sensibilities that they see his style everywhere, even in the distant past.[88] At one surreal moment in the discussion, Borges's friend Alastair Reid remarked that Borges had invented Kafka (i.e., we now read Borges's style into Kafka's fantasies). If Reid's statement is not literally true, it at least suggests the close association between Kafka and Borges. In 1938, Borges was one of the first to translate any of Kafka's short stories into Spanish. He did so from one of the few volumes of Kafka's collected works that escaped Nazi confiscation. In 1976, Borges told Margaret Boegeman: "I was [in my early writings] aping Kafka. But Kafka was a genius, and I am only a man of letters. I couldn't go on being Kafka."[89] Similarly, in a 1979 interview, Borges told Edna Aizenberg that, in his earliest fictions, especially "The Lottery in Babylon" *(La lotería en Babilonia)* and "The Library of Babel" *(La biblioteca de Babel),* he "tried to be Kafka."[90] Aizenberg notes that in the former of those stories, the name of Kafka appears transformed into the "sacred latrine called Qaphqa" *(una letrina sagrada llamada Qaphqa)*[92] and in another story, "The Secret Miracle" *(El milagro secreto),* Borges has the protagonist live at Kafka's address on Zeltnergasse in Prague (Aizenberg 1, 7, 11 n. 14).

The strongest influence on Borges comes from "At the Building of the Great Wall of China," what Borges calls Kafka's "most memorable" story.[92] Borges describes it thus: "The infinite is multiple: to stop the course of infinitely distant armies, an emperor who is infinitely remote in time and space orders that infinite generations raise an infinite wall to encircle his infinite empire."[93] The pattern of the infinite circle (the limitless encircling wall), what Jung calls a "mandala," is one to which

Borges devotes his essay "The Fearful Sphere of Pascal" *(La esfera de Pascal).* He begins that essay by asserting that all history can be reduced to a few metaphors (e.g., the infinite circle whose center is everywhere, Jung's definition of the Self).[94] Borges ends the essay with a sentence almost identical to the first one except for a few words shifting the emphasis away from the repetition of archetypal metaphors to the "different intonations" given them by each author. From Kafka, Borges learned how a writer can strip reality to infinite, eternal patterns, but recognized these raised a major aesthetic question: How could a literature of archetypes be anything but monotonous and tiresome? Many of his best works are devoted to showing how a change in intonation can renew a fossilized pattern, most notably in "Pierre Menard, Author of the Quixote" *(Pierre Menard, autor del Quijote).* It argues that denotation of words depends on the historical context, so that the same passage would have a different meaning if read as sixteenth- or twentieth-century literature. Thus fragments of *Don Quixote* written by the modern author Pierre Menard, even though they are word for word the same as those written by Cervantes, must be interpreted differently. From Kafka's unfinished or fragmentary works (e.g., "At the Building of the Great Wall of China"), Borges had learned that fragmentary compositions inspire the readers to unlimited imaginings.

As with Jung (whose works Borges has much read), these "archetypes" may lead toward an abandonment of the individual Self for identification with a cosmic Self. As with Kafka, however, Borges is ambiguous about this mystical leap of consciousness. In "The God's Script" *(La escritura del Dios),* for example, a prisoner achieves union with God, thus becoming all powerful, but now that he is conscious of the whole universe, the birth and death of galaxies, the shaping of Reality itself, he can no longer concern himself with his individual fate. He cannot bother to free himself from prison. Jung believed that a change of consciousness was a great matter in and of itself. His position derived from a century of German idealism, but like Kafka, Borges leads us to wonder what value there may be in spiritual liberation if it leaves us physically bound. Borges once said to his young friend Richard Burgin, "I believe in God in spite of theology."[95] Borges imagines an incomprehensible divinity shaping our destinies. If at some point—after death, perhaps—we were to understand him, that very revelation would change us so that we would no longer be the same, no longer quite human. Consequently Borges doubts *personal* immortality, while leaving open the possibility of some continuation of consciousness. For Borges, Individuation (identification with the Cosmic Order) is so problematic that he is almost like the next group, those who find religious meaning in their lives through the *absence* of God.

7
Frogs

> Man is a monstrous [*ungeheure*] expanse of marsh. Being stirred by inspiration [*Begeisterung*] affects the general picture as if, in some quarter of the marsh, a small frog plopped into the green water.
>
> —Kafka

> Old pond!
> Frog jumping in
> Water's sound
>
> —Basho

Whether or not Kafka intended this aphorism as a commentary on Basho's haiku, Kafka's insight could well be used as such. Because of Basho's own Zen practice, his poem has habitually been interpreted in terms of the Zen term "emptiness" [*sunyata*], which does not mean vacuum, but rather a view of the world as ecologically interconnected (like a pond or swamp) so that nature is empty of distinctions between the parts. Man himself, Zen proclaims, is not an individual Self but an emptiness indistinguishable from the universal emptiness. Basho's frog appears in one of the poem's lines, sandwiched between lines evoking the pond and the sound of its water, that is, immersed in a nature he affects only momentarily.

These frogs of Basho or Kafka differ from the aforementioned "leopard"-like authors. The latter prowled through many traditions, gaining therefrom a syncretic structure to their writings, very much like the equally leopardian Jung, except where their personal insights modified their understanding of archetypes. For the "frog"-like writers, moments of inspiration or in-spiriting *(Begeisterung)* may make them face experiences of the sort attributed by Jung to archetypes, but the "frog"-like authors minimize or belittle the archetypes because of an acute awareness of the surrounding emptiness, produced by clashing traditions. Although some of the "leopard"-like authors have accepted the idea of emptiness along with their other borrowings from Eastern temples, their works focus more on mythic images, while the "frog"-like writers emphasize the absence of any clear pattern.

In some quarters, the concept of absence has assumed the place of the sacred, generating new faiths and even denominational arguments, as with Keiji Nishitani scolding Sartre for advocating the wrong kind of nothingness.

> Although [Sartre] considers [nothingness] the foundation of [psychology], it is still considered like a wall projected in the base of the ego, or like a springboard on which the ego is standing. His nothingness is turned into a basic factor that shuts the ego up within itself.[1]

In *Absolute Nothingness*, another member of this school of philosophy writes:

> We can see how the spectrum of [Japanese] meanings given to nothingness stretches from what is *unknown* because man has closed himself off from it and is therefore ignorant of it, to what is *unspeakable* and *unknowable* in the face of which man is powerless, despair or trust in it as he might. At this end of the spectrum, man can only endure if he lets himself go in order to find himself in selflessness.[2]

Sartre does not realize (as a Japanese, Buddhist philosopher would have), that the idea of emptiness precludes the existence of an ego.

As in the preceding chapter, Snyder's "Cold Mountain Poems" served as an introduction to the "leopard"-like authors, so one of my favorite passages from Italo Calvino's novel *The Castle of Crossed Destinies (Il castello dei destini incrociati)* may help to introduce some of the more widespread meanings of emptiness and absence:

> The kernel of the world is empty, the beginning of what moves in the universe is the space of nothingness, on absence is constructed what exists, at the bottom of the Grail is the Tao.[3]

First, Calvino's phrase, "on absence is constructed what exists" derives from the vision of absence in terms of a wheel structured around its nave, a pot around its empty space, and a wall around doors and windows, so all things receive form from emptiness, which surrounds them and gives them function.[4] Second, since, as the *Tao te ching* repeatedly asserts, the Tao is ineffable, absence refers to what is not present in texts because it transcends the power of words. Not only is this second aspect of absence a major theme in Calvino's book but it is also an obsession of much recent criticism. Harold Bloom, for example, has turned even tradition (the conventions that give meaning to a work) into an indefinable, transcendental signifier.

> What Ein-Sof [the without-end, first manifest as *Ayin,* nothingness] or the Infinite Godhead was to the Kabbalists, or the Imagination was to the Romantic

> poets, tradition is now for us, the one literary sign that is not a sign, because there is no other sign to which it can refer.[5]

The third meaning of absence is the aforementioned Zenist emptiness (interconnectedness), which has been developed in postmodern philosophy by the followers of Nishida Kitarō and introduced into literary criticism by such ecumenical figures as Robert Magliola, whose Roman Catholic/Deconstructionist/Buddhism was discussed in my previous book. Fourth, since Calvino's experimental novel was inspired by a 1968 symposium on the structure of the narrative, his seeing the root of meaning in the void recalls an idea that structuralism derives from Freud and other theoreticians by way of Lacan—the notion that meaning itself comes from absence. If we were all still cradled in the womb with all our wants fulfilled, we would not need to invent words. All our terms are but means of naming what we lack. Also for structuralists, absence constitutes their version of the Collective Unconscious, a place where all untapped possibilities are stored.[6] In Calvino's *Castle of Crossed Destinies,* absence refuses to stay hidden. The repressed and suppressed rise; the feminine revolts against the masculine, the wild against the city, the sea against the land, the dead against the living, until all order disappears in the Kafkaesque reshuffling.

Modern criticism busily constructs order or rather orders, since disagreement in the critical community is notorious. Behind this order or these orders, there is an awe of what cannot be ordered. One might hypothesize that however secular postmodern literature chooses to be, its paradigms, the models with which it plays, will still be the Sacred Reality that it rejects—but this hypothesis would itself, no doubt, be rejected by the following authors, who have doubts about virtually everything.

Albert Camus

Born in Algeria to an illiterate French father and barely educated Spanish mother, the future Nobel Prize winner Albert Camus, unlike most of his early friends, managed to attend high school. There he learned the Latin, English, and polished French necessary for admission to higher education.[7] At university, he wanted to become a professor, a hope ultimately quashed by tuberculosis. Consequently, beyond occasional money from miscellaneous sources (e.g., from the bourgeois parents of his drug-addicted, first wife), he had to turn to writing for an income. His *oeuvre* reflects all these factors: the intercultural, interlinguistic, interclass tensions of Algeria; the heated, philosophical polemics of French academia; his sometimes disturbed domestic life; and the lonely concerns of the modern, professional writer.

One of his first works to bring this mixture to a significant conclusion was *The Myth of Sisyphus (Le mythe de Sisyphe),* published in 1942. In its first section, "Absurdity and Suicide," it begins with a question that he ends by associating with the fiction of Kafka, but it is also a problem Camus's existence had so often posed to him, "whether life is or is not worth living."[8] In the second section, "Absurd Walls," Camus sees the issue thus: the human mind longs for unity (a comprehensible, anthropomorphic universe), while reality—at least at present—offers only differences (*Essais* 110; *Myth* 17). His solution is what he calls the "absurd."

> This world in itself is not reasonable, that is all that can be said. But what is absurd is the confrontation of this irrational and the wild longing for clarity whose call echoes in the human heart. The absurd depends as much on man as on the world. For the moment it is all that links them together. It binds them one to the other as only hatred can weld two creatures together. (*Essais* 113; *Myth* 21)

Essentially, Camus offers an inversion of Christianity. He ridicules the Christian rapprochement of man and God through love and substitutes hatred. For this reason, in his concluding section, "Hope and the Absurd in the Work of Franz Kafka," he praises *The Trial,* which seems to him a brilliant exposition of universal hostility. Conversely, Camus condemns *The Castle,* where, he suspects, Kafka has become a Kierkegaardian and has sold out to God. Bernard Groethuysen, one of Kafka's first champions in France, told Camus not to mistake Kafka's Judaism for Kierkegaardian Christianity.[9] At the current level of Kafkan scholarship, one may say that Kafka was neither precisely Christian nor Jewish. Indeed, his works had much in common with Camus's fictions.

Consider Camus's retelling of the agony of Sisyphus (condemned in the very bottom of Hades, endlessly to raise a crushing boulder). Like Kafka's "Prometheus," Camus's "Sisyphus" juxtaposes many contradictory versions of the tale, each, presumably, from a different Greek cult, but, by simply listing them without cultural explanation, Camus deliberately disorients readers, preparatory to his final paradox, "One must imagine Sisyphus happy." Like Kafka's story "A Commentary," where a Taoist tale stands invisibly behind the story of a Prague policeman (Introduction, *supra*), so Camus has apparently concealed an Oriental source behind a Greek myth. A paper delivered by the Japanese philosopher Shūzō Kuki at Pontigny in 1928 (a decade before Camus began his "Sisyphus") explains Oriental religion by contrasting it with Greek theology.

> That the Greeks say damnation in the myth of Sisyphus has always appeared superficial to me. . . . Everything depends on the subjective attitude of Sisyphus. His good will, a will firm and sure in ever beginning anew, in ever rolling the rock, finds in this very repetition an entire system of morals and, consequently, all its happiness.[10]

Kuki explains, "It is the enterprise itself that interests us, not the goal," and Camus, in a footnote earlier in *The Myth of Sisyphus,* alludes to the Oriental doctrine of *l'indifférence des oeuvres*—the idea that one should act, but not to achieve a goal (*Essais* 145; *Myth* 64), though he never mentions Kuki. The happiness of Sisyphus in Hades forms the climax of Camus's *Myth,* yet it does not suit those positivist passages where Camus atheistically denies an Afterlife, nor does Camus's "Sisyphus" really fit within Greek mythology. For Camus, Sisyphus must be linked to *the whole universe* through hate, while the Greek Sisyphus has his mutual tie of animosity merely with Zeus—one of many gods. In Oriental religions, however, one reads of Boddhisattvas who blissfully meditate in hell or of Hindus who achieve liberation either through love *(bhakti)* or (much more rarely) hate. Where, as often in the Orient, the Divine Ground of existence is impersonal, what matters is the intensity of one's relationship to It, not whether one loves or despises It. Like Kafka, Camus, however, does not wish simply to import Oriental philosophy but to arrive at its conclusions either by working through Occidental tradition—or seeming to do so.

Originality is important to both of them, not merely, one presumes, as a matter of pride, but also because an incomprehensible world is by definition fresh and unpredictable. Consequently, when Camus's former teacher Jean Grenier charged Camus with borrowing from Kafka in Camus's *The Stranger* (composed simultaneously with *The Myth of Sisyphus*), Camus refused to admit the indebtedness.[11] Interestingly, Camus allowed the Kafka section to be excised from the first edition of *The Myth of Sisyphus,* but perhaps to placate Nazi censors who might have objected to a discussion of a Jewish author. Camus's denial of Kafkan influence on *The Stranger* sounds somewhat tendentious when one thinks of its Kafkaesque obscurities as well as the comparably absurd legal systems in it and in *The Trial.*[12] Like Kafka, Camus achieves a complexity that appears simple because of his relatively short sentences until one tries to analyze his precise meaning. In the novel's ending, for example, the protagonist, Mersault, clearly states his longing for the crowd at his execution to greet him with shouts of hate. Why? So that he may better feel the "tender indifference of the world" *(tendre indifférence du monde),* with which he feels a "fraternal" kinship.[13] The word *indifférence* is exceedingly well chosen, combining as it does the many, mutually exclusive ideas that Camus wishes to harmonize: (1) a world as passionless as Mersault; (2) a universal, fraternal unity such that differences no longer exist (the etymological meaning of *indifférence*); (3) the antagonism between Mersault and the world (since in common parlance—the language in which much of the book is written—*indifférence* connotes hostility, a usage linking the *indifférence* to the hatred of the crowd).

In other words, Camus's description of Mersault's mood falls into pieces if one looks at it carefully. It is as complex as Mersault's *indifférence* toward his mother (or Camus's own ambivalence toward his unaffectionate, quiet mother—her silences perhaps related to the fact that French was not her native language). In the concluding (Kafka) section of *The Myth of Sisyphus* Camus asserts,

> A symbol is always in general and, however precise its translation [from the writer's mind to paper], an artist can restore to it only its movement: there is no word-for-word rendering. (*Essais* 201; *Myth* 124)

In an approximately contemporary notebook, Camus condemns "a psychology which concentrates on details" and in another entry, likens composition to translation from the Unconscious.[14] Thus, he postulates the existence of paradoxical psychological patterns that can only be known in general and cannot be described precisely. In the section on "Absurd Walls" in the *Myth of Sisyphus,* Camus identifies certain themes of frustrated desire for unity (e.g., "the stranger who . . . comes to meet us in the mirror") to be found in "all literatures and all philosophies" (*Essais* 108–9; *Myth* 15–16). With these truly universal themes, he contrasts pseudo-archetypes peculiar to the West (e.g., Don Juan), patterns that future Occidental writers should resist. It is a pity that, like Kafka, Camus's interest is that of philosophical fictionalist rather than psychologist, because his intuition (the inherent relationship of true archetypes to the One) could offer a fresh way of approaching Jung (see part 3). Far from being concerned with systematizing Jung, however, Camus does not try to chart the Unconscious, but instead would prefer that the Unconscious remain an undefined medley of all the conflicting emotions that his ruminations have evoked in him. His advocacy of the Absurd has promulgated an emptinesslike concept in the West (even if Camus's Absurd is mixed with a few Jungian elements that hearken back to chap. 6).

Jean-Paul Sartre

Raised by a German-Protestant grandfather (inventor of the Berlitz language method),[15] Jean-Paul Sartre spent much of his childhood in the family's vast, multilingual library or in converse with the French-Catholic remainder of his family. He took his formal education in France except for a year at the University of Freiburg (Germany); nonetheless, he gravitated toward German philosophy. Indeed, his own atheist Existentialism (with its emphasis on self-examination of conscience) seems partly derived from the German-Protestant tradition, like the almost equally secularized philosophy of his cousin (and fellow Nobel Prize winner) Albert Schweitzer. On the other hand, Sartre's Communist sympathies might be seen as distantly reflecting Catholic communalism and, more obviously, the French wave of antifascism that swept so many Gallic intellectuals into Marxism. During the Occupation, Sartre openly published, with Nazi approval, writings steeped in Germanic influence, particularly Heidegger (who became a supporter of Hitler). Simultaneously, Sartre covertly published anti-Nazi articles and belonged to the Resistance. How did this intercultural tension make him feel? *Nausea,* the title of his first and best-known novel (1938), expresses (perhaps autobiographically) the physical revulsion accompanying anomie. The novel's protagonist, Antoine Roquentin, succumbs to this malady in Indo-China (where Sartre's father died) after Roquentin has devoted years to study and travel throughout Europe and Asia. In this "nausea," conceptual boundaries, for example, the distinction between separate objects and those between animate and inanimate beings have collapsed. Roquentin feels dead; mere things seem to him to be alive. Language no longer adequately describes the world. "My words are dreams, that is all."[16] His symptoms sound almost identical to those of Hoffmannsthal's famous character Lord Chandos, whose breakdown also may have arisen from multicultural studies; there are further precedents in Kafka's stories of physical revulsion and linguistic collapse.[17]

As late as 1953, Alfred Stern presumed the influence of Kafka on the repeated imagery of sudden metamorphosis in *Nausea,* for example. "He will go to a mirror and open his mouth; and his tongue will have become an enormous live centipede."[18] Such a presumption remained quite reasonable until 1974, when Sartre told his *amoureuse* Simone de Beauvoir that, although Kafka "influenced [him] profoundly," *Nausea* appeared before that influence began.[19] In a 1939 diary, Sartre wrote that since September of that year he had "read or reread" *The Castle, The Trial,* and *In the Penal Colony.*[70] Perhaps hearing his *Nausea* compared to Kafka's works made Sartre rush to read the latter. One confusing note, however, arises from a 1949 interview Sartre gave to Maja Goth. According to her, he not only admitted a great debt to Kafka, whose world (he said) he tended to laicize *(laïciser le monde Kafkaïen);* Sartre also talked of how Kafka helped the French to understand Kierkegaard during the 1930s[21]—an odd thing for him to say if he had not encountered Kafka until the last year of that decade.

Instead of directly describing the world in a secular manner, did Sartre covertly import "laicized" versions of religious motifs into his own works? A number of critics, most persuasively Stuart Charmé, have suggested something very like this. Charmé finds within Sartre's literary biographies the archetypal patterns that Eliade and Jung attribute to hagiography.[22] This discovery is particularly noteworthy, since Sartre's Existentialism makes him object to any psychological theory (e.g., of "archetypes") that removes men's fate from their voluntary control. Nonetheless, Joseph Halpern has made a very strong case that Sartre's literary criticism should be read as fictions, shaped by Sartre's unconscious dread of anything soft, passive, or feminine (including beautiful style), qualities he repressed within himself transmuting them into what Jungians call the "archetype" of the Shadow (though Halpern does not use that term).[23] Sartre, though, was very slow in realizing that his views were governed by stock patterns, only recognizing during the composition of his autobiography *Les mots* that his literary career had been governed by his desire to see writers as virile hero figures, hacking their way through the shapeless darkness, never wasting their time on mere stylistic polish.[24] Only in his last years did he admit the existence of an Unconscious.[25] Previously, the most he acknowledged was that people fail to conceptualize parts of their lives: they simply accept what comes unthinkingly or delude themselves by rationalizing away anything unpleasant. This rationalizing (what Sartre calls "bad faith") was the only unconscious activity Sartre originally recognized. Despite Sartre's inclinations, his works can be seen in Jungian terms, but all this necessarily means is that he was not able to break very far from the stereotypes of his culture. His "nausea" evoked by any touch of chaos meant that he could never venture very far into the Kafkaesque mode before trying to reduce his experiences to logic. He felt drawn toward Unity (which he considered a basic human desire), but he stopped just short of overt theologizing. In *Being and Nothingness (L'être et le néant),* he writes:

> The passion of man is the reverse of that of Christ, for man loses himself as man in order that God may be born. But the idea of God is contradictory and we lose ourselves in vain. Man is a useless passion [*l'homme est une passion inutile*].[26]

He believed that nature was absurd, unbound by any consistency or rule, but he refused to apotheosize the dreaded absurdity of the world.

André Breton

Leader of the Surrealists (to the extent that this anarchic group ever had one), André Breton helped to shape their goal: *dépaysement,* literally, being away from one's country (a word Lévi-Strauss later applied to anthropology). *Dépaysement* meant to Breton bewilderment and the sense of the marvelous *(merveilleux)* generated by breaking free from familiar associations.[27] Some of the Surrealists actually had left their countries, notably Salvador Dali, whom Breton once thought of as embodying "the Surrealist spirit."[28] Considering the interregional animosities of France, even Breton's childhood changes of residence from Normandy to Brittany to the outskirts of Paris may have left him slightly *dépaysé*. For him, though, *dépaysement* chiefly denoted a poetic technique involving the suggestive juxtaposition of disparate images to produce an altered state of consciousness. His method of composition also involved decreased consciousness, primarily through automatic writing, a technique derived from word association that he conducted as a psychiatric ward nurse in Saint-Dizier (1916). Breton felt drawn to the exotic as in his volume entitled *Xénophiles (Lovers of the Foreign)*. Its poems praise Oceanic idols and magic masks in his art collection.

Closer at hand but equally strange, the works of Kafka imported into France from the late 1920s also evoked his praise. Breton's 1937 article entitled "Heads of Storm" *("Têtes d'orage")* includes a discussion of Kafka's "capital interrogation of all times" and is followed by Kafka's story "Odradek" with pictures by Max Ernst.[29] In *Anthology of Black Humor* (*Anthologie de l'humour noir,* 1940), Breton devotes a chapter to Kafka's humor, which, according to Breton, "traces cabalistic formulas in the air with blue letters."[30] Even though Kafka's calm style differs markedly from Breton's wild juxtapositions, both authors create dreamlike, darkly humorous fantasies, so there is no tremendous surprise in Breton's seeing Surrealism as Kafkaesque.

The reference to Kabbala, however, is more interesting. Breton's friend Michel Carrouges traces to the Kabbala what he calls "the cornerstone of the surrealist cosmology, the living focal-point of real and surreal."[31] Concerning this focus, Breton writes:

> Everything leads us to believe that there is a certain point in the spirit from which life and death, real and imaginary, past and future, communicable and incommunicable are no longer perceived as contradictories. It would be vain to look for any other motivation in surrealist activity than the hope of determining this point.[32]

This notion resembles the cosmologies that Kafka and Jung (particularly the latter) produced during World War I. Like Jung, Breton sees coincidences not as mere accident but as synchronicities traceable to this point, what Carrouges calls Breton's "*link* . . . between personal unconscious, collective unconscious, and even cosmic unconscious." Like Kafka, Breton believes man to be simultaneously fallen and unfallen (e.g., Breton's poem "No Paradise Is Lost") since this point offers an eternal

Eden, whereas everyday life most evidently offers none. Breton's attitude toward "archetypes" is harder to educe. Cauvin asserts, "Jungian psychology offers many more affinities with Breton than does Freud's, despite Breton's seeming unfamiliarity with, and perhaps deliberate ignorance of, Jung's work" (340 n. 13). In and of itself, this statement seems plausible but it follows Cauvin's discussion of anima and animus archetypes in Breton, terms that Cauvin uses in a non-Jungian manner, leaving one wondering if Cauvin is himself really familiar with Jung. The problem, however, lies even more with Breton. Consider, for example, his poem "If I Were You. . . ." (*A ta place. . . .*) from his collection *Airwater (L'Air de l'eau).* The poem might be read as a love poem spoken by a man to a woman, but the identities of speaker and addressee anomalously shift into one another as the former imagines himself in the place of the latter. Running throughout the poem is a "Leitmotif" of a knight who is saving a damsel in distress but it is called a "Leitmotif . . . of metro exits" and the knight is made of straw (*Poems* 106–7). Breton did not want his poems reduced to analysis and so made them particularly resistant to it. Perhaps the common ground between saving knights and metro exits is that both lead toward freedom (although any number of other possibilities may seem equally probable to a reader). The knight is of straw and the speaker tells the "you" *(tu)* of the poem not to trust such a knight. Indeed, a distrust of stereotypes (e.g., the rescuing knight) runs throughout the poem. Where Jung looks to "archetypal" figures for guidance, Breton (like Kafka) characteristically emphasizes their dreamlike strangeness and untrustworthiness. Thus even though Breton expects his weird juxtapositions to lead toward a "universal symbolism," he seeks patterns that can only be intuited, not ones that psychology can define (even as vaguely as Jung does).

Jacques Derrida

"[O]ne of Derrida's earliest, most haunting memories was his sense of extreme isolation as the child of a largely 'assimilated' Jewish family during a time of mounting persecution and racial violence."[33] Born in French Algeria (1930), Jacques Derrida, after an early fascination with Sartre and Camus and after a higher education in France and America, became what might be called an "experimental fictionalist," though his works have also been considered literary criticism and philosophy.[34] In addition to creative play with typography in his essaylike fictions, he has innovated in other media, including a cassette on which he and the actress Carole Bouquet read (one might almost say dramatize) his work "Fire the Ash" *(Feu la cendre).* His international vogue has been spread both by fine translations of his writings (which he supervises with unusual attention) and by his reading his intriguing compositions to audiences around the globe. The year 1982 brought him to Prague, where he "participated in an 'unofficial' seminar, visited Kafka's grave and worked on . . . [an opus] whose title—'Before the Law'—took on a certain retrospective irony."[35] The atmosphere was explosive, because Czech literature and literary criticism had long been entwined in politics. In 1963, an effort in Prague to rehabilitate Kafka's fictions (condemned as *petit bourgeois* by the Communist party) resulted in a controversial conference. A few participants dared hint that alienation (like that described by Kafka) existed under Communism as well as Capitalism. Since they were allowed to live, the public response was immediate.

> Kafka, who had been a matter of vital interest to a small minority, suddenly became a household word in Prague. His works were published in large editions: the literary journals, radio and television programmes, examined his legacy: and there was talk of staging *The Trial* and *The Castle*. On his birthday an official delegation honoured his grave; and in 1964 a Kafka exhibition was held in Prague and opened by his friend Max Brod. When the play *Who's Afraid of Virginia Woolf* was staged in Prague, the title was rendered as *Who'd be Afraid of Kafka*.[36]

The answer to who feared Kafka came in the form of Soviet tanks, and Czech liberalization was long postponed. Since then, some Western intellectuals (Sartre among them) have tried to rehabilitate Kafka in Eastern Europe, but Socialist governments resisted successfully, at least until the sweeping liberalizations that began in 1989. Consequently, even in 1982, the "unofficial" seminar raised certain tensions reflected in Derrida's "Devant la loi."

In it, he writes, "A man from the countryside, I too here find myself before a law to which I shall doubtless never gain access."[37] Who is this "I," sharing the fate of Kafka's *"Mann vom Lande"*? In a translation for Americans, Derrida adds, "I was to appear before the law in Prague, accused of drug trafficking" (131). This alludes to an actual incident involving Derrida, probably, as Christopher Norris argues, on "a trumped-up charge" (11). Thus the "I" has something in common with Derrida himself—but it is not precisely he. Derrida, the cosmopolitan, is hardly "a man from the countryside."[38] For the purpose of clarity, I shall call this rustic persona "D." (in the manner of Kafka's K., also a comically obtuse fellow struggling to understand "Before the Law"). D. differs both from Derrida and from what Wayne Booth calls the "implied [or, as more-cautious critics would say, inferred] author," an author's "second self," the figure who seems to stand behind his books.[39] While the Derridian implied or inferred author apparently believes that the conventions of literature are "always already" "uncertain" (to coin two of his favorite clichés), D., however, says:

> A slightly heavy accent needs to be placed on certain axiomatic trivialities or on certain presuppositions [the conventions of literature]. I have every reason to suppose that we shall readily agree upon them at first, even if I mean later to undermine the conditions of such a consensus. (Derrida 129; Ronell 129)[40]

Far from having "every reason to suppose that we shall readily agree," the implied or inferred author in previous books has been undercutting that agreement and precipitating what has come to be called the "crisis" in literary criticism. Next, D. loses confidence, admitting that he has spoken "a little rashly" in assuming that he and his British audience (or American readership) belong to the "same culture." Indeed, in the single page preceding D.'s reference to the "same culture," D. has already presented first a quotation from Montaigne in sixteenth-century French, second, what might best be called a prose poem in modern French on the question of citation, and, third, an English translation of Kafka's German story "Before the Law" *("Vor dem Gesetz").* Thereafter, D.'s Kafkaesque plight (struggling to control his words despite the Deconstructionist ambience) becomes the frame story (or, more precisely, "storyless story" as he calls it). Into this, he sets digressions ranging from brief allusions to the medieval Holy Grail romances to a relatively developed treatment of Freud's *Totem and Taboo.* In the inconclusive conclusion, D. quotes Kafka's character, who comments on the parable, "The script is immutable and the commentaries often merely express the despair that this causes" (Ronell 149). Since this character is a strange priest who thinks that "Before the Law" is part of Scripture, one need not take his words as Kafka's position.

They do, however, accord with the attitude toward literature often expressed by the Derridian implied or inferred author. Within "Devant la loi" itself, D. comes to believe, "We could never explain the parable of a so-called literary narration with the help of semantic contents originating in philosophy or psychoanalysis, or drawing on some other source of knowledge" (Derrida 185; Ronell 143). His evidence of this is largely confined to showing that D.'s own Freudian reading of the parable sounds farfetched (as Freudian readings often do). This hardly proves the failure of all psychoanalytic criticism. He adds, "The fictitious nature of this last récit robs us of every event [for analysis]." This statement is self-contradictory: in a "philosophical" fiction ("Devant la loi"), D. comments on a fiction *(Vor dem Gesetz)* asserting that no such comment (as he, himself, is making) is possible. Furthermore, despite his doubts about psychology, in at least one case D.'s own words are particularly susceptible to Jungian analysis. Where Kafka has the man from the country seek an impersonal, grammatically neuter Law, D. uses the feminine gender of the word "Law" *(Loi)* in French as an excuse to personify it in *anima* imagery that the English translator makes even more explicit (Derrida 179; Ronell 137). D. then recalls that the German is neuter, so that his elaborate feminization of it tells more about his own psychic state than about Kafka's text. The implied or inferred author has D. fall into archetypal thinking only so that such thinking can then be exposed—part of a Deconstructionist crusade against belief in the archetypal. The very scope of this crusade, however, suggests that vast numbers of authors (the ones Deconstructionists pride themselves in exposing) have fallen under the spell of "archetypes"—the condition Jung spent his life documenting. Are Derrida and Jung reconcileable? Jung's archetypes seem to be precisely the kind of mystical sources that Deconstruction considers nonexistent. Actually, however, since Jung deemed them ineffable, Jungian therapy may in practice eliminate any reference to psychological sources.

> Whereas Freud valued dreams as providing access to the infantile sources of conflict and placed demand upon patients for a *linear* type of free association leading back to the infantile substructure, the . . . therapist . . . [may] employ a *radial* type of association to amplify the immediate meaning of each dream element. This altered method of "free" association was originally delineated by Jung. Freud asked, "What is the dream caused by?" Jung asked, "What does the dream mean?"[41]

This Jungian understanding of meaning has much in common with Derridian *desemination,* where meaning proliferates despite the rootlessness of existence.

Nathalie Sarraute

Having moved frequently between Russia and France during her first few years, Nathalie Sarraute became bilingual, while she later learned English and German well enough to attend Oxford and the Berlin Faculty of Letters. She writes in French, but with no allegiance to its shibboleths. Indeed, she was the first to write a "New Novel." Clichés that the monolingual speaker would take for granted she sees as masking a flux of what she calls "tropisms," the psychological patterns with which people jockey for control over one another. Beneath these "tropisms" (each person's struggles for identity and solidarity), she believes a soulless void lies gaping.

According to her essay "De Dostoievski à Kafka," the latter writer most brilliantly evoked emptiness and alienation, thereby becoming the precursor of her whole generation of writers. She sees him as being (like her) a Jew among foreigners. One might expect her to identify strongly with him. She feels, nonetheless, somewhat closer to Dostoevsky, though his empathic sensitivity—the trait for which she reveres him—is associated with his dream of uniting Russians in a Christian fellowship, which she has no desire to share.[42] Given a choice between (what seems to her) Kafka's totally bleak vision and Dostoevsky's awareness of life, her preference for the latter becomes understandable. Consequently, Kafka enters her works in an ironic fashion. In one of her most typical novels, *Martereau,* for example, the timid and effeminate narrator does initially identify with Kafka's Joseph K. (i.e., with Kafka). Overpowered by the personalities of his own uncle and of Martereau, Sarraute's narrator likens their way of walking on either side of him to the two "gentlemen," who, at the end of Kafka's novel *The Trial,* escort Joseph K. to his execution. Then Sarraute's narrator realizes that this likeness comes entirely from his own imagination.[43] Because of Kafka's rejection of psychology, his characters are simpler than Sarraute believes life to be. Craving this simplicity, the narrator of *Martereau* imagines that its title character is a monolithic, indeed, "archetypal" Father Figure. Note that for Sarraute, stereotypes seem "archetypal" not by reflecting psychological depth (the Jungian assumption) but by being (or seeming to be) two-dimensional characters. Nonetheless, the narrator's almost pathological fascination with Martereau sounds like Jung's descriptions of someone projecting an archetype.

In one of her most daring fictions, *Between Life and Death (Entre la vie et la mort),* Kafka appears less through his works than through her presentation of the legend of his life, particularly his inability to make his father take his writing seriously.[43] She uses him as an example of the insecure author, but her whole book shows this type to be so diverse as hardly to earn the name of type. Thus she brings against structuralism (and indirectly against Jung) the ultimate challenge that life (at least as depicted in her novels) does not conform to any typology. To raise this charge, however, she has written fiction without plot or coherent characters, going thereby even further than Kafka in her iconoclasm.

Alain Robbe-Grillet

Because of traditionalism in French education, Alain Robbe-Grillet underwent the usual curriculum of Greek and Latin before he could begin the scientific training that eventually brought him baccalaureates in mathematics and natural science, a certificate in machining, and a degree in agricultural engineering.[45] His moving from one technological specialty to another may evidence dissatisfaction with any of them but also may have something to do with traumatic events of the time, primarily the Nazi conquest, which forced him to do factory labor in Germany, interrupting his education. Like many anti-Nazi Frenchmen, he tried communism for a brief while. He ended, however, disliking any systematic approach to life: psychological, ideological, scientific, or humanistic—a disillusionment that influences his approach to Kafka and to his own writings. Climaxing his major manifesto, *For a New Novel,* he argues that Kafka's works are not allegories but should be read primarily for their surface detail. "The visible world of his novels is certainly for him the real world, and what is behind (if there is something) seems without value, faced with the manifest nature of objects, words, etc."[46] Actually, Kafka doubted the reality of the visible world rather than of the "something" beyond. As Robbe-Grillet rightly says, however, details in Kafka's stories do become all the more vivid because their relationship to anything beyond themselves remains unclear. Robbe-Grillet's literary technique is Kafkaesque in that he also deliberately keeps his works from making systematic sense.[47]

Since Robbe-Grillet tries to resist systematization, including psychology, any agreement between him and Jung's work is doubly significant. Consider, for example, Robbe-Grillet's first published novel, *The Erasers (Les gommes).* It begins describing:

> [one] day's events . . . [which] begin their task, gradually encroaching upon the ideal order, cunningly introducing an occasional inversion, a discrepancy, a confusion, a warp, in order to accomplish their work: a day in early winter without plan, without direction, incomprehensible and monstrous.[48]

The day sounds like a nightmare version of the Saturnalia, that classical holiday when society was temporarily inverted and confused as a break from dull, winter routine. Robbe-Grillet finds himself in the midst of a paradox. He wants to show a collapse in the order of his time (political, scientific, artistic, etc.) but anthropological evidence strongly suggests that each culture actually does work chaos into its structure—an expression of the human desire to include everything. His attempt to innovate echoes all previous innovations, seemingly repeating age-old "archetypes." One of these patterns reputedly (but not actually)[49] universal is Oedipus: in *The Erasers,* a detective, seeking a murderer, follows puzzling clues, for example, a painting of Thebes and a drunk who asks the Sphynx's riddle. Finally, like Oedipus, the detective finds that he is himself the murderer. In order to reconcile these reverberations of Oedipus with Robbe-Grillet's insistence on novelty, the critics Olga Bernal and Ilona Leki argue that the allusions are not really allusions. "The references to Oedipus are glimpses of the trap Robbe-Grillet does not want the reader to fall into."[50] This sounds as if the reader has a choice, but Robbe-Grillet is, in essence, demanding, don't think about Oedipus—

rather like saying, don't think about sex. Once Robbe-Grillet has broached the subject, literate readers are caught. The semiliterate (those unfamiliar with the classical heritage) are unlikely to bother with his book in the first place, unless they are required to do so by teachers, who will duly command them not to think about Oedipus and then probably spend a class period explaining the Oedipal myth. Jungians (and Freudians) would consider such an explanation almost unnecessary, Oedipus being allegedly an inescapable part of the human condition. As the finally insane protagonist incoherently mumbles fragments from the plot of Oedipus, the novel ends:

> Around him the familiar specters dance their waltz, like moths circling a lampshade and bumping into it, like dust in the sun, like little boats lost at sea, lulling to the sea's rhythm their delicate cargo, the old casks, the dead fish, the rigging and tackle, the buoys, the stale bread, the knives and the men. (*Gommes* 264; *Erasers* 256)

In this summary passage, the adjectives "old," "dead," and "stale" are apt, for the intercultural confusion of *The Erasers* goes beyond Bakhtinian "carnival" to a postmodern Lent that will not end in Easter celebration. The circular dance of this passage resembles the mandala or labyrinth. In discussing Robbe-Grillet's labyrinths (particularly *In the Labyrinth*), Ben Stoltzfus feels obligated to mention Jung among others.

> The circular pattern of most labyrinths puts them in the category of the Jungian mandala—a universal symbol of central importance to the psychic experience of man. . . . Bachelard, like Jung, believes that the figure of the labyrinth is an archetype for feelings of disorientation linked to childhood. . . . [As evidenced by their labyrinthine imagery], [t]he works of Joyce, Kafka, Beckett, Borges, Sartre, and Robbe-Grillet, among many others, reflect today's alienation, disorientation, and ennui.[51]

Do the orienting mandala and the disorienting labyrinth belong to the same "archetype," as Stolzfus assumes or different ones as Ionesco alleges? (We shall return to this point in chap. 9). Stolzfus also notes the extensive use of alchemical imagery in Robbe-Grillet's more recent work, *Souvenirs du triangle d'or* (32–44), and alchemical treatises form the literature in clearest conformity with Jungian psychology. Why does Robbe-Grillet introduce these "archetypal" patterns into his works? In order to make descriptions of objects fresh and vivid, he must break their customary associations. Jung writes of the Oedipal pattern:

> The impression made by . . . [remarking this archetype] may be likened to the uncanny feeling which would steal over us if, amid the noise and bustle of a modern city street, we were suddenly to come upon an ancient relic—say the Corinthian capital of a long-immured column, or a fragment of an inscription. A

> moment ago, and we were completely absorbed in the hectic, ephemeral life of the present; then, the next moment, something very remote flashes upon us, which directs our gaze to a different order of things. (*GW* vol. 5, par. 1)

The sudden horror of Oedipus confronted with his past; the confusion of being lost in a maze; the bewildering, magical imagery of alchemy—these are all patterns that contravene the drift of quotidian existence (a contravention common to "archetypes"). Similarly, Robbe-Grillet sometimes has characters who have died inexplicably appear once-again alive. He considers the New Testament a precursor of his New Novel.[52] In his book *For a New Novel,* he rejects the notion of the Unconscious inspiration of writers, specifically because of its theological associations. "The novelist, more than a creator in the strict sense [would], thus [be] a simple mediator between ordinary mortals and an obscure power, a force beyond humanity, an eternal spirit, a god" (11). At least according to Leki, however, Robbe-Grillet admits that his "Unconscious" actually does play a part in his composition process (146). His experience of composition and the needs of his writing nudge him toward a Jungian position, against his inclinations.

Philip Roth

> "I have out-Kafkaed Kafka"
>
> —Roth, *The Breast*

> Dr. Kafka calls and takes my Aunt Rhoda to a movie. I am astonished, both that he calls and that she goes; it seems there is more desperation in life than I have come across yet in my fish tank.
>
> —Roth, " 'I Always Wanted You to Admire My Fasting'; or, Looking at Kafka"

> What I started to say about Kafka, about reading Kafka, is that stories of obstructed, thwarted K.'s banging their heads against invisible walls, well, they suddenly had a disturbing new resonance for me.
>
> —Roth, *The Professor of Desire*

According to Philip Roth, his own *Portnoy's Complaint* is not merely a semiautobiographical account of his own Jewish childhood in Newark but is also modeled on the comic family in Kafka's "Metamorphosis."[53] Ever since this disclosure, the relationship of the two authors has occasioned much discussion as in Morton P. Levitt's "Roth and Kafka: Two Jews"[54] and Roth's own story " 'I Always Wanted You to Admire My Fasting'; or, Looking at Kafka." The latter begins with the forty-year-old Roth gazing at a picture of forty-year-old Kafka and wondering how the latter's last year could have been the least miserable in his life. "As Franz Kafka awoke one morning from uneasy dreams he found himself transformed in his bed into a father, a writer, and a Jew" (255). Roth largely derives this notion of relative happiness or hopefulness from Kafka's last story, "The Burrow." That tale concerns a burrowing labyrinth-builder, expecting imminent destruction from a hidden enemy. Roth's suggestion of anticipated happiness comes from his very Freudian assumption that the burrow itself represents Kafka's contemplation of Dora Dymant's (his companion's) private parts: "a fantasy of a hidden orifice that promises 'satisfied desires,' 'achieved ambition,' and 'profound slumber,' but that, once penetrated and in one's possession, arouses the most terrifying and heartbreaking fears of retribution and loss" (257). For Roth, the enigmatic "Burrow" has the same theme as so many of his own novels, sexual fantasy and repression. Next, he imagines what life might have been like for Kafka if the latter had emigrated to America, briefly dated Roth's Aunt Rhoda, been rejected by her as *meshugeh* (crazy), and finally died an unmarried, total failure. Roth has a rich imagination.

In *The Professor of Desire,* he includes another imaginary Kafka. While visiting Prague, the protagonist, David Kepesh, a university teacher like Roth himself, dreams that he learns previously undisclosed erotic information about Kafka from a prostitute. During the dream, Kepesh thinks that being in Prague helps him to realize more fully that Kafka was real, "and," the character Kepesh continues erroneously, "so am I real, nobody is making me up, other than myself" (188). Having frequently taught Kafka's works, Kepesh (like Roth) has written a paper on "spiritual starvation" in Kafka's fictions. Kepesh has come to Prague "by way of Vienna—and the house of Sigmund Freud" (165); thus, once in Prague, Kepesh not surprisingly interprets Kafka's starvation in a Freudian manner as more sexual than spiritual—a theory mildly ridiculed by one of the "many [Czechs who] survive almost solely on Kafka" (169) in a country that became a Kafkaesque nightmare. Does eroticism truly represent repressed Reality for Roth? Throughout his works, Roth admittedly refers obsessively to Freud but only in parody, as in *Portnoy's Complaint,* where a psychoanalist supposedly listens to over two hundred pages of agony before finally saying: "Now vee may perhaps to begin. Yes?"[55] In *The Breast,* David Kepesh, metamorphosed into a giant breast, wants to believe that his sensuality and study of Kafka are responsible for his malady, but he is repeatedly told that his condition is not psychosomatic. In Roth's *Zuckerman Bound,* the protagonist, another seeker after Kafka, suffers from debilitating but inexplicable pains, which he tries, again unsuccessfully, to consider psychosomatic. Although Roth consistently sexualizes the Unknown (from whence come these agonizing transformations), libido, despite its ubiquity, ultimately functions as a symbol for transcending the fictions people substitute for Reality. As early as his second book, *Letting Go* (1951), Roth has two characters argue over whether religion persists in a Jewish atheist's Unconscious. For Jung (perhaps an influence on this passage), the Unconscious is inherently religious, but Roth leaves the argument unresolved. Even while making Jewishness pervasive throughout his novels, Roth generally walls out Judaism. What meaning does he find in all the pain he portrays? In *Zuckerman Bound,* the title character approvingly quotes Kafka's words. "I believe that we should read only those books that bite and sting us. If a book we are reading does not rouse us with a blow to the head, then why read it?" (380). Then Zuckerman insists that this principle of confronting what is painful should be confined to literature. Zuckerman calls the search for disturbing meaning in life "mythomania." He acts as if one could distinguish ultimately between imaginary and Real. Nonetheless, in Roth's works, no clear-cut line divides fiction from fact. As in Kepesh's dream, we are at least partly the fictions that we create (even though Roth ignores the possibility of any other Creator). In Roth's bizarre autobiography, *The Facts,* his own fictional character Zuckerman writes to him:

> My guess is that you've written metamorphoses of yourself so many times, you no longer have any idea what *you* are or ever were. By now what you are is a walking text.[56]

Comparably, Kafka wrote, "[I] am made of literature." (*F* 304).

Vladimir Nabokov

Raised in a trilingual (English/French/Russian) family, Vladimir Nabokov was linguistically prepared for a life of exile when politics forced him from his native Russia. He subsequently lived in Western Europe, then America, and finally Switzerland. His first nine novels were composed in Russian, the rest in English. One of his more recent biographers, Andrew Field argues:

> [In *After Babel,*] George Steiner has put forward the view that Nabokov's multilingualism is the determining fact of both his life and his art. It is a very important fact, to be sure, but I don't think Steiner's case can be sustained as anything but opinion, because Nabokov said and believed firmly that he didn't think in any language but in images, and that a phrase in Russian or English would only form after the fact, like the ocean of his brainwaves. One of his denigrations of Freudianism was that there is a great deal more to an ocean than the breaking of its waves.[57]

Nabokov's attitude toward multilingualism, however, was even more complex than Field suggests. Nabokov was acutely aware that in the imprecisions of translation from one language to another, sometimes the images may be lost. K,[58] the mad commentator in *Pale Fire,* for example, searches in vain for the source of the book's title ("And her pale fire she snatches from the sun," *Timon of Athens,* IV, iii, 440). What makes that search particularly ironic is that he has *Timon of Athens* IV, iii, 440, lying open in front of him. Why doesn't he recognize it? Because it is allegedly in a "Zemblan" translation, which he then laboriously retranslates into the line, "He steals his silvery light from the sun."[59] (The final irony is that the "Zemblan" language cited frequently throughout K.'s commentary does not exist.) Even within a single (real) language, comparable problems may arise. Nabokov's character John Shade (the reputed author of the poem *Pale Fire*) temporarily bases his hope of immortality on the presumption that in two near-death experiences the revivified patients both glimpsed the numinous image of a "white fountain." Actually, in one of the cases, the patient wrote "mountain," which a careless typographer linotyped as "fountain" (*Pale Fire* 61–62). In other words, Nabokov occasionally comes close to a Jungian interest—images transcending language—but he knows that these images—or to use Field's metaphor—"waves"—are communicated, if at all, only by breaking on the dangerous rocks of actual words.

Like Jung and Kafka, Nabokov objects to Freudian theory: the exclusively sexual interpretation of the vagaries of communication, for example, puns or "Freudian" slips. To what extent can Nabokov probe beyond that level? During his academic career, Nabokov chose to teach one of his favorite works: Kafka's "Metamorphosis," which Nabokov analyzed thus:

> The trinity, the triplet, the triad, the triptych are obvious art forms such as, say, three pictures of youth, ripe years, and old age, or any other threefold triplex subject. Triptych means a picture or carving in three compartments side by side, and this is exactly the effect that Kafka achieves, for instance, with his three rooms in the beginning of the story—living room, Gregor's bedroom, and sister's room, with Gregor in the central one. Moreover, a threefold pattern suggests the three acts of a play.[60]

Unlike Jung, Nabokov's numerology makes no search for profound meanings but sees the "trinity" as merely one of many "art forms" with no communicable relationship to psychological or theological depths. Considering the often-noted similarity between the layout of Gregor's and Kafka's family flat, one might more plausibly contend that the "three rooms" are essentially autobiographical. Nabokov's remark, however, is at least relevant to his own works, for example, the following scene from *Pale Fire,* concerning John Shade, his wife, and daughter:

> The point is that the three
> Chambers, then bound by you and her and me,
> *Now* form a triptych or a three-act play
> In which portrayed events forever stay. (46)

Shade's daughter (who slid into madness) is like Gregor (whose metamorphosis has sometimes been taken as a metaphor for mental illness), but the more important point is the narrator's desire to see the triple image as part of an eternal pattern, one that will "forever stay." Desire for such archetypal presences runs throughout Nabokov's works (e.g., in *Lolita,* H. H.'s imagining that the title character is no mere little girl but a nonhuman, "demoniac . . . nymphet").[61] Nabokov, however, always shows that images of eternity or eternal youth are never really manifest in life; indeed, he generally seems to recognize (like Kafka) that even art can never deliver them but only parody them in empty gestures. As Leona Toker has argued, however, this emptiness is not necessarily mere aesthetic escapism. Like Schopenhauerian (or Buddhist) emptiness, it may be a way of breaking down an old perception of the world, which, as Nabokov writes, "begins to rot and stink as soon as the act of individual creation ceases to animate a subjectively perceived texture."[62]

Julio Cortázar

Born (1914) of Argentinians living in Brussels, Julio Cortázar at age four returned with his parents to Buenos Aires, where he eventually became a teacher of French and English literature. Despite permanently expatriating to Paris (1951), Cortázar has continued to write in Spanish (except for the numerous foreign allusions, phrases, and quotations, which patchwork his style). He gained international stature through his second novel, *Hopscotch (Rayuela),* which consists of three parts: the first set in Europe; the second in Latin America; and the third, a group of "expendable" *(prescindibles)* chapters, most with no specific setting, reflecting the musings of Morelli, a persona of Cortázar. The book's preface contains a chart showing one way these appended chapters can be interpolated into the first two parts, though the volume constitutes "many books," the exact arrangement of chapters ultimately at the discretion of the reader.

A number of passages in the third part theorize about the function of reader involvement in modern novels, including the following sentences:

> There is a kind of extrapolation through which [certain characters] jump out at us or we at them. Kafka's K. has the same name as his reader, or vice versa.[63]

Not only are readers forced to decide where to insert this section in the novel, but they must deal with the fact that it comes to them through two distorting personae, first Wong, whose words these are and, second, Morelli, whose theories Wong summarizes. Morelli is presented as being somewhat "confused" *(confusa),* while Wong sometimes seems insane. Although all readers are not literally named "K.," Kafka by using such a vague name may lead readers to consider K. an everyman, at once Kafka and themselves, thus the pronouncement of Wong/Morelli makes some sense, indeed is analogous to Cortázar's own practice. His insistence on eliciting readers' involvement in his novel may erode the distinction between his readers, his characters, and himself. At any rate, Morelli rejects the traditional notion that an author stands apart from his readers, transmitting to them a message. "There is no message, only messengers" *(no hay mensaje, hay mensajeros).*[64] A possible source of this remark is Kafka's parable of the children who chose to become messengers instead of kings, so that there was no king and no royal message for them to carry. Cortázar does not unravel the paradox but does manage to give absurdist literature a function: writing that focuses on the relationship between writer and reader (rather than trying to convey a "message") may transform the reader into the writer's "traveling companion," a fellow messenger. *Angst* suffuses the absurdity of messengers without messages, generating the dissatisfaction and bewilderment that the character Talita considers to be "like a trial."[65] The same fear of situations that manage to be both ominous and seemingly pointless, the condition Kafka so perfectly embodied in his *Trial,* persists into Cortázar's next novel, *62: A Model Kit*. In a study of Cortázar, Steven Boldy writes of that novel, "The anguished atmosphere is reminiscent of Kafka."[66]

62: A Model Kit derives its title from its being the realization of a project envisioned by Morelli in chapter 62 of *Hopscotch.* It proposes making into the "impersonal" the interaction between the characters' "subliminal" minds, constituting an interrelationship that can only be seen by a "third eye." Boldy likens this configuration to the "constellation" of internal psychological events and external coincidences that Jung calls "Synchronicity," from "the activation of unconscious archetypes."[67] In *Hopscotch,* Cortázar uses the phrase "archetypal vision" *(visión arquetípica)* to describe one of the character's ravings.[67] Also in *Hopscotch,* Cortázar repeatedly evokes the very Jungian image of his novel/antinovel as a "mandala," through which the characters and readers hop toward "Heaven, Home."[69] But this quest is also like hopscotch, a childish game.

Thus Cortázar's treatment of "archetypal" patterns is, much like Kafka's, marked by incertitude and irony.

Nicanor Parra

The antipoet reserves the right to make contradictory formulations.
—Parra, in a seminar, NYU, 1971

Nicanor Parra, Professor of Theoretical Physics at the University of Chile and winner of numerous prizes for his poetry, has interwoven scientific, literary, and political concerns in his interdisciplinary career, particularly when, after several years of studying in the United States and Great Britain, he began writing what he calls "antipoetry" (published in *Poemas y antipoemas,* 1954, and in subsequent volumes). In one of these antipoems, he complains that he is "not resigned" to a university teacher's "VI(U)DA"—a portmanteau word combining "life" *(vida)* and "widow" *(viuda).* He images his condition as that of a mourning wife with "the corpse of Galileo" (Grossman xxiv). Despite wishing to escape academic concerns, he must derive his widow's mite therefrom. Instead, he wanted to be an antipoet of the people, as one model of which he turned first to Kafka's "metaphysical laughter"[70] (1946), a "wavering between triviality and transcendence."[71] According to Parra, "Kafka is a creator of atmospheres."[72] Instead of trying to stay within a single system of poetic diction, Parra's antipoetry (poetry turned against itself) can include anything from bits of conversation to advertising clichés as long as his antipoems generate the appropriate feeling. Like Kafka's "Description of a Struggle," Parra emphasizes that words have no inevitable relation to their referents. In "Cambros de nombre," for instance, he suggests renaming the sun "Puss-in-Boots" and urges each person to give God a new name (*Obra Gruesa* 83). In a surreal world where ties between word and referent as well as boundaries between reality and fantasy have broken down, Parra, in one antipoem, speaks of losing his "most necessary prejudices" (the preconceptions needed to function in the world) and slipping into a telephone (emblematic of modern communications, which wipe away the old preconceptions), so that he likens the device to an "abyss" *(abismo).*[73] His world has transcendence, for example, the luminous butterfly pursued in his antipoem entitled *"Socorro!"* ("Help!"), yet while the work's speaker is engaged in this chase, he falls down and bloodies his nose (*Obra Gruesa* 178). All the "archetypal" baggage of the poetic tradition (e.g., the butterfly/soul, the "abyss," and God) dissolves in a laughter that Parra considers the only true seriousness. In another antipoem, he explicitly identifies it with "Kafka's [comic] seriousness,"[74] which Parra has strangely metamorphosed into engagé literature, fascinated with the collapse of the capitalist system (through internal contradiction). Nonetheless, he sometimes praises the United States and criticizes Russia.[75] He is (playfully) critical of psychoanalysis, in one antipoem listing "dream analysis" as a vice[76] and, in another antipoem, his persona deems neurosis healthy because it may lead to great accomplishments.[77] From time to time, he ridicules Freud, whose attempt to make patients normal runs counter to Parra's iconoclastic inclinations—an iconoclasm that eventualy caused him to drop the title "antipoet," just as he previously moved beyond other self-definitions.

Abe Kōbō

Born in Tokyo, Abe Kōbō lived in Manchuria until his early twenties when he returned to his native city. Considering that despite massive cultural borrowings from abroad, Japan tends to be both literally and figuratively insular, his being raised on the mainland may have contributed to the alienation central to his works. He philosophizes thus:

> If we seriously delve into the question of where we belong, it turns out that man has no place to belong to except himself. The inquiry into this sense of belonging is a motif found everywhere in my writings, and especially in *The Box Man* I have just finished, I have tried to see what would happen to man if he pursues, to the utmost extent, where he really belongs.[78]

He graduated from medical school (like his physician-father), but he never practiced and his books evidence a strong revulsion for his father's profession—another side to his alienation.

Abe is the only major Japanese writer consistently compared to Kafka. As a youth, Abe read the latter along with some German philosophy.[79] Haniya Yutaka has likened the two authors' spatial imagery.[80] More obvious is their common mood of absurdity and desolation. In his novel *Secret Rendezvous (Mikkai),* for example, the story begins one morning when an ambulance suddenly arrives and kidnaps the narrator's healthy wife while he lies next to her in bed, rather like the inexplicable morning arrest in Kafka's novel *The Trial.* The narrator refers to himself vaguely either as "I" or as "the man" (comparable to the almost equally anonymous K. of *The Trial*). Abe's man works for a vast, invidious, investigative agency, which turns out to be secretly financed by the hospital. Throughout most of the novel, however, this bureaucracy remains as enigmatic as Kafka's courts. Just as a court record in *The Trial* turns out to be pornographic, so, in *Secret Rendevzous,* the doctors' motive for founding a surveillance agency is pure voyeurism—a depravity Abe seems to consider characteristic of the whole medical profession. The narrator tries to resist the mysterious agency that employs him, but ends fruitlessly begging for mercy as he awaits death in a refuse-filled room of the hospital—a conclusion as depressing as K.'s execution.

In *Secret Rendezvous,* the man's search for his wife turns out to be a search for himself—a theme that Abe often uses playfully: Individuation, involving quest for the female side of the psyche, or, as Jung calls it, the "anima." In Abe's masterpiece, *The Box Man,* for example, the title character says of his girlfriend, when she has left him, that "even she" can be found within the "labyrinth" of the cardboard box he wears—a symbol of his fragmented self.[81] Comparably, he once dreamed of losing a betrothed and devoting his life to drawing pictures of her, a pattern common in Occidental Romantic literature, where artistic devotion to the feminine image within the artist's mind sometimes takes the place of ordinary heterosexuality. At another point in *The Box Man,* its title charcter argues, perhaps jokingly, that the girl and another character, "the false box man," are actually unreal. "Of course, only one of the three of us really exists; the one, who is in fact, continuing to write these notes" (*Hako Otoko,* 108; *Box Man,* 100–1). In Jungian terms, the "false box man" or false self would be called the Shadow, the part of himself that the Box Man represses.

The Box Man hopes that when he finally removes the box he will be resurrected in "another [or different] world" *(betsu no sekai)* like a butterfly arising from the chrysalis—an "archetypal" theme of rebirth (*Hako Otoko* 48; *Box Man,* 41). His hope (vaguely modeled on Amida Buddhist belief in rebirth in a Pure Land) is expressed in a three-line poem, somewhat like a haiku, except that, in violation of tradition, the lines are longer (one of the book's modern or postmodern touches, e.g., the inclusion of photographs and bureaucratic documents). Believing that man must find community within himself, Abe almost inevitably has to show a group of imaginary beings (Jung's "archetypal images") within the Box Man's mind. As early as the first Japanese novelistic masterpiece, Lady Murasaki's *The Tale of Genji* (*Genji monogatari,* eleventh century A.D.), the question: " 'Who am I?' [i]n Lady Murasaki's view seems best approached (although not fully answered) by examining the role of love as a means to self-definition."[82] Abe, thus, is not entirely untraditional in seeing the Box Man's self as defined by his love, though Abe is slightly innovative by hinting that the love is an anima image within the man's mind. Japanese Buddhism, however, had already affirmed that all phenomena were simply products of Mind (the *alayavijnana* or Storehouse Consciousness). Furthermore, Abe, with Japanese reticence, refrains from affirming the existence of these archetypal patterns leaving them merely as notions of his decidedly errant characters. Ultimately, his chief focus is on emptiness, most obviously in his recent novel, *The Ark Sakura (Hakobune no sakura).* Like the paranoid, burrowing protagonist of Kafka's *"Der Bau,"* Abe's paranoid, burrowing protagonist (who likes to be called "Mole") spends years booby-trapping his mazelike hole, but unlike Kafka's story, Abe concludes with the Mole's destroying his lair and finding that everything has become transparent, the material world opening on underlying emptiness.[83]

Milan Kundera

> [The character Franz] felt like a rider galloping off into a magnificent void [*nádherného prázdna*].
>
> —Kundera, *The Unbearable Lightness of Being* [*Nesnesitelná Lehkost Bytí*]

> If one were only . . . on a racing steed . . . until . . . one scarcely saw the smooth plain and the horse's neck and head were gone.
>
> —Kafka, "The Wish to Be an Indian"

Prohibited from publishing in his own country, the Czech émigré Milan Kundera lives in France and travels abroad. Denied a Czech audience, he must publish in translations, though he can only supervise these in the four foreign languages that he knows. Like so many of his fellow Czech liberals, Kundera respectfully refers to Kafka from time to time, but their relationship is complex as can be seen by contrasting even the briefest sample of their writing.

In both of these quotations the riders appear to enjoy the ride into vacuity, and for Kafka himself such a journey might have positive significance (mystic self-loss through identification with Reality, though he was ambivalent about such self-destruction). Kundera's oxymoron "magnificent void" is even more ironic, first because the Czech word translated as "void" [*prázdna*] denotes vacuum rather than anything grandly Buddhistic. Second, Franz is trying to forget his wife by "riding" his mistress in a search to transcend the boundaries of his life, a quest harshly criticized by Kundera's narrator. In *The Book of Laughter and Forgetting (Kniha smíchu a zapomnení)* Kundera quotes a question from Goethe's *East-West Divan:* "Is one man alive when others are alive?" Then, Kundera's narrator answers that writers each try to become a universe, such as the "universe of Kafka" *(universu Kafkově),* so that they see the existence of other authors or *"universes"* as a *"threat"* (*Ksz* 115; *BLF* 105). In other words, literature creates separate worlds rather than reflecting the real one. If Kundera's narrator wishes to wall himself away within his private world, he shares this desire with other of Kundera's narrators who remake the influences on them so that they can absorb them more easily. In *The*

Book of Laughter and Forgetting, for example, Kundera describes what for Czechs has become a famous photograph, the meeting (over twenty years after Kafka's death) of the Communist leaders Gottwald and Clementis (in an area of Prague that Kafka had once frequented). The narrator comments, "Gottwald, Clementis, and all the others did not know about Kafka, and Kafka knew they did not know" (*Ksz* 167; *BLF* 157). Could this narrator really look into the minds of the officials and of the long-deceased Kafka in order to know what they understood? For Kundera, remembering is a creative act where fact and fiction merge, permitting the subtle rewriting of his country's history. His Kafka is a "prophet" who foresaw a land without memory.

> Time [*Čas*] in Kafka's novel is the time of a humanity [*lidstva*] that has lost all continuity with humanity, of a humanity that no longer knows anything nor remembers anything, that lives in nameless cities with nameless streets or streets with names different from the ones they had yesterday, because a name means continuity with the past and people without a past are people without a name. (*Ksz* 167; *BLF* 157)

Was Kafka really foreseeing? Typically, in a 1922 Diary, he complains that he must invent substitutes for "ancestors, marriage, and descendants" (*D* 207). His isolation from past, present, and future seems centered on his quarrels with his father, his unwillingness to marry, and his lack of children rather than on a vision of Czech politics two decades later. In *The Art of the Novel,* however, Kundera contends that Kafka seems to predict the future by discovering certain archetypal potentialities in humanity ("power [as] . . . boundless labyrinth," "the file [as] Platonic idea," the accused seeking an offense, "the horror of the comic").[84] Kundera decries the totalitarian rewriting of history, yet the novel he composes in protest against it, *The Book of Laughter and Forgetting,* itself rewrites the past to create his own universe with himself *almost* the totalitarian ruler thereof. What undermines his absolute control of his writings is that they describe and mirror the postmodern condition, the blurring of all boundaries—presented by Kundera as a frightening or depressing condition (perhaps one reason why in interviews and critical writings he longs for neoclassical order and reason). Jan, the book's protagonist, repeatedly feels this blurring. While making love "there was only a fraction of an inch separating intercourse from laughter, and he was terrified of overstepping it; there was only a fraction of an inch separating him from the border, and across the border things no longer had any meaning [*smysl*]" (*Ksz* 222; *BLF* 214). Two pages later, he wonders why "the image of the border keep[s] coming back to him." He thinks that it is because of his age, since each time an act is repeated it loses vitality and consequently the illusion of meaning. The narrator, however, asserts that the boundary between meaning and meaninglessness is omnipresent and that repetition merely makes the boundary visible (*Ksz* 226–27; *BLF* 217–18). A few pages later, at the close of the book, Jan, standing among nudists, feels that he has finally crossed the border into absurdity. In an interview with Philip Roth, not contained in the original Czech version of the novel, but appended to its English translation, Kundera denounces the Communist search for Paradise as inevitably bringing a return to childish inanity. He associates this search with Russia and the East. In contrast, he recalls the "Western" accomplishments of Central Europe, "Bartók's music, Kafka's and Musil's new aesthetics of the novel" (*BLF* 230). He suggests that the (Soviet) Eastern decline into meaninglessness is through forgetting, while the (Kafkan) Western way is through ironic laughter, but, although Kundera seems to make a polemical distinction between them, they merge in their result—meaninglessness. (After examining Kafka's connection with Taoism, I wonder at the choice of him as a representative Western author; indeed, there may not be any major, modern authors completely "Occidental"—if that word has any ultimate significance.) Kundera adds that, by undermining tradition, Western technology also leads toward forgetting the past by declaring it obsolete. Why repeated traditions provide meaning while repeated love-making generates meaninglessness, Kundera does not yet say. *The Book of Laughter and Forgetting* also distinguishes between ironic and fanatical laughter; however, in one surreal scene, a zealous teacher and ironic pupils join in both kinds of hilarity further mixed with tears until teacher and two students become so light that they float through the ceiling—one of many evidences that Kundera has difficulty showing what real, viable life lies beyond the boundary of meaning.

In his next book, *The Unbearable Lightness of Being*, the protagonist (Franz) arrives at the phrase "living in truth" partly as a recollection of one of Kafka's diaries.[85] He becomes "captivated" by the words (*Nlb* 104–5; *ULB* 112), perhaps because Franz is so obviously living a lie. The narrator explains that Franz's mistress cannot "live in truth" so long as her actions are public. Does this mean that Kafka held a similar view? Actually, he asserted the opposite and more paradoxical position that truth was only possible in public (*D* 308). Kundera's narrator sees the problem of truth in terms of Heraclitus's river, never the same from instant to instant, a "semantic river," which, as individuals age, constantly enriches their language through experience, but at the price of making it less communicable. In contrast to this living richness stands "Kitsch" [*kýč*], overly simple, idealized images used to conceal the void beyond meaning: "kitsch is a folding screen set up to curtain off death" (*Nlb* 230; *ULB* 253). In other words, the reduction of life to stock images (kitsch) conceals the truth that everything is perishable, consequently unique, thus irreplaceable. Is Kundera's Kafka (prophet of forgetting and writer about "living in truth") much more complex or true to life than kitsch? But then Kundera does not entirely reject kitsch. His narrator readily admits that stock images do make up an important part of life: traditions. He does not wish these, however, to invade the private sphere, depriving it of its uniqueness. In an interview in *Le monde,* he praises Jung and talks of "myths" in the "collective consciousness"—but, unlike Jung, Kundera does not represent them as messengers from bottomless depths, but simply as stock images, kitsch.[86] Despite Kundera's dislike of dogmas and movements (e.g., his attack on neo-Christianity in his earlier novel *The Farewell Party* or on Romanticism in his even earlier novel *Life Is Elsewhere*), he not only accepts the existence of stock patterns but sometimes writes as if the border beyond them were natural, not arbitrary. Indeed, his introduction to his play *Jacques and His Master* quite vehemently praises neoclassical rationalism. Kundera's fiction moves toward apocalyptic violence, but he does not seem eager for an apocalyptic revelation. Philip Roth even begins this interview with Kundera by asking the latter if he believes that the world will "soon" end. After some banter over the meaning of the word *soon,* Kundera admits that he now sees "Europe as fragile, mortal" (*BLF* 230). Everything is crumbling into Kafkan laughter and Jungian kitsch.

8
Ravens

> Thou Raven, said I, thou Raven of misfortune [*Unglücksrabe*], what doest thou forever in my way . . . it replied . . . even to me the situation has become somewhat uncomfortable.
>
> —Kafka

In three fragments from the same notebook as his apostrophe to the Raven, Kafka calls a pet animal "Nevermore" (*Nimmermehr, H* 138–39; D 115).[1] Apparently, Kafka had read Poe's "The Raven," which ends:

> Take thy beak from out my heart, and take thy form from off my door!
> Quoth the Raven, "Nevermore."[2]

In "A Fratricide," Kafka asks about a passive observer of suffering: "Why did Pallas . . . who was watching it all . . . permit it to happen?" (*BK* 146). Poe writes of his Raven, another passive observer of suffering: "Perched upon a bust of Pallas . . . / Perched, and sat, and nothing more." Kafka's Raven, however, is not merely an echo of Poe's. As previously discussed (chap. 2), Kafka identified with ominous birds, the Raven among them. This identification with the ominous is an autobiographical element, a suggestion that he is trying futilely to rid himself of what Jungians call the "shadow" (the undesirable, repressed side of oneself) while that "shadow" is almost equally unnerved by confrontation with the ego. A reader of Kafka's German would also think of the bird's Teutonic associations: the ill-omened Ravens of Odin, a god of painfully acquired wisdom (costing one of his eyes) and of sacrificial death. His frightening winged-messengers were called Thuginn (thought) and Muninn (memory), a surprisingly modern or postmodern image of consciousness as portentous, a bringer of fear and dread. The Germanic religious answer to the suffering inherent in consciousness was sacrifice, accepting torment as a meaningful part of life. Thus, in the *Havamal* (an Icelandic poetic Edda recorded in the thirteenth century), Odin, this god of scavenging ravens, proclaims:

> I know that I hung in the windy tree
> For nine whole nights,

> Wounded with the spear, dedicated to Odin,
> Myself to myself.[3]

In imitation of his sacred suicide (from which he rose to new life), animals and men were hanged at Upsala, his holy glade. Because of the late date when the Eddas were recorded, exact details of his atoning death may come to us with some Christian coloring, but it is hard to find any religion that completely lacks imagery of sacrifice. Even in the modern period (essentially the nineteenth and first half of the twentieth centuries), praise of sacrifice continued, but largely in secular terms, for example, giving one's life for one's country or suffering for art. By the postmodern period (the 1960s and thereafter), these quasi-religious trappings of patriotism and Romanticism had worn thin. Consequently, there was no longer (if there had ever been) a universally accepted spell to banish the visitations of anxiety. Today, these "leopard"-like authors at least partly find consolation by discovering new meaning in old values. The "frog"-like authors prefer contemporary life to be "empty," even though few Occidentals find a Buddhistic consolation in emptiness. As the Buddha reputedly said:

> When one sees existence, one is afraid; when one sees inexistence one is also afraid. Therefore one should not be attached to existence and should not be attached to inexistence.[4]

A third group of authors is neither fascinated with old values nor with value-free emptiness, but they are obsessed with the horror that humanity contains or that humanity constitutes an inescapable evil. In his gloomiest moods (e.g., his apostrophe to the Raven), Kafka belongs to this group, but his work anticipates not just this somber wing of postmodernism but others as well. Classification of actual literature is always arbitrary, but certain authors do seem especially vulnerable to *Anxt*. These sensitive ones can be termed "raven"-like—or should one, perhaps, call them "swan"-like when their works are beautiful swan songs.[5] Their plaintive laments reduce life to two choices: (1) accept evil, suffering, and death sadomasochistically; or (2) fight a losing battle against the "shadow" inherent within themselves.

Although the charge of sadomasochism is quite common, overt sadomasochism is sufficiently rare so that a single example, Yukio Mishima, may suffice. During his teens, in his poem "Evil Things" *(Magagoto),* he writes, "I waited each evening . . . for evil omens."[6] The speaker's longing for portents contrasts neatly with the Kafkan wish that they depart. After Mishima committed *hara-kiri,* the critic Jun Eto wrote that *Magagoto* "held the clue to all Mishima's literature."[7] Certainly, fantasies of torture and suicide form almost a refrain in many of Mishima's works. In his semiautobiographical *Confessions of a Mask,* for example, the protagonist is flooded with cruel imaginings, including a torture machine where metal points press deeply into the victim's flesh, perhaps modeled after the similar device in Kafka's "Penal Colony." Mishima, however, is seldom really Kafkaesque. Rather than focusing on futile struggles, he more characteristically depicts diabolical successes, such as in *Gogo no eikō* (translated as *The Sailor Who Fell from Grace with the Sea*), where a boy (accompanied by his friends) manages literally to dissect a kindly foster father. In an important biography, John Nathan quotes large numbers of documents to support the supposition that Mishima actually enjoyed the pain of turning himself from a frail intellectual (the hyperconscious self he despised) into a muscle-bound, pseudo-samurai in preparation for a spectacular suicide.[8] Mishima posed as a kind of "leopard," fighting to renew an ancient Japanese culture that had already passed away, but as he was acutely aware, his house and way of dressing were flagrantly Western, and he spent much time visiting the Occident. Even his *Hagakure nyumon,* his book-length treatise on suicide and the samurai ethic, is peppered with English words and allusions to world literature. In a provocative article, "Suicide and the Japanese Postmodern: A Postnarrative Paradigm?" Alan Wolfe has explored some of the ambiguities of Mishima's suicide, diversely seen as political protest, self-parody, or even "pastiche."[9] One thing the death probably was not, however, was an admission of futility and despair. Mishima's work is more often a contrast to Kafkaesque literature than a part of it.

The Kafkaesque, "Raven"-like authors treated in this chapter are not all suicides. Suicide, *per se,* may have virtually any meaning. These authors' writings, however, are haunted by depression and death.

Kurt Vonnegut

One of the best-known American novels of this century words its title page as follows:

SLAUGHTERHOUSE-FIVE
OR
THE CHILDREN'S
CRUSADE
A DUTY-DANCE WITH DEATH
BY
KURT VONNEGUT, JR.
A FOURTH-GENERATION GERMAN-AMERICAN
NOW LIVING IN EASY CIRCUMSTANCES
ON CAPE COD
[AND SMOKING TOO MUCH],
WHO, AS AN AMERICAN INFANTRY SCOUT

HORS DE COMBAT,
AS A PRISONER OF WAR,
WITNESSED THE FIRE-BOMBING
OF DRESDEN, GERMANY,
"THE FLORENCE OF THE ELBE,"
A LONG TIME AGO,
THIS IS A NOVEL
SOMEWHAT IN THE TELEGRAPHIC SCHIZOPHRENIC
MANNER OF TALES
OF THE PLANET TRALFAMADORE,
WHERE THE FLYING SAUCERS
COME FROM.
PEACE.[10]

Central to this mass of detail (announcing the main themes of the book) is one of its least obtrusive ironies, his self-description as a "German-American." That divided identity affected his perspective when he fought against the Germans, became their prisoner, was almost killed by American planes, and finally wrote a book condemning the Allied fire-bombing. In a 1977 interview he expressed his particular ambivalence thus:

> I tried a few words [of German] I knew on our captors, and they asked me if I was of German ancestry, and I said, "Yes." They wanted to know why I was making war against my brothers. . . . I honestly found the question ignorant and comical. My parents had separated me so thoroughly from my Germanic past that my captors might as well have been Bolivians or Tibetans, for all they meant to me.[11]

Slaughterhouse-Five is structured around three captures: that of Vonnegut himself as "GERMAN-AMERICAN," that of Billy Pilgrim by the Germans, and that of Billy by the Trafalmadorian aliens. Although the book deliberately leaves undecidable the question of whether Billy hallucinated that last capture, from time to time Vonnegut suggests that the Trafalmadorians are merely figments of Billy's imagination, fragments of his possibly "SCHIZOPHRENIC" identity. Thus he may have been captured by a part of himself stranger to him than "Bolivians or Tibetans." In other words, Vonnegut transforms his own predicament as a German-American deprived of a Germanic past into some form that metaphorically suggests his ambiguous feelings. In *Mother Night,* for example, the American Howard W. Campbell, Jr. (another Jr. and writer like Vonnegut) ends unsure whether he became a German war criminal or an American hero. Almost equally transparent as a reference to Vonnegut's position as German American, in *Deadeye Dick,* Otto Waltz, despite being a patriotic American, seems like a traitor to his countrymen because he expressed pro-German sentiments before World War II commenced. Although Vonnegut is the most famous veteran of the Dresden bombing, he refused to appear in a film about it because, as he told an interviewer, "I had a German name."[12] In *Palm Sunday: An Autobiographical Collage,* he gently chides his parents for raising him "ignorant and rootless" by withholding his Germanic heritage (21).

On the preceding page he voices a comparably complex attitude toward the Germanic author perhaps most important to him.

> [Despite being nicknamed "K,"], I have never identified with the "K" in Kafka's works, by the way. Having grown up in a democracy, I have dared to imagine that I know at all times who is really in charge, what is really going on. This could be a mistake.

By noting that his trust may be "a mistake," he at that instant identifies with Kafka's K. Comparable jokes occur throughout Vonnegut's works. Central to one another is the Kafkaesque notion that people do not really know who controls them. In *The Sirens of Titan,* for example, the course of human history turns out to have been covertly shaped by an extraterrestrial alien. In *Jailbird,* a bag lady secretly controls the entire American economy. In *Cat's Cradle,* the dictator of a miniscule, largely ignored country destroys the world. In *Slapstick,* unbeknownst to virtually everyone, the destruction of all human life is being effected by invisible, microbe-sized Chinese that enter bodies like germs—a bizarre instance of Vonnegut's alien-within motif.

Appropriately, Vonnegut acts as narrator in the documentary film, *The Trials of Franz Kafka.* It presents the latter's works as foreshadowing the atrocities of World War II—the least scholarly interpretation. More defensibly, Vonnegut's own opus can be seen as partly colored by memories of those horrors, whether described directly or through analogues such as the genocide of the Armenians in *Bluebeard.* An attempted M.A. thesis in anthropology (which, elsewhere, I have argued was seminal to Vonnegut's development)[13] singles out Kafka's "Metamorphosis" to exemplify one of the basic patterns in our culture—things going from bad to worse.[14] For Vonnegut, Kafka represents the depressing side of Germanic culture: an authoritarian world where no one knows the secret conduits of power and where puzzling, terrible misfortunes befall the unfortunate. Vonnegut occasionally makes use of specifically Kafkan images of this nightmare world, as where Campbell likens his condition to a "burrow . . . secret and snug" invaded by an unidentified "something" (cf., Kafka's "Der Bau").[15]

Vonnegut's (irrationally) happy Germanic author *par excellence* is the Jungian-influenced Hermann Hesse—representative of fairy tales and pleasant mysteries. Vonnegut seldom tires of attacking Hessian optimism. In *Slaughterhouse-Five,* the Trafalmadorian view of time (shown by

Vonnegut to be monstrous) comes from the culminating revelation about eternity in Hesse's *Siddhartha.* The book's subtitle, the "Children's Crusade" may derive from Hesse's novel *The Journey to the East.* Although Hesse apparently approves of the quest, he has those characters unsympathetic to the journey call it "The Children's Crusade."[16] *Slapstick* ends with a travesty of Hessian fairy tales, rendered grotesque by being set in a hopeless future. In the essay "Why They Read Hesse," Vonnegut belittles that author, "While his former countrymen were dying and killing in the trenches, Hermann Hesse was being psychoanalyzed by Carl Jung in a multilingual peaceful little land."[17] Vonnegut's critique of Hesse also indirectly constitutes a reaction against Jung. For the latter, fairy tales contain archetypal patterns through which the Collective Unconscious leads the psyche toward Individuation. In the aforementioned attempt at an M.A. thesis, Vonnegut examines the common pattern behind Cinderella and the Judeo-Christian vision of history. His conclusion, however, is not that the pattern is "archetypal" (as Jung believes) but that it is unique to our culture. In a speech he has given at various university campuses, he suggested that the pattern is also pathological.[18] Similarly, in *Mother Night,* Campbell is driven to suicide partly by the Occidental desire that life should be a story with "a beginning, a middle, an end—and, whenever possible, a moral too."[19] In *Deadeye Dick,* the narrator argues for three pages that people and nations may become suicidal if they try to turn life into a shapely tale with a clear-cut end.[20] The heart of *Cat's Cradle* is the Bokononist religion, which gives drama to life by deliberately establishing the persecution of itself in a cruel manner, which Sandbank compares to the torture machine of Kafka's story "In the Penal Colony."[21] Indeed, Vonnegut's books contain some bizarre religions that he invents (e.g., "the Church of God, the Utterly Indifferent" in *The Sirens of Titan*), all of which make their devotees suffer to fit an insane dream of order.

While finding fewer archetypes than Jung does, Vonnegut has much to say about one instinctual drive. "We are full of chemicals which require us to belong to folk societies [close-knit groups], or failing that, to feel lousy all the time."[22] He adds that this insight "explain[s] *everything*" and goes beyond the psychology of Freud. His sources include what Vonnegut learned during drug therapy for clinical depression and also Robert Redfield's anthropology (which Vonnegut studied in Chicago).[23] Nonetheless, Vonnegut's theory of depression and loneliness has, in common with Jungian psychology, the postulation of an unconscious instinct for unity. Jung, however, tended to associate his archetypes with voices of the past while Vonnegut, from a typically deracinated, American perspective, presumes that loneliness expresses a longing for a community of the living. In more buoyant moods he presumes that Kafkan loneliness and *Anxt* can be overcome by democratic, open societies, but, then, as he repeatedly admits, he "can be mistaken."

Salman Rushdie

As Bombay-born émigré in London, Salman Rushdie made controversial literature from his dissatisfaction with the East, the West, and himself:

> As for me: I, too, like all migrants, am a fantasist. . . . Sometimes I . . . see myself as a tree, even, rather grandly, as the ash Yggdrasil, the mythical world-tree of Norse legend. The ash Yggdrasil has three roots. One falls into the pool of knowledge by Valhalla, where Odin comes to drink. A second is being slowly consumed in the undying fire of Muspelheim. . . . The third is gradually being gnawed through by a fearsome beast called the Nidhögg. And when fire and monster have destroyed two of the three, the ash will fall, and darkness will descend. The twilight of the gods: a tree's dream of death.[24]

In *Shame* (from which this extract comes), he prefaces this despairing self-portrait with a description of the hope in the eyes of arriving émigrés. Apparently, it is short-lived because of

> the emptiness of one's luggage. I'm speaking of invisible suitcases, not the physical, perhaps cardboard, variety containing a few meaning-drained mementoes: we have come unstuck from more than land. We have floated upwards from history, from memory, from Time.

He then expands on this image of rootlessness by quoting a remark that Milan Kundera made about Kafka and Czechoslovakia, the nameless, memoryless condition that the former wrote about and the latter embodies. Later, Rushdie quotes Kafka himself, in the end of *The Trial,* where Joseph K. dies shamefully "Like a dog" (*Shame* 126). Rushdie imagines Kafka's words as an "epigraph" before the sordid story of one of his main characters, Sufiya Zinobia Hyder. She is internally gnawed by the "Beast" (comparable to the Jungian "shadow"). Like Dr. Jekyll to Mr. Hyde, Hyder undergoes a "metamorphosis" into this monstrous part of herself (269), becoming a mass murderess, and helping to bring destruction to the government of "Pecavistan"—Rushdie's dangerous parody of his own Pakistan.

In his next novel, *The Satanic Verses,* his vision becomes more bitter and disjointed.

> Most migrants learn, and can become disguises. Our own false descriptions to counter the falsehoods invented about us, concealing for reasons of security our secret selves.[25]

In *Shame,* he is forgiving toward people's fear of aliens and of alterity in general. "What is the most powerful impulse of human beings in the face of night, of danger, of the unknown?—It is to run away." (*Shame* 218). The style is easier, more willing to accept the conventions of English rather than reworking them into a fragmentary, interlingual medium as in *The Satanic Verses.* In the earlier book, the most vivid image of an alien is Hyder's Beast—the monster within everyone. *The Satanic Verses,* however, is an epic catalog of prejudices and their cruel results. Notable among its motifs is *The Alien Show,* a television program, capitalizing on the idea of alien as monster, including "Bugsy the giant dung-beetle from the Crab Nebula who had run away from his father" (Gregor Samsa with perhaps a further allusion to Bruno Schulz's crab metamorphosis). The stars of the show are an Indian actor and Jewish actress until the producer decides that a Western audience would prefer less alien monsters and hires Anglo-Saxons to replace his former stars. Coincident with his being fired, the actor, following a fall he miraculously survives, finds himself literally being transformed into a devil-figure, with horns growing from his forehead. He is told that a similar fate eventually overtakes all colonials in Britain, forced to wear the form that British prejudice forces on them. Biases about Asians are not all overtly negative, though, so one handsome Indian actor, famed for playing gods in Bombay's theological cinema, is transformed into an angel, complete with halo. He finds this role no more congenial than those turned into monsters because he feels compelled to be perfect in a world where Good and Evil are inextricably intertwined. He is forced to reduce life's real comlexity into a crude antithesis between pure Good and Evil, a simplification that he believes underlies Islam even more than Christianity. According to the Bible, Adam fell from eating of the Tree of Good and Evil, but in the Koran "*It was simply a different Tree!*" (354)—or, as Rushdie seems to imply, Evil was another word for difference itself. In a series of dreams (which have not endeared Rushdie to some Moslems), the angel-actor imagines, however, that even the Koran, the Islamic measure of good and purity, may contain Satanic corruptions added by a scribe named "Salman" (Rushdie?). Finding his condition intolerable, the angel-actor kills himself.

In between those two novels, Rushdie wrote a memoir about a trip to Nicaragua, *The Jaguar Smile.* On its first page he declares, "I've always had a weakness for synchronicity."[26] In fiction, this Jungian tenet manifests itself in the pathetic fallacy (which makes external circumstances conform to the characters' psychological condition). He takes that device to fantastic lengths in *The Satanic Verses* with the metamorphoses of the actors into stereotypes—or are they archetypes? Rushdie leaves the question unsettled, but if there are archetypal powers at work, they are not ministering healing but horror.

Edmond Jabès

Born (1912) of Jewish parents in the French-speaking quarter of Cairo, Edmond Jabès, like many other cosmopolitans, was forced to expatriate because of the surge of Egyptian nationalism accompanying the Suez Crisis (1956). Resettling in France, he began to study the Talmud and Kabbala to orient him during his exile, but horror at God having permitted the Holocaust kept him from finding any consolation (or belief) in Judaism. His intense alienation could no longer be expressed even in the surrealism of his early poetry. Consequently, he began his seven-volume, anomalous work, *The Book of Questions (Le livre des questions).* It is a vast play with language as in the final volume, *El, or the Last Book,* where the Hebrew word *El* (God), suggests to him etymologically unrelated French terms, such as *l'* (the) or *ailes* (wings), which then become departure points for further Kabbalistic fantasies mixed with postmodern philosophy and poignant poetry. It is also an experimental novel about two lovers separated by the Nazis, the girl driven mad by her confinement in a concentration camp, the boy very nearly so by their separation. The narrative is fragmented by interpolation of aphorisms and rabbinic commentary—a form Kafka pioneered but never brought to such extremes of agony. Jacques Derrida has generously acknowledged Jabès's influence. "In the last ten years nothing has been written in France that does not have its precedent somewhere in the texts of Jabès."[27] Despite probing the problematic nature of writing with all the subtlety of the Deconstructionists, Jabès never relinguishes an anguished search for truth, enunciated by his persona, Yukel, a narrator in *The Book of Questions.*

> It is the whole truth I wanted to express. And truth is a scream, a stubborn, ineradicable image which pulls us out of our torpor. An image which overwhelms or nauseates us.[28]

It is an attitude toward literature comparable to Kafka's aphorism:

> The books we need are the kind that act upon us like a misfortune . . . that make us feel as though we were on the verge of suicide, or lost in a forest remote from all human habitation—a book should serve as the ax for the frozen sea within us.[29]

In the final volume of *The Book of Questions,* Jabès quotes Kafka's epigram: "It is up to us to accomplish the negative. The positive is given."[30] By this point, Jabès's work has attained sufficient negativity so that he begins one of its sections, "I must warn you: writing leads to suicide."[31] Conversely, Jabès also writes, "Our body decays when it is suddenly robbed of its language."[32] In an interview he said that when he finished *The Book of Questions:*

> That night I had one of my most violent asthma attacks. And it was the phrase "comes to an end" that brought it on. It had thrown me into a terrible panic. The doctor had to come at three in the morning to give me a shot. I almost couldn't breathe.[33]

As if his life depended on it, he began writing a new series of works, in the same self-tormented, self-tormenting manner. The heart of his works, though, is *El, or the Last Book.* It arises principally from the image, repeated throughout the volume, of God as a point, a period, a circle without diameter, a holy mandala identical with nothingness, the empty origin of everything. Jabès strips away the world of appearances, leaving the archetypal, and then subjects even that to question. In an interview, Jabès has explained:

> In the Kabbalah it says, "God reveals himself in a dot," and by making this reference, the whole work of deconstruction seems to uncover a totality. But the totality can never be shown. Totality is an idea . . . and it can be shown only through fragments.[34]

Jabès's position is reminiscent of the preceding chapter—the sacred as absence—but with a nuance more disquiet, a greater frenzy to question the nightmare of existence.

Samuel Beckett

An Anglo-Irish Nobel Prize winner who writes sometimes in French and sometimes in English (interspersed with occasional Latin, German, and Italian), Samuel Beckett defies easy classification. Whether he translates his own works from English to French or from French to English, his renderings range between almost painful literalism and complete adaptation. In *En attendant Godot,* for example, in a dialogue between the suicidal tramps (otherwise scrupulously translated), three lines concerning the godlessness of the French school system are completely absent from his English version *(Waiting for Godot).*[35] Marjorie Perloff begins an article on Beckett's bilingualism with the latter's remark that, early in his career, he shied away from English because "you couldn't help writing poetry in it,"[36] while he prefers to be unpoetic, austere, even awkward, producing the "literature of the unword," one of Beckett's own phrases that she interprets as a self-reference. Beckett's statements about his artistic intentions and his remarks within his fictions seem to indicate that for each of his works he sees an ineffable original, imperfectly represented by the words of French or English. In a 1937 German letter, for instance, he states a desire to rend language "in order to get at the things (or the Nothingness) behind it."[37] Comparably, throughout the second part of his novel *Molloy,* and most emphatically at its ending, his character Moran tries to deal with an interior voice speaking in an incomprehensible language. "But in the end I understood this language. I understood it, I understood it, all wrong perhaps."[38]

In comparing his works to Kafka's, Beckett again refers to what lies beneath the surface of the words. "Kafka's form . . . *seems* to be threatened the whole time—but the consternation is in the form. In my work there is consternation behind the form, not in the form."[39] On one level, this contrast appears apt. Kafka, indeed, did credit the possibility of transcendent peace behind the troubled realm of illusion, but, as with his "In the Caravansery," any home that can be imaged is unsatisfactory. In *The Castle,* for instance, the protagonist's problem appears to be the impossibility of reaching the inner recesses of the establishment, but unsettling rumors undermine its reputation even though it remains largely unpenetrated. In Beckett's *Watt,* the title character actually manages to reside in the *Castle*-like home of Mr. Knott—finding it dissatisfying. Kafka's Abrahams do not manage to begin their sacred journey; Beckett's Moran in *Molloy* finally manages to drag his son on the suicidal mission—which neither can truly complete. In *The Unnameable (L'innomable),* Beckett again ventures further than Kafka by depicting timeless Reality with relative directness. Nonetheless, Beckett repeatedly admits (both in his own person and in his fictions) that he does not know what lies Beyond. Thus the "consternation" may as easily arise from the problems of translating Reality as in the Reality Itself. In their agitation about the ultimate nature of "things (or Nothingness)," he and Kafka agree.

Eva Metman has already tried to reduce Beckett's treatment of self-tortured tramps and cripples to Jungian categories, but not very successfully.[40] Like Kafka, Beckett borrows patterns from world literature only to present them ironically.[41] The closest Beckett comes to furnishing his own notion of "type" is in *Watt,* where the title character tries to describe an ineffable experience by saying that it was as if a man and his son had come to tune a piano, had talked for a while, and left: casual conversation and cacophony, seemingly chosen to sound as little like an archetype (biblical or Jungian) as could be found. Watt calls this experience the "type" for all such happenings in Knott's house; then, a few pages later, Watt admits that the experiences were really quite different. Nevertheless, the very fact that Beckett chooses to joke about key family relations and link them to religion and mythology indicates that he continues to be fascinated by these images.

Tom Stoppard

Born in Czechoslovakia (1937), Tom Stoppard (born Straussler) first moved with his family to Singapore (1939). Because of an imminent Japanese invasion, his mother, brothers, and he emigrated to India (1942), while his father died in the war. In Darjeeling, India, Tom attended a multiracial academy and his mother married Kenneth Stoppard. The latter eventually sent Tom to school in Nottinghamshire, then Yorkshire. As an adult, Tom Stoppard has lived enough of the time in England to be classified as a British writer, but journalism and other activities have often drawn him elsewhere. He spent six months in Berlin, for example, the year he began his best-known drama, *Rosencrantz and Guildenstern Are Dead.* His plays have become evermore daring in the exploration of multicultural discord. In the first scene of his *Travesties* (1974), several minutes go by while his characters Lenin, Tzvara, and Joyce talk (respectively) in Russian, Dadaist nonsense verse, and Joycean multilingual puns mixed with Latin and German. Stoppard's next drama, *Dirty Linen* (1976), contains a long conversation in French, Latin, and Spanish. Even in *Rosencrantz and Guildenstern Are Dead* (1966), much of the play's absurdity derives from sudden shifts between modern and Shakespearean English (the latter described as "a language which makes up in obscurity what it lacks in style").[42] In most of his works, such chaos makes his characters despair at ever organizing their lives—a lack of control reflected in their wandering speeches. Typically, Rosencrantz's ruminations about death lead him to begin (but leave unfinished) jokes about two converts to Christianity, then about a Christian, a Moslem, and a Jew, then about a Hindu, Buddhist, and a lion tamer. The implication of each truncated witticism is that traditional religious views of life after death have been rendered uncertain by the multitude of conflicting faiths. Before he can make this or any other point, however, he nervously changes the subject, at one point shouting toward the wings of the stage:

> All right, we know you're in there! Come out talking! *(Pause.)* We have no control. None at all. . . . (He paces.) What ever became of the moment when one first knew about death. . . . We must be born with an intuition of mortality. (71)

He keeps expecting actors to emerge from the wings and force him back into Shakespeare's *Hamlet,* for he is partly aware that he is a character in a drama. Furthermore, as he and other characters remark, each human being also plays a part inevitably ending in death—a part perhaps written by God whose existence (or at least intention), nonetheless, remains suspect. In a certain sense, the "divine" author behind *Rosencrantz and Guildenstern Are Dead* is simply Shakespeare, and in that sense, Stoppard's play chronicles the dissolution of British culture and its Shakespeare-olatry in a pluralistic United Kingdom. His characters, however, repeatedly suggest a larger metaphysical scope. Composed about the same time as *Rosencrantz and Guildenstern Are Dead,* Stoppard's novel, *Lord Malquist and Mr. Moon,* more directly confronts postmodern *Anxt.* Moon, who feels his "whole life is a process of suicide" is also bent on murder, carrying a bomb to kill some one or group in protest because of "the sheer volume and numbers of the things we're filling [life] up with, and people, its all multiplying madly and no one is controlling it because it's all got too big."[43]

Panicked by the crowd, Moon "could not synchronize real time with time in his head" (5) like Kafka who, during a 1922 breakdown, complained that the inner and outer clocks kept different times (*T* 522). Comparable Kafkaesque disruptions of internal and external temporality lie behind the anachronisms that characterize Stoppard's works (e.g., in his novel, where an eighteenth-century lord and nineteenth-century American cowboys seem to have been set loose in a twentieth-century London). In an interview with Giles Gordon, Stoppard (responding to charges that his works were too derivative) remarked, "It would be very difficult to write a play which was totally unlike Beckett, Pirandello and Kafka."[44] Since Kafka was not a playwright, his inclusion seems particularly significant. Tim Brassell and Kenneth Tynan have both noted that a sense of confinement in an incomprehensible universe links the works of Kafka and Stoppard.[45]

The most significant difference between Kafka and Stoppard is that the latter is even more leery of stock or "archetypal" images than the former. Kafka's story "The Hunter Gracchus," for example, comically explores the implications of a death boat. Contrastingly, when Stoppard's Rosencrantz asks if death might be a boat, Guildenstern quashes this fancy immediately.

> No, no, no. . . . Death is . . . not. Death isn't. You take my meaning. Death is the ultimate negative. Not being. You can't not-be on a boat. (108)

Rosencrantz at first tries to argue, but then loses heart and turns to thoughts of suicide. For Kafka and Jung, a change of perspective could bring about salvation—a union with the Indestructible or Collective Unconscious (respectively). Some of Stoppard's characters share this hope, as, for instance, a "Player" in *Rosencrantz and Guildenstern Are Dead,* who believes that through art "occasionally . . . there escapes a thin beam of light that, seen at the right angle, can crack the shell of mortality" (83). Reference to this "angle" runs through a number of works, but no character finds it, for, in Stoppard's world, neither art nor psychoanalysis offers a skeleton key to the universal prison.

Elias Canetti

Elias Canetti, winner of the 1981 Nobel Prize in Literature, was born in Bulgaria (1905) of Jewish parents, who conversed in German with each other and spoke Ladino (fifteenth-century Spanish mixed with some Turkish) to the children. His wet nurse knew only Rumanian; many of the servants understood only Bulgarian. He also encountered Russian, Greek, Albanian, Armenian, and Turkish. Once a week, a band of Gypsies (who terrified him) arrived at his home, perhaps adding a few words of Romany to his domestic babel. Since his relatively secular family at least observed the principal Jewish festivals, he presumably absorbed a smattering of Hebrew. He had tellingly little to say of it, though, in his account of his youth, *The Tongue Set Free (Die gerettete Zunge),* from which this biographical information comes. Indeed, he has never expressed much warmth toward the Hebrew God, whom Canetti (at least metaphorically) blamed for linguistic diversity.

> The fact that there are *different* languages is the most sinister fact in the world. It means that there are different names for the same things; and one would have to doubt that they are the same things. All linguistics hides the striving to reduce all languages to *one*. The tale of the Tower of Babel is the tale of the second Fall of Man. . . . God's deed was the most diabolical ever committed.[46]

When Elias was six, his family moved to Manchester, forcing him to learn English. After his father's death, his mother took him to Vienna (1911). Previously, his parents had deliberately kept German from him as a language for their secrets. Finally time had come for him to study it, but his normally kind mother devised a traumatically difficult teaching method coupled with painful insults almost as if she were administering a verbal rite of passage. He thereafter wrote in German, despite spending most of his life in England (where he returned in 1938). Apparently to his surprise, even his early memories transferred into German. He describes the process thus:

> It is not like the literary translation of a book from one languag[e] to another, it is a translation that happened of is own accord in my unconscious, and since I

> ordinarily avoid this word like the plague, a word that has become meaningless from overuse, I apologize for employing it in this one and only case.[47]

Like Kafka, he sounds wary of depth psychology, the discipline that has allegedly overused the concept of the Unconscious, but, as he notes, the mysteries of language required his selecting the term.

In addition to wariness of psychology, Kafka and Canetti had so much in common as polyglot Jewish writers that the former greatly influenced the latter. Canetti confirmed their connection.

> My self-confidence halts in front of a few, very few figures of intellect. . . . It is really those who saw something more important beyond their achievement, something unattainable, so that their achievement seemed to shrink until it disappeared. . . . One such figure is Kafka, and he has affected me more profoundly than Proust, who achieved incomparably more.[48]

More specifically, Canetti reported concerning his own major novel *Auto-da-Fé (Die Blendung),* a work that gradually slips into Kafkaesque absurdity, as the protagonist becomes more self-destructive.

> I had just finished the eighth chapter of *Auto-da-Fé,* now titled "Death," when Kafka's *Metamorphosis* came into my hands. Nothing more fortunate could have happened to me at this point. . . . I bowed to this purest of all models, knowing full well that it was unattainable, but it did give me strength.[49]

Despite some contradiction concerning Kafka's accomplishment, both passages associate him with the "unattainable" *(unerreichbar).* Canetti insists on Kafka's uniqueness.

> Of all writers, he is the only one never to be infected by power; he never exercises any kind of power whatsoever. He has stripped God of the final vestiges of fatherliness. What remains is a dense and indestructible net of qualms concerning the life rather than the demands of the begetter.[50]

Canetti wrote a monograph-length study of Kafka's *Letters to Felice,* perhaps inspired by the striking similarities between that book and Canetti's own *Auto-da-Fé,* both the protracted struggle of a writer for autonomy against the woman in his life. The protagonist of the novel is a Sinologist and the *Letters to Felice* reveal Kafka's extreme Sinophilia. Canetti deems Kafka to be "the only essentially Chinese writer to be found in the West," partly because of Kafka's stories about small animals. In conversations with Canetti, the Sinologist Arthur Waley concurred, citing Kafka's combining "'natural' Taoism" with Confucian "ritualism."[51] Considering that to Occidentals Chinese culture connoted the small and delicate, Canetti's references to Kafka can be reconciled. Kafka has produced a small body of work in contrast with Proust, but Kafka's writings achieve a certain perfection in their lack of pretension. They epitomize a "Chinese" humility—an empathy with moles, bugs, and dogs—a total renunciation of human power. Elsewhere, Canetti describes renunciation of power thus:

> Man must learn to be many men consciously and to keep them all together. . . . Instead of ruling others, he will have to rule over his own personae; they will have names, he will know them, he will be able to order them about.[52]

In Canetti's chief scholarly work, *Crowds and Power (Masse und Mach),* the fruit of most of his life, he contrasts the "kings" (who rule masses of people) and the "shamans" (who imagine themselves transformed into many beings). Canetti portrays the former as villains, the latter as more sympathetic figures though they fall short of Kafka, since their transformations are unconscious, causing them to mislead their patients into superstition. These kings and shamans sound much like Jung's extraverts and introverts, except that Canetti sees them more as social roles than as psychological types. The central concept in Canetti's book is social: the crowd—which repeatedly brings to his mind the vast throngs addressed by Hitler. Aside from three very sketchy pages in *The Archetypes of the Collective Unconscious,* Jung—a product of his individualistic Protestant heritage and his psychiatric practice with individual patients—has little to say about crowds. Although Canetti and he spent most of their lives ransacking world literature, religion, and anthropology for myths and customs, they approached virtually the same material from complementary perspectives. Consequently, Canetti's psychology can sometimes illuminate literary problems that remain opaque to Jung's.

Consider, for example, Kafka's *Metamorphosis.* Since for Jung the archetypes "of transformation" (one of his most common epithets for the archetypes) are "psychic organs," his prime emphasis is how psychological transformations (identifications with various beings) work to heal the patient. It is very hard to see Kafka's *Metamorphosis* as a story of healing. Canetti, however, imagines the origin of psychic transformation in escape: an animal plays dead to fool the pack chasing it. Eventually, this skill at role playing and imagination developed, he hypothesizes, into the shamanic trance, where the shaman, in unconscious escape from self-torture, envisions himself transformed into a crowd of beings simultaneously or successively. One of the most common interpretations of *Metamorphosis* is that Samsa has become an insect to escape his demanding family, but the inevitable objection to such an interpretation has been that transformation into an insect is a preposterous escape. Canetti's researches (even though he did not himself apply them to *Metamorphosis*) have the value of suggesting that Samsa's alteration conforms to a widespread fantasy of fleeing, as in those fairy tales where the prey changes into various animals and objects to elude the pursuers.

Both Jung and Canetti see the need to unify the multitude of transformations and personae within the individual but for Canetti this is secondary to rendering people powerless, so they will stop hurting each other. Canetti's repeated desire for unity (e.g., wanting *one* language and seeking to keep the personae together) is tempered by his horror at how people achieve unity in destructive crowds. For him, terror lies at the heart of the human condition. He begins *Crowds and Power* by stating that

> there is nothing that man fears more than the touch of the unknown. He wants to see what is reaching towards him, and to be able to recognize or at least classify it.[53]

Unity becomes merely an escape into a mob from this Kafkaesque fear. There, in a kind of intoxication, one accepts the touch of others (as second best to what Canetti considers the universal preference: being the sole survivor of the human race). The mood is far from Jung's optimism—and perhaps even more pessimistic than Kafka himself.

John Berryman

Raised in Oklahoma, thereafter educated in New York and England (Cambridge), John Berryman, despite renouncing his father's last name (Smith), never managed to escape the shadow of the latter's suicide when John was fifteen. On the surface, this trauma hardly explains why John dwelt on it all his life, ending in suicide. According to Kohut's theories, however, a boy generally models himself after his father. In Berryman's case, at any rate, thoughts of suicide became a typical way of dealing with failure and stress. At seventeen, for example, in response to an attack by two bullies, he tried to throw himself in front of a train. The bullies saved him, thereby halting their attack[54]—and reinforcing his suicidal attitude. The most important part of his life, his best poetry, which earned him fame and grants, consists largely of overt or covert suicide notes. If he had simply described his problems directly (e.g., his guilt over committing adultery), he would hardly have garnered much sympathy from his readers. Instead, he makes intercultural alienation a metaphor for his feelings of pain and isolation. In his justly famous poems, *The Dream Songs,* he shifts from black to standard English, and moves the locale around the world, with himself as the perpetual stranger. His autobiographical novel *Recovery* reveals his identification with the Jews (even though he was not by ancestry Jewish). He learned Hebrew and contemplated converting from Catholicism to Judaism, whose followers (like American blacks) are proverbially associated with alienation and persecution. *Recovery* also focuses on his membership in AA. He quotes from the AA manual, "We admitted . . . that our lives had become unmanageable."[55] He writes of turning to God for help, but, as in *The Dream Songs,* where his persona "Henry" succinctly remarks, "God's Henry's enemy,"[56] so also in *Recovery,* Berryman's religious worries continue. Indeed, the very title of that novel may be distinctly ironic, although its present condition (left unfinished by his own suicide) leaves the question moot.

Understandably, Berryman long felt attracted to Kafka. In 1938, at the beginning of his career, Berryman tried to interest his family in that writer, chatted with Edwin Muir about the progress of the Kafka-translation project, read most or all of Kafka's works available in English, and wrote a work in imitation of them. (According to Richard Kelly, it was Berryman's poem, "Prague.")[57] In *The Dream Songs,* one of Berryman's personae speaks of "Kafka, old pal," as a man who was best able to achieve virtuosity in German *because* it was foreign to him (332). In a later Dream Song, Berryman's persona identifies with "Kafka & all his tribe" (369). Also in *The Dream Songs,* Berryman quotes twice from the 1953 edition of Janouch's *Conversations with Kafka.*[58] Finally, like Kafka, Berryman had serious doubts about Freudianism—and with more knowledge of it, for he had undergone a lengthy Freudian analysis.

The gist of these doubts appears in Dream Song 327, which derides Freud for not realizing that dreaming reflected a mental life larger than those memories on which psychoanalysis dwelt. Somewhat ambiguously, he suggests that psychology can only be understood by those "troubled by the Fall." One must recall that Berryman's own psychoanalyses had not completely annulled his religious faith. In *Recovery,* he writes:

> Some of my best work I can't claim any credit for, it flowed out all by itself, or in fact by His [God's] moving. But I couldn't see Him interested in the individual life in the ordinary way. Now I did.[59]

However, according to Haffenden, this experience (the "Now" described in *Recovery*) caused him to write in *Love and Fame* that he identified "with everybody, even the heresiarchs"[60]—hardly a return to orthodox faith. He ended, then, a little like Jung, stressing the religious connection of the psyche, but with an eclectic religiosity. In *Recovery,* directly after consideration of what Jung calls the "Unconscious," his persona finds in his reading what would normally be termed "coincidences," but they seem to him more than that, that is, synchronicities or miracles (153). As to the Jungian archetypes, though, his poetry plays with the major religious symbols in perpetual irony and ambiguity. Perhaps the closest he comes to an experience of the archetypal is in *Recovery* when the persona imagines his failures hovering above him "like the Platonic essences" (205). Only his failures remained transcendentally real to him.

Sylvia Plath

At one time or another, both parents of the Pulitzer-Prize-winning poet Sylvia Plath taught German, their first language (though the mother also gave classes in high-school English).[61] In Sylvia's confessional poem "Daddy," she speaks of a reaction against her father so intense that even the German language became for her "obscene."[62] In that stanza, she repeats the German word for I *(Ich)* over and over as if it were itself an obscenity, a reminder of her unsure sense of self, divided between the traditionalism of her Teutonic parents and the modern mores of her native America. In her alienation, although she was not actually Jewish, she likens herself to a Jew being persecuted by the Nazis—an image also employed in her justly famous poem "Lady Lazarus." As Judith Kroll has demonstrated, the latter poem may owe much to Kafka's story "The Hunger Artist," both works describing their protagonists as professionally suffering in a fatal public display.[63]

Kafka, as German-speaking Jew at odds with that language, serves as one model for her predicament. His works also provide paradigms for her nightmare-haunted style. In 1957, she said that she planned to write a story "like Kafka, simply told, symbolic, yet realistic. How one is always and irrevocably alone."[64] The loneliness and attempted merger of the real and symbolic appear in most of her writings—as in those of her literary circle. According to Keith Sagar and Leonard Scigaj, Kafka influenced the poetry of Plath's husband, Ted Hughes, who eventually became Poet Laureate of Britain.[65] Even her friend Anne Sexton may have contributed to her interest in Kafka, at least in the following instance. In the autumn of 1962, Sexton published the collection of poems, *All My Pretty Ones,* its second epigraph a passage from a letter by Kafka to Oscar Pollak. (It attracted a number of "raven"-like authors, perhaps because of its comparison of reading to suicide.) On 1 February 1963, Plath rearranged its images of ax, remote forest, still water, and literature in her poem "Words." Literature (the "Words" of the title) is seen as like the echo of an ax in a remote forest, the interior world explored by the poet. Against this activity, the wood tries to reestablish itself as, she says, a still pool strives to preserve its immobility. She concludes that words eventually run wild, separate from their author, while the water (a traditional image of the Unconscious as with Kafka's "frozen sea within") remains unmoved, an expanse from which the "fixed stars" control one's life. Kafka's lines are not entirely despondent: however painful, literature may break into the internal stillness like an ax. In contrast, Plath despairingly expects no permanent effect from those ax strokes. Typical of her mood at the time (less than two weeks before her suicide), she compares a rock to a partly devoured skull. Her next poem, "Contusion," concludes with an ocean juxtaposed with the image of a mirror (another "frozen sea"). In her last poem, "Edge" it is "the woman" who is immobile:

perfected
. . . dead. . . .

Why does she believe the stillness will win? What, in "Words," does she mean by "fixed stars"? These questions (which turn out to be interrelated) lead to another prime but not necessarily benevolent influence on her poems—Jung. The trail proceeds first to her 1960 poem "Magi." In a BBC broadcast she introduced it thus:

> Abstractions, by definitions, are withdrawn from life and formulated in despite of life's minute and vital complexities. In this poem, "Magi," I imagine the great absolutes of the philosophers gathered around the crib of a newborn baby girl who is nothing but life.[67]

In the poem, she alludes to Plato, thereby suggesting a connection between these abstractions and Platonic Ideas, but unlike the latter (and like Jungian archetypes) her absolutes are personified. They are Magi seeking a "star." For Plato the stars are gods, which, as we have seen (in chap. 3) manipulate the Ideas, but Plath has the "star," some undefined goal or power, manipulating the personifications (like the relationship between an archetype and archetypal images in Jungian theory). Four months later (in "Heavy Women"), the Magi (pejoratively described as "gray") appear again, this time matched by the women of the title, who are said to dwell among "the archetypes." In "Three Women," the Magi-like characters (representatives of abstraction attending a birth) are the maternity-ward doctors. They allegedly crave everything to be "holy" and "flat." Under the influence of these Magi, one woman imagines flat "hieroglyphs" of Oriental languages ("Arabic" and "Chinese"). Although in "Daddy," the only partly familiar German was disturbing, in "Three Women," the even less familiar Arabic and Chinese leave the character locked in her "dead self," refusing "to be more, or different." Finally, in "Words," the stars that "Govern," have become "fixed" in still water. How could these static malevolences have come from Jung's dynamic archetypes of transformation?

During her college years, Plath perused Jungian theory in connection with her honors' thesis on "double personality," but she was examining other psychological theories as well. In 1962, she "was quite possibly reading or rereading [Jung]," and at some time she copied out passages from one of his books "relevant to her concerns near the end of her life."[68] Ted Hughes was another possible source of information on Jung since, early in Hughes's career, he had read all of the Jungian corpus available in English.[69] Nonetheless, her attitude that abstractions are static, antisexual, and deadly is pure Freud. This is her problem: her late poetry expresses growing faith in the power of the archetypes—her mind apparently accepts their existence—yet she revolts against them with a Freudian sensibility. In Jungian theory, the archetypes are, in a sense, midwives, helping the individual give birth to a new, more dynamic personality after a lonely struggle. In "Three Women," the mysterious, "flat" doctors terrify the first woman, because she senses that she is expected "to be more, or different" and fears that in these doctors' care she will be engulfed by eternity. Ultimately, she feels reassured by contemplating "normality," the thought that her newborn son will grow up and marry (Freud's view of normality), while she abhors the thought that her boy might become "exceptional," a hermit of the mountaintop or "desert." Jung, however, was fascinated by mystic figures and saw them as models for the latter part of each human life. One usually thinks of Freud's reaction against archetypal theory as intellectual—his condemning it as unscientific—but, as Jungians have frequently recalled, Freud did accept the existence of "archaic vestiges." He simply refused to pay much attention to them. Plath does not seem to have had that option. During her last months, she told Hughes that she had seen God on a number of occasions.[70] These visitations apparently did not bring her any beatitude. At least in her poetry, she does not glory in the strange, difficult-to-translate language of the Unconscious; she imagines the call from the beyond to be merely the voice of death.

Anne Sexton

After a series of mental breakdowns, Anne Sexton (née Harvey) began writing poetry and perusing world literature. In a 1960 letter, she specifically mentions reading Kafka.[71] As already noted, her own collection of poems, *All My Pretty Ones,* quotes his lines describing necessary books as those which act like axes breaking through an internal "frozen sea."[72] A 1963 letter of Sexton to Brother Dennis Farrell quotes from Kafka's letters to Milena, where Kafka with typical strangeness writes that epistolary kisses do not reach the recipient of a letter but are intercepted by ghosts. In a 1963 letter, after criticizing her own poetry as exhibitionistic, Sexton states:

> I understand Kafka. I understand Rilke. Only through them can I understand myself. The life story or better named, the case history, is only the machine, a Kafka machine. It makes me want to hide, back in the room where I was locked.[73]

Although she employs the psychoanalytic term *case history* for confessional literature, she does not see such literature precisely as therapy but as a way of confronting painful truths that are as likely to destroy as save her. Like the prisoners in Kafka's penal colony, who could only discover their crimes by feeling them inscribed on their bodies by a torture machine conceived by a lunatic, Sexton explores the interconnections of guilt, suffering, language, and madness.

In her most famous works, she does this in verses that read almost like a transcription of personal experience, but in her 1971 collection entitled *Transformations* she confronts what Estella Lauter has called the "transpersonal."[74] Maxine Kumin, at whose urging *Transformations* was written, describes that book as exploring "a kind of collective unconscious".[75] She adds:

> It struck me that Anne's poems based on fairy tales went one step further than contemporary poets' translations from languages they did not themselves read but apprehended through a third party. Their poems were *adaptations;* hers were *transformations.* (xxviii)

Sexton mentions the Jungian author Hesse in her dedication of the book. Nonetheless, she begins *Transformations* with the statement that reading Hesse does not suffice to furnish "The Gold Key" to psychic unity. In "Rumpelstiltskin," an updating of a traditional tale like Kafka's "Poseidon," her first sentence declares that in "many" people an aged, tiny, twisted man (Rumpelstiltskin) struggles "to get out." Is this being the Jungian *animus* (a woman's psyche appearing to her as a male figure)? Sexton describes Rumpelstiltskin as childlike, monstrous, "asexual," a representative of physical desire, a "Doppelğanger," bisexual, and patriarchal ("papa"). It would not be hard to select from this mélange of attributes some that would support identifying this dwarf with the Jungian *animus* or other archetypes, for example, the Hermaphrodite or the Child (or even the Freudian Id). Jung confronted equally heterogeneous groupings. He tried to find a single archetype as the key to each complex, though he often had to admit to "contamination." Where, within the Rumpelstiltskin complex, lies the "Gold Key" to power over it? According to Jung, that fairy tale exemplifies the idea that knowing a name conveys power (*GW* vol. V, par. 274). Sexton concludes her tale with the discovery of Rumpelstiltskin's name, but she focuses on the death agonies of the little man who is for the second time termed the queen's "Doppelgänger."

As in a later section of *Transformations* where the party is called a dying "Kafka beetle," so also in "Rumpelstiltskin" the princess outwardly seems powerful and victorious but at the cost of her "Doppelgänger," her inner self, which lies dead. Hesse and Jung try to make language into therapy. Sexton, however, presents a parable where finding the correct name brings outward control but inner annihilation. Jung sometimes stopped treatment if he felt that patients would be destroyed by analysis, but he inherited the "talking cure" from Freud as Sexton inherited the Kafkan task of turning psychic disturbance into literature (despite equally Kafkan misgivings). A few years after Sexton's version of this story, the West German Rosemarie Kunzler composed a feminist revision of the tale. Her heroine intelligently abandons the evil men in her life "[runs] out into the great wide world and [is] saved."[76] Sexton, though, offers no happy ending but only the discovery of the mysterious name Rupelstiltskin—a nonsense word akin to others in German that signify rattling or rumbling. It is different in practically every version of the tale and traceable, according to Joseph Grimm, to a children's game called "Rumpele stilt."[77] Its ridiculousness stands as a climax to Sexton's struggle to designate, delineate, or define the multiform psyche within.

Susan Sontag

Educated at the University of Chicago, Berkley, Harvard, and Oxford, Susan Sontag has subsequently traveled extensively. She made films in Sweden and Israel (the former in Swedish) and visited North Vietnam in the midst of the Vietnam War. Although not a Communist, she wanted to empathize with the Vietnamese, yet, for most of her stay, she could not help but feel that their Marxist ideology was naive and overly optimistic—her characteristic ambivalence.[78] From time to time throughout her career, she has vaguely alluded to her own faith in progress, even her belief in miracles,[79] but these glimmers of hope are again and again submerged in darkness and despair. In an as-yet unpublished lecture on "Traditions of the New," she typically concluded, "It is true that the modern is liberating . . . and it is also true at the same time that there is something deeply wrong with the modern."[80] Near the beginning of her speech she remarked, "I'm never entirely sure [of what I think]." Her writings counterpoint an almost overwhelming assertiveness with such disarming hesitancy as in *Against Interpretation*, where she admits that she sometimes only believes what she is writing when she writes it.[81]

At the root of this hesitancy lies a desire to problematize the relationship of author and text—partly from a structuralist conviction that books should be treated as autonomous structures—but perhaps also from a personal desire for privacy. There is, for example, an overwrought tone at the end of the following:

> We know that . . . the "K." of *The Trial* and *The Castle* [is not] identical with Kafka. We are not satisfied. It is the author naked which the modern audience demands, as ages of religious faith demanded a human sacrifice.[82]

Kafka is one of her stock examples of the writer as an embodiment of narcissism and melancholy. Although writing is a profession popularly assumed to involve communication, she associates it with reticence.

> The mark of the Saturnine temperament is the self-conscious and unforgiving relation to the self, which can never be taken for granted. . . . (Hence, this is an apt temperament for artists and martyrs, those who court "the purity and beauty of a failure," as Benjamin says of Kafka.)[83]

On the next page, she continues:

> Dissimulation, secretiveness appear a necessity to the melancholic. . . . Using a word that was also applied to Kafka by those who knew him, Scholem speaks of "the almost Chinese courtesy" that characterized Benjamin's relations with people.

She sees in Kafka's notebooks "an exquisite commitment without mockery to his own anguish."[84] Repeatedly, in *Illness as Metaphor,* Kafka's tuberculosis stands as an example of a writer who felt his disease was a form of suicide.[85] Since she is herself a writer, it is hard not to wonder to what extent her denigrating remarks about writers are meant to be autobiographical. Certainly her critical works manifest a fascination with morbidity and decadence, for example, *Illness as Metaphor* (a book-length study of literary references to tuberculosis and cancer), *Under the Sign of Saturn* (essays on writing as mental illness), and even *Styles of Radical Will* (the very title of which reduces radicalism—including her own—to a matter of fashion). This cynicism is also apparent in her fictions. Her first novel, *The Benefactor,* concerns a young French decadent named Hippolyte, who proclaims:

> I am looking for silence, I am exploring the various styles of silence, and I wish to be answered by silence. "You might say," I concluded gaily, "that I am disemboweling myself."[86]

The disemboweling consists of trying to penetrate his own (psychic) interstices, meditating on his dreams but without psychologically interpreting them (since interpretation would distance him from them). Weirdly guided by them, he tries to "help" his benefactress first by selling her as a slave to a lecherous old Arab and then, perhaps, by trying to kill her. What exactly happens, however, is uncertain because he has contradictory memories. His world of nebulous transgressions and distant punishments resembles his description of a criminal.

> It takes a long time for the consequences to catch up with the act. Then one must go on repeating oneself, and boring others, in the interval between act and consequences. This is when people say, he is insatiable. And sometimes . . . there are no consequences, and one has the impression of not being alive at all. (107)

The clause "he is insatiable" echoes the remark made by the guard to the man from the country in Kafka's story "Before the Law." Indeed, Hippolyte's whole image (waiting for a justice that may never come) recalls that parable.

Even more darkly Kafkaesque is Sontag's next novel, *Death Kit*. While Hippolyte allowed his dreams to disorganize his life, Diddy, the protagonist of *Death Kit,* is himself in constant flux, as symbolized by his acquiring a new epithet on practically every page, for example, "Diddy the Discouraged," or "Diddy the Eclectic."[87] He spends most of the book thinking about suicide and waiting for justice to overtake him for a murder he may have committed, perhaps more than once. (He's not sure.)

Near the end of the book, he sees or hallucinates a vast series of famous pessimistic quotations in several different languages, which are called "carrion wisdom" (295–97). These graffiti—despite presenting stereotypes or "archetypes"—cannot redeem him. What is Sontag's attitude toward the archetypal? In *Against Interpretation,* she alludes to Jungian Individuation as a "hopeful theme" (i.e., an overly optimistic one) akin to the lunatic theories of Antonin Artaud and Gnosticism (272). In *Illness as Metaphor,* she goes further, listing Jung as one of those who falsely promised "a temporary triumph over death" through psychological means (55). She assumes that the mind cannot affect the body—that scientific studies to the contrary must have fallen under a popular delusion. Why does she make such a strange assumption, contrary to the weight of evidence?[88] Despite or because of her own eclecticism (the swarm of disparate allusions that embellish her essays), she seems to long for a simplicity threatened by psychology, Jungian or otherwise. Perhaps, she even projects this simplicity on those who attract her, for example, the Vietnamese or her vision of Kafka in her essay, "The Aesthetics of Silence."

> The narratives of Kafka . . . seem puzzling because they appear to invite the reader to ascribe high-powered symbolic and allegorical meanings to them and, at the same time, repel such ascriptions. Yet when the narrative is examined, it discloses no more than what it literally means. The power of the language

> derives precisely from the fact that the meaning is so bare. (*Styles of Radical Will* 29)

Ralph Waldo Ellison

On leave from travels in the merchant marine and under the inspiration of readings in American, British, and European literature,[89] the Oklahoma-born musician Ralph Waldo Ellison, began (in 1945) his novel, *Invisible Man,* winner of the 1953 National Book Award. In an essay on Harlem roughly contemporaneous with the composition of *Invisible Man,* he speaks of black intellectuals (like himself) as having "examine[d] their lives through the eyes of Freud and Marx, Kierkegaard and Kafka, Malraux and Sartre."[90] One of the first books to bring such examination to literary fruition, his novel continues to earn him one honor after another, including the Medal of Freedom (1969), *Chevalier de l'order des artes et lettres* (1970), and the National Medal of Arts (1985), though, aside from a few short stories and occasional pieces, he seems to have suffered from a massive writing block thereafter. Charles Johnson calls *Invisible Man* "the modern Ur-text for black fiction."[91] Johnson, himself, has written a masterful novel more or less in that Ellisonian mold of philosophical black fictionalizing—*Oxherding Tale,* which begins with epigraphs from Kafka, the Zen Oxherding Pictures, the Rig Veda, and Saint Augustine as preparation for his phenomenological dissection of the slave experience.[92] Nonetheless, in one important particular, Johnson criticizes Ellison:

> *Invisible Man* is a one-idea book that works its magic by carefully unpacking its central idea that meaning cannot be fixed, that Being is formless, a field of imagination and possibility that defies intellectual systemization; and by using Freudian references to the subconscious to demolish first the nineteenth-century bourgeois myths created by Booker T. Washington, then other naive optimisms of the Industrial Age, and at last the twentieth-century belief in collective action . . . as a panacea for social ills. . . . But . . . Ellison gets the point wrong, or backward: it is not reality or the world that is formless and fluid but human perception—consciousness itself that allows us infinitely to perceive meaning as a phenomenon of change, transformation, and process; it is Mind (the subject pole of experience), not Matter (the object pole), that gives the perceived world a polymorphous character.[93]

For the Idealist tradition of Kafka's parables and Ellison's *Invisible Man,* however, all that we know is based on perceptions and intuitions: if these perceptions and intuitions are amorphous then so is *our* world. For that tradition, the existence of matter is only a hypothesis, unprovable and irrelevant, since even if matter exists, we will never know what it is in and of itself. All the chapters in *Invisible Man* are variations on what ends the first of them, the nightmare of life as impenetrable deception. A little boy who has seemingly won a competition for blindfolded fighters thereafter goes to sleep and dreams that what he has won is an envelope containing a Chinese boxlike series of envelopes continuing "endlessly."[94] Ellison's experience of composition was itself unnervingly uncontrollable, but maddeningly slow inspiration. He was trying to compose a more conventional novel, while an inner "voice" compelled him to produce *Invisible Man*.[95]

In that novel, his examples of alienation are predominantly from black experience, yet he concludes, "Who knows but that, on the lower frequencies, I speak for you" (439). In an interview when the conversation turned to the function of racial stereotypes in literature, Ellison said, "In fiction, stereotypes partake of archetypes. And to the extent that stereotypes point to something basically human, they overlap."[96] During the composition of *Invisible Man,* Ellison's notion of the archetypal derived largely from his reading of Lord Raglan's study *The Hero,* which, like Propp, finds a series of patterns (in Raglan's case, twenty-two) common to heroic myths. For Raglan, these patterns derive from an early stage when (according to Raglan's theory) all myths were sacred dramas. Both unprovable and unlikely, this theory is not particularly attractive in and of itself, but it provoked Ellison to think of how people need heroes as models. Ironically, those heroes probably never existed except as literary characters, shaped by the structure of literature itself. Ellison then made the absence of heroes, the illusory nature of archetypes, into the fundamental theme of *Invisible Man,* where the search for identity does not bring Jungian Individuation, but a treadmill of Kafkaesque despair.

Walter Benjamin

Born in Berlin (1892) of an assimilated Jewish family, Walter Benjamin, before his suicide (1940), spent much of his life as a perpetual tourist: "seldom would he remain in any of his favorite European haunts for longer than a few months at a time."[97] Wanderlust or constant flight also marks his essays because of their T. S. Eliot-like technique of obsessive allusion and quotation, ever leading away from their main subjects into remote implications and associations. As James Rolleston has observed, Benjamin considered these flights to be a way of unmasking the composite nature of reality, "the multiple languages at work in any given present."[98] Thus, he first rejoiced in his multicultural situation, but he felt it involved certain responsibilities, "The Task of the Translator" *(Die Aufgabe des Übersetzers),* as he called it in a 1923 essay. For that "Task," Benjamin argues, the translator must shatter "decayed barriers [*morsche Schranken*] of his own language" to discover what lies beyond.[99] In the future, Benjamin prophesies, all religions of the world (presumably the mystical traditions within them) will transform each linguistic system into a pure revelation.[100] This idea will sound particularly strange to those who assume that mysticism transcends words, but Benjamin follows the Jewish assumption that religion, mystical or otherwise, will typically consist of textual commentary, designed to harmonize the current world and its languages with the Divine. According to Benjamin, even before the apocalyptic moment, an Enlightened vision of Reality can be generated by perusing texts to expose the idiosyncratic conventions of each tongue, thereby eliminating all distortion in their description of Reality. If Benjamin had maintained this faith (owing much to his fascination with Kabbalistic mysticism), he would belong in chapter 6, but within the next decade his vision became darker. His friend Hans Mayer has explained:

> In 1932, according to Scholem, Benjamin, after revising a will, contemplated suicide for the first time. He was about to turn forty years old and considered himself a total failure. Benjamin's image of Kafka developed concomitant with this experience, once again in the form of an identification, so that his interpretation became stamped with the concept of failure.[101]

Benjamin's 1934 essay, "Franz Kafka: On the Tenth Anniversary of His Death" *(Franz Kafka: Zur zehnten Wiederkehr seines Todestages)* emphasizes Kafka's remark to Max Brod that there was "plenty of hope, an infinite amount of hope—but not for us."[102] In this 1934 essay, Benjamin presumes that Kafka meant that there was no hope for those caught within "the family circle" (even though, in context, Kafka had not been talking about families but about the contrast between humanity and God, so that "us" means humanity). Benjamin's interpretation is consonant with his new self-doubt—his fear that textual study will not bring revelation to such bourgeois individuals as himself. He continued, nonetheless, to assume that there was "plenty of hope" for humanity—an optimism he mistakenly thought he shared with Kafka. Gradually, he began to identify humanity's hope with that of Marxism in bringing a world revolution—but one from which he, still struggling to extricate himself from bourgeois values, was unlikely to profit. And the rise of Nazism made even that revolution seem very distant. With the intention of revising his 1934 Kafka article, Benjamin "kept an extensive archive in which he preserved all written communications and conversations that could be construed as reactions to the essay" (Mayer 201). In 1938, Benjamin sent a letter to Gershom Scholem virtually retracting the 1934 essay and realizing that Kafka had not meant that there was any hope for mankind (Mayer 208).

At his death in 1940, Benjamin left many unfinished projects, most notably his *Passagen-Werk,* an analysis of the shopping arcades of Paris, which he saw as the material embodiment of a capitalist ideology or mythology, leading him to theorize about myths in general. He intended the latter to include refutations of other myth theories, including Jung's. Theodor Adorno, for whom the work was being written, however, refused to commission the section attacking Jung, because Adorno doubted that Benjamin would be sufficiently critical. Benjamin accepted the existence of a Collective Unconscious, a concept that Adorno considered tainted with implicit fascism.[103] Benjamin, nonetheless, was relatively critical of the idea of eternal recurrence that holds so important a place in the writings of Jung and Eliade. Benjamin argues:

> Eternal recurrence is an attempt to link two antinomic principles of happiness with each other: namely that of eternity and that of the yet once again.—The idea of eternal recurrence conjures up out of the misery of time the speculative idea (or phantasmagoria) of happiness.[104]

Where Jung and Eliade emphasize the psychological value of symbolic repetition as a way of realizing that happiness, Benjamin, trying to be a loyal materialist, considers mythological thinking too high a price to pay for an illusory beatitude, which, despite the obfuscation of reactionaries, is allegedly doomed to deteriorate into boredom and impotence.[105] Since his theorizing is part of an unfinished work, one cannot know what form his dialectic between myth and history might have eventually assumed. Even in fragmentary form, his notes suggest that he wished to offer a corrective to the atemporal interpretation of myth so common in Jungian circles. In championing the claims of time against those of eternity, however, he, at the moment of his suicide, seems to have left happiness as a mere phantasmagoria and human life as little more than futility.

Part III
Toward Reconstruction

9
An Approach to Religions in Literature

From Eliade's Hindu/Christian syncretism to the weird cults Vonnegut invents in his novels, a heterodox religiosity permeates much of the Kafkaesque. In order to analyze this spiritual diversity, we need a series of terms for describing religions—a project Jung attempted, but not without theological (among other) controversies. Those proportionately few scientists and traditional scholars who bother to mention him at all generally deem him an obscurantist and self-appointed shaman. The sociologist Daniel Lawrence O'Keefe, for example, classifies Jungians as part of the "magical medical complex" along with "snake handlers, faith healers, holy rollers, logolaliacs, primal screamers and other commotions [sic]."[1] Pious authors, however, frequently accuse Jung of being too traditionally scholarly and scientific to give an unbiased hearing to the claims of religion. Typically, Harold Coward scolds Jung for being skeptical about the alleged magic and mystical visions of advanced yogins.[2] Comparably, in a 1979 letter, the very Christian, Southern novelist Walker Percy admitted his borrowings from Jung, but criticized Jung for not giving sufficient attention to the historical truth of Christ's Incarnation.[3] With such writers as Percy, Fuentes, and Le Guin openly admitting some affinity with Jung, and others (e.g., Robbe-Grillet) coming to Jungian conclusions against their ideological inclinations, a *prima facie* case can be made for connecting Jungian psychology and *belles lettres.* Nonetheless, considering the many criticisms of Jung (which occupy so much of the preceding sections), some divergence from the paleo-Jungians (old-style Jungians) seem inevitable, especially since Jung did not propose a rigorous theory.

How definite should a psycho-religious-literary theory be? By structuralist standards, Jung's "empirical" discoveries seem to be too loose and anecdotal; however, in the poststructuralist epoch, they encounter the opposite objection of rigidity because of his archetypal *structures.* Although no theory of psyche or soul could satisfy everyone from positivist to Deconstructionist to fundamentalist Christian, one useful approach is to view Jung's data from a new perspective. Instead of speculating about archetypes in the depths of the Unconscious, a post-Jungian method might well focus on phenomena we know something about: language, consisting of structures germane to literature, Scripture, ritual, and psychoanalysis—or more precisely, languages, since we are concerned with the multicultural. Citing the growing scholarly interest in language *per se,* Hans-Georg Gadamer writes of "the priority of the domain . . . in which all consciousness and all knowledge articulates itself."[4] Jung was certainly aware of what he called the "transcendent function," the faculty of the unconscious for creating linguistic symbols in any language (*Psychological Types,* 480, 510–23), but it always remained for him rather shadowy and mysterious. Paz's gnomic remarks about language as a Collective Unconscious or Broch's barely begun search for the unconscious "Logos" (logical structures) behind language take us along the same route, but not very far. Jacques Lacan, who "spent some time with Jung,"[5] but never met Freud, composed a psycholinguistic theory of the "collective field of the imagination" and its "forms," reminiscent of Jung's "Collective Unconscious" and its "archetypes,"[6] but Lacan insisted that his theory was faithfully Freudian. Lacan is notoriously obscure. Take, for example, his most famous pronouncement, "The unconscious is structured in the most radical way like a language."[7] Considering the vast diversity of languages and linguistic structures, Lacan's phrase "a language" is far from self-evident. What proof is there that the whole Unconscious has a single structure? When Canetti's Unconscious translated his memories from Landino into German, it presumably contained both tongues as well as the others he knew (not to mention the workings of the nervous system and cognitive dissonance that resisted linguistic encoding). Where does a baby learn the rules of language(s)? Primarily by hearing varied utterances associated with the personalities of the speakers and probably representing considerable diversity in idiolect or even dialect.

Behind all these conflicting linguistic paradigms in the Unconscious, however, there lies the ability to perceive, remember, and use structured images. All forms of human communication have patterns in common, apparently including the following four: **repetition, metaphor, metonymy,** and **antithesis.** First, language acquisition involves recognizing the **repetition** of words, grammatical forms, etcetera. When cryptographers try to decipher a code, they begin with the textual repetitions, confident that any language contains them. Next, Jacobson's famous distinction between **metaphor** and **metonymy** has gained prominence because some mental patients lack the ability to use one *or* the other, strongly suggesting that each is a separate part of the human mind. For this and for other reasons, Deconstructionists assume that language is inherently figurative. Finally, according to Saussure, in choosing a word, one inevitably selects it by unconsciously contrasting it with all other words stored in one's memory. For a skilled author, this pursuit of the *mot juste* may be very subtle, but on its simplest level it involves **antitheses,** for example, that the Saharan summer is usually hot rather than cold, dry rather than wet, and so on. In *Fundamentals of Language,* Jakobson and Halle divide sounds according to binary pairs, a method that may have inspired Lévi-Strauss's division of myth into dyads and Lacan's assumption that language is dyadic.[8] Similarly, differential linguistics assumes the existence of bipolar opposites in all languages.

Jung believed that, in addition to physical instincts, people have many spiritual ones, the "Archetypes," but his evidence of the latter (roughly comparable motifs found in many cultures) can most simply be explained as images of common human experiences (e.g., parental authority, hunger, and light) organized and intensified by these four aspects of language.

Repetition

As suggested in chapter 4, the rhythm of music, the meter of poetry, and the repetitive routines of daily life provide a sense of reassuring structure.[9] In studying Melanesian magic, the pioneer anthropologist Bronislaw Malinowski noted its singsong rhythm and rhetorical repetitions of incantation, characteristics found worldwide.[10] Jung and Eliade have garnered tomes of evidence supporting the notion that so-called "primitive" societies try to orient themselves by repeating patterns that they consider to be primordial. One of these "archetypal" patterns particularly worth noting is the circle. *Anadiplosis,* a rhetorical term for repetition, means "doubling back";[11] the geometrical expression of the doubling back, endless repetition or "Eternal Return" (to use Eliade's favorite phrase), is the circle, the mandala, a pattern so widespread as to be plausibly deemed universal. Lacan describes language as "rings of a necklace that is a ring in another necklace made of rings" (502/153). His very style suggests the interminable repetition inherent in rings or circles, but his interconnecting them makes language into a labyrinth. While a single circle is the simplest path of repetition, an intricate mesh or maze is the most complex, therefore the most frustrating and trying. In *A Remembered Future,* Harold Fisch struggles with his preliminary reading of Jung by which he expects the repetitive, "archetypal" structures in literature to be circular, moving from time into eternity. At his first glance, this simple version of Jung seems to him true to literature, for *Finnegan's Wake* ends with its opening line, revenge dramas concern "getting back" at enemies, and so on. Fisch's close readings, however, reveal that literary repetitions are complicated by ambiguities and subtle changes.[12] The circle has become a labyrinth. Like Jung in his "Answer to Job," Fisch hypothesizes, "Under the stress of historical crisis, archetypes undergo structural modification" (14). Although archetypal images change from writer to writer, the Jungian "archetypes" themselves are presumably of genetic origin and thus must evolve, a vastly slower process than the relatively quick changes discerned by Fisch (or by Jung in his "Answer to Job"). In post-Jungian terms, however, one would expect what Fisch found: each repetition different, reflecting not merely the course of the text itself but the historical context as well. Following Deleuze, J. Hillis Miller distinguishes between "Platonic" repetition "grounded in a solid archetypal model," and "Nietzschian" repetition, where only an undefinable "ghostly" something is repeated.[13] Following Kierkegaard, John M. Neary mentions other kinds of repetition, including Christian grace, where something is restored but in such a surprising manner that the emphasis is on the newness of the event.[14] The varieties of repetition are potentially endless.

Metaphor

Metaphor or analogy may evoke a sense of interconnectedness and wholeness. One need think only of Michel Foucault's studies of analogy in Renaissance thought to recall how, carried far enough, a system of analogies once related the whole world to a unifying God (every rock, plant, and animal given spiritual meaning, e.g., the pelican as an *imago Christi* allegedly feeding its flesh to its young). What relationship do such metaphors have to archetypes? Concerning a childhood memory Jung writes:

> It was as though she [the maid] belonged not to my family but only to me, as though she were connected in some way with other mysterious things I could not understand. This type of girl later became a component [*Aspekt*] of my anima. (*Er* 15; *M* 8)

Thus he believed that "this type of girl" was added to his anima archetype by way of analogy with people he actually met, especially the one in childhood. He maintained, nonetheless, that the anima was autonymous, completely out of the control of his conscious ego. What was he really describing? One clue may lie in "transitivism," the radical identification of one person with another. Lacan writes:

> During the world of this [infantile] period, one will record the emotional reactions and the articulated evidences of a normal transitivism. The child who strikes another says that he has been struck; the child who sees another fall, cries. Similarly, it is by means of an identification with the other that he sees the whole gamut of reactions of bearing and display, whose structural ambivalence is clearly revealed in his behaviour, the slave being identified with the despot, the actor with the spectator, the seduced with the seducer. (*Ecrit* 113/19)

Transitivism shows how weak the boundaries of the self may be. In a dream, you unconsciously manipulate (identify with) all the characters, yet, to the degree that you are conscious, you may even be frightened of some of them. During waking hours, children play with imaginary companions and authors create characters, which may even take on a life of their own against the author's conscious intentions. In multiple personalities, a patient identifies with one persona after another. A fragmented psyche or even multiple personalities often result from the trauma of child abuse. In 1907, Jung wrote to Freud:

> My veneration for you has something of the nature of a "religious" crush because of its undeniable erotic undertone. This abominable feeling comes from the fact that as a boy I was the victim of a sexual assault by a man I once worshipped. (*Freud-Jung Letters,* letter 49j, October 28)

Jung expresses the fear that Freud will also betray or break from him and when this break actually occurred, Jung, in the midst of a narcissistic crisis, a radical fragmentation of self, began conversing with visionary beings he later labeled archetypes (see *Memories, Dreams, Reflections* chap. 6). Jung believed that these "archetypes" could take possession of an individual in a process Jung called "inflation." Like multiple personalities, inflation involves identification with what I consider to be an imaginary construct, except that in inflation there is only one such construct rather than many. In medical terms, fragmentation is presumed to be bad, but a literary critic generally assumes that identification with characters is proof that the book is good, and as we have seen, Canetti wanted humanity to be afflicted with multiple personalities so that they would be too distracted to seek worldly power. The archetypal images that Jung mentions most commonly may actually be fantasy beings (e.g., *senex, puer, anima,* and *animus*) formed on analogy with real persons (e.g., guardians, playmates, and lovers). Since the underlying process of their creation is universal, the images are comparable where the cultures provide similar models. Kafka, however, finding role models and even coherence itself problematic, wrote that metaphors made him despair at becoming a writer (*D*2 200–1).

Metonymy

A third basic component of language is what Jakobson calls "metonymy," the relationship between contiguous images. It helps to explain another widespread pattern in folklore, the notion that when two things normally in contact with one another are separated, they continue to influence each other. Thus a voodoo practitioner may gather the hair of potential victims, assuming it will give power over them. In modern and postmodern literature, however, as numerous studies have shown, metonymic images predominate in realism, metaphoric ones in fantasy. This can best be explained by thinking of one of the most significant divisions of the metonymic mode, synecdoche (taking a part for the whole). In secular life, desire is typically synecdochic:[15] each person acquires one possession or role after another—a new car, a partnership in a law firm—in hope one day to "have it all," as popular cliché phrases this longing. Thus the most secular literature lavishes loving detail on all the miscellaneous objects of the world, the possessions to be obtained. In the midst of life, some people realize that they will never "have it all." Jung was one of the first to diagnose this midlife crisis and show how it may lead to a more introspective, religious turn of mind.

Antithesis

Jung calls antitheses the "contraries" and presumes them to be universal. In *Aion,* he writes, "Equivalent opposites are necessary conditions inherent in the act of cognition" (*GW,* vol. IX, par. 112). Since the Unconscious is defined as other than consciousness, in simplest terms the former is imagined to be the opposite or complement of the latter. If a man thinks of his conscious self in terms of his masculinity, he is likely to personify the Unconscious as its opposite, a mysterious feminine being, the anima. If, however, he imagines consciousness to be his daytime self, then unconsciousness is the dark, nocturnal, shadow side, the repressed portion of his mind. Traditionally, human beings contrast themselves with animals; thus, the Unconscious might be seen as a lurking beast, for example, Hesse's Steppenwolf. Since the Unconscious might impinge on consciousness, there are many fantasies of becoming one's antithesis: man transformed to woman (e.g., Teresias) or to his shadow side (e.g., Jekyll and Hyde), or to an animal (e.g., werewolf). Concerning one psychic transformation, Jung writes, "Men can argue in a very womanish way, too, when they are anima possessed and have thus been transformed into the animus of their anima" (*GW,* vol. IX, par. 29). Jung presents much literary and clinical evidence to suggest that the Unconscious is imagined as the opposite of consciousness. The problem with his typology begins when he tries to go beyond this generalization and divide these images into separate "archetypes."

Are there any such "archetypes" that Jung missed? Since his death, fantasies about machines have become more commonplace, especially in Japanese comics and animated cartoons, where weak human beings turn into their opposites, powerful robots. In traditional Chinese literature, Chuang Tzu dreamed he was a butterfly and, on awaking, wondered if he was a butterfly dreaming he was Chuang Tzu. Kaze Shinobu's graphic story "Heart and Steel" (*Epic,* 1 [February 1982]: 92–97) ends, "I no longer know whether I am a robot, who wishes to become human . . . or a woman who is dreaming she is a robot." The proliferation of mechanical images is exactly what a post-Jungian theory would expect given the growing prominence of machines in our world, but it is evidence against the paleo-Jungians. By evolutionary theory, such an entity as a new Jungian archetype ought to take millennia (or more) to evolve, not a few decades.

A different problem lies in the animus (a woman's Unconscious represented as a numinous male figure). Particularly in Romantic literature, Jung found a wealth of anima figures ("soul mates," *epipsychidions, femmes fatales,* etc.). As feminists have repeatedly remarked, evidence for an animus is arguably more slight. One study has already identified significantly fewer animus figures in works by women than anima figures in works by men.[16] Some evidence for an animus does exist, nonetheless, including the testimony of numerous women who became Jungian analysts and some (albeit ambiguous) representation in the arts, for example, Sexton's Rumpelstiltskin. Young girls are generally presumed to fantasize about knights in shining armor, religious leaders, rock stars—the usual examples of animus figures. One might expect that the animus would either exist (with as much evidence as the anima) or not exist (thereby lacking any evidence). The actual situation, however, is easy to explain. Male political and social dominance has meant that a man has not had to pay quite as much attention to what a woman was really like in order to dominate. Consequently, a man could easily imagine the feminine as his diametrical opposite (an anima), while only a less experienced or perceptive woman was as likely to confuse the men around her with her own Unconscious. Understandably, the anima had its literary heyday in the nineteenth-century Occident, when custom did everything it could to prevent men from knowing the real nature of women. In China, however, traditional art has more often represented the (complementary) opposite of man as nature, particularly the landscape, rather than as some enchantress or seductress. The tendency to describe experience in terms of antitheses appears to be inborn, while the exact nature of them apparently derives from each culture. Even the distinction between consciousness and the unconscious is one of these simplifying antitheses, for what we really experience (as Jung himself occasionally admitted)[17] is a continuum from most to least conscious cerebral activity, rather than a mind neatly chopped into ego, personal unconscious, Collective Unconscious, etcetera.

What Lies Behind these Four Aspects of Language?

Throughout his works, Jung implied that the purpose of archetypes is to unify conscious and unconscious into a Self—most obviously in his last magnum opus, *Mysterium coniuntionis,* a study of numinous conjunctions. To what extent are these four characteristics unifying? To say an event is a **repetition** is to consider it in some sense the same as its antecedent. **Metaphor** or analogy arises from a similarity. With **metonymy** (particularly synecdoche) contiguous parts are joined into a whole. While the world (according to most theories of physics, both ancient and recent) is a flux, and while language (according to the deconstructionists) offers only differ*a*nce, these first three characteristics are predicated on the idea of sameness. But what of **antithesis?** It often represents the process of unification in the dynamic moment just before victory is attained. As with Bruno Schulz's "blissful antinomies," literary **antithesis** tends to be emotional, for example, two lovers uniting or, less pleasantly, two sides forming for Armageddon. Whether its image is marriage or the extermination of the dissidents, it moves toward unity. But is unity ever attained? In New England, as the Puritan fervor abated, there was a drift toward Unitarian (belief in One Divine Person, not a Trinity) Universalism (belief that sinners and saints alike will be united in Salvation). More recently, as life has grown more competitive again, the drift has been toward Fundamentalist moral rearmament against Satan's legions. A true Romantic, Blake was fascinated by antithesis as in *The Songs of Innocence and of Experience: The Contrary States* or *Jerusalem,* where he imagined the uniting process going on eternally, his vision of heaven. A more dispirited writer, Kafka considered antitheses shallow and left himself a note to try to avoid them (*D1* 157). At any rate, antitheses *simplify* the real diversity of the world into an exciting dichotomy, at least sometimes preparatory to unification, or liquidation of the opposition, which amounts to much the same thing. Thus all four functions may have a direction: away from what Derrida calls differ*a*nce and consequently toward nondiffer*a*nce.

Derrida coined differ*a*nce from the French word *différer,* from which the English terms "differ" and "defer" are derived. They were originally seen to be integrally related ideas, both suggesting division and separation. What then is nondiffer*a*nce? Absence of difference and deferment: Absolute Unity, Identity, Presence, Plenitude. It is infinite and eternal because, if it were bounded, then one might look beyond it, interfering with constant homogeneity. It stimulates each sense to the fullest, for it lacks all shadings and differentiations. To the eyes, it is pure light, the luminousness common to mystical and *near*-death experiences. To the ear it is a thunderous roar, as in the Old Testament where the voice of God is imaged as thunder. Taking a few of its aspects (mostly its constancy), Freud presumed that a longing for nondiffer*a*nce was nostalgia for the uterus or a death impulse, but neither womb nor tomb has much in common with it. Christian hymns about Eternal Life are not evidence of Freudian *thanatos,* a supposed desire to be a rotting corpse. In "The Hunter Gracchus: A Fragment," Kafka speaks of the basic human craving for connection or coherence, *Zusammenhang* (*B* 334). According to Janouch, Kafka said that a "Great Coherence" was the idea underlying all religions. Janouch's Kafka associated it with *Tao,* a word which is treated as if it were not a word (e.g., the first verse of the Tao Te Ching), just as Derrida deliberately makes differ*a*nce orthographically strange to separate it from other words. So also, nondiffer*a*nce cannot fit neatly in any semantic system, for no single word or image can adequately describe something beyond the differ*a*nce of language and the flux of physical existence.

These elusive opposites, differ*a*nce and nondiffer*a*nce, are related respectively to two types of cognitive dissonance relevant to literary criticism: (1) the undecideable, what Roland Barthes calls "the obtuse meaning" (defined in a manner comparable to Derridean differ*a*nce);[18] and (2) Jung's "synchronicity," images that, whatever their logical classification, acquire an additional, inexplicable yet meaningful interrelationship (a token of universal unity, i.e., non-differ*a*nce). Take, for example, the story that began this study, "A Commentary," by Kafka. In his obliqueness, the policeman recalls the mysteriousness that Kafka attributed to his own father, but the officer's specific behavior is not very much like Hermann Kafka's. Is the policeman a malevolent fiend? A benevolent sage? A lunatic? Probably, the point will never be settled, for he seems to embody differ*a*nce. Kafka's vogue comes also from synchronicity, his victims of unreachable authority figures seeming to predict the subsequent condition of millions under arbitrary rulers (for Vonnegut, the Nazis; for Kundera, the Communists). The pleasure of perusing Kafkaesque literature comes both from intriguing differ*a*nce and unprovable synchronicity, a glimpse of that nondiffer*a*nce or radical unity that, according to Janouch's Kafka, underlies all religions. To what extent are all religions—or, at least to what extent is all religious language—alike?

In *Pilgrim's Regress,* C. S. Lewis tells how his conversion to theism (and eventually Christianity) was occasioned by the realization that

> The human soul was made to enjoy some object that is never fully given—nay, cannot even be imagined as given—in our present mode of subjective and spatio/temporal experience. This Desire was, in the soul, as the Siege Perilous in Arthur's Castle—the chair in which only one could sit. And if nature makes nothing in vain, the One who can sit in this chair must exist.[19]

Lewis's inkling of One beyond space, time, and the self (i.e., subjectivity), sounds here like nondiffer*a*nce because it is so vague (representing an early stage in his Christian faith). As soon as one moves into somewhat more definite language (the Orthodox dogmas that he eventually accepted), the unifying blur gives way to slightly clearer images: Infinite, Eternal God creating mankind in the Divine likeness; God, in Whom we live and move and have our being; the very Flesh and Blood of God entering the bodies of the communicants; the Holy Spirit (God) and Kingdom of Heaven dwelling within the saved. Similarly, in Islam, a few sufis have spoken with pantheistic vagueness, but the average adherent relies on Koranic images of man related to God only through the former's total submission and the latter's Will. Similarly, Jewish monotheism insists that man and God are contractually joined rather than identical, but this covenant may be very close as in the Kabbalistic mystic's *devekuth* (clinging to God, the *Ayin Sof* [Without End] and *Shadai* [Eternal]). In Hinduism, the Upanishadic Divinity, Brahman, sounds indistinguishable from nondiffer*a*nce, while everyday Hindu religion involves instead a vivid pantheon of integrally and intricately related gods. The nature of a culture is to divide the world into specifics; thus, not surprisingly, ordinary adherents are concerned with the *relationship* between these specifics, while those who for one reason or another transcend or transgress cultural boundaries (the mystics) *may* go on to a vision of unity. It is not the province of Religions in Literature to decide between pantheism and alternative theologies—or, indeed, to confine itself to theologies *per se*.

Early Buddhist literature, for instance, offers a change from theistic phrasing. Instead of revering what Lewis calls "Sweet Desire," the longing to find absolute constancy in this or any world is condemned as a delusion and the root of suffering. Interestingly, by the time the Buddhist Pali Scriptures reached their present form, eradicating this desire was said to earn Nirvana, a state described in a vague, hesitant, negative way, again resembling nondiffer*a*nce.[20]

Taoism offers another variation. The Tao is the coherence of all things and is said to be constant or eternal, yet continuous change characterizes it. Thus Tao consists not merely of nondiffer*a*nce but of differ*a*nce as well. Similarly, Mahayana, a later form of Buddhism, proclaims that taken to their limits, the opposites, Samsara (the world of differ*a*nce) and Nirvana (its antithesis) are identical:

> The limits of *nirvāna* are the limits of *samsāra*
> Between the two there is not the slightest difference
> *(nirvānasya ca ya kotih samsaranasya ca*
> *na tayor antaram kimcit susūksmam api vîdyate).*[21]

In Zen (a sect of Mahayana Buddhism) this means that the adept has an experience of extreme differ*a*nce, followed by a vision of sameness, *Byōdō-kan,* the realization that all beings are identical in their Buddha-nature, the potential to attain Nirvana.[22] Eventually, the Zenist is able to experience *satori,* radical sameness, and difference simultaneously. Although Zen describes this Enlightenment as the "Everyday Mind," *satori* is more profound than the commonsense notion that life is somehow the same, somehow different. The latter can best be termed *monotony,* a stylistic word describing events as having the same tone, yet without any experience of perfection, completion, or wholeness. Life being calmed until it approximates stasis (as in the slow-motion ballet of tai chi) may suggest nondiffer*a*nce as may acceleration to blurring speeds; between these two extremes hangs monotony, where ecstasy is most difficult.

Translating religious language into a common vocabulary (as I am doing) unfortunately involves (like any translation) the loss of important nuances, but the need for even a superficial mutual understanding throughout the world is so great that I believe I am justified in describing religious literature with such terms as *differ*a*nce*, *nondiffer*a*nce*, *repetition, metaphor, metonymy, antithesis, imagery,* and *monotony.* I do not suggest that all religions are the same but merely that religious literature (the way each faith explains itself) derives (albeit, each in its own way) from aspects of language itself. Such a terminology is particularly useful in treating Kafkaesque heterodoxy. The major religions each have a vast body of explanatory writings. Camus's "tender indifference of the world," Beckett's "thing or nothing behind language," and so on, have a less clear cultural context (because of the multicultural backgrounds of the authors). Thus, without translation, the phrases may appear to naive readers like the meaningless gibberish of lunatics. The oxymoron "tender indifference," however, is an apt image, since nondiffer*a*nce involves a feeling of relatedness (Camus's anthropomorphical metaphor "tender") and of sameness ("indifference" being etymologically the antithesis of "difference"). Beckett sensibly hesitates between "nothing" and "something" to describe the transcendence that fascinates him because, being beyond language, nothing can be predicated about it, even its being. Rather than any specific culture, these authors may reflect the dynamics of bilingualism itself. As Beaujour summarizes recent research:

> In tests of divergent thinking of cognitive flexibility, bilinguals have rather consistently been found to outperform monolinguals. . . . Bilinguals themselves frequently mention a greater awareness of the relativity of things.[23]

Deriving from the same psycholinguistic functions no more limits literature than do the laws of acoustics constrain music. Indeed, even so relatively small a part of world literature as the Kafkaesque can be subdivided, perhaps endlessly. The foregoing threefold categorization, however, comes simply from major religious patterns.

First, works by the "leopard"-like authors evoke nondifferance by way of imagery arranged according to repetition, metaphor, metonymy, and antithesis, but since these writings are postmodern, they follow this traditional path in an innovative manner. Eliade's book *The Old Man and the Bureaucrats*, for example, makes the reader want to escape its seemingly aimless digressiveness by focusing on the eternal return of mythical and metaphoric motifs. The French avant-garde originally asumed that Eliade's friend Ionesco was a great absurdist because they enjoyed not being able to make head nor tail of his plays. When, with *Rhinoceros*, he committed the heresy of being relatively clear, many critics were disappointed and angry, considering that he had sold out his convictions to attract a larger audience. Actually, his beliefs were even more conservative, as with his imagery of light, presumed to be a parody of heaven, yet intended to evoke his mystical experiences of "transcendental roots." Similarly, Broch's dying Virgil finds within his nightmares imagery of *puer, anima,* and even an angel, leading him toward the One. For Octavio Paz (and apparently also for his friend Carlos Fuentes), literature reflects the heroic journey through life's labyrinth to the Center. Thomas Mann and Hermann Hesse follow the Jungian line fairly closely, except for the former's inclination to be a "religious humorist." More perverse, heeding a "friendly celestial power," the protagonist of Landolfi's story "The Mute" seeks to unite with his anima "wholly and eternally" by killing the girl on whom he has projected it. Bruno Schulz presents archetypes only to move beyond them, past the gnostic Creator-Demiurge, to the unnameable God. Steinbeck's novel *The Winter of Our Discontent* depicts humanity still unconsciously reenacting paleolithic religious rituals (to which each person responds differently). Believing life to have many discoverable meanings, Joyce Carol Oates moves us even closer to the next group, those who agree with her that existence has no one significance, but insist that the meanings are invented, not discovered. Her vision of life as a heroic quest for meanings, nonetheless, keeps her from entirely abandoning past seekers, including the archetypal theorists and the monistic mystics. Finally, Borges investigates the implications of mystical Individuation and "believe[s] in God in spite of theology." His extreme playfulness, though, almost puts him in the next camp.

The "frog"-like authors (who constitute the next group) seek the antithesis or even the negation of tradition, a radical emptiness comparable to Zen. With Sartre and Camus, the stance is grim and tough-minded, because they are painfully tearing themselves away from Christian culture. André Breton is less tied to the past except in its giving him precedents to seek the "Hegelian" focal point of the spirit. Profiting from his predecessors's struggles with tradition, Derrida generally manages an easy playfulness, though his pervasive use of religious language (albeit in parodied form) and his crusade against logocentricity have often been seen as crypto-religious, a relic of Judaic idol smashing—perhaps also a tendency in Nathalie Sarraute's iconoclasm and Philip Roth's battles against Jewish tradition itself. Alain Robbe-Grillet argues for an untraditional worldview, yet finds himself writing something very like Jungian alchemical mysticism. Even the arch-aesthete Nabokov, a mocker at most verities, seems to have struggled with a desire for eternal patterns. Julio Cortázar did much to smash the traditional form of the novel, yet his *Hopscotch* repeatedly describes itself as a "mandala," leading toward "Heaven, Home." Nicanor Parra's antipoetry apparently retains God, but with each person giving Deity a new name. Abe Kōbō's Box Man, despite leaving aside the forms of ordinary life, wishes to be reborn in "another world," an echo of the Amida Buddhist hope of palingenesis into the Pure Land, where one can easily gain Nirvana. Milan Kundera is tearing himself away from communism, which he sees as a kind of religion, based on archetypal thinking, that he cannot entirely avoid. To the limited extent that he ever seems troubled by this inability, he resembles such an author of the next group as Vonnegut, particularly because of their common tendency to break narrative into dryly ironic fragments.

Finally come the "raven"-like authors. In their works, life is a barely tolerable monotony—not the mere dullness of a rainy day, but a dismal foreshadowing of doom, drawn by something within them. In Kurt Vonnegut's *Slaughterhouse-Five,* he describes the book (his most successful) as a failure and himself as paralyzed and lost, turned to a "pillar of salt." His comic, monotonous refrains (e.g., "And so it goes") mark the passing of his dull, fat protagonist, Billy Pilgrim, from one misery to another in a hell world, where there is no free will or end to pain. In *Shame,* Salman Rushdie describes himself as a tree, whose roots are slowly being consumed in the subterranean depths. The novel's first chapter, "The Dumb-Waiter," introduces its fat, insomniac protagonist, who is "courting Disaster." Some three hundred pages later in the chapter "Judgment Day," he

> saw the abyss open up beneath his feet, felt the vertigo come as the world dissolved. "I confess," he cried, but it was too late. He tumbled into the black fire and was burned. (314)

Edmond Jabès, despite his fascination with Kabbalistic dreams of Unity, believes that it is his duty as writer to pursue any "image which overwhelms or nauseates us," particularly the death camps. Beckett seeks a "literature of the unword," grounded on "consternation." Tom Stoppard's works despairingly reject the possibility of what he seems to desire, an art to "crack the shell of mortality." Canetti's one novel, the vast *Auto-da-Fé,* chronicles the lingering decline of a bibliophile toward suicide and the burning of his own library. Despite some manic moments while identifying "with everybody, even the hersiarchs," John Berryman's poetry echoes the odd notion that he is somehow condemned by his father to suicide, like Kafka's Georg Bendemann. Plath's poetry reflects a gradual surrender to the archetypal "stars" of her fate. For Anne Sexton, life is a "Kafka machine" making her wish to be locked away. Susan Sontag's corpus largely concerns slow diseases of mind and body in a sick society. Ralph Elison's *Invisible Man* tellingly evokes the drab life of a young man, carrying with him a "recommendation" that dooms him to unemployment and alienation. For the later Walter Benjamin, after his Kabbalistic religiosity had cooled, happiness was merely a "speculative idea."

With the possible exception of Jabès and Benjamin, the members of this third group are masters of dark comedy. Beginning in the 1950s, the Dutch psychoanalyst Johan Leonard Arndt encouraged his patients to compose fantasies in which they exaggerated their complaints until they finally ended by laughing them away.[24] For the "raven"-like authors, however, humor seems to be only a palliative. How does one escape depression? Eliade outgrew his juvenile bouts with it, perhaps by constructing his History of Religions to serve as an "orientation." Among the many authors that I have not discussed, T. S. Eliot wrote his *Wasteland* (or, as it was originally called, "He Do the Police in Many Voices") to register his horror at cultural diversity and transitoriness. Even that work, however, ends with a possibility of hope, and his subsequent conversion to conservatism (as Anglican, Royalist, and Classicist) largely protected him from the Kafkaesque condition. By the time of the *Four Quartets,* his orientation was so secure that he could integrate form and formlessness, equating the fire (symbol of earthly mutability) and rose (symbol of heavenly grace).[25] Another once-depressed author who largely avoided becoming Kafkaesque, the French poet Francis Ponge writes:

> Vigny has said: every man has seen the wall which confines his spirit. As to me . . . it is not a wall, it is a precipice. . . . What does a man who suffers from vertigo do when he arrives at the edge of a precipice? Instinctively, he looks only at what is closest. . . . If his trouble is authentic, or even if he falls in the abyss, like Kafka . . . he does not speak of it; he speaks of all but that; he looks only at what is closest.[26]

Kafka, of course, does write of his condition; but, after leaving the sanatarium to which he was confined after his collapse, Ponge devotes his poetry to small, domestic objects, described in a manner, Derrida has shown,[27] reflecting the provincial limitations of French language and culture. Vonnegut's thesis adviser (who eventually committed suicide), once told an anthropology class that the common denominator of all the arts was the artist's belief, "I can do very little about the chaos around me, but at least I can reduce to perfect order this square of canvas, this piece of paper, this chunk of stone." Vonnegut comments:

> Everybody knows that.
> Most of my adult life has been spent in bringing to some order sheets of paper. . . . This severely limited activity has allowed me to ignore many a storm. It has also caused many of the worst storms I ignored.[28]

This knowledge, however, was not much help to him at least until after he began chemical therapy for depression. He kept feeling that he, like all human beings, was genetically engineered to desire a sense of wholeness that passed away with "Folk Societies." More recently, though, with *Bluebeard,* he gives a hint of hope that art can bring many people together, albeit temporarily and only if it is the kind of work (like Vonnegut's later novels) scorned by the critics.

To what extent can literature fulfill the desire for Unity? The next chapter applies the foregoing approach to a concrete example, Kafka's "At the Building of the Great Wall of China."

10
Behind the Great Wall

> Dark, dark, see the Great Wall's beginning,
> Where, according to all, in days of yore,
> Strife raised will and spirit [*ch'i*].
>
> —Wang Chang-Ling, "Border-Post Song" (c. 750 A.D.)

According to Paul Raabe, Kafka's story "At the Building of the Great Wall" (to be abbreviated as "BGW" hereafter) was of paramount importance to Kafka himself.[1] It subsequently was one of his most influential works, for example, on Borges. Especially since Kafka abandoned his original plan to tell *The Castle* in the first person, "BGW" remains among his longest fictions where the narrator is "I" (though, as always, narrative perspective shifts). The first paragraph *seems* to begin on a note of triumph and in the third person omniscient: the fortification has been completed *(beendet),* its walls stretching from southeast and southwest to the north, where they have united *(vereinigt).* Complementary "worker-armies" have met, joining East and West, North and South. This union of compass points, however, is not, as a Jungian might expect it, at the center of a circle. Rather, the segments merge at a distant border—if at all. Within a few sentences, the narrator admits that he has been exaggerating, as have also the perfidious Chinese leadership, who declared the wall finished while gaps *(lücken)* existed. A story has arisen—according to the narrator, perhaps merely a "legend"—that breaks remain. While "BGW" commenced with a sense of architectonic wholeness and narrational omniscience, both intimations disappear together. (In actual Chinese history, after centuries of fragmentary construction, small old walls were partly interconnected into a great one, which then decayed and was rebuilt. This occurred during four major periods between 217 B.C. and 1644 A.D., without ever forming an entirely continuous structure, so the narrator's doubts are justified.)

Not until the second paragraph does the narrator identify himself. Even then, he does not do so with the humble "I," but purports to speak for "we, the builders"—though he feels forced to admit that this group knows less about the wall than even the ignorant barbarians, who migrate near it.

Despite this qualification, he returns to grandiose imagery of the infinite and eternal. The builders sought not only to construct a wall too vast for them to measure but also one that would last an uncountably long time. Consequently, it must embody "the architectural wisdom of all known ages and peoples." This greatest possible union of space, time, and knowledge was to serve as a bulwark against the impatience of the barbarians, as changeable as grasshoppers or locusts *(Heuschrecken),* but it actually excited them to greater movement. Without yet revealing the reason, the narrator explains that this "wisdom" has resulted in the wall's being built in fragments, which tribesmen may destroy before the segments connect.

In thus announcing the absurdity and futility of the project, what is Kafka's tone? When he read his works to his friends, they often laughed appreciatively. Some Occidental (particularly American) readers may not notice this comedy, both because they cannot hear the wry way that he publicly read his works and because attitudes toward humor vary from culture to culture. In his classic of anthropology, *The Silent Language,* Edward T. Hall explains:

> In general, American humor is a binary type of humor, which is either on or off. In the Far East, however, one encounters a continuum, a wide spectrum of subtle degrees of enjoyment.[2]

Kafka's dry self-mockery was more like the latter, examples of which he had allegedly seen in the whimsies of Chuang Tzu, the probable model for the hyperbolic style of "BGW." In one instance of this hyperbole, Kafka's narrator insists that there had to be a skilled architect supervising every four unskilled laborers.[3] This distrust of common people anticipates later remarks. It satirizes the narrator, apparently an aloof mandarin, both ridiculously contemptuous of the masses and naive in assuming that the workers received "good money." Historically, if the laborers received close supervision, it had less to do with their ignorance than with their unwillingness. The stone-layers, in press gangs of almost two million laborers at a time, were often starving, usually selected either by a draft or as a punishment for dissent. As the Chinese poet Yin Geng wrote, "The blood of the builders flowed by like a moat."[4] The Chinese call their wall the "Longest Cemetery on Earth."[5] No wonder that their god of walls governs the boundary between life and death![6]

The First Major Digression: A Reminiscence

Significantly, the third paragraph opens with the third-person pronoun "One" *(Man),* which in Kafka's "Letter to the Father" signaled moments of stress. Instead of directly answering the question posed by the second paragraph (why the wall was built in such an absurd manner), the narrator digresses to earlier times, especially his own childhood. For thirty years before his birth, in preparation for the building, masonry became the chief science, all others measured in accordance with it. Although the prestige of disciplines has varied relative to one another from age to age, the only time when absolute preeminence existed was with theology in the Occidental Middle Ages, so he is inherently comparing masonry and religion—not an original analogy. The Masonic Order is based on it, with Master Builder as God and elaborate geometrical symbology. Regarding Freemasonry, Kafka wrote the following sentence fragment: "The possible truth that there is in every discourse and doctrine" (*D2* 230). Later in "BGW," the wall building develops its own strange metaphysics, but the analogy with religion is more immediately relevant to a childhood incident related by the narrator. As boys, so young that they could barely walk, he and his classmates were commanded to erect a wall of pebbles. Then the teacher, forsaking the proverbial dignity of Chinese pedagogues, pulled up his robes, ran against the structure, and smashed it so that he could scold them. In tears, they ran to their parents. This repeats the motif of faulty unity and scattering (the pebbles and the children), but the cause of this breakdown here is fanaticism. The narrator recounts the incident to reveal this "Geist der Zeit," spirit or mind of the time. The idea of a *Zeitgeist* is charged with Hegelian associations, part of a theory of how history moves from contradiction to an ultimate synthesis of spirit and matter in eternity. We are left, however, only with weeping children—"a trivial incident," the narrator calls it—but considering Kafka's familiarity with Freud and the importance Kafka himself assigned to childhood experiences, the incident cannot be easily dismissed.

In the fifth paragraph, the digression shifts forward from the narrator's childhood. Because of the fifty years' preparation preceding actual wall building, a generation of masons went to their graves without ever having done the work for which they trained and the next generation of masons (that of the narrator) were filled with impatience. To assuage this, the wall was built in fragments, with the mason given awards and movement to a new location every five years (Kafka's synchronistic anticipation of the Chinese five-year plans). Fortification, which in the West is primarily an economic, political, logistical, and military concern, becomes here a question of the builders' "faith in themselves, in the wall, in the world" (237). As this is revealed, the narrator significantly shifts from the first to the third person, trying to make this most subjective of reasons sound objective. His tone grows hyperbolical again: the traveling masons' seeing mountains leveled, forests hewn, temples filled with the prayers of the pious for a speedy completion. They were made thereby into "eternally hopeful children," ready for new labor. The emotionalism of the prose swells. First, the events fostering their confidence are contiguous occurrences on their journey (e.g., meeting credulous officials, encountering the faith of their own families, being accompanied by banner-waving multitudes). By the end of the paragraph, however, the narrator crosses over into metaphor: the wall arises from a "ring of brothers"; the "endless leagues of China" have become a single body with the same blood. That these metaphors are mixed and clichéd distances sophisticated readers from them. The mob's cry of "Unity! Unity!" sounds as dangerous as the mass movements of Kafka's day that eventually evolved into Nazism. At the same time, Kafka's teasing play with the idea of unity throughout the story may tantalize even sophisticated readers with a desire for coherence.

The Tower of Babel

After a transitional paragraph, the narrator again begins a paragraph with a third-person pronoun *(Zunächst muss man . . . sagen),* presenting his compulsion to digress as something "one must" do. He begins an analogy between the wall and the Tower of Babel, the biblical prototype for fall into pluralism. Indeed, the allusion itself is polycultural, jarringly introducing a reference to Hebrew Scripture into the Chinese setting. Admittedly, the presence of Jews in China was well-known. Admittedly also, there are those who read the whole story as Judaic, the wall as an allegory of the Talmud.[7] Nonetheless, at least on the surface, "BGW" has been Chinese to this point and the Chinese Jews (whom Kafka never mentions) tended to be largely assimilated in the larger culture rather than China's being Judaized. To a biblical literalist, of course, the Tower of Babel was a real event that all people should have remembered. Kafka, however, introduces the tower not as fact but as part of a scholar's hypothesis. Although the Bible attributes the abandonment of the tower to divine displeasure at man's trying to gain an eternal name for himself (Gen. 11:1–9) and the subsequent multiplication of languages (i.e., scrambling of names) thereafter, this scholar *(Gelehrter)* disagrees. He contends that the true cause was mechanical: a faulty foundation, the Great Wall being needed as the first story of the structure. The narrator wonders why the scholar confused the desire for a spiritual tower into the heavens with a literal building. Furthermore, the narrator adds, the scholar's metaphysical/physical plan should require a circular wall (i.e., a mandala), something the wall is not. Why should his weird notion have allegedly become popular in China? Kafka's next paragraph explains that "human nature" is so mutable that without some vast metaphor or myth of unity, it will destroy itself and everything else, including the wall. The narrator writes that the people will tear themselves to pieces "in all heavenly directions" *(in all Himmelsrichtungen)*. The phrase is German, yet imitates the Chinese idiom "all under heaven" (available to Kafka in translation) and recalls the Hebrew of Gen. 11:9, describing mankind's being dispersed throughout all the earth. In "BGW," the narrator ridicules the scholar's use of myths as metaphors. If the latter wishes a spiritual ascent into the heavens, he is ridiculous to ground his hope in the Tower of Babel (or the Great Wall of China).

The Tower of Babel is the biblical type of people fragmented and disoriented because of a problem with language—an image that obsessed Kafka. In his story "The City Coat of Arms" *(Das Stadtwappen)*, there is a plurality of tongues even before the construction of the tower of Babel, yet the people come together to erect a path to heaven—or rather to think of such a project, since they deem the idea more important than the deed. While procrastinating, they lavish all their time on the workers' city, fighting over the quarters, and longing, nonetheless, that it be destroyed by a fist from heaven. This disturbingly merges traditional Judeo-Christian imagery of the hand of God with a fist on a coat of arms, perhaps one noted by Jirí Grusa's study of Kafka's relationship to Prague.[8] In "The Pit of Babel" *(Der Schacht von Babel)*, people desire to lower themselves, humbly or perversely seeking deeper levels of abasement, as if toward Hell. George Steiner comments on this fragment and "BGW."

> The foundations of the Tower preoccupy Kafka even more than the edifice itself. "The Burrow," his last story, and an unmistakable comment on the relation of the writer to language and reality, shows how the Tower may be seen from its interior, spiraling galleries.[9]

Like "BGW," "The Burrow" begins with an announcement of completion and success, which is undermined by each successive sentence. The structure contains a "Castle Keep," like a tower (albeit an inverted one), but it has at least "two centers" and consists of a deliberately confusing labyrinth to bewilder the maker's enemies. Instead of accomplishing this goal, he lies terrified, hearing echoing sounds from who knows where, disorienting him. In *The Lost One* (*Der Verschollene,* originally translated as *Amerika*), the Tower of Babel is one of the fragmentary novel's subtexts. According to Jewish tradition, if a hod carrier fell from the Tower of Babel and died, the fellow workers did not mourn the passing[10]—an image that Kafka uses concerning a worker's death at an unfinished building. Like Babel, that edifice is said to rise into heaven *(zum blauen Himmel ragten . . . in den Himmel ragten)*. The character Therese weeps at one of these seemingly unimportant references to heaven, but there is appropriateness to her emotional response in that image if, linked to the builders' indifference to her mother's fatal accident in the construction, the words about a building rising into heaven are seen to repeat the biblical typology of oppression and evil (as in the common German expression *Sündenbabel*). In the American melting pot (or as German idiom renders it *Babel von Sprachen*), those who have not mastered English are condemned to such work as building the skyscrapers, the American babels, that loom throughout the book. Also in "BGW," the mad desire to build stands implicitly condemned "as regards divine approval," though the people think otherwise.

The High Command

After ridiculing the scholar's Tower of Babel, the narrator, with the impersonal phrase, "It is possible," introduces an equally doubtful notion of his own. He bulwarks the following supposition by announcing it in the first-person plural, but heistantly, feeling need to defend that usage:

> We—and here I speak in the name of many people—did not really know ourselves until we had carefully scrutinized the decrees of the high command, when we discovered that without the high command neither our book learning nor our human understanding would have sufficed for the humble tasks which we performed in the great whole. (*C* 239)

Although he knows no one familiar with the names of the "High Command," he hypothesizes the existence of such a leadership, for without them the people could not work together "in the great whole" (*C* 239). In that mysterious bureaucracy, "all human thoughts and desires revolved in a circle, and all human aims and fulfillments in a countercircle" (*C* 240). Are these two circular movements like those in the *T'ai Chi* (*yin* and *yang* symbol), the Taoist emblem of wholeness? Or are Kafka's circles in opposition to one another, the eternal conflict of what we desire and what we attain? A luminence from the Divine (comparable to the light in "Before the Law") radiates the High Command, but it is merely reflected—a bad sign if one recalls Plato's parable of the cave. According to Jung, fantasies often take a compensatory form, the powerless man, for example, dreaming of the powerful. The narrator is among those who "did not know ourselves" except in contrast to these fantasied beings, whose imagined decrees have become the people's dearest belief.

The People's Faith

Contemplating the omnipotence of the High Command, the narrator renounces his previous explanation of the wall's piecemeal construction, since, given their great power, the leadership could have acted more expeditiously if they desired. According to the "best" people, one should not try to understand the High Command, even though "one can neither speak of injury nor non-injury [from such contemplation]." This sentence beginning with another shift to the third person directly precedes a new digression in the form of an extended simile. When human thought considers the High Command, it is like a stream overflowing its banks. In other words, the concern exceeds the nature of thought, leading to a shapelessness (like the "nebulous" plans for a Tower of Babel proposed by the scholar). Since the analogy of the Tao to water is fundamental to Taoism, similitudes involving rivers are common in the Taoist texts that Kafka allegedly owned. Those texts are notoriously paradoxical, but not more than Kafka, who suddenly has the narrator renounce the river simile he has just given as no longer adequate. Disturbingly, the narrator, born in the south of China (cf., Chuang-Tzu's *Southern Land of Blossoms*), now denies his previous contention that the wall was built against northern barbarians, since no one in the South could believe the northern enemy would ever reach the bottom of China. Since the workers from the south have themselves been at the northern border, one might presume that they would realize that barbarians could also make an equally long journey southward. The narrator's people, however, are incorruptibly provincial. To them the Tartars are mythical devils, credible only to children. In place of the similtude of the river, the narrator offers his own belief: the High Command is omniscient (aware of the people's most petty doings) as well as eternal "and the decision to build the wall likewise." The distinction between the petty (the common people) and the great (those close to Tao) may come from the opening chapter of Chuang Tzu, which stresses that the latter are incomprehensible to the former. Kafka's narrator has been making his reasoning more and more religious until his vision of the High Command (ridiculous from a secular point of view) is presented in terms comparable to arguments for Providence—but the High Command is not God. It may act, as the narrator says, in the reflected light of divine worlds, but that is not the same as being divine. Far from acquiring a supernal unity, the world now consists of the divine, the High Command, and the people unable to fathom the mysteriously forwarded commands. According to the narrator, the wall and its gaps (*lücke,* meaning also loopholes in law) have been eternally predestined. The idea might be compared to Blake's notion that time is the mercy of eternity. In other words, the gaps and delays in our lives protect us from Eternity, where individuality succumbs to nondiffer*a*nce. Comparably, a very important part of Talmud is finding the eternally preordained loopholes in the Law by which God's Justice is reconciled with his Mercy. In relation to Kafka's aphorisms (dating from about the same period as "BGW"), these gaps or loopholes are like the rationalizations that protect mankind from disappearing into the Divine Order.

The age of wall building and its enthusiasm have passed, so that the narrator more recently has "occupied [himself] almost exclusively with the comparative history of races" (242). This preoccupation also implies alienation, perhaps even more so. The preceding concerns the "endless leagues" of China, the Middle Kingdom. It is so vast that the Chinese have traditionally had little interest in anything beyond it—except for the need to banish barbarians—and the narrator seems to doubt their existence. Now, he sees the Chinese as simply one race among many, all of interest to him. Each paragraph of "BGW" represents a subtly greater alienation, so that, by this point, the initial presumptions have faded away, and the coherence of the whole is being strained beyond the breaking point. At this juncture, even a proto-Nazi narrator who studies races to prove the superiority of his own would be less surprising than Kafka's disinterested racial theorist. He is impressed by the oddness of his own people. Among their racially "unique" institutions is the empire itself, which even the court misunderstands. Further down, "the eternal truths remain eternally invisible in this fog of confusion" (242). The people devote the time to the "nature gods," whose ceremonies order the year. But no believer in such beings would ever call them "nature gods." They would be given their proper names (or even more pious circumlocutions), not anthropologically reduced to theological species, whose ceremonies have become to the narrator purely aesthetic phenomena, "beautiful and rich" (presumably the way Kafka himself appreciated myths and *Märchen*). Aside from these ceremonies, religious speculation relates to the emperor—but not the present one. Information arrives invariably late by way of "pilgrims" and sailors traversing "sacred rivers," who happen upon the far south, bringing word of some former dynasty. The narrator speculates about the emperor's appearance, the court intrigues, etcetera, preparing the way for the following "legend" *(Sage)*, called such in keeping with the narrator's anthropological viewpoint.

The Imperial Message

The narrator switches to the second-person familiar (used for children, people one knows intimately, holds in contempt, or all three). The legend's style is at first ornate, thus more what is commonly called "Oriental" than the preceding, "You" are termed "the insignificant shadow cowering in the remotest distance before the imperial sun." Although the word "distance" denotes separation, the metaphoric antithesis of emperor and you as "sun" and "shadow" implies complementarity. The comparison of emperor to sun is quite traditional, as in a poem by Tu Fu contained in Heilmann's anthology (57). With the emperor dying, "all the obstructing walls" have been eliminated, and his message to you, repeated and confirmed, has been witnessed by a "ring" of princes. This metaphor of communication, wholeness, nondiffer*a*nce, gives way to metonymies (the remaining delays and obstructions even the strongest messenger would encounter at each stage of his impossible journey). Ultimately you sit in the evening dreaming the message. The explicit opening metaphor of emperor as sun has given way to a more ambiguous implicit metaphor (the evening chosen to suit the disappearance of that sun). You dream the message, which may mean that the message actually reaches you or that you simply imagine that it does.

The incident is reminiscent of Kafka's before-mentioned story, where children all choose to be royal messengers rather than kings, so that there is no royal person from whom messages may be transmitted. Meister Eckhart writes:

> The other person, who is hidden within us, is the inner person. Scripture calls this person, a new person, a heavenly person, a young person, a friend, and a royal person. This person is meant when our Lord says that "a man of royal birth went to a distant country to be appointed king, and afterward he returned.[11]

Through love of worldly action, Kafka's children, however, refuse to become kings, and the imperial messenger, hindered by the press of worldly existence, never arrives. In a sense, Eckhart's king is eternal, yet Eckhart writes of someone appointed king (i.e., identifying with the Psychic Center). Comparably, one might write of the king's dying, when communication with this Center passed from consciousness and remained only in dreams. In Hebrew, which Kafka had just started to learn, the words king *(MLK)* and messenger *ML'K*) have a punning closeness to one another. For Kafka, the two roles seem also to be related: the children can choose one or the other; the Chinese messenger bears the imperial sun, the sign of the dead king whom he represents.

The Czech scholar and novelist Jirí Grusa equates Kafka's wall with the Prague Hunger Wall, constructed in the fourteenth century to give work to the starving, for which reason no one cared that it was "full of holes."[12] His interpretation (although not explaining the whole of "BGW") is relevant to this matter of dreaming, for while looking at the area of the Hunger Wall (on the Laurenziberg slopes), Kafka had the following thoughts:

> I found that the most important or the most delightful [hope] was the wish to attain a view of life (and—this was necessarily bound up with it—to convince

> others of it in writing), in which life, while still retaining its full-bodied rise and fall, would simultaneously be recognised no less clearly as a nothing, a dream, a dim hovering. (DS 292)

The phrasing makes no explicit reference to China. Indeed, the odd word "hovering" may recall that Eckhart defines God as a "hovering being and . . . nothingness" *(überswebende wesen und . . . nihtheit).*[13] The legend of the Imperial Message, nonetheless, like his Laurenziberg musings is dreamy, a quality Europeans associated with China—and with a little justification. Kafka, for example, had read in Heilman, the following lines by Li-Tai-Po:

> If life is a dream
> Why should I strive and bother!
> I—I remain intoxicated all day
> And if I begin to sway
> Then I sink down asleep by my door.[14]

As so often in Heilmann's collection, not Confucian industriousness but Taoist laissez-allez predominates. Particularly Taoist is Kafka's image of the empire as ungoverned. Taoist texts repeatedly explain that the emperor should not actually rule but simply follow the Tao so that his subjects will do likewise. How perfectly consonant with this ideal is an empire where the only contact between central government and provincials is the latter's evening dreams. As the twenty-ninth chapter of the *Tao Te Ching* states, "All below heaven [the empire] is a vessel too spiritual to be mastered." Wars do not disturb Kafka's provincials. They laugh at news of distant revolt, told to them in a dialect they misunderstand. To them, "Peking and its Emperor are . . . a cloud . . . peacefully voyaging beneath the sun in the course of ages." Voyaging on clouds is a characteristic of Taoist immortals, including the mythic Taoist emperor Huang-Ti, mentioned in a poem in Heilmann's anthology (31–33). The provincial village leads "a life on the whole free and unconstrained" yet "pure"—an excellent description of Taoist conduct. Momentarily taking a Confucian standpoint, the narrator first condemns the "weakness" of people and government; then he changes to a Taoist stance, finding himself forced to admit that the vast size, diversity, and corrupt administration gives the country its unity. This image of good coming from weakness is typically Taoist, as in the thirty-sixth chapter of the *Tao Te Ching:* "the submissive and weak will overcome the hard and strong" (*Lau* 95). Finally, the narrator indefinitely postpones his inquiry lest further questions leave the people confused. He says that continued inquiry "would undermin[e] not only our consciences, but, what is far worse, our feet." The image is a fairly common one not only in Kafka's writings but in others' at approximately that period, for example, Chesterton's definition of "Impressionism" as "another name for that final skepticism, which can find no floor to the universe."[15] The twentieth poem of the *Tao Te Ching* enjoins, "Exterminate learning and there will no longer be worries" (*Lau,* 76).

Possibly Related Fragments

Brod assumed that "BGW" was intended to be a larger work, containing not merely the episodes already cited, but also other fragments, though exactly which ones is as much a matter of controversy as whether such a relationship exists. "The News of the Building of the Wall," the most relevant, is a childhood reminiscence about its narrator's father, who heard that a great wall was to be built to protect the emperor from infidels and demons. This diverges from "BGW" in that the latter does not make the emperor the cause of the wall. "The Conscription of Troops" lacks any specifically Oriental details, but does concern a mysterious empire where the subjects are willing to suffer conscription or any other oppression (indeed, young girls go for miles to see an effete nobleman persecute people and are only disappointed when he fails to notice them). "The Problem of Our Laws" also concerns all-powerful nobles, this time resembling the High Command. "The Emperor" tells of a man who doubted the ruler's descent from the gods but without doubting the emperor's divine mission. (Heilmann's anthology alludes to the Emperor's title as Son of Heaven) (57). The title character of "The Imperial Colonel" rules entirely by a gaze that sounds much like Kafka's descriptions of his father's. These fragments differ from "BGW" in that they all concern various powerful authority figures, raised to supernal (Jung would say "archetypal") proportions, while "BGW" manages to reduce the Emperor to a dreamy inconsequence. Without these fragments, "BGW" stands well on its own. Its ending paradoxically offers a silent intuition of unity. Just as in Greek mythology, Semele found Zeus' thunderous, shining, burning Presence deafening, blinding, and fatal, so silence and emptiness, the antithesis of nondiffer*a*nce sometimes become symbols for what humanity's limited sense would perceive in its Presence.

Each of the Kafkaesque authors (discussed *infra*) had a different attitude to the structuring elements of language (the "archetypal" repetitions, metaphors, metonymies, and antitheses) which can be resisted, parodied, or embraced but never discarded before a story's final silence. The variety of these authors (Kafka among them) strongly suggests that the psyche is less clearly structured than Jung thought, but language, including religious language, is inescapably composed of determining elements, a proper concern of intercultural studies.

Why should there be such studies? Another of the allegedly related fragments, "An Old Page," comes close to answering the question. Its narrator, a Chinese cobbler, explains to his own surprise, despite the great distance to the frontier, that foreigners (northern nomads) have entered the capitol. Actually, Beijing is relatively near to the wall, though the cobbler might conceivably inhabit one of the earlier capitols. At any rate, like the narrator of "BGW," he has been ridiculously complacent. Now, however, he has gone to the other extreme, saying that he is living in *der letzten Zeit,* which may be literally rendered "the last age," a phrase in keeping with the Apocalyptic scene that he describes. (The story's title, however, highlights the irony that evocation of the End, which in each age seems *au courant,* is actually an old, as-yet unrealized nightmare.) The nomads have not sacked and burned the city. They disturb daily life only to the extent that the Chinese consider them filthy, frightening, and incomprehensible. They speak a language likened to the shrieks of jackdaws—one of those birds with which Kafka identifies, so that the nomads are, in this one respect, like Kafka's proverbially wandering Hebrews, always hated by the indigenous population. The narrator complains that they do not respect the Chinese "way of living and our institutions" (*C* 416); thus, he presumes, communication is impossible. He does not think of learning the nomads' culture, but assumes they have none. Possibly, they steal, though "you cannot call it taking by force." He particularly objects to their terrifying eating habits, as savage as those of the (anti-Semitic) Cossacks, in an account that, as Binder has noted, Kafka read (*Kafka Kommentar* 221). Horror at the barbarian feast leaves the narrator in an odd state of mind. Although the emperor actually stays sequesterd in an enclosed garden, the cobbler imagines seeing him at the castle *(Schloss)* window (like the mysterious stranger at the casement in the closing moment of *The Trial*). Kafka's probable sources, as uncovered by Binder, include passages about the Chinese emperor in a "holy seclusion" and about God's waiting for an age to close (*Kafka Kommentar* 221). The narrator longs for the stability the emperor once represented. Ceremonial military processions from the royal palace, however, no longer occur. The cobbler thinks the whole problem a "misunderstanding," seemingly a naive understatement, but the Chinese bias against foreigners may be the chief misunderstanding behind the situation. Without intercultural studies, will anyone in a polycultural age escape such an error? Just as the Great Wall, the most ambitious boundary in history, could not protect Chinese culture from foreign influences, so in Kafka's day (and even more in our own) all frontiers have proved permeable. As usual, Kafka trusted in the mystery of education as a possible solution. He wrote Felice:

> The study of languages can be based on the fact that it constitutes the first practical step toward a love of humanity, which expresses itself in the true realization of inner hospitality in detachment from the narrowness of one's own

> feelings, and in entering an alien point of view, thus creating tolerance and humility. (*F* 508)

This process, however, is far from inevitable. Although Jung himself was a multilingual savant, even his most admiring biographers do not claim "humility" for him, and his "tolerance" never reached the latest standards. Despite the fact that his closest followers were a group of educated women (the "Jungfräu" as jealous male colleagues called them), he personally made sexist remarks about "animus-ridden" blue stockings, and published such statements as the following:

> No one can get around the fact that by taking up a masculine profession, studying and working like a man, woman is doing something not wholly in accord with, if not directly injurious to, her feminine nature. . . . I do not mean merely physical injury, but above all psychic injury. (*GW X,* par. 117)

In a lecture that he later published, Jung said of "the Negro . . . he has probably a whole historical layer less than you. The different strata of the mind correspond to the history of the races."[16] Some present Jungians have discovered precedents in Jung's writings for a less biased view of society (for, in this as in practically everything else, he was not consistent). Unfortunately, his approach to psychology leads to a dilemma: if the "archetypes" are not sufficiently definite to form sexual and other stereotypes, then those "archetypes" must be so nebulous as to be of little, analytical value. One of Jung's more politically liberal interpreters, Eric Neumann, for example, defined "archetypes" as "formless psychic structures"[17]—Neumann's escape from Jungian conservatism into equally Jungian paradox and obscurantism. Instead of the word *archetypes,* there is need to substitute less loaded terms, such as *repetition, metaphor, metonymy,* and *antithesis*—categories that have proven their worth in many schools of hermeneutics. In his classic book *The Anatomy of Criticism,* Northrop Frye tried to unite all literary criticism with his own archetypal variety as the cornerstone. The time was premature for such a synthesis. At present, the hope of union seems even less, since it must now reconcile structuralism and deconstruction as well as an indeterminate number of other approaches. Nonetheless, an examination of what has previously been called "archetypal" (as in the present study) is still a reasonable step toward a truly new criticism that can glimpse what lies beyond the great wall of faulty preconceptions and limited views.

Notes

Introduction

1. Heinz Politzer provides a photocopy of the manuscript in *Franz Kafka: Parable and Paradox* (Ithaca, N.Y.; Cornell University Press, 1962), facing p. 1. The estimated date of composition is from Hartmut Binder, *Kafka Kommentar: zu sämtlichen Erzählungen* (Munich: Winkler, 1975), p. 298.

2. E.g., F. M. Dostoevsky, *Sobranie sotsineniy,* vol 5; *Prestypienie i nakazanie* (Moscow: Gosduarstvenooe Izadatel'stvo Khudozhesivennoy Literatury, 1957). Mikhail Bakhtin writes of such sudden events, "[Dostoevsky] 'leaps' over [historical and biographical time], concentrating action in *'crisis points, turning points and years,'* i.e., when the moment loses its temporal limitations." in *Problems of Dostoevsky's Poetics,* trans. R. W. Rotzel (n.p.; Ardis, 1973), p. 124. Among others remarking this device, Sidney Monas sees Dostoevsky's repetitious use of "suddenly" as a motif of discontinuity. Translator's Preface, *Crime and Punishment,* by Fyodor Dostoevsky, trans. Sidney Monas (New York: New American Library, 1968), p. vii.

3. In less mature works, Kafka himself had leaned on this cliché, e.g., in his first publication, *Betrachtung* (1912), where the Dostoevskian "suddenly" appears as an abrupt transition in the fictions *Entlarvung eines Bauernfängers, Der Plötzliche Spaziergang,* and *Der Kaufmann.*

4. The situation might have been doubly jolting if the clock were that of the Prague Jewish Town Hall, which runs counterclockwise. Although the idea of a psychic breakdown at the sight of a clock was new, Kafka had previously used the commonplace image of resetting a watch to match a public clock (the Marienschange of Prague) in *Wedding Preparations in the Country* and Kafka would habitually come late each day to his 2:00 P.M. date with Max Brod at the Powder Tower. See Jírí Grusa, *Franz Kafka of Prague,* trans. Eric Mosbacher (New York: Schocken, 1983), pp. 9, 68. As to the image of consulting a policeman, Peter Mailloux notes that eleven years before "A Commentary," Kafka had asked directions from three policemen and finally gone to the police station. *A Hesitation Before Birth: The Life of Franz Kafka* (Newark: University of Delaware/London: Associated University Press, 1989), p. 154.

5. Politzer, pp. 1–22.

6. Gustav Janouch, *Conversations with Kafka,* trans. Goronwy Rees, 2nd ed. rev. (New York: New Directions, 1971), pp. 152–55.

7. *Confucius: Confucian Analects, The Great Learning & The Doctrine of the Mean* [bilingual edition], trans. James Legge (Oxford: Clarendon, 1893; reprint, New York: Dover, 1971), p. 333. Legge translates the Chinese as: "Give up *your vain pursuit.* Give up *your vain pursuit.*" The italicized phrase, however, is Legge's interpolation.

8. Kungfutse [Confucius], *Gespräch (Lun Yü),* trans. Richard Wilhelm (Jena, Germany: Eugen Diedrichs, 1923), p. 203.

9. Dsuang Dsi [Chuang Tsu], *Das Wahrebuch vom Südlichen Blutenland* (Nan Hua Duschen Ging), trans. Richard Wilhelm [Jena, Germany; Eugen Diederichs, 1912; reprint. Leipzig, 1940), p. 36. *The Texts of Taoism,* trans. James Legge, Sacred Books of the East, nos. 39 and 40 (London: Oxford University Press, 1891; reprint, as one volume, New York: Julian Press, 1959), p. 269.

10. Ibid., p. 502.

11. *Lao Tzu: "My words are very easy to understand" (Tao Te Ching* [Chinese and English] Commentary by Man-jan Cheng, trans. Tam C.Gibbs (Richmond, Calif.; North Atlantic Books, 1981), chapter 1, p. 23. All references to the Chinese version of the *Tao te*

ching are to this edition and translations are mine unless otherwise specified. I have consulted Paul J. Linn's analysis of textual variation between the Ma-wang-tui, Wang Pi, and Fu versions of the *Tao te ching* in his book, *A Translation of Lao Tzu's Tao Te Ching and Wang Pi's Commentary* (Ann Arbor: University of Michigan Press, 1977), pp. 157–76; as well as Lao-Tzu, *Te-Tao Ching: A New Translation Based on the Recently Discovered Ma-wang-tui Texts,* trans. Robert G. Henricks (New York: Ballantine, 1989).

12. Paul de Man, *Allegories of Reading* (New Haven, Conn.: Yale University Press, 1979), p. 205. Clayton Koelb has applied to Kafka's story another passage from *Allegories of Reading,* de Man's description of rhetoric as allowing a passage to embody "two incompatible, mutually self-destructive points of view" (131). Clayton Koelb, *Kafka's Rhetoric: The Passions of Reading* (Ithaca, N.Y.: Cornell University Press, 1989), p. 10.

13. Ritchie Robertson, *Kafka: Judaism, Politics, and Literature* (Oxford: Clarendon, 1985), p. 4.

14. Elizabeth Klosti Beaujour, *Alien Tongues: Bilingual Russian Writers of the "First" Emigration* (Ithaca, N.Y.: Cornell University Press, 1989), p. 17.She does not connect these "visio-spatial disabilities" to any literary motif, for she is merely summarizing sources, which include Eta Schneiderman and Chantal Desmaraia, "A Neuropsychological Substrate for Talent in Second Languge Acquisition," in *The Exceptional Brain: The Neuropsychology of Talent and Special Abilities* ed., L. K. Obler and D. A. Fern (New York: Guilford, 1988), pp. 103–26, 115–16. See also N. Geshwind and A. Galaburda, "Cerebral Laterilization—Biological Mechanisms, Associations, and Pathology," *Archives of Neurology* 42 (1985): which argues that, since polyglots devote a larger-than-normal share of the right-brain hemisphere to language, other right-brain functions (e.g., spatial perception) are correspondingly impaired.

15. Jacques Lacan, "La séminaire sur 'La lettre volée,'" *Le Psychoanalyse* 2 (1956): 1–44.

16. Jung's notes for these lectures were privately printed in Zurich, 1959–60. James W. Heisig notes the "abortive" nature of these lectures in Heisig's excellent *Imago Dei: A Study of C. G. Jung's Psychology of Religion* (Lewisburg: Bucknell University Press/London: Associated University Presses, 1979), p. 146.

17. Jung, Preface, to Jolande Jacobi, *The Psychology of C. G. Jung* (London: Routledge and Kegan Paul, 1969), p. ix.

Chapter 1. At the Frontier

1. Jos van Meurs with John Kidd, *Jungian Literary Criticism, 1920–1980* (Metuchen, N.J.: Scarecrow, 1988).

2. Max Brod, *Franz Kafka: Eine Biographie,* 2d ed (New York: Schocken, 1946), p. 118, trans. by G. Humphreys (chapter 1 to 7) and Richard Winston (chapter 8), as *Franz Kafka: A Biographie,* 2nd ed. (1960; reprint. New York: Schocken, 1963).

3. Gertrude Marvin Williams, *Priestess of the Occult: Madame Blavatsky* (New York: Knopf, 1946), pp. 222–57, et passim.

4. Wilheim Emrich, *Franz Kafka: A Critical Study of His Writing,* trans. Sheema Zeben Buehne (New York: Ungar, 1968), p. 7.

5. In the biblical sense, the word *"translated"* comes ultimately from the Vulgate rendering of the original Greek term *"metéthē"* in Heb. 11:5 as "translatus," a Latin expression meaning not merely to be transferred but also to be used figuratively, to be rendered from one language into another, and even to be delayed. This last seems particularly appropriate to the fact that the hunter has been in the act of dying for centuries. That, after his classical studies, Kafka, an ardent Bible-reader in Roman Catholic Austria, could have had this Latin word in mind is possible but not demonstrable.

6. Malcolm Pasley, "Zu Kafkas Interpunktion," *Euphorion* 75/4 (1981). 490.

7. Freud's choice of metaphor is interesting not only in terms of his own analyses of similar images but also in the light of Klaus Theweleit's studies. He massively documents

how in Germanic lands at approximately that period the image of a flood became associated with various threats to male-dominated, "Aryan" culture, e.g., racial minorities, aggressive women, and political liberalism, Theweleit, *Male Fantasies,* trans. Stephen Conway in collaboration with Erica Carter and Chris Turner, vol 1: *Women, Floods, Bodies, History* (Minneapolis: University of Minnesota Press, 1987), pp. 429, et passim.

8. Jung believed that in his late teens, philosophical studies beginning with Schopenhauer caused him to switch from introversion to extraversion (*Er* 75). Since Jung invented the introversion/extraversion classification, he is presumably as well qualified as anyone to categorize himself according to it, and, at least in comparison to Kafka, Jung certainly sounds extraverted.

9. Mailloux, p. 48.

10. Gilles Deleuze and Félix Guattari, *Kafka: Toward a Minor Literature,* trans. Dana Polans, Foreword by Reda Bensmaîa, Theory and History of Literature, no. 30 (Minneapolis: University of Minnesota Press, 1986), p. 19.

11. Edward Upward, "Sketch for a Marxist Interpretation of Literature," in *The Mind in Chains: Socialism and the Cultural Revolution,* ed. C. Day Lewis (London: Frederick Muller, 1937), p. 42. I owe this example to Shimon Sandbank, *After Kafka: The Influence of Kafka's Fiction* (Athens: University of Georgia Press, 1989), p. 114.

12. Apparently, she represented an alien type that attracted him. According to Sabina Spielrein, "Jung had been fond of a dark-haired hysterical girl called S. W., who always described herself as Jewish (but in reality was not). . . . This girl was deeply rooted in him and she was [Spielrein's] prototype." Spielrein continues that Jung also talked about an attachment to Freud's eldest daughter, Mathilde. Aldo Carotenuto, *A Secret Symmetry: Sabina Spielrein between Jung and Freud,* trans. Arno Pomerans, John Shepley, and Krishna Winston (New York: Pantheon, 1982). According to Vincent Brome, Jung was able to sustain his sanity during his collapse through an affair with Toni Wolff, a beautiful young Eursasian who collaborated with him in his researches. *Jung* (London: Macmillan, 1978), pp. 129–38. Among others, Colin Wilson discusses Jung's alleged sexual adventures, *C. G. Jung: Lord of the Underworld* (Wellingborough, Northamptonshire, U.K.: Aquarian, 1984), pp. 89, et passim. In his autobiography, Jung traces his anima imagery to a black-haired, olive-skinned maid who fascinated him in his childhood because of her strangeness compared to the blonde, fair women more common in his canton. (*Er.* 15; *M* 8–9). Perhaps, as in his intellectual pursuits, he was attracted by this very element of strangeness.

13. Carotenuto, p. xvii.

14. Ibid., p. 107. Jung also partly blamed his relationship with Spielrein on Gross. Martin Green, *The von Richthofen Sisters* (New York: Basic, 1974), p. 43.

15. Carotenuto, p. 86–90, 110.

16. Ibid., p. xlii.

17. Susan Handelman, *The Slayers of Moses: The Emergence of Rabbinic Interpretation in Modern Literary Theory* (Albany: SUNY, Press, 1982). She asserts that traditional Hebraic thought made no distinction between words and things, because God created language coextensive with the world it describes and because the Hebrew term for *"word" DBR* means both signifier and signified. Thus, when Foucault's book entitled *Words and Things (Les mots et les choses)* was translated into Hebrew, the two nouns had to be rendered by the one word *DBR,* as has been observed in Andre Neher, *L'Exil de la parole, du silence biblique au silence d'Auschwitz* (Paris: Edition du Seuil, 1970), p. 99. trans. by David Maisel as *The Exile of the Word: From the Silence of the Bible to the Silence of Auschwitz* (Philadelphia: Jewish Publication Society of America, 5741/1981). p. 92.

18. Solomon Grayzel, *A History of the Jews: From the Babylonian Exile to the Present* (New York: New American Library, 1968), p. 606.

19. Ibid.

20. Brome, P. 24.

21. Ernst Pawel, *The Nightmare of Reason: A Life of Franz Kafka* (New York: Farrar, 1984), p. 314.

22. Nahum N. Glatzer, *The Loves of Franz Kafka* (New York: Schocken, 1986), p. 46.

23. One of the principal sources of her anger was the fact that, as Jung later much

regretted, he wrote to her mother promising not to seduce Sabina if the mother sent him "10 francs" a session for psychiatric services rendered. Bruno Bettelheim, "Commentary," in Carotenuto, p. xxix.

24. Even so assiduous a researcher as Hartmut Binder can find no secure biographical link between Kafka and Jung other than the *possibility* that the former might have seen mention of the latter in a magazine article or heard of the latter from Otto Gross. *Motiv und Gestaltung bei Franz Kafka* (Bonn: Bouvier, 1966), pp. 94–109; *Kafka: Der Schaffensprozess* (Frankfurt am Main, Germany: Suhrkamp, 1983), pp. 44–46.

25. Walter Scott, ed. and trans., *Hermetica: The Ancient Greek and Latin Writings which Contain Religious or Philosophical Teachings Ascribes to Hermes Trismegistus*, vol. 1: *Texts and Translations* (Boulder, Colo,: Hermes House, 1982; reprint. Boston: Shambhala, 1985). pp. 140–41.

26. James Strong. "Hebrew and Chaldee Dictionary," *The New Strong's Exhaustive Concordance of the Bible* (New York: Nelson, 1984), p. 99.

27. David Burrell, *Analogy and Philosophical Language* (New Haven, Conn.: Yale University Press, 1973), pp. 10, 122, 197. Burrell praises Aquinas's skill in training the mind to make unverifiable analogical judgments. For examples of Aquinas's treament of analogy, see *Summa contra gentiles*, 1., 32–35; and the Index to *Summa theologiae*. The only memorable competitor to Aquinas's work with analogy was Duns Scotus's theory that the "concept of being" *(conceptus entis)* applies in the same sense to both God and man, yet they manifest "being" differently—the first infinitely, the second finitely. His theory has failed to achieve general acceptance, nor has any other hypothesis succeeded. Duns Scotus, *Philosphical Writings* (New York: Nelson, 1962), pp. 20–21.

28. Burrell, p. 19; Mary Hesse, *Science and the Human Imagination* (London: SCM, 1954), pp. 84, et passim.

29. In a note to that text, Jung and/or Pauli remarks, "I must again stress the possibility that a relationship between body and soul may yet be understood as a synchronistic one." Consequently, far from being rare, synchronisity would be the fundamental condition of man's being in the world. "Two Chapters from the Interpretation of Nature and the Psyche," in *C. G. Jung, Psyche and Symbol*, ed. Violet S. de Laszlo (Garden City, N.Y.: Doubleday, 1958), p. 261, n. 46.

30. Martin Buber, *The Philosophy of Martin Buber*, ed. Paul Arthur Schilpp (La Salle, Ill.: Open Court, 1967), pp. 742–43.

31. Quoted in Brod p. 94; and Winston, p. 74.

32. Pawel, p. 176.

33. Brome, pp. 250–51.

34. Rudy Rucker, *Infinity and the Mind: The Science and Philosophy of the Infinite* (Toronto: Bantam, 1982), pp. 177–78. Rucker likening Gödel to Kafka was inspired by a comparison of the two in Simon Kocher, "In Memorian Kurt Gödel," *The Mathematical Intelligencer* (July 1978): 182–85.

35. Ralph Waldo Emerson, "Self-Reliance," *Selected Prose and Poetry*, ed. Reginald L. Cook, 2nd ed. (New York: Holt, 1950), p. 78.

36. Brome, pp. 217–24.

37. Ian Barbour, *Myths, Models and Paradigms: A Comparative Study of Science and Religon* (New York: Harper, 1974), p. 95.

38. E. A. Bennet, *Meetings with Jung: Conversations Recorded During the Years 1946–1961* (Zurich: Daimon, 1985), p. 95.

39. Jung, *Analytical Psychology: Its Theory and Practice* (New York: Random, 1968), p. 69.

40. Summarized in "Dr. Jekyll, Señor Hyde," *Psychology Today* 21 (December 1978): 16.

41. Julien Green, "My First Book in English," *Le langage et son double* (Paris: Editions de la Difference, 1985). p. 232.

42. Tzvetan Todorov, "Bilinguisme, dialogisme, et schizophrenie," *Du bilinguisme* (Paris: Denoëel, 1985), pp. 11–26, 29. Translation mine. These two literary examples of division in bilinguals (Green and Todorov) are also cited in Elizabeth Klosty Beaujour, *Alien*

Tongues: Bilingual Russian Writers of the "First Emigration" (Ithaca, N.Y.: Cornell University Press, 1989), pp. 46–48.

Chapter 2. Autobiographical Investigations

1. Articles interpreting Kafka as primarily writing about the act of writing include Stanley Corngold, *"Kafka's Die Verwandlung: Metamorphosis of the Metaphor," Mosaic* III, 4(1970): 91–106, and D. Cohn, "Castles and Anti-Castles or Kafka and Robbe-Grillet," *Novel* (Fall 1971). 185. Naturally, the flood of Deconstructionist reinterpretations of Kafka focus on the difficulties of communication, but Kafka's writing block also sometimes appears in general studies of that problem such as Tillie Olsen, *Silences* (New York: Laurel/Seymour Lawrence, 1983), pp. 26, 31–33, 176, 197.

2. The word *aufbauen* not only suggests architecture but also academic research as in *Aufbaustudium* research studies. Etymologically, *Untersuchung* means a seeking beneath something, while it presently denotes various kinds of investigations including legal ones as in the word *Untersuchungsgefangener,* a prisoner awaiting trial; thus, an untranslatable aspect of the passage is the precise way in which it echoes themes of tunneling and building as well as legal and academic research that pervade Kafka's major works. Consequently, the passage is another instance of the complementary relationship between Kafka's inability to write and his writing.

3. *The Confessions of Augustine,* eds. John Gibb and William Montgomery (New York: Garland, 1980), p. 293, trans. by Rex Warner as *Confessions* (New York: New American Library, 1963). pp. 226–27.

4. Ibid., p. 446; Warner, p. 348.

5. Lawrence Byrne, "Writing God's Story: Self and Narrative Structure in Augustine's Confessions," *Christianity and Literature* 38 (Spring 1989), 23; Roy Shafer, "Narration in the Psychoanalytic Dialogue," in *On Narrative,* ed. W. J. T. Mitchell (Chicago: University of Chicago Press, 1980). p. 46.

6. Robertson, p. 126.

7. Heinz Politzer, *Franz Kafka: Parable and Paradox,* 2nd ed. (Ithaca, N.Y.: Cornell University Press, 1966), pp. 174–75; Johannes Urzidil, *Da geht Kafka* (Zurich: Artemis, 1965), p. 33; Marthe Robert, *Seul, comme Franz Kafka* (Paris: Calmann-Lévy, 1979), p. 163.

8. Brome, P. 291. Charles E. Osgood, "Semantic Differential Technique in the Comparative Study of Cultures; Osgood and Zella Luria, "A Blind Analysis of a Case of Multiple Personality Using the Semantic Differential," in *Semantic Differential Technique: A Sourcebook,* eds. James G. Snider and Osgood (Chicago: Aldine, 1969), pp. 303–32, 505–17.

9. Klaus Wagenbach, "Kafka's Castle?" in *The World of Franz Kafka,* ed. J. P. Stern (New York: Holt, 1980), p. 146.

10. Brod, p. 25.

11. One of my graduate students actually asked me the original question: "Since Kafka handed the letter to his mother, why do people think that it was written for his father?" As Walter Sokel observes, some anti-Freudian psychoanalysts have seen the letter as "a deliberate caricature of Freud's fundamental doctrine [the Oedipal relationship of child and parents]," "Freud and the Magic of Kafka's Writing," in *The World of Franz Kafka,* ed. Stern (New York: Holt, 1980), p. 146. Ritchie Robertson adds, "The sons in [Kafka's] stories, far from killing their fathers, do not even rebel against them" (26). In this rejection of the Oedipal model, Robertson echoes Roy Pascal, but neither offers a more adequate psychological paradigm to replace the discarded one. Pascal, *Kafka's Narrators: A Study of His Stories and Sketches* (New York: Cambridge, 1982). p. 48.

12. Books seeing the empirical core of Jung's teaching include both works by former Jungians who are now dissident (cited throughout Samuels's *Jung and the Post-Jungians)* and also works from other schools such as Peter Homans's application of Heinz Kohut's theories of Self-Psychology to Jung in Homans's *Jung in Context* (Chicago: University of Chicago Press, 1979), pp. 80–84. Heinz Kohut diagnoses Kafka as fragmented because he lacked the responsive environment necessary for the unification of self.

> Even a hostile empathic environment is vastly preferable to an indifferent one. That is why Kafka, in a sense, is the literary representative of our time. Over and over again, he describes the vacuum that surrounds Mr. K., the everyman of our times.

Kohut, *Self Psychology and the Humanities: Reflections on a New Psychoanalytic Approach,* edited and introduced by Charles B. Strozier (New York: Norton, 1985), p. 222.

13. Pawel, p. 383.

14. John Hibberd, *Kafka in Context* (London: Studio Vista, 1975), p. 11.

15. Comparably, two independent psychological studies have demonstrated that "God the Father" more nearly connotes "mother" to modern adherents than "father." A. Godin and M. Hallez, "Parental Images and Divine Paternity": *Lumen Vitae* 19 (1964): 253–84; A. Vergote and A. Tamayo, *Parental Figures and the Representation* (The Hague: Mouton and Leuven University Press, 1980).

16. Mary Ann Mattoon, *Jungian Psychology in Perspective* (New York: Macmillan, 1981), p. 115.

17. Nathan A. Scott, Jr., "The New *Trahison Des Clercs:* Reflections on the Present," *The Virginia Quarterly Review* (Summer 1986): 419.

18. Brome, p. 108.

19. In Jungian usage, the persona is the whole system or method by which an individual adapts to the world.

20. If one knows (1) that Kafka was embarrassed by his own thinness; (2) that he thought of writing as a form of prayer; and (3) that he felt nervous about exposing himself by publishing, one can guess that the emaciated Supplicant who prays exhibitionistically is a self-travesty.

21. The Tower of Babel, which typologists related to the original Fall, was thought to have brought the undoing of the direct relationship between signifier and signified that Jewish tradition believed God had initially established. Noah's drunkenness, the first artifically altered consciousness, is also typologically associated with the Fall and traditionally signified the return of imperfection after the Flood had washed the earth clean. Thus, the Tower of Babel and Noah's drunkenness are traditionally related to each other as in Milton's *Paradise Lost,* bk. 12, 13–106, where the Archangel Michael, in retelling biblical history, skips from the first of these events to the second. In "Kafka and the Place of the Proper Name," Mark Anderson summarizes various attempts by critics to explain Kafka linking the Tower of Babel and Noah's drunkenness, including Anderson's own search for phallic images in the two. *The Journal of the Kafka Society of America* 9 (June/December 1985): 10–13.

22. Jean Jaffen adds that Kafka's Hebrew name, Amschel, comes probably from the German "Anselm" but might be associated with the German "Amsel," which means "blackbird." *The Jewish Mystic in Kafka* (New York: Peter Lang, 1987), p. 24.

23. This distinction between God and Angel depends on whether one refers to Gen. 32. 22–32 or Hos. 12.4.

24. For exemplification, I shall cite a very few of the countless, nineteenth-century versions of Jacob's wrestling. In "Carrion Comfort," Gerard Manley Hopkins's speaker first presumes that he confronts the demon "Despair," then learns that he is "wrestling with (my God!) my God." An admirer of St. Thomas More, Hopkins, unlike his speaker, knew that to "fight or wrestle" with despair is a "great comfort," bringing one closer to the presence of God. Gerard Manley Hopkins, *Poems,* ed. Robert Bridges (London: Oxford University Press, 1930), pp. 61–62; Thomas More, *A Dialogue of Comfort Against Tribulation,* ed. Leland Miles (Bloomington: Indiana University Press, 1965), p. 84. In Alfred, Lord Tennyson's *In Memoriam,* the speaker "fought with death" (120.4) while elsewhere in the poem God manifests himself as the Angel of Death (85.20). *Poems,* ed. Christopher Ricks (New York: Longman, 1969), pp. 970, 933. In Walt Whitman, "The Song of Myself," "quivering me to a new identity" (1. 618), comparable to Jacob earning a new name, "a red marauder" meeting the speaker alone on a "headland" proves to be "Blind wrestling touch" (1. 641). The "floodgates" open and the "rich showering rain" comes (1. 646—a decorous expression for sex. Some interpreters have read a similar eroticism into Emily Dickinson's comic Jacob poems, but with Whitman the sexuality is no joke but part of a sense of love for humanity as in an 1847 notebook where love for mankind "wrestles as with the knuckles of God." *Leaves of Grass: The First (1855) Edition,* ed. Malcolm Cowley (New York: Viking, 1959; reprint,

1961), pp. 52–54; *The Uncollected Poetry and Prose,* ed. Emory Holloway (Garden City, N.J.: Doubleday, 1921), vol. 2, p. 67. In its own way as strange as Melville's Art/Angel, Hopkins's Despair/God, Tennyson's Death/God, and Whitman's Touch/God is Søren Kierkegaard's Repetition/God in his elusive novella *Repetition,* where he sees the whole book as a "wrestling match" *(brydning)* with the Ineffable. Kierkegaard, *Repetition: An Essay in Experimental Psychology,* trans. Walter Lowrie (New York: Harper, 1941), pp. 133, 142, n. 92.

25. Herman Melville, *Collected Poems,* ed. Howard P. Vincent (Chicago: Packard, 1947), p. 231.

26. Among the many connections between Karl and Kafka, both were aided (in a manner that turned out to be unsatisfactory) by people who had gone from Europe to America and risen in the U.S. government. In Kafka's case, Uncle Jacob was his great-uncle Arnold Weissberger, whose financial success in America had brought him a post as honorary U.S. vice consul. From this eminence, he helped Kafka obtain a dreadful position in a mercilessly demanding insurance company. See Ernst Pawel, *The Nightmare of Reason* (New York: Farrar, 1984), pp. 175–76.

27. Allusions to America as Egypt include the town of Rameses as the fictional setting for a significant portion of the narrative and Uncle Jacob's ironic description of America as a place of "signs and wonders" (*V* 40; *A* 27), a phrase that occurs twice in the Torah, both times referring to the plagues of Egypt.

28. "I am . . . a negro" *(Je suis . . . un négre),* Arthur Rimbaud, *A Season in Hell, The Illuminations: Une Saison en Enfer, Les Illuminations* [bilingual edition], trans. Enid Rhodes Peschel (New York: Oxford, 1973), pp. 52–53. Kafka, however, makes the teenaged vagabond Rossmann a far less lurid character than the teenaged vagabond Rimbaud. The copy of Rimbaud's works in Kafka's possession when he died was published too late to have influenced the composition of *The Lost One,* but that does not preclude the possibility of Kafka's acquaintance with Rimbaud's works and perhaps also with the famous portrait, "Rimbaud, Wounded in Brussels," by Jef Rosman, whose last name could have consciously or unconsciously inspired the choice of the name Rossmann.

29. John Donne. *The Complete Poetry* (New York: New York University Press; London: University of London Press, 1968), p. 392.

30. Wolfgang von Goethe, *Faust* (Garden City, N.Y.: Doubleday 1961), p. 161. All references to *Faust* are to this edition.

31. Emrich, pp. 274–75.

32. Brod, p. 122.

33. In Roman Jakobson, *Selected Writings* vol. 2 (Pais: Mouton, 1971), pp. 237–59. Typical of the modern tendency to find Jung valuable enough to borrow from but not reputable enough to cite, Jakobson calls Word-Association a test for "children" and never mentions Jung (254).

Chapter 3. Myths and *Märchen*

1. G. S. Kirk, *The Nature of Greek Myths* (New York: Penguin, 1974), p. 14.

2. Marshall McLuhan with Hubert Hoskins, "Electric Consciousness and the Church," *The Man and His Message,* eds. George Sanderson and Frank Macdonald (Golden, Colo.: Fulcrum, 1989), 166.

3. Aristotle, *The Metaphysics* [Greek and English], ed. and trans. Hugh Tredennick (Cambridge: Harvard University Press, 1947), chapter 4, pp. 188–89.

4. R. H. Blyth, trans. and Commentary, *Mumonkan* [Chinese English], Zen and Zen Classics, no. 4 (Tokyo: Hokuseido Press, 1966), p. 57.

5. Ibid., p. 61.

6. E.g. Majjhima Nikāya, Sutta 63, 72.

7. D. T. Suzuki looked in vain for a reference to this legend prior to Li Tsun-hsu, *The Records of the Spread of the Lamp* (*Kuang têng lu,* 1029 A.D.), which already judges the story to be unhistorical. *Essays in Zen Buddhism (First Series)* (London: Luzac, 1927), p. 156.

8. Earlier versions attribute the amputation to bandits. Thomas Hoover, *The Zen Experience* (New York: New American Library, 1980), pp. 30, 244.

9. Max Brod, *Franz Kafka: A Biography,* trans. G. Humphreys Roberts and Richard Watson (New York: Schocken, 1963), p. 53; Klaus Wagenbach, *Franz Kafka: Eine Biographie Seiner Jugend 1883–1912* (Bern, Switzerland: Francke, 1958), pp. 38, 58, 125; Ernst Pawel, *The Nightmare of Reason: A Life of Franz Kafka* (New York: Farrar, 1984) p. 350.

10. Janouch, p. 167. Gustavo Benavides, "Prasanga and Double Bind," in *Buddhist and Western Psychology,* ed. Nathan Katz (Boulder, Colo.: Prajña, 1983), p. 201.

11. Edwin Arnold, *The Light of Asia and the Indian Song of Songs (Gita-Govinda)* (Bombay: Jaico, 1949), p. 130. In conversation (Janouch 142), Kafka allegedly used the phrase, "the tension between the circumscribed drop of water and the infinite sea." Although this image of mystical immersion in the Absolute is not unique to Arnold's poem, that work popularized it in English-speaking lands and German ones, where Neumann's translation sold widely, James Whitlark, "Nineteenth-Century 'Nirvana Talk,'" *South Asian Review* 5 (1981): 17–33.

12. E.g., T. J. Reed, "Kafka und Schopenhauer: Philosophisches Denken und dichterisches Bild," *Euphorion* (1965), 160–72; and A. Foulkes, *The Reluctant Pessimist: A Study of Franz Kafka* (The Hague: Mouton, 1967).

13. Recent attempts to solve the enigma of the *Parmenides* include Kenneth M. Sayre, *Plato's Late Ontology: A Riddle Resolves* (Princeton, N.J.: Princeton University Press, 1983), pp. 18–49; Viggo Rossvaer, *The Laborious Game: A Study of Plato's Parmenides* (Oslo: Universatetsforlaget, 1983); and R. E. Allen, *Plato's Parmenides: Translation and Analysis* (Minneapolis: University of Minnesota Press, 1983).

14. William David Ross, *Plato's Theory of Ideas* (Oxford: Oxford University Press, 1953), p. 157.

15. *Lao Tzu: "My words are very easy to understand,"* chapter 80, pp. 226–27.

16. Plato's Pharmacy," *Dissemination,* trans. Barbara Johnson (Chicago: University of Chicago Press, 1981). p. 111.

17. Brod, p. 53.

18. Bertrand Russell, *History of Western Philosophy: And Its Connection with Political and Social Circumstances from the Earliest Times to the Present Day* (New York: Simon, 1945), p. 130.

19. Paul Shorey, *The Unity of Plato's Thought* (New York: Garland, 1979), p. 37.

20.

> [In Plato] the occult knowledge which the shaman acquires in trance has become a vision of metaphysical truth; his "recollection" of past earthly lives . . . has become a "recollection" of bodiless Forms which is made the basis of a new epistemology: while in the mythical level his "long sleep" and "underworld journey" provides a direct model for the experiences of Er the Son of Armenius [another of Plato's myths].

E. R. Dodds, *The Greeks and the Irrational* (Berkeley: University of California Press, 1959), p. 213.

21. To take a modern example, the philosopher Charles Landesman, in the introduction to *The Problem of Universals,* subtly ponders the question of whether the color green has a Universal behind it. Landesman ed., *The Problem of Universals* (London: Basic, 1971), pp. 3–17. If one moves beyond the boundaries of English, the possibility of "green" as a transcendent reality seems preposterous. Ludwig Wittgenstein more sensibly asks: "Which shade is the 'sample in my mind' of the colour green—the sample of what is common to all shades of green?" *Philosphical Investigations,* eds., G. H. von Wright and G. E. M. Anscombe, trans. G. E. M. Anscombe (Oxford: Basil Blackwell, 1953), section 73. A number of languages (including Chinese) have traditionally made no distinction between blue and green. In a diary, Kafka once pondered the related epistemological problem, "Why does one take a rather long time to recognize a color," and noted the shifts from green to blue in his semidark room (*D1* 77–78). The anthropologist Verne F. Ray has charted how Amerindian languages have highly diverse color vocabularies, grouping and separating shades in manners radically different from one another and from English, "Human Color Perception and Behavioral Response," *Transactions of the New York Academy of Sciences* 16 (1953): 98–104. Benjamin

Lee Whorf, "Some Verbal Categories of Hopi," in *Language, Thought, and Reality,* edited and introduced by John B. Carroll, Foreword by Stuart Chase (New York: Wiley/MIT Press, 1956). According to Whorf, Hopi lacks a way of indicating time, but according to C. F. and F. M. Voegelin, "Hopi Domains: A Lexical Approach to the Problem of Selection," *International Journal of American linguistics* (Indiana University Publications in *Anthropology and Linguistics,* memoir 14, 1957), Whorf was partly mistaken. Sometimes Plato seems aware of the blurring of ideas into one another, as in the *Protagoras,* where he identifies Courage and the Good, but since the Greek word *agathos* means both good and brave, he is probably still reifying his own language.

22. Bryan Magee, *The Philosophy of Schopenhauer* (Oxford: Oxford University Press, 1983), p. 239.

23. Wendy Doniger O'Flaherty, *Siva: The Erotic Ascetic* (New York: Oxford University Press, 1973), p. 21.

24. Robert Graves, *The Greek Myths,* vol. 1 (New York: Penguin, 1955), p. 41.

25. Foreword (1981) by Hugh Lloyd-Jones in Humphrey Trevelyan, *Goethe & the Greeks* (Cambridge: Cambridge University Press, 1941: reprint rev. 1981). p. xix.

26. Kurt Weinberg, *Kafkas Dichtungen: Die Travestien des Muthos* (Bern: Francke, 1963), pp. 32–87.

27. Hugh G. Evelyn-White, ed. and trans. *Hesoid, The Homeric Hymns and Homerica* [Greek and English] (Cambridge: Harvard University Press, 1977), p. xv, and vol II. 26–27, p. 81.

28. Ibid., pp. 2–3.

29. Dodds, pp. 46–47; *Republic* 377e–378b.

30. "The Primordial Child in Primordial Times," in *Essays on a Science of Mythology,* p. 56.

31. Evelyn-White, p. 93, n. 3.

32. Homer [attributed], *Ilias* [and] *Odyssee,* eds., J. C. Bruijn and C. Spoelder (Haarlem, Netherlands: H. D. Tjeenk Wilink & Zoon, 1970). p. 740. According to Wagenbach (58), Kafka's school curriculum included "Abschnitte aus Homer," Hartmut Binder argues that Kafka also had a Jewish source, *Die Sagen der Juden,* influencing his restructuring the Homeric story. *Motiv und Gestaltung bei Franz Kafka* (Bonn: Bouvier, 1966). pp. 149–50.

33. Bernard M. W. Knox, *The Heroic Temper: Studies in Sophoclean Tragedy* (1964; reprint. Berkeley: University of California Press, 1983). pp. 56–57.

34. Richard I. Evans, *Conversations with Carl Jung and Reactions from Ernest Jones* (New York: Van Nostrand, 1964), pp. 48–49.

35. Peter Homans, *Jung in Context* (Chicago: University of Chicago Press, 1979), pp. 80–84.

36. Ruth V. Gross, "Rich Text/Poor Text: A Kafkan Confusion," *PMLA* 95 (March 1980): 168–82. Her article contains a decent text of the story, which can be found in less authentic form in *B* 122–23.

37. With the usual structuralist predisposition toward fixed images, Gross sees the boasting as "an archetypal source of amnesia, of a fall into a hellish dreamworld" (173).

38. Max Brod, *Paganism—Christianity—Judaism: A Confession of Faith,* trans. William Wolf (University: University of Alabama Press, 1970), pp. 14, et passim), p. 14.

39. Ernst Pawel, *The Nightmare of Reason: A Life of Franz Kafka* (New York: Farrar, 1984), pp. 74, 91.

40. Wagenbach, pp. 251–63.

41. John Hibberd, *Kafka in Context* (London: Studio Vista, 1975), p. 49.

42. Max Luthi, *Once Upon a Time: On the Nature of Fairy Tales,* trans. Lee Chadeayne and Paul Gottwaldt (New York: Ungar, 1970), p. 145; *Es War Enimal: Vom Wesen des Volksmárchens* (Göttingen, Germany: Vandenhoeck & Ruprecht, 1970), p. 113.

43. Nahum Glatzer, ed., *I Am a Memory Come Alive: Autobiographical Writings,* by Franz Kafka (New York: Schocken, 1974), p. 240.

44. Vladimir Propp, *Morphology of the Folktale,* trans. Laurence Scott (Austin: University of Texas Press, 1968), p. 120.

45. Heinz Rolleke, ed., *Die Alteste Märchensammlung der Brüder Grimm* (Cologne: Fondation Martin Bodmer, 1975), p. 70.

46. John Ellis, *One Fairy Story Too Many* (Chicago: University of Chicago Press, 1983), p. 189. The Grimms rewrote *Volksmärchen* to appeal to their nineteenth-century readers, so that their published versions are in an intermediate state between *Volksmärchen* and *Kunstmärchen*.

47. Hans Christian Andersen, *The Complete Illustrated Stories*, trans. H. W. Dulcken (London: Chancellor, 1983), p. 316.

48. Hartmut Binder, *Kafka-Komentar zu Sämtlichen Erzahlungen* (München, Germany: Winkler, 1975). p. 211.

49. I thank F. Robert Lehmeyer (Associate Professor of German, University of Alabama at Birmingham) and Timothy F. Sellner (Professor of German, Wake Forest University) for their kind help proofreading an earlier version of this section. They are not responsible for any errors that have subsequently occurred.

Chapter 4. A New Kabbala

1. Evelyn Beck, "Kafka's Triple Bind: Women, Jews and Sexuality," in *Kafka's Contextuality* (Baltimore, Md.: Gordion Baltimore Hebrew College Press, 1986), pp. 351–52.

2. Carlo Suarés, *The Sepher Yetsira: Including the Original Astrology According to the Qabala and its Zodiac*, trans. Micheline and Vincent Stuart (London: Shambhala, 1976), p. 38.

3. Hayyim Vital, *Ez Hayyim*, quoted in Hebrew and English in Rabbi Yehuda L. Ashlag, *The Kabbalah: A Study of the Ten Luminous Emanations from Rabbi Isaac Luria*, trans. Rabbi Levi I. Krakovsky (Jerusalem: Research Center of Kabbalah, 1969), p. 89. Vital recorded the sayings of Luria. For bibliographical details, see Gershom Scholem, *Kabbalah* (New York: New American Library, 1974), pp. 424–25.

4. David Blumenthal, *Understanding Jewish Mysticism: A Source Reader* (New York: KTAV, 1978), p. 42.

5. Robertson, pp. 195–96.

6. H. P. Blavatsky, *the Secret Doctrine*, rev. ed. (1888; reprint, Madra, India: Theosophical Publishing House, 1962), vol. 1, p. 292.

7. Quoted in Louis Jacobs, *Hasidic Thought* (New York: Schocken, 1976), pp. 72–73. Comparably, "Moses de Leon mentions a supreme but temporary condition in which the soul finds itself standing before God in a state of contemplation and ultimate bliss without any garment between it and Him" Scholem, p. 160.

8. See Max Kaltenmark, *Lao Tzu and Taoism*, trans. Roger Greaves (Stanford, Calif.: Stanford University Press, 1969), p. 96.

9. Quoted in Edward Hoffman, *The Way of Splendor* (London: Shambhala, 1981), p. 7.

10. The quotation from the *Midrash Leviticus Rabbah* follows H. Freedman and M. Simon, trans. and eds., *Midrash Rabbah*, Gen. vol. 1. (London: Soncino, 1939), based on the Rome edition of 1853–58.

11. Reference to the *Peah* comes from I. Epstein's translation of the *Talmud* (London: Soncino, 1935–48).

12. Andre Neher, *L'Exil de la parole, du silence biblique au silence d'Auschwitz* (Paris: Editions de Seuil, 1970), trans. by David Maisel as *The Exile of the Word: From the Silence of the Bible to the Silence of Auschwitz* (Philadelphia: Jewish Publication Society of America, 5741/1981). With the exception of the opening quotation from II Sam., all translations from the Bible in this subsection are Neher's French and/or Maisel's English, because the former's arguments would sometimes not be comprehensible if another version were substituted. E.g., in place of their "voice of silence" *(voix du silence)* the *soi-dissant* "Authorized" version (which King James never finally authorized) more literally renders *QOL DMMH DQH* a "still small voice." Elsewhere, translations are from the "Authorized" version unless otherwise noted. For a general survey of references to silence in philosophy, see Bernard P. Dauenhauer, *Silence: The Phenomenon and Its Ontological Significance* (Bloomington: Indiana University Press, 1980).

13. Although Kafka's notion may be traced in various forms to antiquity, one of the stages

of its development is probably Hegel, who argues that from the viewpoint of pictorial religious thought, "man . . . is the synthetic ground of [the] existence [of Good and Evil] and their conflict," *Phenomenology of Spirit,* trans. A. V. Miller (Oxford: Clarendon, 1977), section 777, p. 469. Hegel's understanding of what lies beyond mere picture-thinking, however, differs from Kafka's since, unlike the latter, Hegel insists that the relationship between phenomenal and noumenal is comprehensible (section 75, pp. 47–48).

14. In J. M. Robinson, trans. and ed., *The Nag Hammadi Library* (New York: Harper, 1977), 103.9–20.

15. Steven T. Katz, ed., *Mysticism and Philosophical Analysis* New York: Oxford University Press, 1978), pp. 52–53.

16. Kafka's image of absorption is neo-Platonic, probably acquired through his readings in Eckhart and Augustine. In "Language, Epistemology, and Mysticism," Steven T. Katz observes that, since Judaism emphasizes God's transcendence,

> Jewish mystics envisioned the ultimate goal of mystical relation, *devekuth,* not as absorption into God, or as unity with the divine but rather as a loving intimacy, a "clinging to" God.

In *Mysticism and Philosophical Analysis,* ed. Katz (New York: Oxford University Press, 1974), pp. 35–36. See also Sholem, *Kabbalah* (New York: New American Library, 1954); and his article "Devekuth" in *The Messianic Idea in Judaism* ed. Sholem (New York: Anti-Defamation League of the B'nai B'rith, 1972), pp. 203–26.

17. Robert Gordis, *The Book of Job: Commentary, New Translation, and Special Studies,* Moreshit Series, Studies in Jewish History, Literature and Thought, no. 2 (New York: Jewish Theological Seminary of America, 5738/1978), p. 287.

18. Scholem, p. 178.

19. E.g., Omori Sōgen and Terayama Katsujō, *Zen and the Art of Caligraphy: The Essence of Sho,* trans. John Stevens (London: Routledge & Kegan Paul, 1983), pp. 12–19, et passim.

20. Gordis, p. 64. Throughout the remainder of this subsection, I use his translation.

21. Harold Bloom, *Kabbalah and Criticism* (New York: Seabury, 1975), p. 82.

22. F. David Peat, *Synchronicity: The Bridge Between Matter and Mind* (New York: Bantam, 1987), pp. 20–21; H. B. G. Casimir, *Haphazard Reality* (New York: Harper, 1983).

23. Søren Kierkegaard, *Repetition: An Essay in Experimental Psychology,* trans. Walter Lowrie (New York: Harper, 1941), pp. 133, 142, n. 92.

24. In *Advances in the Psychology of Religion,* ed. L. B. Brown (New York: Pergamon, 1985), pp. 8–17.

25. Janet L. Larson, *Dickens and the Broken Scripture* (Athens: University of Georgia, 1985), p. 8; Julian Moynahan, "The Hero's Guilt: The Case of *Great Expectations," Essays in Criticism* 10 (January 1960): 61. As "dissent to Moynahan's reading," Larson cites Dennis Walder, *Dickens and Religion* (Boston: George Allen and Unwin, 1981), p. 203.

26. Charles Dickens, *Great Expectations* (1953; reprint. London: Oxford University Press, 1969), p. 2.

27. Jean-Paul Sartre, *Anti-Semite & Jew* (New York: Schocken, 1965).

28. Robertson, p. 197.

29. Janouch, p. 166. Debate over the accuracy of Janouch's book has raged since its publication, with numerous close acquaintances of Kafka defending it (including Max Brod) and some scholarly works simply dismissing it, e.g., Pawel, p. 72. Among those accusing Janouch of factual errors are Eduard Goldstucker, "Kafkas Eckerman? Zu Gustav Janouchs *Gespräche mit Kafka,*" in Claude David, ed. *Franz Kafka: Themen und Probleme* (Götingen: Vandenhoek and Reprecht, 1980), pp. 238–55; and Hartmut Binder, *Kafka-Handbuch in Zwei Bänden* (Stuttgart, Germany: Kröner, 1979) pp. 554–62. Gregory Triffit, however, has pointed out parallels between the *Conversations* and writings by Kafka unpublished by the date of Janouch's first edition (1951), *Kafka's 'Landarzt' Collection: Rhetoric and Interpretation,* Australian and New Zealand Studies in German Language and Literature, no. 13 (New York: Peter Lang, 1985), pp. 203–4. In my article "Kafka and the Taoist Sages," *Kafka Society Journal* 8 (June/December 1984): 28–34, I have shown some similarities between Kafka's posthumously published works and material added to Janouch's revised edition (though this

edition admittedly appeared in print after the publication of the analogous sections in Kafka's own works). At this point Janouch's work seems far from mere invention, but his testimony about Kafka's religion is presumably an indistinguishable mixture of quotation and paraphrase, the latter probably influenced by Janouch's own liberal Christianity and desire to find a kindred faith in Kafka. Furthermore, even filtered through Janouch's memory, Kafka's oxymoronic praise of Christ as a luminous abyss sounds ironic.

30. See Jan Gorak, *God the Artist: American Novelists in a Post-Realist Age* (Urbana: University of Illinois Press, 1987), pp. 3, et passim.

31. Although the Greek version of this verse lacks the explanatory gloss ("the beginning and the ending") this phrase appears in most translations and is traceable to the Vulgate: "princîpium et finis," Jerome, trans. *Biblia Sacra: vulgatae Editionis* (Rome: Editiones Paulinae, 1957), p. 1272. Luther, e.g., retains the gloss ("Ich bin das A und das O, der Anfang und das Ende"), Martin Luther, trans., *Die Bibel oder die ganze Heilige Schrift des Alten und Neuen Testaments* (Berlin: Britische und Auslandische Bibelgesellschaft, 1923), p. 255.

32. Adam Clarke, *Commentary on the Bible,* abridged by Ralph Earle (Grand Rapids, Mich.: Baker, 1967), p. 1332.

33. Alan Udoff, Introduction, *Kafka's Contextuality,* ed. Alan Udoff (Baltimore: Gordian/Baltimore Hebrew College Press, 1986), p.xxxii.

34. Thomas Merton, *Zen and the Birds of Appetite* (New York: New Directions, 1968), pp. 54–55.

35. Meister Eckhart, *Von der Geburt der Seele:Ausgewähite Schriften und Predigten* (n.p.: Sigbert Mohn, n.d.) p. 112. The spelling of Eckhart's name varies widely.

Chapter 5. Oriental Tales

1. Brome, pp. 191–93.

2. Ronald Gray, *Franz Kafka* (Cambridge: Cambridge Universty Press, 1973), p. 43.

3. James Whitlark, "Nineteenth-Century 'Nirvana Talk,'" *South Asian Review* 5 (1981): 17–33.

4. Alexander Tille, introd. and trans., *Thus Spake Zarathustra* (New York: Macmillan, 1896). p. xi.

5. Richard Wilhelm, trans., *Dschuang Dsi: Wahrebuch vom sudlichen Blutenland* (Nan Hua Dschen Ging) (1912; reprint. Jena, Germany: Eugen Diedrichs, 1923), p. xii.

6. Guy Welbon, *The Buddhist Nirvana and Its Western Interpreters* (Chicago: University of Chicago Press, 1968), p. 187.

7. Welbon, p. 185; John Oxenford, "Iconoclasm in German Philosophy," *Westminster Review* (April 1853). 399.

8. Max Nordau, *Degeneration* (London: William Heinemann, 1895), p. 21. Famous for his book *Die Philosophie des Unbewussten* (Berlin: C. Duncker, 1870), Hartmann differed from Schopenhauer in a few details, e.g., Hartmann's contention that before the Fall of Man, the Will and Reason were united; nonetheless, Hartmann's marshaling persuasive examples to the Schopenhauerian cause generally furthered it.

9. E.g., T. J. Reed, "Kafka und Schopenhauer: Philosophisches Denken und dichterisches Bild," *Euphorion* (1965): 160–72.

10. *F* 119; Max Brod, *Verzweiflung und Erlosung im Werk Kafkas* (Frankfurt am Main, Germany: Schocken, 1959), p. 67; Hans Heilmann, trans., *Chinesische Lyrik,* Die Fruchtschale, no. 1 (München, Germany: Piper,).

11. Marthe Robert, *As Lonely as Franz Kafka,* trans. Ralph Manheim (New York: Harcourt, 1979), p. 19; *F.* 252; Martin Buber, trans., *Chinesische Geister und Liebesgeschichten* (Frankfurt am Main, Germany: Rutten & Loening, 1922).

12. Klaus Wagenbach, *Franz Kafka* (Bern, Switzerland Francke, 1958), pp. 251, 253.

13. Meno Spann, *Franz Kafka* (Boston: Twayne, 1976), pp. 30–31.

14. Gustav Meyrink, *The Golem* (New York: Dover, 1986), p. 191.

15. George Cary, *The Medieval Alexander,* ed. D. J. A. Ross (Cambridge: Cambridge University Press, 1956), pp. 18–20, et passim.

16. M. J. de Goeje, "De Muur van Gog en Magog," Verslagen en Mededeelingen d. koninkl. Akad. van Wetenskapen, Afd. Letterkunde, 3e reeks, Deel V (Amsterdam: n.p. 1888), 87; Andrew Runni Anderson, *Alexander's Gate, Gog and Magog, and the Inclosed Nations* (Cambridge: Mediaeval Academy of America, 1932), p. 92.

17. Anderson, p. 3.

18. Ibid., p. 3.

19. Triffit, p. 208, no. 2.

20. Oliver Impey, *Chinoiserie* (New York: State Mutual Book and Service, 1977), p. 89.

21. James Thomson, *The Castle of Indolence* (London: Millar, 1748). William Booney comments on this passage, "As might be expected, Thomson sees to it that the incomprehensible is presented as a type of sinful deception." *Thorns and Arabesques: Contexts for Conrad's Fiction* (Baltimore: Johns Hopkins University Press, 1980), pp. 12–13.

22. Max Brod believes that the landscape in this story was inspired by Kafka's favorite Japanese woodcut (*B* 312). At Kafka's hands, though, the scene becomes a vague mingling of East and West like Chinoiserie.

23. Robert Buchanan, "The New Buddha," *The North American Review* 140 (1885): 445.

24. Triffit, p. 154.

25. Joseph Campbell, ed., *The Portable Arabian Nights*, trans. John Payne (New York: Viking, 1952), p. 506.

26. Hartmut Binder, *Kafka: Der Schaffensprozess* (Frankfurt am main, Germany: Suhrkamp, 1983), p. 18.

27. Martha Conant, *The Oriental Tale in England in the Eighteenth Century* (New York: Octagon, 1966), p. 227.

28. Hans Heilman, Introduction, *Chinesische Lyrik*, Die Fruchtschale, no. 1 (Munich: Piper, 1905).

29. William Johnston, *The Austrian Mind: An Intellectual and Social History 1848–1938* (Berkeley: University of California Press, 1972), p. 21.

30. Ibid., p. 154.

31. Ibid., p. 170.

32. C. G. Jung, Commentary *The Secret of the Golden Flower*, translated into German by Richard Wilhelm and into English by Cary F. Baynes (New York: Causeway, 1975), p. 83.

33. Robert Walser, *Selected Stories* (New York: Farrar, 1982), p. 27.Among the contemporary European authors read by Kafka, the pseudo-Eastern style was becoming common, as with Knut Hamsun's "dreamlike, lingering poetry of the Orient." Harold Naess, *Knut Hamsun* (Boston: Twayne, 1984), p. 28.

34. Okakura, *The Awakening of Japan* (New York: Century, 1904), pp. 77–78.

35. C. A. S. Williams, *Outline of Chinese Symbolism and Art Motives*, 3rd ed., rev. (Shanghai: Kelly and Walsh, 1941; reprint. New York: Dover, 1976), pp. 132–41.

36. Franz Baumer, *Franz Kafka*, trans. Abraham Farbstein (New York: Ungar, 1971), p. 38. Kafka, though, was far from the first to do so. E. T. A. Hoffman, e.g., included a heroine who assumed serpent form in the Oriental fantasy, "The Golden Pot," and helpful snakes are common in Eastern lore, e.g., in a book of Turkish fairy tales purchased by Kafka, where a serpent prince helps the hero. Theodor Menzel, *Der Zauberspiegel: Türkische Märchen* (Hanover: Orient-Buchhandlung Heinz Lafaire, 1924), pp. 1–18.

37. Henry Wei, *The Guiding Light of Lao Tzu: A New Translation and Commentary on the Tao Teh Ching* (Wheaton, Ill.: Quest, 1982), p. 2.

38. Léon Wieger, *Taoism: The Philosophy of China*, trans. Edward Charles Lucas (Burbank, Calif.: Ohara, 1976).

39. N. G. Girardot, *Myth and Meaning in Early Taoism: The Theme of Chaos (Hun-Tun)* (Berkeley: University of California Press, 1983).

40. E.g., Lao Tzu [attributed], *Dao de ging: das buch des alten vom Sinn und leban*, trans. Richard Wilhelm (Jena, Germany: Eugen Diedrichs, 1911), p. 23, trans. by H.G. Ostwald as *Tao Te Ching: The Book of Meaning and Life* (London: Arkana, 1985), p. 15. The publisher of the English translation even calls Wilhelm's rendering "archetypal," but means it as a compliment (vi).

41. Leon Wieger, *Chinese Characters: Their Origin, Etymology, History, Classification and Signification* (n.p.: Catholic Mission Press, 1915; reprint. New York: Paragon/Dover, 1965), p. 638.

42. E.g., Herta Ramthun, ed., *Bertolt Brecht: Diaries 1920–1922*, trans. John Willett (New York: St. Martin's, 1979), p. 50; Thomas Mann, *Tagebücher 1933–34*, ed. Peter de Mendelssohn (Frankfurt Am Main, Germany: S. Fischer, 1977), p. 158; Adrian Hsia, *Hermann Hesse und China* (Frankfurt am Main, Germany: Suhrkamp, 1974), passim; Ko won, *Buddhist Elements in Dada* [including references to Taoism] (New York: NYU Press, 1977), pp. 85, et passim; and Gershon Weiler, *Mauthner's Critique of Language* (Cambridge: Cambridge University Press, 1979), p. 294. Immediately after translating the works of Chuang Tzu (1910), Buber was fascinated with Taoism, but later he regretted his early endorsement of it. Martin Buber, *Pointing the Way*, trans. Maurice Friedman (New York: Harper, 1957), pp. ix, 31–58.

43. Borges, "Kafka y sus Precursores," p. 187; Han Yu, "La Capture de la Licorne," in G. Margoulies, *Anthologie raisonne de la litterature* (Paris: Payot, 1948), pp. 120–21; *GW*, vol. 12, 466.

44. Benjamin spaced the dialogue together in a single paragraph, but I have changed the format to stress its dramatic nature.

45. See S. G. F. Brandon, "The Weighing of the Soul," in *Myths and Symbols: Studies in Honor of Mircea Eliade*, eds. Joseph M. Kitagawa and Charles H. Long (Chicago: University of Chicago Press, 1969), pp. 91–110.

46. *Tao Te Ching: The Richard Wilhelm Edition*, p. 38.

47. Ibid., p. 13.

48. Baumer, p. 2.

49. Stanley Corngold, ed. and trans., *The Metamorphosis*, by Franz Kafka (New York: Bantam, 1072), p. 64.

50. Clemens Heselhau, "Kafkas Erzählformen," *Deutsche Viertel jahrszeitschrift für Literaturwissenschaft und Geistesgeschichte*, (1952): 363.

51. James Legge, trans., *The Texts of Taoism*, Sacred Books of the East, nos. 39, 40 (London: Oxford University Press, 1891; reprint. as one volume, New York: Julian, 1959), p. 269.

52. Kurt Weinberg, *Kafkas Dichtungen: Die Travestein des Muthos* (Berne, Switzerland: Franke, 1963), pp. 316–17.

53. *The Sayings of Chuang Tzu* (Hong Kong: n.p., 1973), p. 112; Wilhelm, trans., p. 75.

54. *Sayings of Chuang Tzu*, p. 294; Dschwang Dsi, p. 180.

55. Li'a Dsi, *Das Wahre Buch vom Quellenden Urgrund (Tschung Hü Dschen Ging); Die Lehren der Philosophen Lia Yü Kou und Yang Dschur*, trans. Richard Wilhelm (Jena, Germany: Eugen Diederichs, 1921), pp. 46–47.

Chapter 6. Leopards

1. In *Cahiers pour un temps* (Paris: n.p. 1986), p. 18. Translation mine.

2. Uta Liebmann Schaub, "Foucault's Oriental Subtext," *PMLA* 104 (May 1989): 306–16.

3. Jack Kerouac, *The Dharma Bums* (New York: New American Library, 1958). Gary Snyder, "Cold Mountain Poems," *Evergreen Review* 2 (Autumn 1958): 69–80, subsequently published in a number of Snyder's books. For the Chinese, I have used the 1965 edition of the *Ssu-pu ts'ung k'an*. My decision to choose Snyder as an example of postmodernism owes something to "De/Reconstructing the 'I': PostFANTASTICmodernist Poetics," *Journal of the Fantastic in the Arts* 1 (1988): 39–48, where Patrick D. Murphy argues that play with traditions in Snyder's original poetry makes him prototypically postmodern.

4. For Snyder's knowledge of Campbell, see the former's undergraduate essay, *He Who Hunted Birds in His Father's Village: The Dimensions of a Haida Myth* (Bolinas, Calif.: Grey Fox, 1979), p. 113, where Snyder quotes from Joseph Campbell, *The Hero with a Thousand Faces* (New York: Pantheon, 1949), p. 391. Snyder's categorization of spiritual stages is in the essay *He Who Hunted Birds in His Father's Village*, p. 73.

5. James Whitlark, *Illuminated Fantasy: From Blake's Visions to Recent Graphic Fiction* (Madison: Fairleigh Dickinson University Press; London: Associated University Presses, 1988), p. 177.

6. In an interview with Jonah Raskin, Doris Lessing insisted that, although the analysis was successful, its Jungian "terminology" was (at least initially) uncongenial to Lessing, but considering the mystical turn that Lessing's writings have taken, I suspect that the Jungian orientation of her analyst was significant. Lessing, *A Small Personal Voice,* edited and introduced by Paul Schlueter (New York: Knopf, 1974), p. 68.

7. Mircea Eliade, *Ordeal by Labyrinth: Conversations with Claude-Henri Rocquet,* trans. Derek Coltman (Chicago: University of Chicago Press, 1982), pp. 4–5.

8. "Cu Mircea Eliae: despre el si despre alti," in *Rampa* (Bucharest): 5 June 1933, pp. 1, 3; Mac Linscott Ricketts, *Mircea Eliade: The Romanian Roots, 1907–1945,* East European Monographs, no. 248, vol. 1 (New York: Columbia University Press, 1988). p. 13.

9. Eliade, *Autobiography,* Vol. 1: *1907–1937, Journey East, Journey West,* trans. Mac Linscott Ricketts (San Francisco: Harper, 1981), p. 31.

10. Ricketts, p. 12.

11. *Autobiography* p. 29.

12. *Ordeal by Labyrinth,* pp. 70–71.

13. *Autobiography,* p. 213.

14. In David Carrasco and Jane Marie Swanberg, eds., *Waiting for the Dawn: Mircea Eliade in Perspective* (Boulder, Colo.: Westview, 1985), p. 118.

15. Eliade, *The Old Man and the Bureaucrats,* trans. Mary Park Stevenson (Notre Dame: University of Notre Dame Press, 1979). Although not on such a massive level, Eliade does have characters in earlier novels fend off rationalist criticism by claiming that the truth is too large to tell at the moment, e.g., Eliade, *The Forbidden Forest,* trans. Mac Linscott Ricketts and Mary Park Stevenson (Notre Dame: University of Notre Dame Press, 1978), p. 76.

16. E.g., Eliade, *Cosmos and History* (New York: Harper, 1959), pp. viii–ix. When Eliade employs "archetypes" in his own way, his usage is more defensible than Jung's, except that Eliade assumes that the archetypes of each culture inevitably have very much in common—an assumption as problematic as Jung's.

17. Eliade, *Patterns in Comparative Religion,* trans. Rosemary Sheed (New York: New American Library, 1958), p. 197.

18. Claude Bonnefoy, *Entretiens avec Eugène Ionesco* (Paris: Pierre Belfond, 1966), p. 23, trans. by Jan Dawson as *Conversations with Eugène Ionesco* (New York: Holt, 1966), p. 21.

19. Ionesco, *Fragments of a Journal,* trans. Jean Stewart (New York: Grove, 1968), p. 60.

20. Hermann Broch, *Gesammelte Werke,* vol. 6: *Dichten und Erkennen: Essays,* ed. Hannah Arendt (Zurich: Rhein, 1953–61), 164 trans. by Ernestine Schlant as *Hermann Broch,* TWAS 485 (Boston: Twayne, 1978), p. 88. Broch was far less appreciative of Kafka's style than of his "countermyth," and Broch's own rhetorical, long sentences constitute a prose diametrically opposed to Kafka's. See Schlant, p. 173, n. 18.

21. Schlant, p. 9.

22. Broch, *Der Tod des Vergil* (Zurich: Rhein/Suhrkamp, 1958), p. 193, trans. by Jean Starr Untermeyer in collaboration with Broch as *The Death of Virgil* (New York: Pantheon, 1945; reprint. Grosset, 1965), p. 175.

23. Aniela Jaffe, "Hermann Broch, 'Der Tod des Vergil': Ein Beitrag zum Problem der Individuation," in *Studien fur analytischen Psychologie C. G. Jungs: Festschrift zum 80. Geburtstage von C. G. Jung* (Zurich: Rhein, 1955), vol. 2; 288–43.

24. *Hermann Broch-Daniel Brody Briefwechsel 1930–1951* (Frankfurt: Buchhändler-Vereinigung, 1971), p. 195; Schlant p. 73.

25. Schlant, p. 127.

26. Der *Tod des Vergil,* p. 533; *Death of Virgil,* p. 482.

27. Broch, *Gesammelte* Werke, vol. 8: *Briefe* (Zurich: Rhein, 1953–61), pp. 271–72, as trans. in Schlant, p. 121.

28. *Der Tod des Virgil,* p. 253; *Death of Virgil,* p. 230.

29. George Steiner, *After Babel: Aspects of Language and Translation* (London: Oxford University Press, 1975), pp. 319–21.

30. Octavio Paz, *Alternating Current,* trans. Helen R. Lane (New York: Viking, 1973), p. 7.

31. Paz, *Early Poems 1935–1955* [bilingual edition], trans. Muriel Rukeyser et al.

(Bloomington: Indiana University Press, 1973), "Prólogue"/"Prologue" pp. 2–5, "The Endless Instant"/"*No hay salida*?" pp. 124–29.

32. *Alternating Current,* trans. Helen R. Lane (New York: Viking, 1973), p. 16.

33. Ibid., p. 18.

34. Ibid., p. 21.

35. Richard Callan, *Hispania* 60 (1977): 916–26.

36. Ruth Needleman, "Poetry and the Reader," *the Perpetual Present: The Poetry and Prose of Octavio Paz,* ed. Ivar Ivask (Norman: University of Oklahoma Press, 1973), p. 36.

37. Carlos Fuentes, "How I Started to Write," in *The Graywolf Annual Five: Multicultural Literacy,* eds., Rick Simonson and Scott Walker (St. Paul: Graywolf, 1988), p. 85.

38. Ibid., p. 110.

39. Ibid., p. 95.

40. Ibid., p. 104.

41. Ibid., p. 106.

42. Fuentes, *Terra nostra* (Mexico City: Joaquín Mortiz, 1975), trans. by Margaret Sayers Peden as *Terra Nostra* (New York: Farra, 1976); Fuentes, *Aura* [bilingual edition], trans. Lysander Kemp (New York: Farrar, 1975).

43. Fuentes, *Zona Sagrada* (Mexico City: Gabriel Mancera, 1967), p. 6, trans. by Susanne Jill Levine as *Holy Places* (New York: Dutton, 1972), p. 13. Gloria P. Duran, *The Archetypes of Carlos Fuents: From Witch to Androgene* (Hamden, Conn. Archon, 1980), p. 77.

44. Fuentes's English letter (and another from him in Spanish) form the appendix of her book. Duran, p. 202.

45. Ibid., 79. Carl G. Jung, *Psychology and Religion* (New Haven, Conn.: Yale University Press, 1938), p. 34.

46. "How I Started to Write," p. 107.

47. Thomas Mann, "Homage" (*C* xi); Mann's original German version is readily available *Schriften und Reden zur Literatur, Kunst und Philosophie,* vol. 2 (Frankfurt am Main, Germany: Fischer, 1968), p. 376.

48. Mann, *Joseph, der Ernährer, Joseph und seine Bruder,* vol. 4 (Stockholm: Bermann-Fisher, 1943; reprint, Frankfurt am Main: Fischer, 1983), 7–19, trans. by H.T. Lowe-Porter as *Joseph the Provider* (New York: Knopf, 1944), pp. 3–17.

49. Ignace Feuerlicht, *Thomas Mann* (New York: Twayne, 1968), p. 90.

50. *Mythology and Humanism: The Correspondence of Thomas Mann and Karl Kerényi,* trans. Alexander Gelley (Ithaca: Cornell University Press, 1975), p. 100.

51. Mann, *Die Geschichten Jaakobs, Joseph und seine Brüder,* vol 1. (Berlin: Fischer, 1934; reprint. Frankfurt am Main, Germany: Fischer, 1983), p. 7, trans. by H. T. Lowe-Porter as *Joseph and His Brothers* (New York: Knopf, 1939), p. 3.

52. Ralph Freedman, *Hermann Hesse: Pilgrim of Crisis, A Biography* (New York: Pantheon, 1978), pp. 15–26.

53. Hesse, "Kindheit des Zauberers," *Gesammelte Werke,* vol. 8 (Frankfurt: Suhrkamp, 1970), 374–78, trans. by Denver Lindless as "Childhood of the Magician," *Autobiographical Writings* (New York: Farrar, 1971), pp. 6–9.

54. Hesse, *Die Morgenlandfahrt,* in *Gesammelte Werke,* vol. 8 (Frankfurt am Main, Germany: Suhrkamp, 1970), p. 374, trans. by Hilda Rosner as *The Journey to the East* (New York: Farrar, 1956), p. 92.

55. Hesse's *Gesammelte Werke,* vol. 12, 477–91, contains 11 sections on Kafka, ranging from a paragraph to several pages. Perhaps further notable are Hesse's repeated references in *Morgenlandfahrt* to the painter Paul Klee. One of Hesse's readers wrote to Hesse asking if there were a parallel between Kafka and Klee, a letter to which Hesse published a response in 1956 (one of Hesse's many complimentary remarks about Kafka from 1925 on). In that response—a very selective and incomplete reply—Hesse ignored the question about Klee and also ignored most of the questions about Hesse he himself mentions in his preamble to that reply—including one often asked by Hesse's readers—his relationship to Jung. Such unwillingness to answer his readers fully characterizes not merely this response but also those rare occasions when he (begrudgingly and taciturnly) considered the possibility that

his works were Jungian. His denials of significant influence are less interesing than the biographical facts.

56. Freedman, pp. 184–89.

57. Quoted in ibid. p. 225.

58. Quoted in ibid., p. 353.

59. Daniel Halpern, ed., *The Art of the Tale: An International Anthology of Short Stories* (New York: Penguin, 1986), p. 811.

60. *Cancerqueen and Other Stories* pp. 106–14, 145–47.

61. Ibid., p. 18.

62. In Halpern, p. 380.

63. Quoted by Updike in the introduction to Bruno Schulz, *Sanatorium under the Sign of the Hourglass,* trans. Celina Wieniewska (New York: Penguink 1978), p. xiv, abbreviated hereafter as *Hourglass.*

64. *Klepsydra,* p. 339; *Hourglass,* p. 171.

65. In regard to this question of chaos, John Updike quotes a line from Schultz, *The Street of Crocodiles*—a line attributed to the protagonists's father, but that Updike convincingly sees as Schulz's own sentiment. "If, forgetting the respect due to the Creator, I were to attempt a criticism of creation, I would say 'Less matter, more form!" Introduction, *Hourglass,* p. xv. Thus there are limits to the Father's (and perhaps also Schulz's) tolerance of the vast diversity and proliferation of beings found throughout Creation.

66. Arthur Sandauer, *Traité des mannequins,* Les Lettres Nouvelles, no. 15 (Paris; Julliard, 1961), p. 24.

67. *Klepstdra,* pp. 65–69.

68. Introduction, *Hourglass,* p. xvi.

69. Translator's Preface, *Hourglass,* p. xi.

70. Steinbeck ms. at the Humanities Research Center, University of Texas, quoted in Jackson J. Benson, *The True Adventure of John Steinbeck, Writer,* (New York: Viking, 1984), p. 21; letter to Frank and Lynn Loesser, 25 May 1960, quoted in Benson, p. 878.

71. Benson, p. 40.

72. Letter to the Loessers, 25 May 1960, quoted in Benson p. 878.

73. Steinbeck, *The Winter of Our Discontent* (New York: Viking, 1961), p. 49.

74. Letter to the Loessers, Benson, p. 878.

75. Donal Stone, "Steinbeck, Jung, and *The Winter of Our Discontent,*" *Steinbeck Quarterly* 9 (Summer/Fall 1978): 87. Even if one posits the existence of an anima (a very problematic concept), Stone's identification of characters with it is overly reductive. Margie Young-Hunt, e.g., is less a legendary prophetess or seductress than a parody of such anima figures. She represents less a universal than an American type, the aging divorcée, who, as her last name suggests, is in pursuit of vanishing youth. Admittedly, through widespread references to myth and legend, Steinbeck probably does suggest that the American condition is a variant of universal human nature, but his focus is on *our* American crisis.

76. Greg Johnson, *Understanding Joyce Carol Oates* (Columbia: University of South Carolina, 1987), pp. 4–7.

77. Oates, "The Nature of Short Fiction or, The Nature of My Short Fiction," *Handbook of Short Story Writing* (New York: Writer's Digest, 1970), p. xii.

78. Oates, *New Heaven, New Earth: The Visionary Experience in Literature* (New York: Vanguard, 1974), p. 296.

79. Ibid., p. 282.

80. Chapter 40 of *Tao Te Ching,* trans. Gia-Fu Feng and Jane English (New York: Vintage, 1972), as quoted in *New Heaven, New Earth,* pp. 278, 290.

81. Oates, *Marriages and Infidelities* (New York: Vanguard, 1968), p. 361.

82. Oates, *Crossing the Border* (New York: Vanguard, 1976), p. 119.

83. Oates, *Invisible Woman* (Princeton, N.J.: Ontario Review, 1982), pp. 74–75.

84. Oates, "Kafka as Storyteller," *The Complete Stories and Parables,* ed. Nahum N. Glatzer (New York: Quality Paperback Book Club, 1983), p. xviii.

85. *New Heaven, New Earth,,* p. 260.

86. Ibid., p. 117.

87. Jorge Luis Borges, *The Aleph and Other Stories 1933–1969,* ed. and trans. Norman Thomas di Giovani (New York: Dutton, 1970), p. 142.

88. Borges, "Kafka y sus Precursores," *Sus Mejores Pajinas* (Englewood Cliffs, N.J.: Prentice-Hall, 1970), p. 186, trans. by Donald A. Yates and James E. Irby as "*Kafka and His Precursors,*" *Labyrinths: Selected Stories and Other Writings* (New York: New Directions, 1970), p. 199.

89. Margaret Boegeman, "From Amhoretz to Exegete: The Swerve from Kafla to Borges," *Critical Essays on Jorge Luis Borges,* ed. Jaime Alazraki (Boston: G. K. Hall, 1987), p. 174. Boegeman confirmed the bibliographical facts through that 1976 interview with Borges.

90. Edna Aizenberg, "Kafka, Borges and Contemporary Latin-American Fiction," *Newsletter of the Kafka Society of America* 6 (June/December 1982), 11 n. 13.

91. Borges, *Ficciones* (Buenos Aires: Emecé, 1956), p. 61.

92. Borges, ed., *La metamorfosis,* by Franz Kafka (Buenos Aires: Losada, 1938), p. 10, as trans. in Aizenberg, p. 5.

93. Ibid.

94. Preston Harold, *The Shining Stranger* (New York: Dodd, Mead, 1967), p. 380. Jung also defined the Self thus in conversation with Serrano, *Jung & Hesse,* p. 56.

95. Richard Burgin, *Conversations with Jorge Luis Borges* (New York: Holt, 1968), p. 140.

Chapter 7. Frogs

1. Keiji Nishitani, *What Is Religion* (Tokyo: n.p., 1961). p. 52.

2. Hans Walsdenfels, *Absolute Nothingness,* trans. J.W. Heisig (New York: Paulist, 1961), p. 65.

3. Italo Calvino, *Il Castello dei destini incrociati* (Torino, Italy: Einaudi, 1973), p. 97, trans, as *The Castle of Crossed Destinies* (New York: Harcourt, 1976), p. 97. In the Italian, but not in the English version of his work, Calvino reveals that it was inspired by a structuralist conference.

4. *The Canon of Reason and Virtue (Lao-Tze's Tao Teh King)* [Chinese and English], trans. D. T. Suzuki and Paul Carus (La Salle, Ill.: Open Court, 1974), pp. [Chinese] 31, [English] 79–80.

5. Bloom, p. 98.

6. For an early version of this attitude, see Ferdinand de Saussure, *Cours de linguistique generale* (Paris; Payot, 1962), p. 32.

7. Herbert R. Lottman, *Albert Camus: A Biography* (Garden City, N.Y.: Doubleday, 1979), p. 38.

8. Albert Camus, *Essais* (Paris: Gallimard, 1965). p. 198; *Myth of Sisyphus and Other Essays,* trans. Justin O'Brien (New York: Knopf, 1964), p. 123.

9. Lottman, p. 193.

10. Shūzō Kuki, "Considerations on Time," in *Shūzō Kuki and Jean-Paul Sartre: Influence and Counter-Influence in the Early History of Existential Phenomenology,* edited, translated, and comment by Stephen Light, Foreword by Mychel Rybalka (Carbondale: Southern Illinois University Press, 1987), p. 49.

11. Lottman, p. 208.

12. Maja Goth has analyzed the many similarities of tone between these two novels, e.g., narrators who are "neutre, impersonnel et terne," *Franz Kafka et les lettres Françaises (1928–1955)* (Paris: José Corti, 1956), pp. 123–35.

13. Camus, *Étranger* (New York: Pantheon, 1942), p. 171, trans. by Stuart Gilbert as *The Stranger* (New York: Knopf, 1967), p. 154. Gilbert renders *tendre* as "benign," but, given Camus's position, one does better to see *tendre indifference* as like Lao Tzu's Tao, which treats people like straw animals for sacrifice. It is both cruel and benevolent and (perhaps coincidentally) *tendre* in another sense: soft and pliable—one of the reasons it is indefinable.

14. Camus, *Carnets* (Paris: Gillimard, 1962), May 1937, April 1941, trans. by Philip Thody as *Notebooks: 1935–1942* (New York: Modern Library, 1965), pp. 33, 197.

15. Hayden Carruth, Introduction, *Nausea,* by Jean-Paul Sartre, trans. Lloyd Alexander (New York: New Directions, 1964; reporting. Cambridge: Robert Bentley, 1979), p. x.

16. Sartre, *La nausée* (Paris: Gallimard, 1938), p. 54, trans. as *Nausea,* p. 33.

17. The next year after the publication of "The Letter of Lord Chandos" *(Der Brief des Lord Chandos,* 1904), Hugo von Hofmannsthal confessed to his friend Leopold von Andrian that "the letter was inspired by 'a personal inner event' " and by dreaming himself "into the way in which . . . people of the sixteenth century perceived antiquity." Hofmannsthal and Leopold von Andrian, *Briefwechsel,* ed. Walter Perl (Frankfurt am Main, Germany: Fischer, 1968), p. 160; Lowell A. Bangerter, *Hugo von Hofmannsthal* (New York: Ungar, 1977), p. 28. "The Letter" evokes an age of vast country estates and aristocratic leisure for interrelated translation, interpretation, and imitation of the classics—enough intercultural study to risk what Elizabethans considered one major danger of scholarship, "melancholy." His mental state, however, is even stranger than the Renaissance thought that malady to be. He writes:

> The language in which I might be able not only to write but to think is neither Latin nor English, neither Italian nor Spanish, but a language none of whose words is known to me, a language in which inanimate things speak to me and wherein I may one day [in the grave *im Grabe*)] have to justify myself before an unknown judge.

To Hofmannsthal's persona, Chandos, his quasi-aphasia arrived inexplicably. In listing his former achievements, nonetheless, Chandos inadvertently reveals the etiology of the condition. His literary career advanced from poetry largely within his own culture (pastorals) to dreams of unifying the fragments of all ages as a way of self-knowledge. The crisis then ensued: both traditional religion and worldly pursuits could no longer lure his mind from the "void *[Leere,* emptiness]." Alienated from his own culture and thus unable to view his surroundings with "the simplifying eye of habit *[Gweohnheit],*" Chandos sees everything broken into parts—comparable to the Buddhist understanding of existence as *anicca,* a constant flow of fragments. Equally, he has an intense identification with all creation, even poisoned rats—comparable to Buddhist compassion, which in Zen Enlightenment involves a sense that all is mystically one. Hugo von Hofmannsthal, *Gesammelte Werke,* vol. 3 (Berlin: Fischer, 1934), pp. 202, 193, 195, trans. by Mary Hottinger and Tania and James Stern as *Selected Prose,* Bollingen Series, no. 33 (New York: Pantheon, 1952), pp. 133, 134, 140–41.) In other words, moments of mystic insight may cause the conventional boundaries of things to disappear with two results: one sees as fragments what seemed to be whole but these fragments are mutually conditioned, so that one feels integrally related to all of them. *The Mumonkan (Gateless Gate),* a thirteenth-century casebook of Chinese Zen *(Ch'an),* e.g., contains a poem that begins, "[For those who] know the principle, everything is of one household" *(hui tsai shih t'ung i chia).* Paradoxically, as in Hofmannsthal, the poem ends, "[For those who] know the princple, everything is separate and different" *(hui tsai wan pieh kan ch'a).* R. H. Blyth, trans., ed., and comment. *Zen Classics,* p. 135 *[W].* Shimon Sandbank, who ignores Hoffmannsthal and other precursors, considers Kafka the earliest such writer and Sartre's source (13–28).

18. Alfred Stern, *Sartre: His Philosophy and Psychoanalysis* (New York: Liberal Arts, 1953), p. 16.

19. Simone de Beauvoir, trans. Patrick O'Brian (New York: Pantheon, 1984), p. 198.

20. Sartre, *The War Diaries: November 1939/March 1940,* trans. Quintin Hoare (New York: Pantheon, 1984), p. 62. Sartre misquoted the title of *In the Penal Colony.*

21. Goth, p. 138. Metamorphosis, the work closest to *Nausea,* had been translated into French as early as 1928.

22. Stuart L. Charmé, *Meaning and Myth in the Study of Lives: A Sartrean Perspective* (Philadelphia: University of Pennsylvania Press, 1984), pp. 149–57. As Charmé notes (124), Thomas M. King observes that Sartre's works have "an overwhelming theological character that often seems to be unaffected by the atheism that he professes." King, *Sartre and the Sacred* (Chicago: University of Chicago Press, 1974), p. xi.

23. *Critical Fictions: The Literary Criticism of Jean-Paul Sartre* (New Haven: Yale University Press, 1976), pp. 1–18, et passim.

24. Charmé, p. 115.

25. Ibid., p. 58.

26. Sartre, *L'être et le néant: essai d'ontologie phénoménologique* (Paris: Gallimard, 1943), p. 708. trans. by Hazel E. Barnes as *Being and Nothingness: A Phenomenological Essay on Ontology* (New York: Washington Square, 1956), p. 784.

27. Jean-Pierre Cauvin, Introduction; "The Poetics of Andre Breton" in *Poems of André Breton: A Bilingual Anthology,* trans. and ed., Jean-Pierre Cauvin and Mary Ann Caws (Austin: University of Texas Press, 1982), p. xvii.

28. Breton, *Entretiens (1913–1952)* rev. ed. (Paris: Gallimard, 1969), p. 159.

29. Breton," *Têtes d'orage," Minotaure* (Winter 1937), quoted in Goth, p. 14. Goth devotes 50 pages (13–63) to listing references to Kafka by the Surrealists and comparing their sentiments with Kafka's.

30. Breton, *Anthologie de l'humour noir* (Paris: Sagittaire, 1940), p. 77.

31. Michel Carrouges, *André Breton and the Basic Concepts of Surrealism,* trans. Maura Prendergast (University: University of Alabama, 1974), p. 11; Breton, *Manifests du surréalisme* (Paris: Sagitaire, 1946), p. 92.

32. André Breton, *Manifestes du Surréalisme* (Paris: Gallimard, 1969), pp. 76–77. Breton later said that this remark was inspired by Hegel. André Breton, *Entretiens (1913–1952)* (Paris: Gallimard, 1969), p. 151.

33. Christopher Norris, *Derrida* (Cambrige: Harvard University Press, 1987), p. 11.

34. Legend has it that the academic posts held by Derrida at the Sorbonne and elsewhere were as a *philosophy* teacher. Perhaps this association of him with philosophy comes from the defensiveness with which his personae sometimes (but not always) protect that academic field from the incursions of literary critics. See, e.g., his fiction on Paul Valéry in *Margins of Philosophy,* trans. Alan Bass (Chicago: University of Chicago Press, 1982) and the comment on it in Norris, p. 23.

35. Norris, p. 11.

36. A. French, *Czech Writers and Politics 1945–1969* (New York/Boulder: Columbia University Press/East European Monographs, 1982), p. 182.

37. Jacques Derrida, "Devant la loi," in *Philosophy and Literature,* ed. A. Phillips Griffiths, Royal Institute of Philosophy Lecture Series, no. 16, Supplement to *Philosophy* 1983 (London: Cambridge University Press, 1984), p. 178, trans. Avital Ronell and reworked by Derrida in Alan Udoff, ed, *Kafka and the Contemporary Critical Performance: Centenary Readings* (Bloomington: Indiana University Press, 1987), p. 133.

38. The phrase in the French "original" *(campagne continentale)* is even more problematic suggesting that Derrida comes not from the suburbs of El Biar, Algiers (nor from his more recent urban abodes) but from some European country seat.

39. Wayne C. Booth, *The Rhetoric of Fiction* (Chicago: University of Chicago Press, 1961), pp. 71–73. Previous studies of Derrida have noted that he makes errors so glaring that they must be deliberate, most notably Paul de Man, *Blindness and Insight: Essays in the Rhetoric of Contemporary Criticism,* 2nd ed. (Minneapolis: University of Minnesota, 1983.

40. Beginning as it does, "permittez-moi," the French version has a more polite tone than the English. In other words, the D. whom I am analyzing belongs to the Ronell/Derrida English version and differs subtly from the French persona, *je*.

41. C. Scott Moss, *Dreams, Images, and Fantasy: A Semantic Differential Casebook* (Urbana: University of Illinois Press, 1970), p. 277.

42. Nathalie Sarraute, *L'Ere du soupçon: essais sur le roman,* les Essais, no. 80 (Paris: Gallimard, 1956), pp. 9–52.

43. Sarraute, *Martereau* (Paris: Gallimard, 1953), pp. 202, 228, trans. by Maria Jolas as *Martereau* (New York: George Braziller, 1959), pp. 202, 229.

44. E.g., Sarraute, *Entre la vie et la mort* (Paris: Gallimard, 1968), pp. 113, 123.

45. Ilona Leki, *Alain Robbe-Grillet,* TWAS, no. 682 (Boston: TWAS, 1983), pp. 3–4.

46. Robbe-Grillet, *Pour un nouveau roman* (Paris: Les Editions de Minuit, 1963), trans. by Richard Howard as *For a New Novel* (New York: Grove, 1965), p. 165. According to one psychological theory, when people wish to deal with a situation that is unfamiliar, confused, or involving unpleasant responsibility, they may switch their attention from large concerns to details of method. R. R. Vallacher, and D. M. Wegner, *A Theory of Action Identification*

(Hillsdale, N.J. Lawrence Erlbaum, 1985). When he limits his literary focus to such details, Kafka may be suggesting that his personae are lost or childishly avoiding responsibility.

47. Numerous critics have remarked that in one sense or another, Robbe-Grillet's style is Kafkaesque e.g., D. Cohn, "Castles and Anti-Castles or Kafka and Robbe-Grillet," *Novel* (Fall 1971): 19–31; Ingeborg Hoesterey, "The Intertextual Loop: Kafka, Robbe-Grillet, Kafka," in *Kafka and the Contemporary Critical Performance: Centenary Readings;* ed. Alan Udoff (Bloomington: Indiana University Press, 1987), pp. 58–75.

48. Robbe-Grillet, *Les gomes* (Paris: Les Editions de Minuit, 1953), p.11, trans. by Richard Howard as *The Erasers* (New York: Grove, 1964), p. 7. In an article on his works, Robbe-Grillet explains his use of myth and cliché as a means to undermine them and the repressive social order as well, "Order and Disorder in Film and Fiction," trans. Bruce Morrisette, *Critical Inquiry* 4 (1977): 1–20.

49. Even during Freud's lifetime, evidence against the universality of the Oedipal complex proliferated, example, Heisaku Kosawa's paper, "Two Kinds of Guilt Feelings (Ajase Complex)," presented to Freud at the Vienna Psychoanalytic Institute, July 1932, and eventually published in *The Japanese Journal of Psychoanalysis,* 1 (1950). Its argument (that the fundamental Japanese complex differs from the Oedipal pattern) has become influential in Japanese psychology (Herink 21). Anthropological studies have shown even greater psychological variety of family organization throughout the world, particularly with matrilineal cultures where the patriarchal structures of Oedipus may be undermined or absent.

50. Leki, p. 20; Olga Bernal, *Alain-Robbe-Grillet: le roman de l'absence* (Paris: Gallimard, 1964), pp. 52–57.

51. Ben Stoltzfus, *Alain Robbe-Grillet: The Body of the Text* (Madison: Fairleigh Dickinson University Press/Associated University Presses, 1985), pp. 117–18.

52. Leki, p. 5.

53. "On Portnoy's Complaint," interview by George Plimpton, in *Reading Myself and Others,* pp. 21–22.

54. In Sanford Pinsker, ed., *Critical Essays on Philip Roth* (Boston: G. K. Hall, 1982), pp. 245–54.

55. Roth, *Portnoy's Complaint* (New York: Random, 1967), p. 274.

56. Roth, *The Facts: A Novelist's Autobiography* (New York: Farrar, 1988), p. 162.

57. Andrew Field, *VN: The Life and Art of Vladimir Nabokov* (New York: Crown, 1986), p. 32; George Steiner, After Babel (London: Weidenfeld and Nichlson, 1981).

58. In addition to the Kafkan initial K., the commentator ascribes to himself a number of other names including Botkin, Kinbote, and Charles the Beloved. While freely admitting his admiration for Kafka, Nabokov repeatedly insisted that the often-noted, Kafkaesque mood of his early works came before he was familiar with Kafka, but with books after he had taught "Metamorphosis" (such as *Pale Fire*) he could not deny the possibility of Kafka's influence. Even with the early works, the affinity with Kafka is noteworthy.

59. Vladimir Nabokov, *Pale Fire* (New York: Putnam 1962), p. 80.

60. Nabokov, *Lectures on Literature,* ed. Fredson Bowers, introd. John Updike (New York: Harvest/Harcourt, 1980), p.283.

61. Nabokov, *The Annotated Lolita,* ed. Alfred Appel, Jr. (New York: McGraw-Hill, 1970), p. 18.

62. Leona Toker, *Nabokov: The Mystery of Literary Structures* (London: Cornell University Press, 1989), pp. 1–11; Nabokov, *Strong Opinions* (New York: McGraw-Hill, 1981), p. 118.

63. Julio Cortázar, *Rayuela* (Buenos Aires: Editorial Sudamericana Sociedad Anónima, 1963), p. 543, trans. by Gregory Rabassa as *Hopscotch* (New York: Pantheon Books, 1966), p. 478.

64. *Rayuela* p. 543; *Hopscotch,* p. 478.

65. *Rayuela,* p. 292; *Hopscotch,* p. 248.

66. Steven Boldy, *The Novels of Julio Cortázar* (Cambridge: Cambridge University Press, 1980), p. 143.

67. Ibid., p. 116.

68. *Rayuela,* p. 471; *Hopscotch,* p. 414.

69. *Rayuela,* pp. 36, 91, 373–74, 458; *Hopscotch,* pp. 21,73, 321–22, 402.

70. Remarks at a poetry reading, NYU, Maison Française, May 1970, quoted in translation in Grossman, p. 12.

71. Antonio Skarmeta, "El apogeo del antipeota," *Ercilla* (1971): 37. quoted in translation in Grossman, p. 12.

72. Quoted in Grossman, p. 12.

73. Nicanor Parra, "La tramps" [The Trap] in *Obra Gruesa* [Basic Work] (Santiago, Chile: Editorial Universitaria, 1969), pp. 54–55.

74. Parra and Pablo Neruda, *Discursos* [Speeches] (Santiago, Chile: Editorial Nascimento, 1962), p. 14–16.

75. Grossman, p. 41.

76. "Los vicios del mundo moderno," *Antipoems: New and Selected,* ed. David Unger, introduced by Frank MacShane (New York: New Directions, 1985), 20–21.

77. Poem 37 in *Sermons and Homilies of the Christ of Elqui* (Columbia: University of Columbia Press, 1984), pp. 54–55.

78. Abe Kōbō, "the Age which Asks the Question about Our Ultimate Belonging" *[Saichū no kizokyu o tou jidai],* Supplement to *The Box Man [Hakootoko]* (Tokyo: Kinyōsha, 1973), p. 3, trans. by Keiko I. McDonald, in "Contemporary Man's Plight: An Analysis of *The Box Man," Literature East and West* 21 (January/December 1977): 198.

79. "A Note about the Author, in Abe *Box Man [Hakootoko],* trans. E. Dale Saunders (New York: Knopf, 1974), p. 181.

80. Supplement to *the Complete Works of Kobo Abe [Abe Kō bō Zensakuhin],* vol. 2 (Tokyo: Shinchōsha, 1976), p. 4.

81. Abe, *Hako Otoko* (Tokyo: Shinchōsha, 1973), p. 191, trans. as *The Box Man,* p. 1178.

82. J. Thomas Rimer, *Modern Japanese Fiction and Its Traditions: An Introduction* (Princeton, N.J.: Princeton University Press, 1978), pp. 22–23.

83. Abe Kōkō, *The Ark Sakura* (New York: Vintage, 1988), p. 336.

84. Milan Kundera, *The Art of the Novel,* trans. Linda Asher (New York: Grove, 1988), pp. 99–117.

85. Set as the book is within the Prague Spring (the liberalization movement of 1968), the phrase "live in truth" also recalls one of the Czech adjutators for liberalization, Vaclav Havel, whose locally famous essay "The Power of the Powerless" contrasts "living in a lie" and "living in the truth."

86. Quoted in Antonin J. Liehm, "Milan Kundera: Czech Writer," in *Czech Literature Since 1956: A Symposium,* (New York: eds., William E. Harkins and Paul I. Trensky Bohemic, 1980), p. 47.

Chapter 8. Ravens

1. *Collected Works of Edgar Allan Poe,* ed. Thomas Olive Mabbott (Cambridge: Harvard University Press, 1969), p. 364–69.

2. In Kafka's notebook, the pet named "Nevermore" is a dog rather than a raven, but the choice of the name, close to Kafka's fragment about the raven, strongly suggests that Kafka was thinking of Poe's poem.

3. J. G. Frazer, *The New Golden Bough* (New York: S. G. Phillips, 1959), p. 467.

4. From a Mahayana version of the Dhammapada quoted in *Nāgārjuna's Great Perfection of Wisdom Treatise,* trans. Richard H. Robinson, *Early Mādhyamika* (Madison: University of Wisconsin, 1967), p. 60. The verse is not present in the Pali Dhammapada.

5. Ernst Kaiser and Eithne Wilkins translate one of Kafka's fragments with the following beginning:

> You keep talking about death, and yet you do not die.
> And yet I shall die. I am just saying my swan song.

Although the image of the swan is by the translators (*D* 299), while Kafka writes merely of an "ending song" (*Schlussgesang* H 334), their translation may have made explicit an implication of the original.

6. As translated in Henry Scott Stokes, *The Life and Death of Yukio Mishima* (London: Peter Owen, 1975), p. 77.

7. Ibid.

8. John Nathan, *Mishima: A Biography* (Boston: Little, Brown, 1974), pp. xii, 49n, 97, 166, 221n–222n, et passim.

9. Alan Wolfe, "Suicide and the Japanese Postmodern: A Postnarrative Paradigm?" *South Atlantic Quarterly* 87 (Summer 1988): 571–89.

10. Kurt Vonnegut, Jr., *Slaughterhouse Five or The Children's Crusade, A Duty Dance with Death* (New York: Dell, 1966), title page.

11. Vonnegut, *Palm Sunday: An Autobiographical Collage* (New York: Dell, 1981), p. 88 [Vonnegut eventually dropped the "Jr." from his signature.]

12. Ibid., p. 93.

13. James Whitlark, "Vonnegut's Anthropology Thesis," *Literature and Anthropology*, Comparative Literature Series, no. 20 (Lubbock: Texas Tech University Press, 1989), pp. 77–86.

14. *Palm Sunday*, p. 314.

15. Vonnegut, *Mother Night* (New York: Dell, 1961), pp. 109–10.

16. Hermann Hesse, *Die Morgenlandfahrt in Gesammelte Werke*, vol. 8 (Frankfuhrt/Am Main:, Germany Suhrkamp, 1970), p. 35, trans. by Hilda Rosner as *The Journey to the East* (New York: Farrar, 1956), p. 52.

17. Vonnegut, *Wampeters, Foma, & Granfalloons (Opinions)* (New York: Dell, 1976), p. 114.

18. E.g., at Texas Tech University, November 1983.

19. *Mother Night*, p. 136.

20. Vonnegut, *Deadeye Dick* (New York: Delacorte/Seymour Lawrence, 1982), pp. 208–10.

21. Sandbank, p. 140.

22. *Wampeters*, pp. 178–80.

23. Ibid. "Vonnegut's Anthropology Thesis," p. 184.

24. Salman Rushdie, *Shame* (New York: Vintage, 1983), p. 92.

25. Rushdie, *The Satanic Verses* (New York: Viking, 1988), p. 49.

26. Rushdie, *The Jaguar Smile: A Nicaraguan Journey* (New York: Viking, 1987), p. 11.

27. Jacques Derrida, "Edmond Jabès and the Question of the Book," *Writing and Difference*, trans. Alan Bass (Chicago: University of Chicago Press, 1978), pp. 64–78.

28. Jabès, *The Book of Questions*, trans. Rosmarie Waldrop (Middletown, Conn.: Wesleyan University Press, 1972), p. 122. In the Introduction to *The Sin of the Book: Edmond Jabès* (Lincoln: University of Nebraska Press, 1985), p. xiv, Gould cites this passage as one of many pieces of evidence that "at the center of *[The Book of Questions]* lies the shrillest of aphorisms: the scream."

29. Kafka, *I Am a Memory Come Alive: Autogiographical Writings*, ed. Nahum N. Glatzer (New York: Schocken, 1974), p. 7. In "Nomadic Writing: The Poetics of Exile," *The Sin of the Book: Edmond Jabès*, p. 111, Richard Stamelman quotes the beginning of this aphorism in regard to Jabès. The concluding image of breaking through a wall is also applicable, for Jabès starts a section of his work with two aphorisms, one about "the book" and the second as follows:

> "The wall," he also said, "is not in front of us, but inside. There we must strike."

Jabès, *The Book of Questions: El, or the Last Book*, trans. Rosmarie Waldrop (Middletown, Conn.: Wesleyan University Press, 1984), p. 87.

30. Ibid., p. 6.

31. Ibid., p. 77.

32. *Book of Questions*, p. 11.

33. "An Interview with Edmond Jabès," *The Sin of the Book: Edmond Jabès*, p. 17.

34. Ibid., p. 20.

35. Samuel Beckett, *En attendant Godot*, eds. Germaine Brée and Eric Schoenfeld (Paris: Editions de Minuit, 1952; reprint, New York: Macmillan, 1963), p. 13, trans. by Samuel Beckett as *Waiting for Godot* (New York: Grove, 1954), p. 8.

36. Beckett, *Disjecta: Miscellaneous Writings and a Dramatic Fragment,* ed. Ruby Cohn (New York: Grove, 1984), p. 173; Marjorie Perloff, "Une voix pas la mienne: French/English Beckett and the French/English Reader," in Alan Warren Friedman et al, ed., *Beckett Translating/Translating Beckett* (University Park: Pennsylvania State University, 1987), pp. 36–48.

37. *Disjecta,* as translated in the Notes by Martin Esslin, pp. 170–73. Perloff also quotes from this letter (37).

38. *Molloy,* trans. Patrick Bowles in collaboration with the author, in Beckett, *Three Novels* (New York: Grove, 1955), p. 176.

39. *The New York Times,* 6 May 1956, quoted in Ruby Cohn, "*Watt* in the Light of *The Castle,*" *Comparative Literature* 13 (Spring 1961): 154. Probably taking his cue from Beckett's words, Sandbank writes, "In Kafka it was the symbolic meaning of the literal that was lost; in Beckett it is the literal itself" (66). Actually, however, since Kafka sees language as derived from an illusory phenomenal world, he doubts the literal. Other comparative studies of *Watt* with *The Castle* include Cohn, "*Watt* in the Light of *The Castle,*" *Comparative Literature* 13 (Spring 1961): 154–66; Edith Kern, "Reflections on the Castle and Mr. Knott's House: Kafka and Beckett" in *Franz Kafka: His Place in World Literature,* ed. Zyla (Lubbock: Texas Tech University Press, 1971); and Charles Bernheimer, "Watt's in *The Castle*: The Aporetic Quest in Kafka and Beckett," *Kafka Society Newsletter* 6 (June/December 1982): 19–24.

40. Eva Metman, "Reflections on Samuel Beckett's Plays," *The Journal of Analytical Psychology* (January 1960). Melvin Friedman has called her reading "eccentrically Jungian," in his Introduction to *Samuel Beckett Now,* edited and introduced by Friedman (Chicago: University of Chicago Press, 1970), p. 13.

41. E.g., in her article, "The *Magna Mater* Myth in Beckett's Fiction: Subtext and Subversion," in Friedman, pp. 149–54, Angela Moorjani analyzes Beckett's ironic presentation of the Mother Archetype.

42. Tom Stoppard, *Rosencrantz and Guildenstern Are Dead* (New York: Grove, 1967), p. 77.

43. Stoppard, *Lord Malquist and Mr. Moon* (New York: Knopf, 1968), p. 12.

44. Giles Gordon, "Tom Stoppard," *Transatlantic Review* 29 (1968): 23.

45. Kenneth Tynan, *Show People* (New York: Weidenfeld and Nicolson, 1980), p. 83; Tim Brassell, *Tom Stoppard: An Assessment* (New York: St. Martin's, 1985), p. 61.

46. Elias Canetti, *The Human Province,* trans. Joachim Neugroschel (New York: Seabury, 1978), p. 7. The passage is omitted from the German edition, *Aufzeichnungen 1942–1972* (n.p.: Suhrkamp, 1979), where it should have occurred on p. 12.

47. Canetti, *The Tongue Set Free,* trans. Joachim Neugroschel (New York: Seabury, 1979), p. 10.

48. *Human Province,* p. 246; omitted from *Aufzeichnungen 1942–1972.*

49. Canetti, *Das Gewissen der Worte* (Munich: Hanser, 1976), p. 230, trans. by Joachim Neugroschel as *The Conscience of Words* (New York: Seabury, 1979), p. 211.

50. *Human Province,* p. 99; *Aufzeichnungen 1942–1972,* p. 89.

51. *Das Gewissen der Worte,* pp. 137–38; *Conscience of Words,* pp. 120–21. Since *Letters to Felice* appeared after the publication of *Auto-da-Fe,* there is no question of the former's influencing the latter, so the similarities may arise from resemblances between Canetti and Kafka.

52. *Human Province,* p. 76; *Aufzeichnungen 1942–1972,* p. 72.

53. Canetti, *Crowds and Power,* trans. Carol Stewart (New York: Viking, 1966), p. 15.

54. John Haffenden, *The Life of John Berryman* (London: Routledge & Kegan Paul, 1982), pp. 46–47.

55. John Berryman, *Recovery* (New York: Farrar, 1973), p. 19.

56. Berryman, *The Dream Songs* (New York: Farrar, 1969), p. 15.

57. Richard J. Kelly, ed., *We Dream of Honour: John Berryman's Letters to His Mother* (New York: Norton, 1988), pp. 118, 120–22.

58. Haffenden, *John Berryman: A Critical Commentary* (New York: NYU Press, 1980), p. 110.

59. The passage also exists in a slightly different form in Berryman's notes to the book *Recovery*, p. 233.

60. *Life of John Berryman*, p. 370.

61. Linda Wagner-Martin, *Sylvia Plath: A Biography* (New York: Simon, 1987), pp. 17–19.

62. Plath, *The Collected Poems*, ed. Ted Hughes (New York: Harper, 1981), p. 223.

63. Judith Kroll, *Chapters in Mythology: The Poetry of Sylvia Plath* (New York: Harper, 1976), pp. 154–56.

64. *The Journals of Sylvia Plath*, ed. Frances McCullough (New York: Dial, 1982), pp. 166, 169.

65. Keith Sagar, *The Art of Ted Hughes*, 2nd ed. (London: Cambridge University Press, 1978), pp. 1–5; Leonard Scigaj, *The Poetry of Ted Hughes: Form and Imagination* (Iowa City: University of Iowa Press, 1986), pp. 3, 89–90, 119, 173, 179–80, 182, 209, 211.

66. Anne Sexton, *The Complete Poems*. Foreword, Maxine Kumin (Boston: Houghton, 1981), p. 48.

67. Quoted in Plath, p. 290.

68. Kroll, p. 74.

69. Leonard M. Scigaj, *The Poetry of Ted Hughes: Form and Imagination* (Iowa City: University of Iowa Press, 1986), p. 7.

70. Wagner-Martin, p. 240.

71. *Anne Sexton: A Self-Portrait in Letters*, ed. Linda Gray Sexton and Lois Ames (Boston: Houghton, 1977), p. 116.

72. Sexton, *The Complete Poems*. Foreword by Maxine Kumin (Boston: Houghton, 1982), p. 48.

73. *Sexton*, p. 271.

74. Estella Lauter, "Anne Sexton's 'Radical Discontent with the Order of Things,'" quoted in Sexton, p. xxx.

75. Foreword to Sexton, p. xxviii.

76. Rosemarie Kunzler, "Rumpelstilzchen," *Neues vom Rumpelstilzchen*, ed. Hans-Joachim Gelberg (Weinheim: n.p., 1976), pp. 26–28.

77. Heinz Rölleke, ed., *Die Alteste Närchensammlung der Brüder Grimm* (Cologne: Fondation Martin Bodmer, 1975), p. 238.

78. Susan Sontag, *Styles of Radical Will* (New York: Farrar, 1969; reprint. Toronto: Collins, 1987), pp. 205–74.

79. Sontag, *Brother Carl: A Filmscript* (New York: Farrar, 1974), p. xvi.

80. Sontag, "Traditions of the New," speech delivered at Texas Tech University, Lubbock, 25 October 1988.

81. Sontag, *Against Interpretation* (New York: Farrar, 1967), p. viii.

82. Ibid., p. 42.

83. Sontag, *Under the Sign of Saturn* (New York: Farrar, 1980; reprint. Random, 1981), p. 117.

84. *Against Interpretation*, p. 43.

85. Sontag, *Illness as Metaphor* (New York: Farrar, 1978; reprint. Random, 1979), pp. 18, 33, 39, 43, 53.

86. Sontag, *The Benefactor* (New York: Farrar, 1963; reprint. Toronto: Collins, 1987), p. 32.

87. Sontag, *Death Kit* (New York: Farrar, 1967; reprint. 1986), pp. 104, 237.

88. In *Disease, Pain & Sacrifice: Toward a Psychology of Suffering* (Chicago: University of Chicago Press, 1968), pp. 5–15, David Bakan cites fifty-two scientific books and articles presenting statistical and clinical evidence of psychosomatic influence on a host of diseases including cancer and tuberculosis. In his listing of evidence from reputable journals and presses, Bakan is merely including the best-known examples, while, since his book's 1968 publication, the literature has grown enormously. Sontag (in 1978), nonetheless, dismisses it all without detailed analysis or citation of counterevidence.

89. Ralph Ellison, *Going to the Territory* (New York: Random, 1986), p. 289.

90. Ellison, *Shadow and Act* (New York: Random, 1964), p. 284.

91. Charles Johnson, *Being and Race: Black Writing Since 1970* (Bloomington: Indiana University Press, 1988), p. 15.
92. Johnson, *Oxherding Tale* (New York: Grove, 1982), p. v.
93. Johnson, *Being and Race,* p. 16.
94. Ellison, *Invisible Man* (New York: Random, 1947; rpt. 1982), p. 26.
95. *Shadow and Act,* p. xv.
96. *Going to the Territory,* p. 285.
97. Richard Wolin, *Walter Benjamin: An Aesthetic of Redemption* (New York: Columbia University Press, 1982), p. ix.
98. James L. Rolleston, "The Politics of Quotation: Walter Benjamin's Arcades Projects," *PMLA* 104 (January 1989): 16.
99. Walter Benjamin, *Die Aufgabe des Übersetzers, Gesammelte Schriften,* vol. 4, 19 (Frankfurt am Main, Germany: Suhrkamp, 1980), p. 10, trans. Harry Zohn and Hannah Arendt as "The Task of the Translator," *Illuminations* (New York: Schocken, 1969), p. 80.
100. Benjamin, *Gesammelte Schriften,* vol. 4, 14; *Illuminations,* p. 75.
101. Hans Mayer, "Walter Benjamin and Franz Kafka," *On Walter Benjamin: Critical Essays and Recollections,* ed. Gary Smith (Cambridge: MIT Press, 1988), p. 189.
102. Benjamin, "Franz Kafka: *Zur zehnten Wiederkehr seines Todestages,*" *Gesammelte Schriften,* vol. 2, 414, trans. as "Some Reflections on Kafka," in Harold Bloom, ed., *Modern Critical Views* (New York: Chelsea House, 1986), p. 21.
103. Richard Wolin, *Walter Benjamin: An Aesthetic of Redemption* (New York: Columbia University Press, 1982), pp. 179–80, 198–99.
104. Benjamin, *Passagen-Werk,* I:682f, trans. by Winnfried Menninghaus, as "Walter Benjamin's Theory of Myth," in *On Walter Benjamin,* p. 321. My understanding of the *Passagen-Werk* is indebted to Menninghaus's analysis, which she also pursues at length in *Schwellenkunde: Walter Benjamins Passage des Mythos* (Frankfurt am Main, Germany: Suhrkamp, 1986).
105. See Rolleston, p. 23.

Chapter 9. An Approach to Religions in Literature

1. Daniel Lawrence O'Keefe, *Stolen Lightning: The Social Theory of Magic* (New York: Vintage, 1982), p. 3. Considering how important France has been in the formulation of recent critical thought, Dan Sperber remarks:

> Jung's view [of symbolism] is richer and more complex [than Freud's] though [Jung] never gave it a clear and compact formulation to which he might have held. It is customary in France to criticize Jung without ever having studied his work, and to accentuate his weaknesses while ignoring his original contributions, *Rethinking Symbolism,* trans. Alice Morton (Cambridge: Cambridge University Press, 1975), p. 46

2. Harold Coward, *Jung and Eastern Thought* (Albany: SUNY Press, 1985), pp. 185–89, et passim.
3. Letter to Ted R. Spivey, quoted in *Beyond Modernism: Toward a New Myth Criticism* (New York: University Press of America, 1988), p. 512.
4. Hans-Georg Gadamer, "Text and Interpretation," trans. Dennis J. Schmidt and Richard E. Palmer, *Dialogue & Deconstruction: The Gadamer-Derrida Encounter,* eds. Diane P. Michelfelder and Richard E. Palmer (New York: SUNY Press, 1989), pp. 28–29.
5. Francois Peraldi, "Time in 'The Purloined Letter,'" *The Purloined Poe,* p. 337.
6. P. Kugler, *The Alchemy of Discourse* (Lewisburg, Pa.: Bucknell University Press, 1981), p. 41.
7. Jacques Lacan, *Ecrit: A Selection,* trans. Alan Sheridan (New York: Norton, 1977), p. 159.
8. John P. Muller and William J. Richardson, eds. *Lacan and Language: A Reader's Guide to Ecrits* (New York: International Universities Press, 1982), p. 11.

9. At the beginning of his seminar on Poe, Lacan writes: Our inquiry has led us to the point of recognizing that the repetition automatism *(Wiederholungswang)* finds its basis in what we have called the insistence of the signifying chain. We have elaborated that notion itself as a correlate of the ex-sistence (or: excentric place) in which we must necessarily locate the subject of the unconscious if we are to take Freud's discovery seriously. (*Purloined Poe,* p. 28).

Despite the allusion to Freud and Lacan's attempt (elsewhere) to tie this reasoning to early work by Freud, Lacan's insight (that repetition has something to do with the nature of the self) is relatively original and might have been developed along the line I am pursuing here (although Lacan did not do so).

10. Bronislaw Malinowski, *Argonauts of the Western Pacific* (New York: Waveland, 1961), pp. 428–63.

11. Willard Espy, *The Garden of Eloquence: A Rhetorical Bestiary* (New York: Harper, 1983), p. 50.

12. Harold Fisch, *A Remembered Future: A Study in Literary Mythology* (Bloomington: Indiana University Press, 1984), pp. 14, et passim.

13. J. Hillis Miller, *Fiction and Repetition: Seven English Novels* (Cambridge: Harvard University Press, 1982), p. 6.

14. John M. Neary, " 'Ah: Runs': Updike, Rabbit, and Repetition," *Religion and Literature* 21 (Spring 1989): 91.

15. Synecdoches are particularly common in literature describing the relationship of individual and group. If the latter is perceived as relatively homogeneous, then the only threat to its unity is selfishness. Consequently, rituals arise in which individuals surrender something, often what is dearest to them. The sacrificed object or person may be symbolically or actually shared by the group (as in a feast) or submitted to the real or demonic enemies of the group. In the Roman ritual of *devotio,* e.g., a specially chosen soldier was expected to rush to his death in battle, and, in the rare case that he failed to die, a giant image of him was buried and an animal was sacrificed (Burkert, p. 63).

If, however, greater differences divide a group, then the sacrifice may not be communion or submission, but a purge, eliminating the divisive part of the society. In *Tiefenpsychologie und Neue Ethik,* Eric Neumann, e.g., has studied various "scapegoat" rituals as ways of symbolically exiling the Jungian "shadow," the repressed or suppressed element within the society.

If, finally, internal division becomes hopelessly ingrained, then the relationship of part to whole is acquisitive, each individual's trying to possess as much as possible.

16. E.g., Naomi Goldenberg, *The Changing of the Gods: Feminism and the End of Traditional Religion* (Boston: Beneon, 1979); Carol Christ, "Some Comments on Jung, Jungians and the Study of Women," *Anima* 3 (Spring 1977): 14–18; Estella Lauter, "Visual Images by Women: A Test Case for the Theory of Archetypes" in *Feminist Archetypal Theory: Interdisciplinary Re-Visions of Jungian Thought,* eds. Estella Lauter and Carol Schreier Rupprecht (Knoxville: University of Tennessee Press, 1985), pp. 46–83.

17. E.g., "There is nothing definitely unconscious; it is only not present to the conscious mind under a certain light." C. G. Jung, *Analytical Psychology: Its Theory & Practice* (New York: Vintage, 1968), p. 69.

18. Roland Barthes, *Image—Music—Text,* trans. Stephen Heath (New York: Hill and Wang, 1977), p. 54.

19. C. S. Lewis, *The Pilgrim's Regress* (London: Geoffrey Bles, 1933; reprint. Eerdman's, 1987), p. 10.

20. Some modern scholars, noting the lack of the term "Nirvana" in the Edicts of Asoka, have wondered if it actually appeared in the earliest Buddhism, so that the original goal of that faith is open to speculation. The Jungian analysts H. Marvin Spiegelman and Mokusen Miyuki (the latter also a thirteenth-generation Buddhist priest) argue that the goal has always been the union of consciousness and the "unconscious" in a Self. They contend that the Buddhist doctrine of *anatta* (no-self) does not deny the existence of an ego. Their contention seems questionable in terms of the Pali canon, but more plausible vis-à-vis Japanese Buddhism, which occasionally mentions a higher self. J. Marvin Spiegelman and Mokusen Muyaki, *Buddhism and Japanese Psychology* (Phoenix: Falcon, 1985), pp. 127–33, et passim.

21. Nāgārjuna, *Mūlamadhyamakakārikā,* ed. J. W. de Jong (Madras, India: Adyar, 1977), p. 39.

22. Michael S. Diener, Ingrid Fischer-Schreiber, et al., "Byōdō-Kan," *The Encyclopedia of Eastern Philosophy and Religion* (Boston: Shambhala, 1989), p. 57.

23. Beaujour, p. 16. She argues that bilinguals have a permanently greater tendency to separate "sign and referent" and bases her contention on the following published studies: G. L. MacNab, "Cognition and Bilingualism: A Reanalysis of Studies," *Linguistics* 17 (1979): 237. D. Carringer, "Creative Thinking Ability of Mexican Youth: The Relationship of Bilingualism," *Journal of Cross-Cultural Psychology* 5 (1974): 492–504; W. E. Lambert, "Cognitive and Attitudinal Consequences of Bilingual Schooling," *Journal of Educational Psychology* 65 (1973): 86–96; J. MacNamara, "Nurseries, Streets, and Classrooms: Some Comparisons and Deductions," *Modern Language Journal* 57 (1971), 66–84; Veroboj Vildomec, *Multilingualism* (Leiden, Netherlandsd: A. W. Sythoff, 1963).

24. Gerard van den Aardweg, "Exaggeration Therapy," in *The Psychotherapy Handbook: The A to Z Guide to More than 250 Different Therapies in Use Today,* ed. Richie Herink (New York: New American Library 1980), pp. 183–86. Johan L. Arndt, *Genese en Psychotherapie der Neurose,* 2 vols (The Hague: Boucher, 1966).

25. T. S. Eliot, *Complete Poems and Plays 1909–1950* (New York: Harcourt, 1958), p. 145.

26. Francis Ponge, *Le grand receuil:* vol. 2: *Méthodes* (Paris: Gallimard, 1961), 245–47. Translation mine.

27. Jacques Derrida, *Signéponge/Signsponge* [French and English] New York: Columbia University Press, 1984).

28. Kurt Vonnegut, *Palm Sunday: An Autobiographical Collage* (New York: Dell, 1981), p. 100.

Chapter 10. Behind the Great Wall

1. Paul Raabe, *Franz Kafka: Sämtliche Erzahlungen* (Frankfurt am Main, Germany: n.p. 1972), p. 404.

2. Edward T. Hall, *The Silent Language* (Garden City, N.Y.: Anchor/Doubleday, 1973), p. 53.

3. Kafka's one architect for every four laborers is a violation of common sense. Historically, the ratio was one overseer to beat twenty convicts into submission, while architects were far fewer than overseers. Cheng Dalin, *The Great Wall of China* (Hong Kong: South China Morning Post/New China News, 1984), p. 197.

4. As translated in Dalin, p. 197.

5. Jonathan Fryer, *Great Wall of China* (London: New English Library, 1975), p. 64.

6. Without reference to this Chinese notion, Christian Gooden's article on *"BGW"* likens Kafka's Great Wall to the cemetery wall in *The Castle,* which the boys climb for no other reason than the act of climbing itself. Christian Gooden, "The Great Wall of China: The Elaboration of an Intellectual Dilemma," in *On Kafka: Semi-Centenary Perspectives,* ed. Franz Funa (London: Paul Elek, 1976), p. 129.

7. Several scholars have argued that the Great Wall of Kafka's story may parody a rabbinic saying well-known to Kafka: Talmudic commentaries should form a wall around the most sacred scripture, the Torah. E.g., Clement Greenberg, "At the Building of the Great Wall of China," in *Franz Kafka Today,* eds. Angel Flores and Homer Swander (Madison, Wis.: Gordian, 1958), pp. 77–81; and Richie Robertson, *Kafka: Judaism, Politics, and Literature* (Oxford: Clarendon, 1985), p. 174. Robertson also shows that a number of German authors compared the Jews and the Chinese (175).

8. Kirí Grusa, *Kafka of Prague,* trans. Eric Mosbacher (New York: Schocken, 1983), p. 42.

9. *After Babel,* p. 67.

10. Robert Graves and Raphael Patai, *Hebrew Myths: The Book of Genesis* (Garden City, N.Y.: Doubleday, 1963).

11. Fox, p. 510.

12. Grusa, p. 95.

13. Quoted in F. Pfeifer, *Deutsche Mystiker des 14, Jahrhunderts* (Aalen: Scientia, 1962), vol. 2, 319.

14. Heilmann, p. 28. Translation mine. Heilmann renders the title as "Spring Day" *Frühlingstag,* though it might be rendered more fully as "A Homily on Ideals in Life, Uttered in Springtime on Rising from a Drunken Slumber," as in John A. Turner, trans., *A Golden Treasury of Chinese Poetry* [bilingual edition] (Hong Kong: Chinese University Press, 1976), p. 115.

15. G. K. Chesterton, *The Man Who Was Thursday: A Nightmare* (London: Sunpkin, Marshall, Hamilton, Kent, 1908), p. 225.

16. *Analytical Psychology,* p. 51.

17. Eric Neumann, *Art and the Creative Unconscious,* trans. Ralph Mannheim (Princeton, N.J.: Princeton University Press, 1974), p. 82.

Key to Abbreviations

When no translation of Kafka is cited parenthetically in the text, the translation is mine. If a dual language text is cited, a W in square brackets signifies that the translation is, nonetheless, mine. With Jung's *Gesammelte Werke,* since German and English editions have paragraphs numbered identically, the abbreviation *GW* identifies both the German text and the translation in *The Collected Works* (unless a W in square brackets appears, designating that the translation is mine).

Kafka's Works

A — *Amerika.* Edited by Max Brod. Translated by Willa and Edwin Muir. London: Seeker and Warburg, 1949. Reprint. New York: Schocken Books, 1953

B — *Beschreibung eines Kampfes: Novellen, Skizzen, Aphorismen aus dem Nachlass.* Edited by Max Brod. 2nd ed. New York: Schocken Books, 1946.

BK — *The Basic Kafka.* Introduction by Erich Heller. New York: Washington Square Press, 1979.

Br — *Briefe 1902–1924.* Edited by Max Brod. 1954. New York: Schocken Books, 1958.

C — *The Complete Stories.* Edited by Nahum N. Glatzer. 1971; New York: Schocken Books, 1976.

Ca — *The Castle.* Translated by Willa Muir, et al. Definitive edition. 1954. New York: Vintage, 1974.

D — *Dearest Father: Stories and Other Writings.* Translated by Ernst Kaiser and Eithne Wilkins. New York: Schocken Books, 1954.

D1 — *The Diaries of Franz Kafka 1910–1913.* Edited by Max Brod. New York: Schocken Books, 1948.

D2 — *The Diaries of Franz Kafka 1913–1923.* Edited by Max Brod. 1949; New York: Schocken Books, 1965.

E — *Erzählungen.* Edited by Max Brod. 1935. New York: Schocken Books, 1952.

H *Hochzeitsvorbereitungen auf dem Lande: und andere Prosa aus dem Nachlass 1966*. Frankfurt am Main, Germany: Fischer, 1953.

F *Letters to Felice*. Edited by Erich Heller and Jürgen Born. Translated by James Stern and Elisabeth Duckworth. New York: Schocken Books, 1973.

FK *Briefe an Felice und andere Korrespondenz aus Verlobungzeit*. Edited by Erich Heller and Jürgen Born. Frankfurt am Main, Germany: Fischer, 1967.

L *Letters to Friends, Family, and Editors*. Translated by Richard and Clara Winston, New York: Schocken Books, 1977.

M *Letters to Milena*. Edited by Jürgen Born and Michael Müller. Translated by Willi Haas. London: Secker and Warburg, 1953.

Mi *Briefe an Milena*. Edited by Jürgen Born and Michael Müller. Frankfurt am Main, Germany: Fischer, 1952.

O *Letters to Ottla and the Family*. Edited by N. N. Glatzer. Translated by Richard and Clara Winston. New York: Schocken Books, 1982.

OF *Briefe an Ottla und die Familie*. Edited by Hartmut Binder und Klaus Wagenbach. Frankfurt am Main, Germany: Fischer, 1974.

P *Parables and Paradoxes/Parabein und Paradoxe* [German and English]. Edited by Nahum N. Glatzer. 2nd ed. New York: Schocken Books, 1961.

Pr *Der Prozess: Roman*. Edited by Max Brod. 1925. New York: Fischer, 1953.

S *Das Schloss*. Edited by Malcolm Pasley. New York: S. Fischer/Schocken Books, 1982. Unless specified otherwise, all references are to vol. 2, the definitive text.

T *The Trial*. Translated by Willa Muir, et al. Definitive edition. New York: Vintage, 1969.

Ta *Tagebücher*. Edited by Max Brod. New York: Schocken, 1948.

V *Der Verschollene*. Edited by Jost Schillemeit. 2 vols. New York: S. Fischer/Schocken Books, 1983. Unless specified otherwise, all references are to vol. 2, the definitive text of the novel.

Jung's Works

Er *Erinnerungen, Träume, Gedanken*. Recorded and edited by

Aniela Jaffé. Zürich: Rascher, 1963. At Jung's request, this autobiography was excluded from *GW*.

GW *Gesammelte Werke*. 20 vols. Zürich: Rascher, 1959–1967. *The Collected Works.* Edited by Gerhard Adler, Michael Fordham, and Herbert Read. William McGuire, executive editor. Translated by R. F. C. Hull (volume 1 was translated by Leopold Stein in collaboration with Diana Riviere). The entire edition constitutes Bollingen Series 20. 1953–67: Reprint. New York: Pantheon Books/Bollingen Foundation/Princeton University Press, 1967–79.

MDR *Memories, Dreams, Reflections.* Recorded and edited by Aniela Jaffé. Translated by Richard and Clara Winston. Rev. ed. New York: Vintage, 1973.

Except when quoting Wilhelm, I use the Wade system of transliteration from Chinese but omit indications of tones, because they can be confused with note numbers.

Bibliography

Abe, Kōbō. "The Age which Asks the Question about Our Ultimate Belonging" *[Saisū no kozoku o tou jidai], Supplement to The Box Man [Hako otoko]*. Tokyo: Kinyōsha, 1973.

———. *Supplement to the Complete Works of Kōbō Abe [Abe Kōbō Zensakuhin]*. Vol. 2. Tokyo: Shinchōsha, 1973.

———. *The Ark Sakura*. New York: Vintage, 1988.

———. *Hako otoko*. Tokyo: Shinchōsha, 1973.

Aizenberg, Edna. "Kafka, Borges and Contemporary Latin-American Fiction," *Newsletter of the Kafka Society of America* 6 (June/December 1982): 11 n. 13.

Al-Issa, Ihsan and Wayne Dennis, eds. *Cross-Cultural Studies of Behavior*. New York: Holt, 1970.

Alazraki, Jaime. *Critical Essays on Jorge Luis Borges*. Boston: G. K. Hall, 1987.

Allen, R. E. *Plato's Parmenides: Translation and Analysis*. Minneapolis: University of Minnesota Press, 1983.

Analects of Confucius, The. Translated and edited by Arthur Waley. New York: Vintage, 1938.

Andersen, Hans Christian. *The Complete Illustrated Stories*. Translated by H. W. Dulcken. London: Chancellor, 1983.

Anderson, Andrew Runni. *Alexander's Gate, Gog and Magog, and the Inclosed Nations*. Cambridge: Mediaeval Academy of America, 1932.

Anderson, Mark. "Kafka and the Place of the Proper Name," *The Journal of the Kafka Society of America* 9 (June/December, 1985): 10–13.

Aristotle. *The Metaphysics* [Greek and English]. Translated and edited by Hugh Tredennick. Cambridge: Harvard University Press, 1947.

Arkins, Brian. *Sexuality in Catullus*. New York: Georg Olms, 1982.

Arndt, Johan L. *Genese en psychotherapie der neurose*. 2 vols. The Hague: Boucher, 1966.

Arnold, Edwin. *The Light of Asia and The Indian Song of Songs (Gita-Govinda)*. Bombay: Jaico, 1949.

Ashlas, Yehuda L. *The Kabbalah: A Study of the Ten Luminous Emanations from Rabbi Isaac Luria*. Translated by Rabbi Levi I. Krakovsky. Jerusalem: Research Centre of Kabbalah, 1969.

Augustine, St. *The Confessions [Confessionum]*. Edited by John Gibb and William Montgomery, New York: Garland, 1980. Translated by Rex Warner as *Confessions*. New York: New American Library, 1963.

Bakan, David. *Disease, Pain & Sacrifice: Toward a Psychology of Suffering*. Chicago: University of Chicago Press, 1968.

Bakhtin, Mikhail. *Problems of Dostoevsky's Poetics*. Translated by R. W. Rotsel. N.p.: Ardis, 1973.

Bangerter, Lowell A. *Hugo von Hofmannsthal*. New York: 1977.

Barbour, Ian. *Myths, Models, and Paradigms: A Comparative Study of Science and Religion*. New York: Harper Publications, 1974.

Barthes, Roland. *Image—Music—Text*. Translated by Stephen Heath. New York: Hill and Wang, 1977.

Baumer, Franz. *Franz Kafka.* Translated by Abraham Farbstein. New York: Ungar Publishing Co., 1971.

Beaujour, Klosti Elizabeth. *Alien Tongues: Bilingual Russian Writers of the "First" Emigration.* Ithaca, N.Y.: Cornell University Press, 1989.

Beckett, Samuel. *Disjecta: Miscellaneous Writings and a Dramatic Fragment.* Edited by Ruby Cohn. New York: Grove Press, 1984.

———. *En attendant Godot.* Edited by Gemaine Bree and Eric Schoenfeld. Paris: Editions de Minuit, 1952. Translated by Beckett as *Waiting for Godot.* New York: Grove Press, 1954.

———. *Three Novels.* Translated by Patrick Bowles and Beckett. New York: Grove Press, 1955.

Benjamin, Walter. *Illuminations.* New York: Schocken Books, 1969.

———. *Gesammelte Schriften.* 12 vols. Frankfurt am Main, Germany: Suhrkamp, 1980.

Bennet, E. A. *Meetings with Jung: Conversations Recorded During the Years 1946–1961.* Zurich: Daimon, 1985.

Benson, Jackson J. *The True Adventure of John Steinbeck, Writer.* New York: Viking Press, 1984.

Bernal, Olga. *Alain Robbe-Grillet: le roman de l'absence.* Paris: Gallimard, 1964.

Bernheimer, Charles. "Watt's in the Castle: The Aporetic Quest in Kafka and Beckett," *Kafka Society Newsletter* 6 (June/December 1982): 19–24.

Berryman, John. *Recovery.* New York: Farrar, 1973.

———. *The Dream Songs.* New York: Farrar, 1969.

Biblia sacra: vulgatae editionis. Translated by St. Jerome. Rome: Editiones Paulinae, 1957.

Bickman, Martin. *The Unsounded Centre: Jungian Studies in American Romanticism.* Chapel Hill: University of North Carolina Press, 1980.

Binder, Hartmut. *Kafka-Handbuch in zwei Bänden.* Stuttgart, Germany: Dröner, 1979.

———. Kafka-Komentar zu Sämtlichen Erzählungen. Munchen: Winkler, 1975.

———. *Kafka: Der Schaffensporzess.* Frankfurt am Main, Germany: Suhrkamp, 1983.

———. *Motiv und Gestaltung bei Franz Kafka.* Bonn: Bouvier, 1966.

Blavatsky, H. P. *The Secret Doctrine.* Rev. ed. 2 vols. Madras, India: Theosophical, 1888. Reprint, 1962.

Bloom, Harold. *Kabbalah and Criticism.* New York: Seabury, 1975.

Blumenthal, David. *Understanding Jewish Mysticism: A Source Reader.* New York: KTAV, 1978.

Blyth, R. H., trans. and comment. *Mumonkan* [Chinese and English]. Zen and Zen Classics, no. 4. Tokyo: Hokuseido Press, 1966.

Bodkin, Maud. *Psychological Studies of Imagination.* London: Oxford University Press, 1934.

Boldy, Steven. *The Novels of Julio Cortázar.* Cambridge: Cambridge University Press, 1980.

Bolles, Edmund Blair. *Remembering and Forgetting: Inquiries into the Nature of Memory.* New York: Walker, 1988.

Bonnefoy, Claude. *Entretiens avec Eugène Ionesco.* Paris: Pierre Belfond, 1966. Translated by Jan Dawson as *Converstions with Eugène Ionesco.* New York: Holt, 1966.

Bonney, William. *Thorns and Arabesques: Contexts for Conrad's Fiction.* Baltimore: Johns Hokins University Press, 1980.

Booth, Wayne C. *The Rhetoric of Fiction.* Chicago: University of Chicago Press, 1961.

Borges, Jorge Luis, ed. *La metamorfosis by Franz Kafka.* Buenos Aires: Losada, 1938.

———. *Labyrinths: Selected Stories and Other Writings.* New York: New Directions, 1970.

———. *Sus mejores pajinas.* Englewood Cliffs, N.J.: Prentice-Hall, 1970.

———. *The Aleph and Other Stories 1933–1969*. Translated and edited by Norman Thomas di Giovani. New York: Dutton & Co., 1970.

———. *Ficciones*. Buenos Aires: Emecé, 1956.

Brassell, Tim. *Tom Stoppard: An Assessment*. New York: St. Martin's Press, 1985.

Breton, André. *Anthologie de l'humour noir.* Paris: Sagittaire, 1940.

———. *Entretiens (1913–1952)*. Rev. ed. Paris: Gallimard, 1969.

———. *Manifestes du surrealisme*. Paris: Sagitaire, 1946.

———. *The Poems of André Breton: A Bilingual Anthology*. Translated and edited by Jean-Pierre Cauvin and Mary Ann Caws. Austin: University of Texas Press, 1982.

Broch, *Gesammelte Werke*, vol. 8. *Briefe*. Zurich: Rhein, 1953–61.

Broch, Hermann. *Der Tod des Vergil*. Zurich: Rheinuhrkamp, 1958. Translated by Jean Starr Untermeyer with Hermann Broch as *The Death of Vergil*. New York: Pantheon Books, 1945.

———, and Daniel Brody. *Hermann Broch-Daniel Brody Briefwechsel 1930–1951*. Frankfurt: Buchhändler-Vereinigung, 1971.

———. *Gesammelte Werke*. Vol. 6. *Dichten und Erkennen: Essays*. Edited by Hannah Arenndt. Zurich: Rhein, 1953–61.

Brod, Max. *Franz Kafka: Eine Biographie*. 2nd ed. New York: Schocken, 1946. Translated by G. Humphreys (chap. 1 to 7) and Richard Winston (chap. 8) as *Franz Kafka: A Biography*. 2nd ed. 1960. Reprint. New York: Schocken Books, 1963.

———. *Paganism—Christianity—Judaism: A Confession of Faith*. Translated by William Wolf. University: University of Alabama Press, 1970.

———. *Verzweiflung und Erlosung im Werk Kafkas*. Frankfurt am Main, Germany: Schocken Books, 1959.

Brome, Vincent. *Jung*. London: Macmillan, 1978.

Brown, L. B., ed. *Advances in the Psychology of Religion*. Oxford: Pergamon, 1985.

Buber, Martin. *Pointing the Way*. Translated by Maurice Friedman. New York: Harper, 1957.

———. *The Philosophy of Martin Buber*. Edited by Paul Arthur Schilpp. La Salle, Ill.: Open Court, 1967.

Buchanan, Robert. "The New Buddha," *The North American Review* 140 (1885): 445.

Burgin, Richard. *Conversations with Jorge Luis Borges*. New York: Holt, 1968).

Burns, W. " '*In the Penal Colony*': Variations on a Theme by Octave Mirbeau," *Accent* 17 (1957): 45.

Burrell, David. *Analogy and Philosophical Language*. New Haven: Yale University Press, 1973.

Byrne, Lawrence. "Writing God's Story: Self and Narrative Structure in Augustine's Confessions," *Christianity and Literature* 38 (Spring 1989): 23.

Callan, Richard. "," *Hispania* 60 (1977): 916–26.

Calvino, Italo. *Il Castello dei destini incrociati*. Turin, Italy: Einaudi, 1973. Translated as *The Castle of Crossed Destinies*. New York: Harcourt, 1979.

Campbell, Joseph, ed. *The Portable Arabian Nights*. Translated by John Payne. New York: Viking, 1952.

———. *The Hero with a Thousand Faces*. New York: Pantheon Books, 1949.

Camus, Albert. *Carnets*. Paris: Gallimard, 1962. Translated by Philip Thody as *Notebooks: 1935–1942*. New York: Modern Library, 1965.

———. *Essais*. Paris: Gallimard, 1965.

———. *L'Etranger*. New York: Pantheon Books, 1942.

———. *Myth of Sisyphus and Other Essays*. Translated by Justin O'Brien. New York: Knopf, 1964.

Canetti, Elias. *Das Gewissen der Worte*. Munich: Hanser, 1976. Translated by Joachim Neugroschel as *The Conscience of Words*. New York: Seabury, 1979.

———. *Die gerettete Zunge: Geschichte einer Jugend*. Munich: Carl Hanser, 1977. Translated by Joachim Neugroschel as *The Tongue Set Free*. New York: Seabury, 1979.

———. *Die Provinz des Menschen: Aufzeichnungen*. Munich: Carl Hanser, 1973. Translated by Joachim Neugroschel as *The Human Province*. New York: Seabury, 1978.

———. *Masse und Macht*. Hamburg: Claasen, 1960. Translated by Carol Stewart as *Crowds and Power*. New York: Viking, 1966.

Carotenuto, Aldo. *A Secret Symmetry: Sabina Spielrein between Jung and Freud*. Translated by Arno Pomerans, John Shepley, and Krishna Winston. New York: Pantheon Books, 1982.

Carrasco, David and Jane Marie Swanberg, eds. *Waiting for the Dawn: Mircea Eliade in Perspective*. Boulder, Col.: Westview, 1985.

Carrouges, Michel. *André Breton and the Basic Concepts of Surrealism*. Translated by Maura Prendergast. University: University of Alabama Press, 1974.

Cary, George. *The Medieval Alexander*. Edited by D. J. A. Ross. Cambridge: Cambridge University Press, 1956.

Casimir, H. B. G. *Haphazard Reality*. New York: Harper & Publishers, 1983.

Charmé, Stuart L. *Meaning and Myth in the Study of Lives: A Sartrean Perspective*. Philadelphia: University of Pennsylvania Press, 1984.

Chesterton, G. K. *The Man Who Was Thursday: A Nightmare*. London: Sunpkin, Marshall, Hamilton, Kint, 1908.

Christ, Carol. "Some Comments on Jung, Jungians and the Study of Women," *Anima* 3 (Spring 1977): 14–18.

Chuang Tzu. *Dschuang Dsi: Wahrebuch vom sudlichen Blutenland*. Translated by Richard Wilhelm (Nan Hua Dschen Ging). Jena: Eugen Diederichs, 1912. Reprint. 1923.

———. *The Sayings of Chuang Tzu* [Chinese and English]. Hong Kong: N.p. 1973.

Clarke, Adam. *Commentary on the Bible*. Abridged by Ralph Earl. Grand Rapids, Mich.: Baker, 1967.

Coe, Richard. *Samuel Beckett*. New York: Grove Press, 1969.

Cohn, D. "Castles and Anti-Castles or Kafka and Robbe-Grillet," *Novel* (Fall 1971): 185.

Cohn, Ruby. "*Watt* in the Light of *The Castle*. *Comparative Literature* 13 (Spring 1961): 154.

Conant, Martha. *The Oriental Tale in England in the Eighteenth Century*. New York: Octagon, 1966.

Confucius: *Confucian Analects, The Great Learning*. Translated by James Legge. Oxford: Clarendon, 1893. Reprint. New York: Dover, 1971.

Corngold, Stanley, ed. and trans. *The Metamorphosis*, by Franz Kafka. New York: Bantam, 1972.

———. "Kafka's *Die Verwandlung:* Metamorphosis of the Metaphor," *Mosaic* III, 4 (1970): 91–106.

Cortázar, Julio. *Rayuela*. Buenos Aires: Editorial Sudamericana Sociedad Anónima, 1963. Translated by Gregory Rabassa as *Hopscotch*. New York: Pantheon, 1966.

Coward, Harold. *Jung and Eastern Thought*. With Contributions by John Borelli, J. F. T. Jordens, and Joseph L. Henderson. New York: SUNY Press, 1985.

Dalin, Cheng. *The Great Wall of China*. Hong Kong: South China Morning Post/New China News, 1984.

Daly, Martin. Rev. *Archetypes: A Natural History of the Self by Anthony Stevens*. New York: Morrow, 1982, *BioScience* 34 (October 1984): 587.

Dauenhauer, Bernard. *Silence: The Phenomenon and Its Ontological Significance*. Bloomington: Indiana University Press, 1980.

David, Claude, ed. *Franz Kafka: Themen und Probleme*. Göttingen, Germany: Vandenhoek and Ruprecht, 1980.

Deleuze, Gilles and Félix Guattari. *Kafka: Toward a Minor Literature*. Foreword by Reda Bensmaïa. Theory and History of Literature, no. 30, Minneapolis: University of Minnesota Press, 1986.

Deleuze, Gilles. *Masochism: An Interpretation of Coldness and Cruelty, Together with the Entire Text of* Venus in Furs by Leopold von Sacher-Masoch. Translated by Jean McNeil. New York: Braziller, 1971.

Derrida, Jacques. *Dissemination*. Translated by Barbara Johnson. Chicago: University of Chicago Press, 1981.

———. *Margins of Philosophy*. Translated by Alan Bass. Chicago: University of Chicago Press, 1982.

———. *Signéponge/Signsponge* [French and English]. New York: Columbia University Press, 1984.

———. *Writing and Difference*. Translated by Alan Bass. Chicago: University of Chicago Press, 1978.

Dickens, Charles. *Great Expectations*. London: Oxford University Press, 1953. Reprint. 1969.

Dodds, E. R. *The Greeks and the Irrational*. Berkeley: University of California Press, 1959.

Donne, John. *The Complete Poetry*. With introduction, notes, and variants by John T. Shawcross. New York: New York University Press/London: University of London Press, 1968.

Dostoevsky, Fyodor. *Crime and Punishment*. Translated by Sidney Monas. New York: New American Library, 1968.

———. *Sobranie Sotsineniy.*, Vol. 5: Prestyplenie i nakazanie. Moxcow: Gosudarstvennoe izdatelbstvo khvdozhestvennoy literatury, 1957.

Dr. Jekyll, Señor Hyde," *Psychology Today* 21 (December 1987): 16.

Dudley, Guilford. *Religion on Trial: Mircea Eliade & His Critics*. Philadelphia: Temple University Press, 1977.

Durán, Gloria B. *The Archetypes of Carlos Fuentes: From Witch to Androgene*. Hamden, Conn.: Archon, 1980.

Eckhart, Meister. *Von der Geburt der Seele: Ausgewählte Schriften und Predigten*. Sigbert Mohn,

Eliade, Mircea. *Autobiography*. Vol. 1. *1907–1937, Journey East, Journey West*. Translated by Mac Linscott Ricketts. San Francisco: Harper, 1981.

———. *Cosmos and History*, New York: Harper, 1959.

———. *Images and Symbols*. Translated by Philip Mairet. New York: Sheed and Ward, 1961.

———. *Ordeal by Labyrinth: Conversations with Claude-Henri Rocquet*. Translated by Derk Coltman. Chicago: University of Chicago Press, 1982.

———. *Patterns in Comparative Religion*. Translated by Rosemary Sheed. New York: New American Library, 1958.

———. *The Forbidden Forest*. Translated by Mac Linscott Ricketts and Mary Park Stevenson. Notre Dame: University of Notre Dame Press, 1978.

———. *The Old Man and the Bureaucrats*. Translated by Mary Park Stevenson. Notre Dame: University of Notre Dame Press, 1979.

Eliot, T. S. *Complete Poems and Plays 1909–1950*. New York: Harcourt, 1958.

Ellis, John. *One Fairy Story Too Many*. Chicago: University of Chicago Press, 1983.

Ellison, Ralph. *Going to the Territory*. New York: Random, 1986.

———. *Invisible Man*. New York: Random, 1947. Reprint 1982.

———. *Shadow and Act*. New York: Random, 1964.

Emerson, Ralph Waldo. "Self-Reliance," *Selected Prose and Poetry*. Edited by Reginald L. Cook. 2nd ed. Holt, 1950.

Emrich, Wilhelm. *Franz Kafka: A Critical Study of His Writings*. Translated by Sheema Zeben Buehne. New York: Ungar Publis, 1968.

Espy, Willard. *The Garden of Eloquence: A Rhetorical Bestiary*. New York: Harper, 1983.

Evans, Richard I. *Conversations with Carl Jung and Reactions from Ernest Jones*. New York: Van Nostrand, 1964.

Evelyn-White, Hugh G., ed. and trans. *Hesiod, The Homeric Hymns and Homerica* [Greek and English]. Cambridge: Harvard University Press, 1977.

Ferber, Rafael. *Zenons Paradoxien der Bewegung und die Struktur von Raum un Zeit*. Zetamata, Monographien zur Kalassischen Altertumswissenschaft, no. 76, Munich: C. H. Beck, 1981.

Ferruccio, Rossi-Landi. *Ideologies of Linguistic Relativity*. The Hague: Mouton, 1973.

Feurlicht, Ignace. *Thomas Mann*. New York: Twayne, 1968.

Field, Andrew. *VN: The Life and Art of Vladimir Nabokov*. New York: Crown, 1986.

Fisch, Harold. *A Remembered Future: A Study in Literary Mythology*. Bloomingon: Indiana University Press, 1984.

Fischer-Schreiber, Ingrid, Franz-Karl Ehrhard, Kurt Friedrichs, Michael S. Diner. *The Encyclopedia of Eastern Philosophy and Religion*. Boston: Shambhala, 1989.

Flores, Angel and Homer Swander, eds., *Franz Kafka Today*. Madison: University of Wisconsin Press, 1958.

Frazer, J. G. *The New Golden Bough*. Edited by Theodor Gaston. New York: S. G. Phillips, 1959.

Freedman, H. and M. Simon, ed. *Midrash Leviticus Rabbah*. London: Soncino, 1939.

Freedman, Ralph. *Hermann Hesse: Pilgrim of Crisis, A Biography*. New York: Pantheon, 1978.

French, A. *Czech Writers and Politics 1945–1969*. New York/Boulder: Columbia University Press/East European Monographs, 1982.

Friedländer, M. *Die religiösen Bewegungen innerhalb des Judentums im Zeitalter Jesu*. Berlin: n.p. 1905.

Friedman, Alan Warren, ed. *Beckett Translating/Translating Beckett*. University Park: Pennsylvania State University Press, 1987.

Friedman, Melvin, ed. and introd. *Samuel Beckett Now*. Chicago: University of Chicago Press, 1970.

Fryer, Jonathan. *Great Wall*. London: New English Library, 1975.

Fuentes, Carlos. *Aura* [bilingual edition]. Translated by Lysandra Kemp. New York: Farrar, 1975.

———. *Terra Nostra*. Mexico City: Joaquín Mortiz, 1975. Translated by Margaret Sayes Peden as *Terra Nostra*. New York: Farrar, 1976.

———. *Zona Sagrada*. Mexico City: Gabriel Mancera, 1967. Translated by Suzanne Jill Levine as *Holy Place*. New York: Dutton, 1972.

Gadamer, Hans-Georg. "Text and Interpretation." Translated by Dennis J. Schmidt and Richard E. Palmer. *Dialogue & Deconstruction: The Gadamer-Derrida Encounter*. Edited by Diane P. Michelfelder and Richard E. Palmer. New York: SUNY Press, 1989.

Gelberg, Hans-Joachim, ed. *Neues vom Rumpelstilzchen*. Weinheim: n.p. 1976.

Girard, René. *Violence and the Sacred*. Translated by Patrick Gregory. London: 1977.

Glatzer, Nahum N. *The Loves of Franz Kafka*. New York: Schocken, 1986.

Godin, A. and M. Hallez. "Parental Images and Divine Paternity," *Lumen Vitae* 19 (1964): 253–84.

Goethe, Johann Wolfgang von. *Iphigenia in Tauris*. Translated by John Prudhoe. New York: Barnes & Noble, 1966.

———. *Faust*. Garden City, N.Y.: Doubleday, 1961.

Goldenberg, Naomi. *The Changing of the Gods: Feminism and the End of Traditional Religion*. Boston: Beneon, 1979.

Gorak, Jan. *God the Artist; American Novelists in a Post-Realist Age*. Urbana: University of Illinois Press, 1987.

Gordis, Robert. *The Book of Job: Commentary, New Translation, and Special Studies*. Moreshit Series, Studies in Jewish History, Literature and Thought, no. 2. New York: Jewish Theological Seminary of America, 5738/1978.

Gordon, Giles. "Tom Stoppard," *Transatlantic Review* 29 (1968): 23.

Goth, Maja. *Franz Kafka et les lettres Françaises (1928–1955)*. Paris: José Corti, 1956.

Gould, Eric. *The Sin of the Book: Edmond Jabès*. Lincoln: University of Nebraska Press, 1985.

Graves, Robert. *The Greek Myths*. Vol. 1. New York: Penguin, 1955.

Gray, Ronald. *Franz Kafka*. Cambridge: Cambridge University Press, 1973.

Grayzel, Solomon. *A History of the Jews: From the Babylonian Exile to the Present*. New York: New American Library, 1968.

Green, Martin. *The Von Richthofen Sisters*. New York: Basic, 1974.

Greenwald, Anthony. "The Totalitarian Ego: Fabrication and Revision of Personal History," *American Psychologist* 35 (July 1980): 603–18.

Griffiths, A. Phillips, ed. *Philosophy and Literature*. Royal Institute of Philosophy Lecture Series, no. 16, Supplement to *Philosophy* 1983. London: Cambridge University Press, 1984.

Gross, Ruth V. "Rich Text/Poor Text: A Kafkan Confusion," *PMLA* 95 (March 1980): 168–82.

Grossman, Edith. *The Antipoetry of Nicanor Parra*. New York: NYU Press, 1975.

Grusa, Jírí. *Franz Kafka of Prague*. Translated by Eric Mosbacher. New York: Schocken, 1983.

Günther, V. J. Helmut Koopmann, Peter Pütz, Hans Schrimpf, eds., *Untersuchungen zur Literature als Geschichte: Festschrift für Benno von Wiese*. Berlin: 1973.

Haffenden, John. *John Berryman: A Critical Commentary*. New York: NYU Press, 1980.

———. *The Life of John Berryman*. London: Routledge & Kegan Paul, 1982.

Hall, Edward T. *The Silent Language*. Garden City, N.Y.: Anchor/Doubleday, 1973.

Halpern, Daniel, ed. *The Art of the Tale: An International Anthology of Short Stories*. New York: Penguin, 1986.

Halperin, Joseph. *Critical Fictions: The Literary Criticism of Jean-Paul Sartre*. New Haven: Yale University Press, 1976.

Handelman, Susan. *The Slayers of Moses: The Emergence of Rabbinic Interpretation in Modern Literary Theory*. Albany: SUNY Press, 1982.

Harkins, William E. and Paul I. Trensky, eds. *Czech Literature Since 1956: A Symposium*. New York: Bohemia, 1980.

Harold, Preston. *The Shining Stranger*. New York: Dodd, 1967.

Hartmann, Karl Eduard von. *Die Philosophie des Unbewussten*. Berlin: C. Duncker, 1870.

Hegel. *Phenomenology of Spirit*. Translated by A. V. Miller. Oxford: Clarendon, 1977.

Heilmann, Hans. Trans. *Chinesische Lyrik*. Die Fruchtschale, no. 1. Munchen: Piper, 1905.

Heine, Heinrich. *Sämtliche Schriften*. Munich: Carl Hanser, 1968.

Heisig, James W. *Imago Dei: A Study of C. G. Jung's Psychology of Religion*. Lewisburg: Bucknell University Press/London: Associated University Press, 1979.

Heller, Erich. *Franz Kafka*. New York: Viking, 1974.

Herink, Richie, ed. *The Psychotherapy Handbook: The A to Z Guide to More than 250 Different Therapies in Use Today*. New York: New American Library, 1980.

Hesse, Hermann. *Die Morgenlandfahrt*. In *Gesammelte Werke*. Vol. 8. Translated by Hilda Rosner as *The Journey to the East*. New York: Farrar, 1956.

———. *Gesammelte Werke*. Vol. 8. Frankfurt am Main, Germany: Suhrkamp, 1970.

———. *The Journey to the East*. New York: Farrar, 1956.

———. *Autobiographical Writings*. Translated by Denver Lindless. New York: Farrar, 1971.

Hesse, Mary. *Science and the Human Imagination*. London: SCM, 1954.

Hibberd, John. *Kafka in Context*. London: Studio Vista, 1975.

Hoffman, Edward. *The Way of Splendor*. London: Shambhala, 1981.

Hofmannsthal, Hugo von. Gesammelte Werke. Vol. 3. Berlin: Fischer, 1934. Translated by Mary Hottinger and Tania and James Stern as *Selected Prose*. Bollingen Series, no. 33. New York: Pantheon, 1952.

Hofmannsthal, Hugo von and Leopold Andrian. *Briefwechsel*. Edited by Walter Perl. Frankfurt am Main, Germany: Fischer, 1968.

Homans, Peter. *Jung in Context*. Chicago: University of Chicago Press, 1979.

Homer [attributed]. *Ilias* [and] *Odyssee*. Edited by J. C. Bruijn and C. Spoelder. Haarlem, Netherlands; H. D. Tjeenk Willink & Zoon, 1970.

Hoover, Thomas. *The Zen Experience*. New York: New American Library, 1980.

Hopkins, Gerard Manley. *Poems*. Edited by Robert Bridges. London: Oxford University Press, 1930.

Hsia, Adrian. *Hermann Hesse und China*. Frankfurt am Main, Germany; Suhrkamp, 1974.

Impey, Oliver. *Chinoiserie*. New York: State Mutual Book and Periodical Service, 1977.

Ionesco, Eugène. *Journal en miettes*. Paris: Mercure de France, 1967. Translated by Jean Stewart as *Fragments of a Journal*. New York: Grove, 1968.

Ivask, Ivar, ed. *The Perpetual Present: The Poetry and Prose of Octavio Paz*. Norman: University of Oklahoma Press, 1973.

Jabés, Edmond. *Le livre des question*. Paris: Editions Gallimard, 1963. Translated by Rosmaire Waldrop as *The Book of Questions*. Middletown, Conn.: Wesleyan University Press, 1972.

———. *The Book of Questions: El, or the Last Book*. Middletown, Conn.: Wesleyan University Press, 1984.

Jacobs, Louis. *Hasidic Thought*. New York: Schocken, 1976.

Jacobi, Jolande. *The Psychology of C. G. Jung*. London: Routledge and Kegan Paul, 1969.

Jaffe, Aniela, ed. *Studien analytischen Psychologie C. G. Jungs: Festschrift zum 80. Geburtstag von. C. G. Jung*. Zurich: Rhein-Verlag, 1955.

Jaffen, Jean. *The Jewish Mystic in Kafka*. New York: Peter Lang, 1987.

Jakobson, Roman. *Selected Writings*. Paris: Mouton, 1971.

Kanouch, Gustav. *Conversations with Kafka*. Translated by Goronwy Rees. 2nd ed. rev. New York: New Directions, 1971.

Jerome, St. Trans. *Biblia sacra: vulgatai editionis*. Rome: Editiones Paulinae, 1957.

Johnson, Charles. *Being and Race: Black Writing Since 1970*. Bloomington: Indiana University Press, 1988.

———. *Oxherding Tale*. New York: Grove, 1982.

Johnson, Greg. *Understanding Joyce Carol Oates*. Columbia: University of South Carolina Press, 1987.

Johnston, William. *The Austrian Mind: An Intellectual and Social History 1848–1938*. Berkeley: University of California Press, 1972.

Kaltenmark, Max. *Lao Tzu and Taoism*. Translated by Roger Greaves. Stanford, Calif.: Stanford University Press, 1969.

Katz, Nathan. Ed. *Buddhist and Western Psychology*. Boulder, Colo.: Prajña, 1983.

Katz, Steven T., ed. *Mysticism and Philosophical Analysis*. New York: Oxford University Press, 1978.

Kelly, Richard J., ed. *We Dream of Honour: John Berryman's Letters to His Mother*. New York: Norton, 1988.

Kerouac, Jack. *The Dharma Bums*. New York: New American Library, 1958.

Kierkegaard, Sóren. *Repetition: An Essay in Experimental Psychology*. Translated by Walter Lowrie. New York: Harper, 1941.

King, Thomas M. *Sartre and the Sacred*. Chicago: University of Chicago Press, 1974.

Kirk, G. S. *The Nature of Greek Myths*. New York: Penguin, 1974.

Kitagawa, Joseph M. and Charles H. Long, eds. *Myths and Symbols: Studies in Honor of Mircea Eliade*. Chicago: University of Chicago Press, 1969.

Knox, Bernard M. W. *The Heroic Temper: Studies in Sophoclean Tragedy*. Berkeley: University of California Press, 1964. Reprint. 1983.

Kocher, Simon. "In Memoriam Kurt Gödel," *The Mathematical Intelligencer* (July 1978): 182–85.

Kohut, Heinz. *Self Psychology and the Humanities: Reflections on a New Psychoanalytic Approach*. Edited and introduced by Charles B. Strozier. New York: Norton & Co., 1985.

Kroll, Judith. *Chapters in a Mythology: The Poetry of Sylvia Plath*. New York: Harper, 1976.

Kugler, P. *The Alchemy of Discourse*. Lewisburg, Pa.: Bucknell University Press, 1981.

Kundera, Milan. *Kniha smíchu a zapomneni*. Toronto: Sixty-Eight Publishers, 1981.

———. *Nesnesitelná Lehkost Bytí*. Toronto: Sixty-Eight Publishers, 1985. Translated by Michael Henry Heim as *The Unbearable Lightness of Being*. New York: Harper, 1984.

———. *The Art of the Novel*. Translated by Linda Asher. New York: Grove, 1988.

Kurz, Gerhard. *Traum-Schrecken: Kafkas literarische Existenzanalyse*. Stuttgart, Germany, Metzler, 1980.

Lacan, Jacques. *Ecrit: A Selection*. Translated by Alan Sheridan. New York: W. W. Norton and Co., 1977.

———. "Le séminaire sur 'La lettre volée,'" *Le Psychoanalyse* 2 (1956): 1–44.

Landesman, Charles, ed. *The Problem of Universals*. London: Basic, 1971.

Landolfi, Tommaso. *Cancerqueen and Other Stories*. Translated and introduced by Raymond Rosenthal. New York: Dial, 1971.

Lao Tzu [attributed] and Wang Pi. *A Translation of Lao Tzu's Tao Te Ching and Wang Pi's Commentary*. Translated by Paul J. Lin. Ann Arbor: University of Michigan Press, 1977.

Lao Tzu [attributed]. *The Canon of Reason and Virtue (Lao-Tze's Tao Teh King)* [Chinese and English]. Translated by D. T. Suzuki and Paul Carus. La Salle, Ill.: Open Court, ;1974.

———. *Dao De Ging: Das Buch des Alten vom Sinn und Leben*. Translated by Richard Wilhelm. Jena: Eugen Diederichs, 1911.

———. *The Guiding Light of Lao Tzu: A New Translation and Commentary on the Tao Teh Ching*. Translation and commentary by Henry Wei. Wheaton, Ill.: Quest, 1982.

———. *My Words are very easy to understand" [Tao Te Ching]* [Chinese and English]. Commentary by Man-jan Cheng. Translated by Tam C. Gibbs. Richmond, Calif.: North Atlantic, 1981.

———. *Tao Te Ching: The Book of Meaning and Life*. Translated by H. G. Ostwald from Richard Wilhelm's German translation and commentary.

———. *Te-Tao Ching: A New Translation Based on the Recently Discovered Ma-wang-tui Texts*. Translated and introduced by Robert G. Hendricks. New York: Ballantine, 1989.

Larson, Janet L. *Dickens and the Broken Scripture*. Athens: University of Georgia Press, 1985.

Lauter, Estella and Carol Schreier Rupprecht, eds. *Feminist Interdisciplinary Re-Visions of Jungian Thought*. Knoxville: University of Tennessee Press, 1985.

Leki, Ilona. *Alain Robbe-Grillet*. TWAS, no. 682. Boston: Twayne, 1983.

Lessing, Doris. *A Small Personal Voice*. Introduced and edited by Paul Schlueter. New York: Knopf, 1974.

Lewis, C. S. *The Pilgrim's Regress*. London: Geoffrey Bles, 1933. Reprint. Eerdman's, 1987.

Li'a Dsi, *Das Wahre Buch vom Quellenden Urgrund (Tschung Hü Dschen Ging); Die Lehren der Philosophen Lia Yü Kou und Tang Dschu*. Translated by Richard Wilhelm. Jena: Eugen Diederichs, 1921.

Light, Stephen, ed. *Shūzō Kuki and Jean-Paul Sartre: Influence and Counter-Influence in the Early History of Existential Phenomenology*. Foreword by Mychel Rybalka. Carbondale: Southern Illinois University Press, 1987.

Linn, Paul J. *A Translation of Lao Tzu's Tao Te Ching and Wang Pi's Commentary*. Ann Arbor: University of Michigan Press, 1977.

Lottman, Herbert R. *Albert Camus: A Biography*. Garden City, N.Y.: Doubleday, 1979.

Luther, Martin, trans. *Die Bibel oder die ganze Heilige Schrift des Alten und Neuen Testaments*. Berlin: Britische und Ausladische Bibelgesellschaft, 1923.

Luthi, Max. *Es War Einmal: Vom Wesen des Volksmärchens*. Gottingen: Vandenhoeck & Ruprecht, 1970. Translated by Lee Chadeayne and Paul Gottwaldt, as *Once Upon a Time: On the Nature of Fairy Tales*. New York: F. Ungar, 1970.

Magee, Bryan. *The Philosophy of Schopenhauer*. Oxford: Oxford University Press, 1983.

Mailloux, Peter. *A Hesitation Before Birth: The Life of Franz Kafka*. Newark: University of Delaware Press; London: Associated University Presses, 1989.

Maimon, Salomon. *Lebensgeschichte*. Edited by Jakob Fromer. Munich: n.p. 1911.

Maimonides, Moses. *The Guide of the Perplexed*. Translated by Shlomo Pines. Chicago: University of Chicago Press, 1963.

Malinowski, Bronislaw. *Argonauts of the Western Pacific*. New York: Waveland, 1961.

Man, Paul de. *Allegories of Reading*. New Haven: Yale University Press, 1979.

———. *Blindness and Insight: Essays in the Rhetoric of Contemporary Criticism*. 2nd ed. Minneapolis: University of Minnesota Press, 1983.

Mann, Thomas and Karl Kerényi. *Mythology and Humanism: The Correspondence of Thomas Mann and Karl Kerényi*. Translated by Alexander Gelley. Ithaca, N.Y.: Cornell University Press, 1975.

Mann, Thomas. *Joseph und seine Brüder: Die Geschichten Jakobs*. Vol. 1. Berlin: Fischer, 1934. Reprint. Frankfurt am Main, Germany: Fischer, 1983. Translated by H. T. Lowe-Porter as *Joseph and His Brothers*. New York: Knopf, 1939.

———. *Joseph und seine Brüder: Joseph, der Ernährer*. Vol. 4. Stockholm: Bermann-Fischer, 1943. Reprint. Frankfurt am Main, Germany: Fischer, 1983. Translated by H. T. Lowe-Porter as *Joseph the Provider*. New York: Knopf, 1944.

———. *Schriften und Reden zur Literatur, Kunst und Philosophie*. Frankfurt am Main, Germany: Fischer, 1968.

———. *Tagebücher 1933–34*. Edited by Peter de Mendelssohn. Frankfurt am Main, Germany: S. Fischer, 1977.

Margoulies, G. *Anthologie raisonne de la litterature Chinoise*. Paris: Payot, 1948.

Mattoon, Mary Ann. *Jungian Psychology in Perspective*. New York: Macmillan, 1981.

McDonald, Keiko I. "Contemporary Man's Plight: An Analysis of *The Box Man*," *Literature East and West* 21 (January/December 1977): 178.

McLuhan, Marshall. *The Man and His Message*. Edited by George Sanderson and Frank Macdonald. Golden, Col.: Fulcrum, 1989.

Melville, Herman. *Collected Poems*. Edited by Howard P. Vincent. Chicago: Packard, 1947.

———. *Moby-Dick*. Edited by Harrison Hayford and Hershel Parker. New York: Norton, 1967.

Mendoza, Ramón G. *Outside Humanity: A Study of Kafka's Fiction*. New York: University Press of America, 1986.

Menninghaus, Winnfried. *Schwellenkunde: Walter Benjamins Passage des Mythos*. Frankfurt: Suhrkamp, 1986.

Menzel, Theodor. *Der Zauberspiegel: Türkishce Märchen*. Hannover, Germany: Orient-Buchhandlung Heinz Lafaire, 1924.

Merton, Thomas. *Zen and the Birds of Appetite*. New York: New Directions, 1968.

Meurs, Jos van with John Kidd. *Jungian Literary Criticism, 1920–1980*. Metuchen, N.J.: Scarecrow, 1988.

Meyrink, Gustav. *The Golem*. New York: Dover, 1986.

Mitchell, W. J. T. Ed. *On Narrative*. Chicago: University of Chicago Press, 1980.

More, Thomas. *A Dialogue of Comfort against Tribulation*. Edited by Leland Miles. Bloomington: Indiana University Press, 1965.

Moss, C. Scott. *Dreams, Images and Fantasy: A Semantic Differential Casebook*. Urbana: University of Illinois Press, 1965.

Moss, C. Scott. *Dreams, Images and Fantasy: A Semantic Differential Casebook*. Urbana: University of Illinois Press, 1970.

Moynahan, Julian. "The Hero's Guilt. The Case of *Great Expectations*," *Essays in Criticism* 10 (January 1960): 61.

Muller, John P. and William J. Richardson, eds. *Lacan and Language: A Reader's Guide to Ecrits*. New York: International University Press, 1982.

Murphy, Patrick D. "De/Reconstructing the 'I': PostFANTASTICmodernist Poetics," *Journal of the Fantastic in the Arts* 1 (1988): 39–48.

Nabokov, Vladimir. *Lectures on Literature*. Edited by Fredson Bowers. Introduction by John Updike. New York: Harvest/Harbrace, 1980.

———. *Pale Fire*. New York: Putnam, 1962.

———. *Strong Opinions*. New York: McGraw-Hill, 1981.

———. *The Annotated Lolita*. Edited by Alfred Appel, Jr. New York: McGraw-Hill, 1970.

Naes, Harold. *Knut Hamsun*. Boston: Twayne, 1984.

Nathan, John. *Mishima: A Biography*. Boston: Little, Brown, 1974.

Nagarjuna. *Mūlamadhyamakārikā*. Edited by J. W. de Jong. Madras, India, Adyar, 1977.

Neary, John M. " 'Ah: Runs': Updike, Rabbit, and Repetition," *Religion and Literature* 21 (Spring 1981): 91.

Neher, André. *L'Exil de la parole, du silence biblique au silence d'Auschwitx*. Paris: Editions du Seuil, 1970. Translated by David Maisel as *The Exile of the Word: From the Silence of the Bible to the Silence of Auschwitz*. Philadelphia: Jewish Publication Society of America, 5741/1981.

Nishitani, Keiji. *What Is Religion?* Tokyo: n.p. 1961.

Nordau, Max. *Degeneration*. Translated by. London: William Heinemann, 1895.

Norris, Christopher. *Derrida*. Cambridge: Harvard University Press, 1987.

Oates, Joyce Carol. *Crossing the Border*. New York: Vanguard, 1976.

———. *Handbook of Short Story Writing*. New York: Writer's Digest, 1970.

———. *Invisible Woman*. Princeton, N.J.: Ontario Review, 1982.

———. *Marriages and Infidelities*. New York: Vanguard, 1968.

Obler, L. K. and D. A. Fein, eds. *The Exceptional Brain: The Neuropsychology of Talent and Special Abilities*. New York: Guilford, 1988.

O'Flaherty, Wendy Doniger. *Siva: The Erotic Ascetic*. New York: Oxford University Press, 1973.

Okakura. *The Awakening of Japan*. New York: Century, 1904.

O'Keefe, Daniel Lawrence. *Stolen Lightning: The Social Theory of Magic*. New York: Vintage, 1982.

Olsen, Tillie. *Silences*. New York: Laurl/Seymour Lawrence, 1983.

Omori Sōgen and Terayama Katsujō. *Zen and the Art of Calligraphy: The Essence of Sho*. Translated by John Stevens. London: Routledge & Kegan Paul, 1983.

Parra, Nicanor. *Antipoems: New and Selected* [bilingual edition]. Edited by David Unger. Introduction by Frank MacShane. New York: New Directions, 1985.

———. *Obra Gruesa*. Santiago, Chile: Editorial Universitaria, 1969.

———. *Sermons and Homilies of the Christ of Elqui* [bilingual edition]. Columbia: University of Columbia Press, 1984.

——— and Pablo Neruda. *Discursos*. Santiago, Chile: Editoral Nascimento, 1962.

Pascal, Roy. *Kafka's Narrators: A Study of His Stories and Sketches*. New York: Cambridge, 1982.

Pasley, Malcolm. "Zu Kafkas Interpunktion," *Euphorion* 75/4 (1981): 490.

Pawel, Ernst. *The Nightmare of Reason: A Life of Franz Kafka*. New York: Farrar, 1984.

Paz, Octavio. *Alternating Current*. Translated by Helen R. Lane. New York: Viking, 1973.

———. *Early Poems 1935–55* [bilingual edition]. Translated by Muriel Rukeyser, Paul Blackburn, Lysander Kemp, Denise Levertov, William Carlos Williams. Bloomington: Indiana University Press, 1973.

Peat, F. David. *Synchronicity: The Bridge Between Matter and Mind*. New York: Bantam, 1987.

Pfeiffer, F. *Deutsche Mystiker des 14. Jahrhunderts*. Aalen: Scientia, 1962.

Pinsker, Sanford, ed. *Critical Essays on Philip Roth*. Boston: G. K. Hall, 1982.

Plath, Sylvia. *The Collected Poems*. Edited by Ted Hughes. New York: Harper, 1981.

———. *The Journals of Sylvia Plath*. Edited by Frances McCullough. New York: Dial, 1982.

Plato. *Republic*. Edited by James Adam. 2nd ed. with introduction by D. A. Rees. New York: Cambridge University Press, 1965.

———. *Theaetetus* [and] *Sophist* [Greek and English]. Translated by Harold Fowler. Cambridge: Harvard University Press, 1952.

———. *Works*. Vol. 2. Translated by Henry Davis. London: Henry G. Bohn, 1849.

Poe, Edgar Allan. *Collected Works*. Edited by Thomas Ollive Mabbott. Cambridge: Harvard University Press, 1969.

Politzer, Heinz. *Parable and Paradox*. Ithaca, N.Y.: Cornell University Press, 1962.

Propp, Vladimir. *Morphology of the Folktale*. Translated by Laurence Scott. Austin: University of Texas Press, 1968.

Ramthun, Herta, ed. *Bertolt Brecht: Diaries 1920–1922*. Translated by John Willet. New York: St. Martin's Press, 1979.

Ray, Verne F. "Human Color Perception and Behavioral Response." *Transactions of the New York Academy of Sciences* 16 (1953): 98–104.

Reed, T. J. "Kafka and Schopenhauer" Philosophisches Denken und dichterisches Bild," *Euphorion* (1965): 160–72.

Ricketts, Mac Linscott. *Mircea Eliade: The Romanian Roots, 1907–1945*, East European Monographs, no. 248, vol. 1. New York: Columbia University Press, 1988.

Rimbaud, Arthur. *Une saison en enfer/Les illuminations/A Season in Hell/The Illuminations*. Translated by Enid Thodes Peschel. New York: Oxford University Press, 1973.

Rimer, J. Thomas. *Modern Japanese Fiction and Its Traditions: An Introduction*. Princeton: Princeton University Press, 1978.

Rölleke, Heinz, ed. *Die Alteste Märchensammlung der Brüder Grimm*. Cologne: Fondation Martin Bodmer, 1985.

Robbe-Grillet, Alain. *Les gommes*. Paris: Les Editions de Minuit, 1953.

———. *Pour un nouveau roman*. Paris: Les Editions de Minuit, 1963. Translated by Richard Howard as *for a New Novel*. New York: Grove, 1965.

Robert, Marthe. *As Lonely as Franz Kafka*. Translated by Ralph Manheim. New York: Harcourt, 1979.

Robertson, Ritchie. *Kafka: Judaism, Politics, and Literature*. Oxford: Clarendon, 1985.

Robinson, J. M. Translated and edited as *The Nag Hammadi Library*. New York: 1977.

Robinson, Richard H. *Early Mādhyamika*. Madison: University of Wisconsin Press, 1967.

Rolleke, Heinz, ed. *Die Älteste Märchensammlung der Brüder Grimm*. Cologne, Germany: Fondation Martin Bodmer, 1975.

Rolleston, James L. "The Politics of Quotation: Walter Benjamin's Arcades Projects," *PMLA* 104 (January 1989): 16.

Ross, William David. *Plato's Theory of Ideas*. Oxford: Oxford University Press, 1953.

Rossvaer, Viggo. *The Laborious Game: A Study of Plato's Parmenides*. Oslo: Universatetsforlaget, 1983.

Roth, Philip. *Portnoy's Complaint*. New York: Random, 1967.

———. *Reading Myself and Others*. New York: Farrar, 1975.

———. *The Breast*. New York: Bantam, 1973.

———. *The Facts: A Novelist's Autobiography*. New York: Farrar, 1988.

———. *The Professor of Desire*. New York: Farrar, 1977.

Rucker, Rudy. *Infinity and the Mind: The Science and Philosophy of the Infinite*. Toronto: Bantam, 1982.

Rushdie, Salman. *Shame*. New York: Vintage, 1983.

———. *The Jaguar Smile: A Nicaraguan Journey*. New York: Viking, 1987.

———. *The Satanic Verses*. New York: Viking, 1988.

Russell, Bertrand. *History of Western Philosophy: And its Connection with Political and Social Circumstances from the Earliest Times to the Present Day*. New York: Simon & Schuster, 1945.

Sagar, Keith. *The Art of Ted Hughes*. 2nd ed. London: Cambridge University Press, 1978.

Sandbank, Shimon. *After Kafka: The Influence of Kafka's Fiction*. Athens: University of Georgia Press, 1989.

Sarraute, Nathalie. *Entre la vie et la mort*. Paris: Gallimard, 1968.

———. *L'Ere du soupçon: essais sur le roman*. Les Essais, no. 80. Paris: Gallimard, 1956.

———. *Martereau*. Paris: Gallimard, 1953. Translated by Maria Jolas as *Martereau*. New York: George Braziller, 1959.

Sartre, Jean-Paul. *Anti-Semite & Jew*. New York: Schocken, 1965.

———. *L'être et le néant: essai d'ontologie phénomenologique*. Paris: Gallimard, 1943. Translated by Hazel E. Barnes as *Being and Nothingness: A Phenomenological Essay on Ontology*. New York: Washington Square Press, 1956.

———. *La nausée*. Paris: Gallimard, 1938. Translated by Lloyd Alexander as *Nausea*. Introduction by Hayden Carruth. New York: New Directions, 1964. Reprint. Cambridge: Robert Bentley, 1979.

———. *The War Diaries: November 1939/March 1940*. Translated by Quintin Hoare. New York: Pantheon, 1984.

Saussure, Ferdinand de. *Cours de linguistique generale*. Paris: Payot, 1962.

Sayre, Kenneth M. *Plato's Late Ontology: A Riddle Resolved*. Princeton, N.J.: Princeton University Press, 1983.

Schaub, Uta Liebmann. "Foucault's Oriental Subtext," *PMLA* 104 (May 1989): 306–16.

Schlant, Ernestine. *Hermann Broch*. TWAS, no. 485. Boston: Twayne, 1978.

Schneidau, Herbert. *Sacred Discontent: The Bible and Western Tradition*. Berkeley: University of California Press, 1976.

Scholem, Gershom. *Kabbalah*. New York: New American Library, 1974.

———. *The Messianic Idea in Judaism*. New York: Anti-Defamation League of the B'nai B'rith, 1972.

Schulz, Bruno. *Sanatorium under the Sign of the Hourglass*. Translated by Celina Wieniewska. Introduction by John Updike. New York: Penguin, 1978.

———. *Sklepy Cynamonowe; Sanatorium pod Klepsydra*. Krakow, Poland: Wydawnictwo Literackie, 1957.

———. *Traité des mannequins*. Translated and introduction by Arthur Sandauer. Les Lettres Nouvelles, no. 15. Paris: Julliard, 1961.

Scigaj, Leonard. *The Poetry of Ted Hughes: Form and Imagination*. Iowa City: University of Iowa Press, 1986.

Scott, Nathan A., Jr. "The New *Trahison Des Clercs:* Reflections on the Present," *The Virginia Quarterly Review* (Summer 1986): 419–38.

Scott, Walter, ed. and trans. *Hermetica: The Ancient Greek and Latin Writings which Contain Religious or Philosophical Teachings Ascribed to Hermes Trismegistus*. Vol. 1: *Texts and Translations*. Boulder, Colo.: Hermes House, 1982. Reprint. Boston: Shambala, 1985.

Scotus, Duns. *Philosophical Writings*. New York: Nelson, 1962.

Secret of the Golden Flower, The. Translated into German by Richard Wilhelm and into English by Cary F. Baynes. Commentary by C. G. Jung. New York: Causeway, 1975.

Serrano, Miguel. *Jung & Hesse: A Record of Two Friendships*. New York: Schocken, 1966.

Sexton, Anne. *Anne Sexton: A Self Portrait in Letters*. Edited by Linda Gray Sexton and Lois Ames. Boston: Houghton, 1977.

———. *The Complete Poems*. Foreword by Maxine Kumin. Boston: Houghton, 1981.

Shorey, Paul. *The Unity of Plato's Thought*. Chicago: Garland, 1903.

Simonson, Rick and Scott Walker, eds. *The Graywolf Annual Five: Multicultural Literacy*. St. Paul: Graywolf, 1988.

Skarmeta, Antonio. "El apogeo del antipoeta," *Ercilla* (1971): 37.

Smith, Gary, ed. *On Walter Benjamin: Critical Essays and Recollections*. Cambridge: MIT Press, 1988.

Snider, James S. and Charles E. Osgood, eds. *Semantic Differential Technique: A Sourcebook*. Chicago: Aldine, 1969.

Snyder, Gary. "Cold Mountain Poems," *Evergreen Review* 2 (Autumn 1958): 69–80.

———. *He Who Hunted Birds in His Father's Village: The Dimensions of a Haida Myth*. Bolinas, Calif.: Grey Fox, 1979.

Sontag, Susan. "Traditions of the New." Speech delivered at Texas Tech University, Lubbock, 25 October 1988.

———. *Against Interpretation*.

———. *Brother Carl: A Filmscript*. New York: Farrar, 1974.

———. *Death Kit*. New York: Farrar, 1967. Reprint, 1986.

———. *Styles of Radical Will*. New York: Farrar, 1974.

———. *The Benefactor*. New York: Farrar, Straux and Giroux, 1963. Reprint, Toronto: Collins, 1987.

———. *Under the Sign of Saturn*. New York: Farrar, Straus and Giroux, 1978. Reprint, New York: Random, 1979.

Spann, Meno. *Franz Kafka*. Boston: Twayne, 1976.

Spiegelman, J. Marvin and Mokusen Miyuki. *Buddhism and Japanese Psychology*. Phoenix, Ariz.: Falcon, 1985.

Spivey, Ted R. *Beyond Modernism: Toward a New Myth Criticism*. New York: University Press of America, 1988.

Steinbeck, John. *The Winter of Our Discontent*. New York: Viking, 1961.

Steiner, George. *After Babel: Aspects of Language and Translation*. London: Oxford University Press, 1975.

Stern, Alfred. *Sartre: His Philosophy and Psychoanalysis*. New York: Liberal Arts, 1953.

Stern, J. P. *The World of Franz Kafka*. New York: Holt, 1980.

Stevens, Anthony. *Archetypes: A Natural History of the Self*. New York: Morrow, 1982.

Stokes, Henry Scott. *The Life and Death of Yukio Mishima*. London: Peter Owen, 1975.

Stoltzfus, Ben. *Alain Robbe-Grillet: The Body of the Text*. Madison: Fairleigh Dickinson University Press/Associated University Presses, 1985.

Stone, Donal. "Steinbeck, Jung, and *The Winter of Our Discontent*," *Steinbeck Quarterly* 9 (Summer/Fall 1978): 87.

Stoppard, Tom. *Lord Malquiest and Mr. Moon*. New York: Knopf, 1968.

———. *Rosencrantz and Guildenstern Are Dead*. New York: Grove, 1967.

Strong, James. *The New Strong's Exhaustive Concordance of the Bible*. New York: Nelson, 1984.

Suarès, Carlo. *The Sepher Yetsira: Including the Original Astrology According to the Qabala and Its Zodiac*. Translated by Micheline and Vincent Stuart. London: Shambhala, 1976.

Suzuki, D. T. *Essays in Zen Buddhism* (first series). London: Luzac, 1927.

Talmud. Translated by I. Epstein. London: Soncino, 1935–48.

Tennyson, Alfred. *Poems*. Edited by Christopher Ricks. New York: Longman, 1969.

Texts of Taoism, The. Translated by James Legge. Sacred Books of the East, nos. 39, 40. London: Oxford University Press, 1891. Reprinted as one volume, New York: Julian, 1959.

Theweleit, Klaus. *Male Fantasies*. Translated by Stephen Conway in collaboration with Erica Carter and Chris Turner. Vol. I: *Women Floods, Bodies, History*, Minneapolis: University of Minnesota Press, 1987.

Thomson, James. *The Castle of Indolence*. London: Millar, 1748.

Tille, Alexander, introd. and trans. *Thus Spake Zarathustra*. New York: Macmillan, 1896.

Toker, Leona. *Nabokov: The Mystery of Literary Structures*. London: Cornell University Press, 1989.

Trevelyan, Humphrey. *Goethe & the Greeks*. Foreword by Hugh Lloyd-Jones. Cambridge: Cambridge University, 1941. Reprint revised, 1981.

Triffit, Gregory. *Kafka's 'Landarzt' Collection: Rhetoric and Interpretation*. Australian and New Zealand Studies in German Language and Literature, no. 13. New York: Peter Lang, 1985.

Turner, John A. *A Golden Treasury of Chinese Poetry* [bilingual edition]. Hong Kong: Chinese University Press, 1976.

Tynan, Kenneth. *Show People: Profiles in Entertainment*. New York: Simon & Schuster, 1979.

Udoff, Alan, ed. *Kafka's Contextuality*. Baltimore, Md.: Gordion Press/ Baltimore Hebrew College Press, 1986.

———. *Kafka and the Contemporary Critical Performance: Centenary Readings*. Bloomington: Indiana University Press, 1987.

Vergote, A. and A. Tamayo. *Parental Figures and the Representation of God*. The Hague: Mouton Leuven University Press, 1980.

Vonnegut, Kurt. *Deadeye Dick*. New York: Delacorte/Seymour Lawrence, 1982.

———. *Mother Night*. New York: Dell, 1961.

———. *Palm Sunday: An Autobiographical Collage*. New York: Dell, 1981.

———. *Slaughterhouse Five or The Children's Crusade: A Duty Dance with Death.* New York: Dell, 1966.

———. *Wampeters, Foma & Granfalloons (Opinions).* New York: Dell, 1976.

Wagenbach, Klaus. *Franz Kafka: Die Erzählungen.* Frankfurt: Fischer, 1961.

———. *Franz Kafka: Eine Biographie seiner Jugend 1883–1912.* Bern, Switzerland; Francke, 1958.

Wagner-Martin, Linda. *Sylvia Plath: A Biography.* New York: Simon & Schuster, 1987.

Waldenfels, Hans. *Absolute Nothingness: Foundations for a Buddhist-Christian Dialogue.* Translated by J. W. Heisig. New York: Paulist, 1980.

Walder, Dennis. *Dickens and Religion.* Boston: George Allen and Unwin, 1981.

Walser, Robert. *Selected Stories.* New York: Farrar, 1982.

Weiler, Gershon. *Mauthner's Critique of Language.* Cambridge: Cambridge University Press, 1979.

Weinberg, Kurt. *Kafkas Dichtungen: Die Travestien des Mythos.* Bern; Switzerland: Francke, 1963.

Welbon, Guy. *The Buddhist Nirvana and Its Western Interpreters.* Chicago: University of Chicago Press, 1968.

Whincup, Greg, trans. *The Heart of Chinese Poetry.* New York: Doubleday, 1987.

Whitlark, James. "Kafka and the Taoist Sages," *Journal of the Kafka Society of America* 8 (June/December 1984): 28–34.

———. "Kafka's Babel," *Journal of the Kafka Society* of America 13 (1989): forthcoming.

———. "Kafka's 'Country Doctor' as Neo-Romantic Fairy Tale." *The Shape of the Fantastic: Selected Essays from the Seventh International Conference on the Fantastic in the Arts.* Edited by Olena H. Saciak (Westport, Conn.: Greenwood, 1990.

———. *Illuminated Fantasy: From Blake's Visions to Recent Graphic Fiction.* Madison: Fairleigh Dickinson University Press/London: Associated University Presses, 1988.

———. "A Post-Jungian Approach to Kafka," *Journal of the Kafka Society of America,* 9 (June/December 1985): 149–60.

———. "Nineteenth-Century 'Nirvana Talk." *South Asian Review* 5 (1981): 17–33.

———. "Vonnegut's Anthropology Thesis." In *Literature and Anthropology.* Comparative Literature Series, no. 20. Lubbock: Texas Tech University Press, 1989.

Whitman, Walt. *Leaves of Grass: The First (1855) Edition.* Edited by Malcolm Cowley. New York: Viking, 1959. Reprint. 1961.

———. *The Uncollected Poetry and Prose.* Edited by Emory Holloway. Garden City, N.J.: Doubleday, 1921.

Whorf, Benjamin Lee. *Language, Thought, and Reality.* Edited and introduction by John B. Carroll. Foreword by Stuart Chase. New York: John Wiley/MIT Press, 1956.

Wieger, Leon. *Chinese Characters: Their Origin, Etymology, History, Classification and Signification.* Catholic Mission, 1915. Reprint. New York: Paragon/Dover, 1965.

Wiesel, Ellie. *The Golem: the Story of a Legend.* Translated by Anne Borchardt. New York: The Story of a Legend. New York: Summit, 1983.

Williams, C. A. S. *Outline of Chinese Symbolism and Art Motives.* 3rd ed., rev. Shanghai: Kelly and Walsh, 1941. Reprint. New York: Dover, 1976.

Williams, Gertrude Marvin. *Priestess of the Occult: Madame Blavatsky.* New York: Alfred A. Knopf, 1946.

Wilson, Colin. *C. G. Jung: Lord of the Underworld.* Wellingborough, Northamptonshire, U.S.: Aquarian, 1984.

Wittgenstein, Ludwig. *Philosophical Investigations.* Edited by G. H. von Wright and G. E. M. Anscombe. Translated by G. E. M. Anscombe. Oxford: Basil Blackwell, 1953.

Wolfe, Alan. "Suicide and the Japanese Postmodern: A Postnarrative Paradigm?" *South Atlantic Quarterly* 87 (Summer 1988): 571–89.

Wolin, Richard. *Walter Benjamin: An Aesthetic of Redemption*. New York: Columbia University Press, 1982.

Won, Ko. *Buddhist Elements in Dada*. New York: New York University Press, 1977.

Zyla, Wolodymyr, ed. *Franz Kafka: His Place in World Literature*. Comparative Literature Series. Lubbock: Texas Tech University Press, 1971.

Index